Contributions to Economics

The series *Contributions to Economics* provides an outlet for innovative research in all areas of economics. Books published in the series are primarily monographs and multiple author works that present new research results on a clearly defined topic, but contributed volumes and conference proceedings are also considered. All books are published in print and ebook and disseminated and promoted globally. The series and the volumes published in it are indexed by Scopus and ISI (selected volumes).

More information about this series at http://www.springer.com/series/1262

Lei Delsen
Editor

Empirical Research on an Unconditional Basic Income in Europe

Springer

Editor
Lei Delsen
Department of Economics
Radboud University
Nijmegen, The Netherlands

ISSN 1431-1933　　　　　　ISSN 2197-7178　(electronic)
Contributions to Economics
ISBN 978-3-030-30046-3　　　ISBN 978-3-030-30044-9　(eBook)
https://doi.org/10.1007/978-3-030-30044-9

© Springer Nature Switzerland AG 2019
This work is subject to copyright. All rights are reserved by the Publisher, whether the whole or part of the material is concerned, specifically the rights of translation, reprinting, reuse of illustrations, recitation, broadcasting, reproduction on microfilms or in any other physical way, and transmission or information storage and retrieval, electronic adaptation, computer software, or by similar or dissimilar methodology now known or hereafter developed.
The use of general descriptive names, registered names, trademarks, service marks, etc. in this publication does not imply, even in the absence of a specific statement, that such names are exempt from the relevant protective laws and regulations and therefore free for general use.
The publisher, the authors, and the editors are safe to assume that the advice and information in this book are believed to be true and accurate at the date of publication. Neither the publisher nor the authors or the editors give a warranty, expressed or implied, with respect to the material contained herein or for any errors or omissions that may have been made. The publisher remains neutral with regard to jurisdictional claims in published maps and institutional affiliations.

This Springer imprint is published by the registered company Springer Nature Switzerland AG.
The registered company address is: Gewerbestrasse 11, 6330 Cham, Switzerland

Preface

The Unconditional Basic Income (UBI) is an old idea, which recently re-emerged as a hot topic of debate. The fierce discussions between proponents and opponents about the desirability and feasibility of a UBI lack an empirical basis, and there is scarce empirical research on the UBI. To mark my retirement on 21 June 2018 from the Department of Economics and Business Economics of the Nijmegen School of Management (NSM) at the Radboud University, I organised an international farewell seminar on the UBI. This seminar took place on 22 June 2018 in the Elinor Ostrom Building of the NSM in Nijmegen, the Netherlands. The seminar entitled "Empirics in Europe of the Unconditional Basic Income (UBI)" hosted several Dutch and international researchers who represented the results of their laboratory experiments, field experiments and survey analyses on UBI. Financial support of the International Office of the Radboud University and the NSM is kindly acknowledged. The chapters in this book are based on the presentations in the seminar, complemented with an introductory chapter.

In the beginning of my scientific career, among others in my 1995 Ph.D. thesis on atypical employment, and in several scientific papers, I was sceptical about the UBI. Full employment and a high activity rate are conditions *sine qua non* for a sustainable welfare state in general and a maintainable social security system in particular. High employment rates are a core condition for a successful future of the welfare state, both for fundamental reasons of social cohesion and individual self-esteem, and for reasons of economic sustainability. The introduction of a UBI would mean that policymakers should acknowledge that it is no longer possible to offer the entire labour force a paid (full-time) job. It also means abolishment of the obligation to look for employment and the end of the right to work. In the midst of the 1990s, the prospects for a return to the conditions prevailing before 1973 were poor. I argued that a general saturation, demographic developments and environmental problems may cause bottlenecks for economic growth. Important changes in the labour supply and in the sectoral distribution of employment were eroding the full-time, full-year concept. In addition, advances in information technology made it imperative to re-examine the old concept of full employment. I recommended a new concept of full employment: a legal right to a basic amount of work, the right to at least a part-time job for all people in the workforce, combined with the stipulated right to a (partial) basic income guaranteed by the government.

Dehumanisation of work continued. For an increasing number of (self)employed, work lost its intrinsic value as well as its extrinsic value. In-work poverty increased faster than employment. The growth of low-paid insecure employment resulted in more income inequality. Flexible work turned out to be worse than being unemployed. More recently, I have become more in favour of the introduction of a UBI as part of a solution. This is mainly due to the development of the national welfare state in the direction of a "participation society" (with the Netherlands as league leader), which requires more involvement of citizens in their municipalities and neighbourhoods, but also because of the increasing number of atypical jobs and growing income and wealth inequality. In a 2017 report for the Science Council of Japan, I concluded: "The 1965 Social Assistance Act, the final social safety net, was the crowning piece of the Dutch welfare state. The basic income may become the crowning piece of the participation society".

The aim of this book is to scrutinise and comment on the main issues of the UBI, to contribute to the knowledge basis on the UBI and to support better informed, evidence-based, policymaking. In recent years, the UBI has attracted renewed attention in academia, as well as in public discussions, and much has been written on the possible consequences of a UBI. This book, however, is the first edited volume on the UBI in Europe which offers international comparative research findings. Among other topics, it includes analyses of survey data on preferences for a UBI in the European Union, the political feasibility of a UBI in the European Union, the first empirical findings of the UBI-related field experiments in the Netherlands, the main motives behind the planned basic income pilots in four municipalities of Scotland and results of laboratory experiments on the behavioural effects of UBI. Presenting contributions from Dutch and international researchers, the book provides scientific answers to the question of whether a UBI is desirable and feasible in Europe.

Maastricht/Nijmegen, The Netherlands Lei Delsen
June 2019

Acknowledgements

I want to thank Anisa Holmes, Data Journalist and Communications Manager at Dalia Research GmbH in Berlin, for providing the data set of the 2017 basic income survey in the European Union. Thanks are also due to Julika Frome and Aniek Schouten for their editorial assistance. Last but not least, I want to express my gratitude to Springer, Yvonne Schwark-Reiber in particular, for the smooth cooperation in finalising the book.

Contents

1   **Unconditional Basic Income and Welfare State Reform in Representative Democracies** 1
Lei Delsen

2   **Individual Preferences for the Unconditional Basic Income in the European Union** 29
Lei Delsen and Rutger Schilpzand

3   **Is a Basic Income Feasible in Europe?** 61
Genevieve Shanahan, Mark Smith, and Priya Srinivasan

4   **Exploring Benefits and Costs: Challenges of Implementing Citizen's Basic Income in Scotland** 81
Michael Wlliam Danson

5   **Job Search, Employment Capabilities and Well-being of People on Welfare in the Dutch 'Participation Income' Experiments** 109
Ruud Muffels and Erwin Gielens

6   **The Who and the Why? Selection Bias in an Unconditional Basic Income Inspired Social Assistance Experiment** 139
János Betkó, Niels Spierings, Maurice Gesthuizen, and Peer Scheepers

7   **Experimental Economics: A Test-Bed for the Unconditional Basic Income?** 171
Sascha Füllbrunn, Lei Delsen, and Jana Vyrastekova

8   **Experimental and Game Theoretical Analyses of the Unconditional Basic Income** 201
Toshiji Kawagoe

Author Index 221

Subject Index 229

List of Figures

Fig. 3.1	Public support for a UBI policy in Europe by country (2016) (Note: % of population in favour or strongly in favour of having a UBI scheme in their country). Source: European Social Survey (2016), Lee (2018), and Fitzgerald (2017)	64
Fig. 5.1	Inequality of outcomes across latent clusters of welfare recipients partaking in Dutch trust experiments	127
Fig. 5.2	Yearly (actual) exit probabilities for 11 Dutch cities in % of total population on January 1 moving out from social assistance into a paid job, 2016–2018	130
Fig. 5.3	Predicted exit probabilities of social assistance beneficiaries by benefit (SA) duration, June 1, 2016–June 1, 2018 in four experimenting cities. Source: Municipal BUS (social assistance benefit statistics) data 2015–2018	131
Fig. 5.4	Predicted exit probabilities of people in Apeldoorn/Epe and Oss moving in before June 1, 2016 and exit after June 1, 2016 by having a minimum education level or not. Source: Municipal BUS (social assistance benefit statistics) data 2015–2018	133
Fig. 7.1	Outcomes of investments with probabilities (Screenshot)	188
Fig. 7.2	Feasible outcomes of investments (Screenshot)	189
Fig. 8.1	The relationship between earned income (Y) and post-tax income (Z)	206
Fig. 8.2	The average of earned income in the UBI and the NIT schemes	207
Fig. 8.3	Example of a 4 × 4 Sudoku puzzle (**a**) a 4 × 4 problem (**b**) the problem correctly solved	209

List of Tables

Table 2.1	Comparison of Dalia Research sample statistics and EU population statistics	32
Table 2.2	Descriptive and bivariate statistics of all survey variables	38
Table 2.3	Behaviour of respondents; effect of UBI on his/her own work choices (single choice) (percentage)	43
Table 2.4	Ordered probability to vote in favour of UBI in the European Union	46
Table 2.5	Multi-level models explaining the likelihood to vote in favour of UBI in the European Union	52
Table 3.1	A feasibility framework for a UBI in Europe	66
Table 3.2	Basic income initiatives by stage of development in 28 EU member states, January 2016–March 2019	70
Table 3.3	Elements of basic income initiatives in 28 EU member states, January 2016–March 2019	71
Table 3.4	Public support for basic income policy in Europe	73
Table 4.1	At-risk-of-poverty rate in Europe by poverty threshold—EU-SILC	85
Table 4.2	Poverty rates across the UK, after housing costs (AHC)	85
Table 4.3	Illustrative UBI schemes to match a floor and two poverty benchmarks for Scotland, 2017–2018	101
Table 5.1	Social assistance (SA) (target) population and participants of the Dutch trust experiments (Article 83 and Not-Article 83 municipalities)	115
Table 5.2	Operationalisation of the health and well-being measures (acronyms and brief questionnaire wording)	120
Table 5.3	Operationalisation of the other outcome measures	121
Table 5.4	Operationalisation of indicators of motivation and abilities regarding paid work	123
Table 5.5	Profiles of survey respondents participating in four Dutch trust experiments: results of LCA model estimations (N = 1474)	123

Table 5.6	Job search and perceived employment chances of the participants in four of the Dutch trust experiments	124
Table 5.7	Fit indices for the LCA model estimations in four Dutch trust experiments	126
Table 5.8	Perceived living conditions at the first survey based on the various outcome measures by LCA cluster	128
Table 5.9	Predicted exit probabilities of experiment participants, non-participants and withdrawals for the period between June 1, 2016 and June 1, 2018 in Apeldoorn/Epe, Oss, Tilburg and Wageningen	133
Table 6.1	Summary of demographic, household and allowance factors explaining biases in participation in the Nijmegen social assistance experiment	151
Table 6.2	Descriptive statistics of explanatory variables in the Nijmegen social assistance experiment	156
Table 6.3	Likelihood to participate and not to participate in the Nijmegen social assistance experiment, Chi square and Cramer's V	157
Table 6.4	Likelihood of participation in the Nijmegen experiment, logistic regressions with individual, household and allowance characteristics, N = 6010	159
Table 6.5	Summary of statistical significance ($p < 0.05$) of variables explaining differences between participants and non-participants in the Nijmegen social assistance experiment	160
Table 7.1	Endowment allocation to assets A, B and C across tasks and treatments (in percent of endowment)	190
Table 7.2	Rank of arguments for and arguments against UBI	192
Table 7.3	When is UBI important?	193
Table 7.4	Impact of UBI on own work choices	194
Table 7.5	UBI referendum voting behaviour of employed and unemployed	194
Table 8.1	Average earned income under conditions A (no scheme) and B (UBI or NIT scheme)	207
Table 8.2	Lottery choices in the Multiple Price List (MPL) method	211
Table 8.3	A typical choice task in the Social Value Orientation (SVO) test	212
Table 8.4	Average number and standard deviation (SD) of correctly solved problems in each of the four trials	213
Table 8.5	Raw data of experiment 2	215
Table 8.6	Estimation results of regression of personality traits on labour effort	215
Table 8.7	Payoff matrix of the UBI game with M type agents (willing to get married) and B type agents (willing to participate in labour market)	217

Chapter 1
Unconditional Basic Income and Welfare State Reform in Representative Democracies

Lei Delsen

Abstract An increase in income and wealth inequality does not only have negative social and economic consequences, it is also a threat to the functioning of our democracies. The debate on the introduction of an Unconditional Basic Income (UBI) is beset with unanswered questions, with conjectures and unproven beliefs that call for additional research by economists and a uniform definition. The current distribution-and-income-based national welfare state could be transformed into a 'prosperity state', in which the economy is designed around delivering the capabilities for human flourishing. The introduction of a UBI, funded by progressive consumption and wealth taxes, should be on the research agenda of economics, and on the policy agenda in representative democracies. It has the potential to enlarge the economic pie, and to improve the distribution of income, for it reflects the contribution to society. Empirics on UBI are limited. Moreover, research is mainly focussed on short-term labour market effects, poverty and income inequality reduction, and there is some attention for health and well-being. However, the long-term effect on the environment are fully disregarded. The aim of this book is to scrutinise and comment on some of the main issues of the basic income, to contribute to the knowledge basis on the basic income, and to support better informed—evidence-based—policy making, and to bring a better world about.

Keywords Welfare state reform · Economic science · Prosperity state · Unconditional basic income · Human flourishing · Sustainable economy

---

"Even though the market is socially embedded in its organization, it is thus not socially embedded in its outcomes." B. van Bavel (2016) *The invisible hand? How market economies have emerged and declined since AD 500*, Oxford: Oxford University Press: 266.

L. Delsen
Department of Economics, Institute for Management Research, Radboud University, Nijmegen, The Netherlands
e-mail: l.delsen@fm.ru.nl

1.1 Introduction

The idea of a basic income has a long history. More than two centuries ago, Thomas Paine was the first to propose an Unconditional Basic Income (UBI) scheme in his 1796 pamphlet *Agrarian Justice*. The UBI system is a radical redesign of the tax regime and the welfare system, and implies a complete redrawing of the relationship between the state, the citizen and nature. In Paine's view, the natural world is the common property of all. Landowners should compensate everyone else by paying a so-called 'ground rent', to be collected as a 10% tax on inheritance. This should be paid out in part as a lump-sum on reaching the age of 21, and in part as an annual payment to each person over the age of 50 and to people with disabilities.

Over the past century, the debate on basic income followed a contra-cyclical pattern: in periods of recession, e.g. the 1930s, 1970s and 1980s, there is more discussion about basic income than in periods of economic prosperity, e.g. the Golden Age of capitalism in the 1950s and 1960s (Groot, 1999). Over time, there was not only an increase in the intensity of the debates, but there was also an increase in the geographical spread of the debates. After World War I, basic income was widely discussed in Europe. In the 1960s and 1970s it became a topic among economists in Europe and North America. In the United States (US) and Canada, the Federal Governments funded Negative Income Tax (NIT) field experiments. After the Great Recession (2007–2009) the discussion on basic income became more intense and more wide, covering again a higher number of advanced countries, and a selection of developing countries. Basic income is now moving up the policy agenda in many countries. In the wake of the global financial crisis, a small but increasing number of Organisation for Economic Cooperation and Development (OECD) countries and member states of the European Union (EU) launched basic income experiments (see Bregman, 2017; Standing, 2017; Torry, 2018; Van der Veen & Groot, 2000; Van Parijs & Vanderborght, 2017; Widerquist, 2017; Widerquist, Noguera, Vanderborght, & De Wispelaere, 2013).[1] The focus of this book will be mainly on Europe.[2]

A uniform definition of basic income is still lacking. The literature offers differing definitions of the basic income under various names, with different objectives, recipients, and levels of the transfer (see Piachaud, 2018; Standing, 2017; Torry, 2018; Van der Veen & Groot, 2000; Van Parijs & Vanderborght, 2017; Widerquist

---

[1] For updates on all existing UBI experiments and basic income policy proposals from around the world, see the Basic Income News service of the Basic Income Earth Network (BIEN) (https://basicincome.org/news/).

[2] Basic income experiments in developing countries are outside the focus of this volume. In the developing world, the interest in basic income mirrors a policy shift in e.g. the World Bank and in developing countries to bundle the various subsidies and targeted transfers into a lump-sum cash transfer to households (Banerjee, Niehaus, & Suri, 2019; Hanna and Olken, 2018). Recent basic income experiments were in India (2010–2011), Namibia (2008/2009–2012), Kenya (2011–2013), Uganda (2017–2019) and Brazil (2018–) (Downes & Lansley, 2018; Haushofer & Shapiro, 2016, 2018). In Iran (2011–) a nation-wide unconditional cash-transfer replaced energy subsidies to distribute natural wealth (Salehi-Isfahani & Mostafavi-Dehzooei, 2018).

et al., 2013). Typically, the terms 'basic income', 'citizen's income' or 'demogrant' have been used by those on the left of the political spectrum, while 'Negative Income Tax' (NIT) has been used by those on the right. The terms 'social dividend', 'national dividend', and 'basic income guarantee' are also used. The discussion about basic income is impeded by this confusing hidden range of options about what basic income is, and what it is not. It also limits the comparability of research results.

The official definition of the basic income by the Basic Income Earth Network (BIEN) is "a periodic cash payment unconditionally delivered to all on an individual basis, without means-test or work requirement" (Basic Income Earth Network, 2015). According to Van Parijs & Vanderborght (2017: 8), a basic income is a form of public assistance paid in cash to all citizens, i.e. legal residents (after a minimal period of legal residency). It is an individual entitlement (not linked to household situation), is universal (no income or means test), and is obligation free (no obligation to work or prove willingness to work). These two definitions do not include an aim, the (uniform or differentiated between adults and children) level (poverty line), spending freedom (unlike in-kind payment or voucher), and no reference is made to taxes to fund the public basic income. Not all basic income schemes and field experiments are tax financed; some are privately funded. Most so-called basic income schemes are not universal. They are limited to e.g. certain parts of the population, a region or village, to age categories or benefit recipients, or a combination of these.

The introduction of a basic income implies a paradigm shift. A basic income, providing a sufficiently high income for all, regardless of their need for support and without work obligations, is fundamentally at odds with the foundations of national welfare systems, where reciprocity—give and take—and need play a crucial role. The fundamental reform requirement, combined with an absence of a uniform definition and varied goals, cultural traditions and values, explain the different positions in the national and international debate on the desirability and feasibility of the basic income. However, there is still only limited empirical evidence to back the arguments by advocates and critics of a basic income. Basic income is beset with unanswered questions, with conjectures and unproven beliefs that call for additional research by economists. The aim of this book is to scrutinise and comment on some of the main issues of the basic income, to contribute to the knowledge basis on the basic income, and to support better informed—evidence-based—policy making, and bring a better world about.

This chapter is structured as follows. Following this introduction, Sect. 1.2 presents definitions of UBI and the alternative institutions, and also addresses the conditions for effective economic policy making and institutional reform. Section 1.3 answers the question why UBI deserves more research and policy attention. Section 1.4 deals with two opposing views on the welfare state: cost factor vs. investment. Section 1.5 discusses an alternative subject matter for economics and economists. A new and different balance, i.e. definition of the optimal situation and the optimal combination of policies and institutions is called for, to replace the narrow economic paradigm. Section 1.6 reviews optimal taxation in relation to UBI. A shift from a flat income tax towards progressive income and preferably progressive consumption tax seems to be consistent with UBI. The advantages and disadvantages of the available approaches to research UBI—macro- and micro-simulations, field and laboratory experiments, and survey research—are reviewed in Sect. 1.7. The chapter concludes in Sect. 1.8 with the structure of the book.

1.2 Definition of the UBI and Its Alternatives

To contribute to a common and uniform definition of basic income, UBI and the alternative institutions to choose from are defined below. The fact that there are alternatives, has implications for empirical research.

Full UBI This model is an unconditional (no means, work or other requirements), universal (all residents, not citizens), individual (not household), periodical (regular intervals), automatical (no need to apply), sovereign (free to spend), tax financed, cash payment (not in kind), at or above the poverty line (high enough to cover all basic needs), provided by the government. This definition implies that UBI replaces (part of) the existing social welfare payments in advanced economies. A full UBI has never been implemented in an EU or in an OECD country. Hoynes and Rothstein (2019) argue that a full UBI is extremely expensive: twice the costs of the current transfer system in the US. Micro-simulations for Finland, France, Italy and the United Kingdom (UK) show that a UBI for everyone, at meaningful but fiscally realistic levels, requires tax rises, as well as a reduction in existing benefits. UBI may results in more, not less income poverty (Browne & Immervoll, 2017; OECD, 2017). The affordability of a UBI scheme depends crucially on the generosity of the scheme. However, the affordability also crucially depends on the way UBI is funded, i.e. on the efficiency of the taxation. For a viable UBI proposal, should we start from the present, or should we start from the desired future?

Partial UBI In this model, the amount allocated is below the poverty line. The amount paid is insufficient to meet a person's basic needs. Several advanced economies implemented unconditional provision of money (cash transfer) to individuals or households on a temporary or permanent basis. These unconditional public transfers include flat rate child, family and pension benefits, and means-tested social assistance. Examples of a permanent and universal partial UBI are the 1982 Alaska Permanent Fund (Goldsmith, 2010) and the 2011 universal and unconditional income transfer in Iran (Salehi-Isfahani & Mostafavi-Dehzooei, 2018). However, in both countries people have to apply.

Negative Income Tax This model integrates social security and taxation. Income below the agreed minimum level is compensated by means of taxation. Earned income is reduced by an implicit tax rate. It provides a basic income guarantee, but it is not universal. Its aim is to replace all current welfare programmes, and represents an alternative to the full UBI. In 1992 in the US, the NIT at the level of the poverty line of a family of four, replacing all welfare programmes would imply half of all families would be 'on welfare' under this NIT. The willingness to pay the required higher taxes by the remaining workers is doubtful, while considerable lower benefit would imply many families are ineligible (Filer, Hamermesh, & Rees, 1996: 67–68).

Participation Income This model is a basic income, but with conditions attached. For example, the beneficiary would have to engage in community service (Atkinson, 1996, 2015). It represents an alternative to the partial UBI. FitzRoy and Jin (2018) argue that the only cost-effective policy for comprehensive welfare is a combination of modest basic income with a job offer by local authorities at less than the minimum wage. Delsen (1995, 1997) proposed a right to a partial basic income, conditional on accepting a part-time job. The public sector acts as the employer of last resort. Micro-simulation results show this socially desirable policy is a 'Robin Hood' type of income and tax policy that is budget neutral, and both effective and economically efficient (Delsen, 2002: 204–206). Administration costs were not considered.

Unconditional Job Guarantee This model is a right to work for all who are willing to work to restore full employment (Klosse & Muysken, 2016; Mitchell & Muysken, 2010; Mitchell & Watts, 2004; Standing, 2017). This right to work is a component of the 1948 United Nations' Universal Declaration of Human Right. In the Unconditional Job Guarantee (UJG), the public sector acts as the employer of last resort. It is an alternative to UBI and NIT, to provide everyone with a minimum standard of living, to address inequality and exclusion, and increase well-being and happiness.

Effective economic policy making requires a coordinated use of a sufficient number of appropriately chosen coherent instruments. For economic policy to be effective, Tinbergen's (1952) 'counting rule'—the number of policy instruments should be equal or higher than the number of policy objectives—should be satisfied. Regulatory policies that shape the relationship between the state, citizens, businesses and nature are necessary complements of economic policies. Coherence concerns the design of institutions according to identical principles. Coherent configuration produces better outcomes: complementarity results from coherence (Schmid & Schömann, 1994). A challenge of reform programmes, like the introduction of a UBI, is therefore to achieve a new type of complementarity between reformed institutions (Amable, 2003, 2009; Hall & Gingerich, 2004; Hall & Soskice, 2001). Hence, UBI can only be one policy instrument, one institution in a package of policies. UBI should be embedded in a coherent policy framework. UBI is not, and cannot, be a panacea for all society's—economic, social, environmental, and political—ills.

Institutions are not politically neutral: they reflect power relations. Institutions are changeable when political will changes. A change in competitive market forces is an important source for these changes in institutions and political will. Institutional choice requires flexible coordination: institutional choice and corresponding policy strategies should reflect the amount and nature of variety in the national context. Markets can be appreciated and assessed in various ways, depending on cultural traditions and values. Thus, institutional choice and corresponding policy strategies will vary from country to country, from time to time (Schmid & Schömann, 1994). In most economics textbooks, no reference is made to power, beyond monopoly and bargaining power. Most economists overlook the power struggle that is always present when the distribution of the Gross Domestic Product (GDP) comes up for discussion (cf. Krehm, 2002; Rothschild, 2002). Economic research on UBI should take the distribution of economic and political power in our societies into account.

Opportunity costs are also important in policy decision making. Opportunity costs are the costs of the alternative choice when making an institutional choice for UBI to replace the current social safety net, and should be part of the empirical research on UBI. Comparative research on the UBI, NIT and UJG is still very scarce. For example, Harvey (2006) estimated for the US that the UJG could not only eliminate poverty more efficiently than a UBI or an equivalent NIT, but that it could also achieve most of the other goals of a basic income guarantee at less costs.

1.3   Why UBI Deserves More Research and Policy Attention

In recent years, the topic of (unconditional) basic income has been attracting attention in politics and in public opinion, inside as well as outside of Europe. Automation, the digital revolution, globalisation and the ongoing economic crisis have led to higher unemployment rates, more job insecurity and weakened social standards in many countries. The current discussion about UBI is also related to growing poverty, income and wealth inequality, and the imbalances between work, family and leisure (Bregman, 2017; OECD, 2017; Torry, 2018). Forecasts indicate that considerable percentages of jobs are at 'high risk' of being automated (Frey & Osborne, 2013; McKinsey Global Institute, 2017). Robots have their impact; low-skilled workers are displaced by technological change. There is ample evidence that less-skilled workers are experiencing stagnation in wages and job opportunities (see Hoynes & Rothstein, 2019).

UBI is also a response to the dissatisfaction with the current social safety net. UBI requires less information and administration costs.[3] In all cash-benefit systems, moral hazard is a significant problem (OECD, 1998a, 1998b). It concerns the incentives for people to be poor—decrease hours worked, decrease income—in order to qualify for social assistance. This inefficient overuse adds to the costs of means-tested social assistance. Negative social stigmatisation may explain why take-up rates of social security are low or rights are not effectuated, i.e. funds are not used. Even the most conservative estimates of non-take-up are above 40%, irrespective of benefit types in the EU countries (Eurofound, 2015).

The recurrent non-take-up rates, the complexity and administrative demand, stigmatisation, and increasing dependency on means-tested benefits and high marginal implicit tax rates discourage families to participate in paid employment. Atkinson (1996) recommends to replace them by a participation income.

---

[3] According to US estimates, the administrative costs of means-testing benefits are four or five times higher than the amount of non-means-tested transfers, such as a UBI (Colombino, 2019).

De Wispelaere and Stirton (2018), however, argue that UBI is to be preferred; both schemes involve the same sort of political trade-offs, while participation income is administratively more demanding than means-tested benefits.

The introduction of a UBI may also solve the moral hazard problems. UBI has the potential to address poverty better than means-tested programmes. A UBI is to be preferred over means-tested programmes and NIT, for it eliminates the stigmatisation effect on the poor, and avoids the unemployment and the poverty trap (Gamel, Balsan, & Vero, 2006). Hence, the introduction of a UBI is efficiency improving, and could act as a basis for human flourishing.

Abolishing means-testing would remove all compliance issues and could easily incorporate non-standard workers. UBI would entail a greater benefit coverage. UBI implies a shift from workfare back to welfare. The effects of basic income schemes on labour supply depend on many context factors and have to be assessed empirically (OECD, 2018). However, replacing all existing working-age benefits by a flat-rate amount (without raising general revenue) in a budget-neutral way would lead to benefit levels below the poverty line in all OECD countries. It may also imply significant losses for disadvantaged groups such as the disabled, as their specific benefits would no longer be targeted. This raises substantial fairness concerns, as some individuals, such as the disabled, have greater needs than others. Top-ups for specific groups, would undermine the appeal of simpler (and cheaper) administration and complete predictability of basic income (OECD, 2018). Conditional (income) support policies that complement UBI remain important.

UBI may result in a decline in labour supply as workers are free to choose non-employment over poorly compensated work. UBI also encourages work sharing by reducing desired working time. For some groups, the higher tax burden required for funding UBI may reduce work incentives. High-income OECD countries with shorter average working hours have smaller ecological footprints, carbon footprints and carbon dioxide emissions: reduction of working time and part-time employment redistribute employment and reduce unemployment rates, cut carbon emissions and the ecological footprint, and give people quality of life, well-being, work-life balance as well as productivity growth (see Knight, Rosa, & Schor, 2013; Pullinger, 2014; Schor, 2005). However, UBI will also increase labour supply, for it reduces unemployment and poverty traps. Employment and working hours may increase in the short-term. UBI offers greater economic security, independence and empowers women. It will reduce the gender division of labour (Delsen, 1995, 1997; Haywood, 2014; Standing, 2017: 168; Torry, 2018: 58–59). Some feminists oppose this view. According to them, labour market activities—paid work—and financial independence are the road to emancipation. They consider UBI hush money, that tempers emancipation and sends women back home (Robeyns, 2000). Research is needed to provide evidence.

UBI may also lead to increased investments in human capital by both young people and adults, and positively impacts the health of children and their development. These human capital effects have long-term implications for labour supply, and may offset the negative short-term effects on labour supply (Hoynes & Rothstein, 2019). UBI will reduce labour supply and increase the wage rate. UBI will also shift labour supply away from unpleasant and precarious jobs to low pay jobs with high amenities, jobs with opportunities for human capital accumulation, and jobs that are more aligned with individual tastes. Wages of low paid, low quality jobs may increase and wages of high paid, high quality may decrease. However, experience with the 1982 Alaska Permanent Fund Dividend shows that the induced immigration exerts a downward wage pressure. It offsets the positive wage effect of the dividend. The wage effect of UBI may also be negative, for it also allows employers to hire dividend-receiving workers at a lower wage rate (Goldsmith, 2010). For the worker, accepting a low paid job is worthwhile under UBI, subsidising the employer. Human capital investment will result in higher wages in the medium and long-run (Hoynes & Rothstein, 2019). The jury is still out. The net effect of UBI on participation rates, employment, working hours, wages, and working conditions is still unclear. Further research is required.

The OECD is an international organisation of 36 countries that accept the principles of free-market economy. Capitalism is an economic system characterised by the following: most of the means of production are privately owned; production for the market; operation to make a profit. The profit motive, along with inheritance law, and supported by contract law, forms the driving force of capitalism. A century ago Irving Fisher (1919) concluded that the inheritance system is a responsible factor for the undemocratic distribution of wealth. It has to do with the transmission of fortunes from one generation to another. The other great factor for the distribution of wealth is the profit system. It has to do with the mushroom growth of a fortune in a single generation. The increasing number of the super rich is inconsistent with democratic ideals, democratic progress and creates hostility.

The gap between the rich and the poor keeps widening. Growth, if any, has disproportionally benefited higher income groups, while lower income households have been left behind (OECD, 2015). In the early 1990s, EU countries copied workfare from the US, the obligation to search for a job to receive welfare benefits. In some EU countries the minimum benefit was pegged well below the poverty line. Lower benefits and workfare are incentives to accept low-paid and flexible work (Betzelt & Bothfeld, 2011; Delsen, van Gestel, & van Vugt, 2000; Hastings & Heyes, 2016). The increasing number of non-standard jobs partly explains the growing income inequality (OECD, 2015). Data on the 28 member states of the EU shows that irregular or on-call hours at employers' discretion, has important detrimental effects on workers' health and well-being, especially those working very short hours (Piasna, 2018). Hohendanner and Krug (2018) found that fixed term contracts have a significant negative effect on self-rated health in Germany. Job insecurity explains this. Having a bad job can be worse for one's health than being unemployed. Chandola and Zhang (2018) found evidence in the UK that formerly unemployed adults who moved into poor quality jobs had elevated risks for a range of health problems, compared to adults who remained unemployed.

In 2000, the world's top 1% held 45.5% of all household wealth. In 2017 this was 50.1%. The richest top 10% of adults own 88% of global assets, while the bottom half of adults collectively own less than 1% of total wealth. The growth of financial assets has outpaced the growth of real assets (homes and land) (CSRI, 2017). There is empirical evidence showing that rising inequality has major negative economic consequences (Cingano, 2014; IMF, 2017; OECD, 2015), causes social and health problems (Rowlingson, 2011; Wilkinson & Pickett, 2009), and has negative consequences for our democracies (Van Bavel, 2016), and hence deserves more research and policy and political attention.

Tackling inequality can make our societies fairer and our economies stronger (OECD, 2015). Ostry, Berg and Tsangarides (2014) found that the overall effect of redistribution is pro-growth. The introduction of a UBI is one important instrument to address poverty and inequality, and can contribute to a more equal sharing of the benefits of economic growth. The impact of UBI depends crucially on the level of the payment, the characteristics of the tax system and the benefit provisions it would replace (Browne & Immervoll, 2017; OECD, 2017).

1.4 Welfare States: From Cost Factor to Investment

In the past few years, UBI has gained traction in the debate on reforming the national welfare states in Europe and elsewhere in the OECD area. A welfare state is a country with a democratic constitution, where production is largely governed by the price mechanism and where the government tries to guarantee its citizens an acceptable standard of living through a combination of consultation, regulation and activation of the budget mechanism. All OECD countries are welfare states. In the scientific literature, welfare states are commonly associated with three mutual exclusive goals: income provision, work incentives and cost minimisation (see e.g. Schiller, 2007). Welfare state design involves trade-offs. Any of these goals can only be achieved by comprising the remaining goal. In this respect, Okun (1975) refers to the 'big trade-off' between efficiency and equality. Redistribution is a 'leaky bucket'. Okun (1975) argues that "any insistence on carving the pie into equal slices would shrink the size of the pie". In his opinion, economic science focuses on enlarging the economic pie, while politics concentrates on dividing it. Well-intentioned social policy interventions may be counterproductive. According to Okun (1975: 1) inequalities in living standard and material wealth "reflect a system of rewards and penalties that is intended to encourage efficiency and channel it into socially productive activity. To the extent that the system succeeds, it generates an efficient society. That pursuit of efficiency necessarily creates inequalities. And hence, society faces a trade-off between equality and efficiency". Moreover, according to Elster (1986: 719), introducing a UBI would be considered unfair and unjust. Most workers would consider it "a recipe for the exploitation of the industrious by the lazy."

Social policy is a 'productive factor' and a 'social investment' (Sinn, 1995, 1996; Varian, 1980). According to Varian (1980), optimal redistributive tax involves trading off three kinds of effects: the equity effect of changing distribution of income, the efficiency effect from reducing incentives, and the insurance effect from reducing the variance of individual income streams. 'Risk' is a production factor; higher risk-taking by individuals means more output for the society (Sinn,

1995, 1996). The welfare state can increase people's willingness to take economic risks, and stimulates independent entrepreneurship. Employability and investments in human capital also require that people take a certain risk.

There is ample empirical evidence in the US, Canada and the EU that social policy is not a leaky bucket. It is an investment, for it increases productivity and promotes risk taking, entrepreneurship, human capital, social peace and the country's competitiveness (Acemoglu & Shimer, 1999; De Grauwe & Polan, 2005; Gottlieb, Townsend, & Xu, 2016; Hombert, Schoar, Sraer, & Thesmar, 2014; Olds, 2016). Government and market are not substitutes but complements: social insurances make growth of markets possible (Rodrik, 1998). This is at odds with the traditional ideas behind neoclassical economics, and the trade-off in particular.

However, the national welfare states are developing in the direction of a 'participation society' (Delsen, 2017). The underlying idea of the participation society is one in which people decrease their dependency on state provision, and instead become self-sufficient or dependent on family and community solidarity. People must take responsibility for their own future and create their own social and financial safety nets. Care and social support are also first and foremost the personal responsibility of citizens. It resembles Titmuss's residual welfare model based on the principle of assistance, i.e. a social security net. Family and the private market are the core. Government is a last and temporary resort, when the private market and the family fall short. Central aim of the residual welfare model is to teach people how to do without it (Titmuss, 1974). In the participation society, unpaid productive work and social services are fundamental; reciprocity in the sense of 'income should be distributed according to productive contributions' loses relevance. In the context of the participation society, the UBI is an income for the individual's contribution to society. UBI implies that working only for money is in the past: everyone works for the society, and contributes to the public good. Laboratory experiments show that students—in a game theoretical situation—behave differently from neoclassical economic predictions: they are willing to contribute to the public good, even in situations where the incentives to free-ride are very strong (Fischbacher, Gärter, & Fehr, 2001). The current distribution and income based national welfare state could be transformed into an efficiency, happiness and environment based 'prosperity state' to achieve and secure sustainable shared prosperity. A prosperity state is a state in which the economy is designed explicitly around delivering the capabilities for human flourishing.

1.5 New Subject Matter for Economics and Economists

The influential definition of the subject matter of economics that still lives in contemporary economics textbooks is by Robbins (1932: 15): "Economics is the science which studies human behaviour as a relationship between ends and scarce means which have alternative uses." "Economics takes all ends for granted." (p. 31).

Ethics was discarded from economics. The individual is the best judge of her or his interests. His definition justified not only the narrowing down of economic theory to the theory of constrained maximisation or rational choice, but also the 'imperialism' of economics into the other social sciences (Backhouse & Medema, 2009).

In recent years, increasing productivity is no longer sufficient in most OECD countries to raise real wages for the typical worker. There are two explanations for this decoupling of real wages from labour productivity. First, increasing wage inequality. Between 1995 and 2014, the ratio of median to average wages has declined in all OECD countries, except Spain and Chile. This reflects the disproportionate wage growth at the very top of the wage distribution. Second, the decline in labour share in two thirds of the OECD countries. The labour share measures the extent to which value added is appropriated by capital (Schwellnus, Kappeler, & Pionnier, 2017). The challenge for future policy is not the quantity of jobs, but the quality of jobs: jobs that pay enough to provide a decent standard of living. Wages fail to capture a big enough piece of the economic pie to ensure everyone gets a fair share of it. Moreover, the pay gap between the Chief Executive Officer (CEO) and the shop floor has negative effects on the motivation of workers (Steffens, Aslam, Peters, & Quiggin, 2018). The trend of absolutely and relatively rapidly increasing executive compensation reflects the increased power of capital relative to labour. This shift has many causes and has been undermining confidence in capitalism. People are becoming concerned that the rising power of big successful companies may be part of the reason for the recent sluggish economic growth and rising income inequality. Although the negative macro-economic implications of rising corporate market power have been modest so far, further increases in the market power of these already powerful firms could weaken investment, deter innovation, reduce labour income shares, and make it more difficult for monetary policy to stabilise output (IMF, 2019).

According to Nobel Lauriat Milton Friedman (1962), capitalism will bring prosperity for all, guarantees freedom and is a necessary condition for political freedom. Free market economy is a condition sine qua non for equality and economic prosperity. A viable basic income proposal simultaneously calls for the establishment of a complementary institutional framework of competitive, open and free markets. Opposite to Friedman, Van Bavel (2016) shows empirically that freedom and equality are necessary conditions for markets to develop. Markets may hamper GDP growth and freedom. Freedom is not a result of markets, but rather a condition for the emergence of markets. New economic elites conquer political and legal power with their wealth, and exclude newcomers. Markets tend to concentrate wealth in the hands of a few, who then distort market mechanisms in their favour, leading to unequal distributions of wealth, and increasing lack of freedom.[4]

---

[4]Van Bavel (2016) analyses the rise and downfall of three market economies: early medieval Iraq, high/late medieval Italy, and the late medieval/early modern Low Countries, and then draws parallels to England and the US in recent times.

This begs the question: will the capitalistic economic system go under due to its internal limits, caused by inevitable internal contradiction, i.e. increasing and then untenable income and asset inequality? It happened before in China and the Soviet Union (see Van Bavel, 2016). Economically, sustainability means avoiding major disruptions and collapses, hedging against instabilities and discontinuities. It always concerns temporality, and longevity, can only be observed after the fact, and there are no direct indicators, only predictors (Costanza & Patten, 1995). According to Nobel Prize winner Simon Kuznets (e.g. 1955) there is a self-regulating mechanism that prevents the end of capitalism. According to Kuznets, income inequality first increases and then decreases during the economic development process, an inverted-U shape. This so-called Kuznets curve was raised to the level of *law by other economists*—opposed to Karl Marx's pessimistic view on capitalism: capitalism does not result in increasing inequality. It fits the Cold War ideological conflict. After World War II, economic growth, i.e. GDP growth, became and still is considered the main policy goal, inspired by Kuznets (1937), a solution to poverty as well as to class struggle, and core for development. The OECD was founded in 1961, and targets for economic growth were set to compete between the East and the West. The European single market established in 1993 seeks economic expansion to increase economic growth in the EU. Ostry, Berg and Tsangarides (2014) conclude that it would be a mistake to focus on growth and let inequality take care of itself.

Many risks associated with climate change have distributional implications. The adaptation measures taken and the mitigation of climate change could also have profound distributional implications, e.g. carbon tax will press more heavily on the poor. Full employment is a condition sine qua non for contemporary welfare states: they are based on an expansionary economic model. Continuous economic growth provides jobs and business opportunities, generates the tax revenues that finance welfare programmes, and provides opportunities that discourage radical demand of wealth redistribution, but is also accompanied by a growing environmental footprint (see e.g. Gough & Meadowcroft, 2011).

This begs the question: will capitalism be the victim of its growth success, because it clashes on the external limits imposed by the environment? The *environmental Kuznets curve* hypothesis postulates an inverted-U shape between GDP per capita and environmental pressure. Thus, the answer to this question is no. However, it happened before, e.g. Easter Island and Maya civilisation (De Grauwe, 2017). The paradox of the market system is that the more successful the market system, the greater the chance that the system encounters environmental limits. There is a self-destructive tendency present in the market system. If the government does not manage the external costs—caused by market activities—to be paid by those who have generated these cost, then the market system will come to its end at some point (De Grauwe, 2017).

Kelly (2012) calls for a redesign of capitalism, i.e. for generative ownership—a generative economy—that aims to create the conditions for the flourishing of life, generating broad well-being, serving the common good, a socially fair and ecologically sustainable economy, to replace the dominant extractive model of capitalism, extracting fossil fuels from the earth, and financial wealth from the economy.

Nature can do without society or economy. However, no society, no economy can do without nature. Almost half a century ago, the economist Barbara Ward stressed the need to simultaneously address the 'inner limits' of human needs and the 'outer limits' of what the earth can sustain (Ward & Dubois, 1972). In Raworth's (2017) 'doughnut economy', the outer ring consists of the earth's environmental limits, the inner ring represents a sufficiency of the resources people need to lead a good life, i.e. the inner and outer social and ecological limits for humans to flourish. The area between the two rings—the doughnut itself—is the "ecologically safe and socially just space" in which humanity should strive to live. The purpose of economics should be to help enter that space and stay there. Anyone living in the hole in the middle of the doughnut is in a state of deprivation, i.e. falls short on life's essentials, as agreed in the Sustainable Development Goals of the United Nations. These essentials of well-being include income, food, clean water, housing, sanitation, energy, education, healthcare, access to work, and political voice. Fitoussi & Stiglitz (2011) recommend a shift in the focus from production and growth to a concern for sustainable human well-being. Economics is then the study of resource allocation decisions and processes, and the forces that guide these: from a human perspective it is about understanding who gets what, under what conditions and why? (McGregor & Pouw, 2019). The human dimension should be introduced into economy and into economics. This involves taking into account the non-monetised as well as the monetised economy, which constitute economic activity.

The introduction of a UBI may be an important institution in the redesign of capitalism, and redirect the focus of economics towards happiness. The UBI is a reward for the contribution to society, to the public good. UBI may contribute to poverty and inequality reduction, to well-being and trust in other people and in institutions, and hence to social cohesion and sustainability. In the next Section, it will be argued that to bring the latter about, progressive taxation is a coherent and complementary institutional choice.

1.6 UBI: From Flat Tax to Progressive Personal Consumption Tax

Mirrlees' (1971) redistributive theory of optimal income taxation is the dominant tax theory. The optimal income tax depends on the distribution of abilities, and it assumes that income is the only indicator of ability. Distaste for inequality and the responsiveness of work and effort to incentives are core factors. For instance, Hoynes and Rothstein (2019) state that given rising inequality and the motivation of offsetting increasing income shares of capital owners, one might prefer to finance UBI through a more progressive tax. In public finance textbooks, the central issue in the design of fiscal policy is this trade-off between equity and efficiency. Marginal tax rates discourage exerting effort, generating efficiency costs (Mankiw, Weinzierl,

& Yagan, 2009). The optimal tax is a lump-sum tax,[5] for it does not result in changes of behaviour or in reallocation of resources. The flat income tax concerns the same marginal tax rate for all income earners. To keep it simple, the flat tax should be combined with a lump-sum transfer for the lower income earners and is close to optimal (Atkinson, 1995; Islam & Colombino, 2018; Mankiw et al., 2009). The level of the flat rate is a political decision. A high flat rate implies the priority is to fight poverty; the tax burden is shifted from low to high income earners, protecting the vulnerable groups (equity). A low flat rate (efficiency) implies the tax burden is shifted from high to low income earners.

The 'just desert theory' (Mankiw, 2010) does not require a distributive motive to increase marginal tax rates. According to the 'just deserts theory' taxation should ensure that individuals receive their social contribution, i.e. individuals' compensation should reflect his or her social contribution. Who contributes more to society— more goods and services—deserves a higher income, it is rightfully his or hers. However, paid employment is not the only resource for state income/government revenues. Also other resources, including land, knowledge, security, and political stability contribute to inter-country differences in productivity. Part of this state income can be divided as a social dividend (Haywood, 2014).

There is a considerable gap between how much different professions are paid and what they contribute to society. UBI can play a positive role in closing this gap. The New Economics Foundation (NEF, 2009) found that some of the most highly paid jobs benefit us least, and some of the lowest paid jobs benefit us most. The least well paid jobs are often those that are among the most socially valuable—jobs that keep our communities and families together. The market does not reward this kind of work well. For instance, leading London City bankers, advertising executives, and tax accountants destroy more social value than the money value they generate, while childcare workers, hospital cleaners, and waste recycling workers generate more social value than they are paid. Bringing a better world about requires a new approach to looking at the value of work: look beyond the narrow mainstream economic notion of productivity—more products and services produced and sold through the market—to quantify its social, environmental and economic value. By making social value creation an important economic and societal goal, we could set the right incentives to maximise net social benefits, ensure a greater return to labour rather than capital, and a more equal distribution of economic resources between workers.

Capitalism is supposed to be the most efficient economic system. However, about 8% of workers perceive their job to be socially useless. An additional 17% seem doubtful about the social usefulness of their job. These, socially useless jobs are not productive, i.e. inefficient. These inefficient jobs are more likely in the private sector than the public sector. The highest share of workers reporting a socially useless job are in finance and law (Dur & van Lent, 2019; Graeber, 2018).

---

[5]In 1990 Margret Thatcher introduced a head tax. It became one of the factors that led to the end of her premiership in the same year, and it was repealed in 1991 by her successor.

High-paying professions have negative externalities. Low-paying professions have positive externalities. These externalities are large and have important implications. There is evidence that arts, engineering, research and teaching generate positive externalities, and finance, management[6] and law generate negative externalities (Lockwood, Nathanson, & Weyl, 2017; Piketty, 2014; Piketty, Saez, & Stantcheva, 2014: 508–512). Raising marginal tax rates for the well-off can be used to incite workers to move into socially (more) productive professions and has an efficiency benefit. Progressive income taxation can be used to reallocate talented individuals from professions that cause negative externalities to those that cause positive externalities and can be considered a social welfare generating Pigouvian optimal tax. Pigouvian subsidies can be used for professions that cause positive externalities. Hence, it is not only solidarity, i.e. the distributional motive, it may also be for pure efficiency reasons to introduce a UBI financed by progressive income tax, i.e. an optimal taxation that fits Mankiw's 'just deserts theory'.

The introduction of the UBI is preferably to be financed by a progressive personal consumption tax. Both are designed according to identical principles, allowing for coherence and complementarity, i.e. compatible combination of policies (Schmid & Schömann, 1994). A progressive consumption tax should replace the progressive income tax, for people should be taxed on what they take out of society (consumption), not on what they contribute to society (income). Advocates of replacing income tax with a progressive personal consumption tax have asserted its superiority to the income tax in terms of fairness, economic efficiency, and simplicity of administration (Graetz, 1979). Moreover, it encourages sustainability (Easterlin, 1974; Frank, 2011; Layard, 2005). The hedonic treadmill (rising aspiration levels) (Brickman & Campbell, 1971) and the positional treadmill (status seeking behaviour) turn economic growth into a rat race (Frank, 1985). Both treadmills indicate that happiness is affected by relative, rather than absolute income levels. Overconsumption is not only a waste of scarce natural resources, it is also accompanied by air, water and soil pollution. However, it shows positive in GDP growth rates. All will benefit from progressive consumption tax on activities that are harmful to society. If consumption were taxed at a progressive rate, we would save more, buy less expensive houses and cars, and feel less pressure to work excessively long hours (Frank, 1997). This improves the quality of our lives.[7] The results of a laboratory experiment by Blumkin, Bradley and Ganun (2012) support the switch from income to consumption tax (value added tax, VAT): less reduction in labour supply plus potential welfare gains and confirm the equity, efficiency and simplicity arguments for a consumption based tax.

---

[6]When market forces can explain the compensation of CEO's externalities are zero. The skyrocketing executive pay can be explained by bargaining power: low marginal tax rates encourage executives to negotiate harder for higher pay; and have little to do with managerial productivity (Piketty et al., 2014).

[7]Consumption tax rates start low and rise more steeply than the current income tax. A top marginal rate of 100% encourages savings and investments. It also reduces income inequality and cures slow growth (Frank, 2011).

UBI may also increase the total amount of wasteful and inefficient expenditure on positional goods, i.e. conspicuous consumption that is detrimental to investments and the longer-term needs of the society (Goldsmith, 2010). There may be a 'mailbox effect': the marginal propensity to consume windfall income is higher than income from other resources (Pech, 2010). The latter depends on how UBI is perceived and the tax scheme, and hence is an empirical question. UBI combined with progressive consumption tax and progressive income tax not only influences consumption, the demand side of the economy, it also impacts the supply side of the economy, the production, and how production is organised.

1.7 Five Types of Research Design to Evaluate the Effects of a UBI

Scientific evidence of the effects of UBI in the EU and OECD countries is limited. Five types of research design have been used by researchers to investigate the empirical consequences of a UBI. All five have benefits and drawbacks.

A first option is to rely on existing survey material and official statistics to analyse the effect of increases in income on e.g. labour supply or poverty. However, existing datasets hardly ever contain information about (periodically) significant exogenous non-earned incomes. This makes it almost impossible to make any inferences from such databases to a UBI situation (see Marx & Peeters, 2004). Sommer's (2016) micro-simulations on Germany secondary data show a positive impact on labour supply as well as poverty rates, in case the means-tested unemployment benefits were replaced with a NIT and calibrated to be both financially feasible and compatible with current constitutional legislation. The International Monetary Fund (IMF) concludes that the fiscal costs depend on the level of UBI. UBI reduces inequality and poverty substantially in advanced and developing countries (IMF, 2017). Simulations of the impact of UBI in Catalonia show that self-financing requires high nominal tax rates. Arcarons, Calonge, Noguera, and Raventós (2004) conclude that the reforms are financially feasible. However, the political feasibility is doubted. Welfare implications of micro-simulations based on representative agent models need not hold for individuals in an economy. Macro-simulations by a Keynesian model show that UBI increases aggregate demand and the size of the economy (Nikiforos, Steinbaum, & Zezza, 2017). The model assumes that the size of the economy is constrained by aggregate demand, and that additional marginal taxes and the UBI have no impact on labour supply. Also, micro-simulation models traditionally omit behavioural responses. They fall foul of the Lucas critique: people may change their expectations and behaviour in reaction to a change in economic policy, and this will shift the parameters of the models used.

A second option is to use surveys of lottery winners. Marx and Peeters (2008) surveyed Belgian lottery winners to research the effect of periodically unconditional life-long income on behaviour. Labour supply effects are limited. Winners are less uncertain about future. Massachusetts State Lottery winners and Swedish lotteries have been used to establish the effect of wealth on labour supply. The negative labour supply response is modest. Lottery prizes concern a specific type of wealth shock. Another drawback is that lottery players may not be representative of the general population. Winners may have a right to remain anonymous. The low number of winners does not allow to assess the macro-impact. Unlike UBI, lottery wins are not funded by taxes (see Cesarini, Lindqvist, Notowidigdo, & Östling, 2017; Imbens, Rubin, & Sacerdote, 2001; Marinescu, 2018).

A third option is to survey people and ask them what their attitude is towards a UBI and what they might do under UBI conditions (see e.g. Dalia Research, 2017; ING, 2016; Northeastern University, 2018). The external validity of the results is limited, since there is an important difference between attitudes (what people say) and behaviour (what people do). Survey responses are influenced by the regional, national macro-economic and welfare state contexts. Responses may also vary with question wording and order. However, surveys on attitudes may provide important insights on decisions that closely resemble voting in elections (Gerber & Green, 2011). The 36 OECD member countries accept the principles of representative democracy. Also all 28 EU member states are representative democracies. In representative democracies public opinions matter. The impact of public opinion on public policy is substantial in democracies (Burstein, 2003). Surveys may provide useful information about the preferences for UBI and what people believe about UBI, the reasons for individuals to support or oppose UBI, as well as on the expected behavioural consequences of UBI. Surveys offer relevant insights to establish the societal desirability as well as the political support, and hence the political feasibility, i.e. the achievability of UBI.

A fourth possibility is to examine existing programmes that resemble a UBI, e.g. the 1982 Alaska Permanent Fund Dividend (Goldsmith, 2010; Jones & Marinescu, 2018), the recently ended field experiment in Finland (Kangas, Jauhiainen, Simanainen, & Ylikännö, 2019), or the recently started trust-based experiments with social assistance in the Netherlands and Germany (HartzPlus).

Field experiments may provide useful information about the causal effects and hence the desirability and feasibility of UBI, i.e. the radical redesign of the tax regime and the welfare system. In field experiments individuals are randomly assigned to treatment and control groups. Random assignment is the only approach to social policy evaluation that assures statistical independence between the treatment being offered and other determinants of outcomes. It is considered the 'gold standard' in social policy evaluation. To enhance and evaluate the external validity, field experiments try to simulate the conditions as closely as possible under which a causal process of a stimulus of policy interest occurs (Gerber & Green, 2011). Social experiments have a number of important limitations. High costs are a major disadvantage of social experiments, and cause concern about funding. The results of these field experiments may be biased due to e.g. selection bias (more motivated participants), randomisation bias (randomisation procedure affects behaviour of potential participants), disruption bias (administrative changes in response to randomisation) and drop-out bias (incomplete treatment). Moreover, the social experiment may change the behaviour of the participants during the programme, the so-called Hawthorne effect. Random assignment may be unethical, because assigning individuals to a control group conflicts with universal access to programmes. Money may be a solution to compensate the ethical concerns (Björklund & Regnér, 1996; Heckman & Smith, 1995, 1996; Killingsworth, 1983: 379).

Past field experiments and research were centred on the macro-economic effect of basic income, labour supply in particular. The US Government funded four NIT field experiments between 1968 and 1978. During 1975–1978 Canada also conducted a NIT experiment (see Burtless, 1986; Killingsworth, 1983: 379–408; Killingsworth & Heckman, 1986; Marinescu, 2018; Pencavel, 1986: 73–82; Robins, 1985; Widerquist, 2018). The negative effects of the NIT experiments on work effort in the US and Canada are limited or absent. The micro studies of the NIT experiments in the US, Canada, and the Cherokee Indians casino dividend, using treatment and control groups, show positive effects of the basic income on social exclusion, on human capital formation, on educational outcomes and on health, and negative effects on criminal activity (Forget, 2011; Hanushek, 1987; Marinescu, 2018). The Alaska dividend has no significant effect on employment, yet increases part-time work. The higher consumption due to the additional income increases labour demand and offsets the negative income effects (Jones & Marinescu, 2018). Results of a randomised field experiment in Mexico show that UBI may lead to increased investments by poor households. A UBI does not only alleviate liquidity and credit constraints. When perceived as a secure and steady source of income over time, risk-averse households will be more willing to invest in riskier but higher return productive activities and increase living standards in the long-run (Gertler, Martinez, & Rubio-Codina, 2012). The first results of the 2017–2019 Finnish partial basic income experiment show no significant employment effects, and that basic income recipients are more positive about the future, their well-being, and the basic income (Kangas et al., 2019).

Field experiments have expiration dates. For instance, the NIT experiments in the US and Canada took place in different pre-internet times, in different contexts. They concern short-term interventions that shed little light on the long-term effects of UBI.[8] Their samples sizes are rather small and their designs are quite similar. The amounts of the UBI are also rather small to establish the macro-economic effects of a UBI. Most field experiments concern partial UBI and UBI-related trials (Hoynes & Rothstein, 2019; Widerquist, 2018). Noguera and De Wispelaere (2006) add two more drawbacks. Field experiments on UBI are susceptible to 'political manipulation', defined as "external interference with the research process or its outcomes for

---

[8]The 1982 Alaska Permanent Fund Dividend has a long duration. The large-scale dividend has served as an important 'automatic stabiliser' for the entire economy of Alaska. It has a positive effect on the birth rate. The reduction of the cost of children (price effect) may be smaller or bigger than the income effect, i.e. value of time also increases with income. Since raising children is a time-consuming activity, the birth rate could fall because of the dividend (Goldsmith, 2010). The Alaska dividend has also had a significant positive effect on the birth weight (Chung et al., 2016). In the US, the NIT treatment increased also the birth weights and decreased the fertility (Marinescu, 2018).

political reasons". Second, a field experiment design entails scientific limitations that impede a genuine understanding of the behavioural effects of UBI in a modern welfare state. While field experiments can teach us a lot about some of the central questions to be considered when implementing a UBI, they nevertheless face considerable constraints that affect both the scope of the research, the range of questions researchers can study in a single field experiment, and the validity and robustness of the results.

Finally, as has been proposed by Noguera and De Wispelaere (2006), one could use laboratory experiments to study the behavioural responses to the introduction of a UBI. Laboratory experiments can enhance the understanding of two behavioural issues: 'judgement' and 'choice' (Camerer & Loewenstein, 2004). Judgement is the ex ante opinion, i.e. to establish under what conditions people support the introduction of UBI. The latter is very relevant for the political feasibility. 'Choice' concerns ex post prediction of economic and social behaviour after introduction of the UBI. The latter is important for the sustainability of a UBI. Laboratory experiments have become one of the main tools used by behavioural economists. These experiments have the advantage of providing a controlled environment to identify causal effects (of treatments) that is not possible to create using other empirical methodologies. Laboratory experiments may have external validity concerns (Virjo, 2006). Laboratory experiments often concern students. Due to this pool bias, the insights from these laboratory experiments may not be generalisable to the field, and the treatment effects may not hold outside the laboratory. Moreover, up until now laboratory experiments mainly concern short-term impacts of UBI (e.g. Haigner, Höchtl, Jenewein, Schneider, & Wakolbinger, 2012; Kawagoe, 2009). Widerquist (2018: 91) even considers laboratory experiments, although popular in economics, not useful for the study of UBI. For policy makers, unlike field experiments, laboratory experiments do not require their commitment to UBI (Stafford, 1986). Unlike short-lived field experiments, laboratory experiments also allow to research long-run consequence of UBI, e.g. on birth rates (Kawagoe, 2009). Students' behaviour in the laboratory is often not different from more relevant real-world pendants (Charness & Kuhn, 2011). Hebst and Mas (2015) show that the results of laboratory experiments can be generalised to the field. Moreover, students can be replaced with a 'relevant' subject pool, e.g. people from throughout the population.

All five approaches have their shortcomings. They may complement each other. For instance, experiments can verify impressions from survey data, and cost-effective laboratory experiment may precede more expensive field research.

1.8 Structure of This Book

In representative democracies, surveys offer relevant insights to establish the societal desirability of the introduction of a UBI. In Chap. 2 Lei Delsen and Rutger Schilpzand research the preferences for UBI in the 28 EU member states. They analyse the extent to which such preferences differ across individuals and countries, and how such differences can be explained. Moreover, they research expected changes in own individual work choices and in the work choices of other people due to the introduction of a UBI.

Core requirements for a successful introduction of a UBI are political will and political support. Also the continuation of a UBI is ultimately a political rather than an economic question. In Chap. 3 Genevieve Shanahan, Mark Smith and Priya Srinivasan explore the political feasibility of basic income policies in the 28 EU member states. They analyse the various types of political feasibility and their interaction.

The next three chapters concern field experiments. In Chap. 4 Mike Danson reviews the main motives behind the planned basic income pilots in four municipalities in Scotland. UBI is a tool for redistribution and a means of solidarity and inclusion: reducing poverty and tackling inequality is the main driver of the Scottish UBI pilot. The chapter also explores the constraints and barriers to launching the pilot experiments.

The Chaps. 5 and 6 deal with ongoing UBI-related social assistance experiments in eleven cities in the Netherlands. Dissatisfaction with the so-called 'active labour-market policies' plays an important role to start these trust-based UBI-related experiments. Although activation policies are decentralised, Dutch municipalities need the consent of the central government to experiment with social assistance. In Chap. 5 Ruud Muffels and Erwin Gielens discuss the history, the design and the first empirical findings of the 'participation income' experiment. In Chap. 6 János Betkó, Niels Spierings, Maurice Gesthuizen and Peer Scheepers theorise and test in detail which selection biases are found in the city of Nijmegen's UBI-related social assistance experiment, and how strong those biases are.

The last two chapters deal with laboratory experiments. Laboratory experiments on UBI are still very limited. In Chap. 7 Sascha Füllbrunn, Lei Delsen and Jana Vyrastekova explore how experimental economics can be used to test UBI policies in order to inform policymakers. They take a detailed look at this method, and how it can help to understand the consequences of a UBI. They also present the results of a small-scale experiment on the effect of the UBI on risk-taking.

Finally, in Chap. 8 Toshiji Kawagoe addresses moral hazard (reduction of labour incentive) and adverse selection (women are willing to get married in order to increase total household income) resulting from UBI in laboratory experiments. He compares UBI and NIT using an evolutionary theoretic game model and analyses it by evolutionary game theory. UBI increases labour supply significantly more than NIT. He also analyses the long-run effects of UBI on marriage and child-bearing choices.

References

Acemoglu, D., & Shimer, R. (1999). Efficient unemployment insurance. *The Journal of Political Economy, 107*(5), 893–928. Accessed June 8, 2019, from http://www.jstor.org/stable/2990832

Amable, B. (2003). *The diversity of modern capitalism*. Oxford: Oxford University Press.

Amable, B. (2009). Structural reforms in Europe and the (in)coherence of institutions. *Oxford Review of Economic Policy, 25*(1), 17–39. https://doi.org/10.1093/oxrep/grp001

Arcarons, J., Calonge, S., Noguera, J. A., & Raventós, D. (2004). *The financial feasibility and redistributive impact of a basic income scheme in Catalonia.* Paper for the 10th congress of the Basic Income European Network (BIEN), Barcelona, 19–20 September. Accessed June 10, 2019, from https://basicincome.org/bien/pdf/2004ArcaronsCalongeNogueraRaventos.pdf

Atkinson, A. B. (1995). *Public economics in action. The basic income/flat tax proposal.* Oxford: Clarendon Press.

Atkinson, A. B. (1996). The case for a participation income. *The Political Quarterly, 67*(1), 67–70. https://doi.org/10.1111/j.1467-923X.1996.tb01568.x

Atkinson, A. B. (2015). *Inequality: What can be done?* Cambridge, MA: Harvard University Press.

Backhouse, R. E., & Medema, S. G. (2009). Defining economics: The long road to acceptance of the Robbins definition. *Economica, 76*(s1), 805–820. https://doi.org/10.1111/j.1468-0335.2009.00789.x

Banerjee, A., Niehaus, P., & Suri, T. (2019). *Universal basic income in the developing world* (NBER Working Paper No. 25598). Cambridge, MA: National Bureau of Economic Research.

Basic Income Earth Network. (2015). *About basic income.* Retrieved May 17, 2019, from https://basicincome.org/basic-income/

Betzelt, S., & Bothfeld, S. (Eds.). (2011). *Activation and labour market reforms in Europe: Challenges to social citizenship.* Houndmills: Palgrave Macmillan.

Björklund, A., & Regnér, H. (1996). Experimental evaluation of European labour market policy. In G. Schmid, J. O'Reilly, & K. Schömann (Eds.), *International handbook of labour market policy and evaluation* (pp. 89–114). Cheltenham: Edward Elgar.

Blumkin, T., Bradley, J. R., & Ganun, Y. (2012). Are income and consumption taxes ever really equivalent? Evidence from a real-effort experiment with real goods. *European Economic Review, 56*, 1200–1219. https://doi.org/10.1016/j.euroecorev.2012.06.001

Bregman, R. (2017). *Utopia for realists. And how we can get there.* London: Bloomsbury.

Brickman, P., & Campbell, D. T. (1971). Hedonic relativism and planning the good society. In M. H. Apley (Ed.), *Adaptation-level theory: A symposium* (pp. 287–302). New York: Academic Press.

Browne, J., & Immervoll, H. (2017). Mechanics of replacing benefit systems with a basic income: Comparative results from a microsimulation approach. *The Journal of Economic Inequality, 15*(4), 325–344. https://doi.org/10.1007/s10888-017-9366-6

Burstein, P. (2003). The impact of public opinion on public policy: A review and an agenda. *Political Research Quarterly, 56*(1), 29–40. https://doi.org/10.2307/3219881

Burtless, G. (1986). The work response to a guaranteed income: A survey of experimental evidence. In A. H. Munnell (Ed.), *Lessons from the income maintenance experiments* (pp. 22–52). Boston, MA: Federal Reserve Bank of Boston.

Camerer, C. F., & Loewenstein, G. (2004). Behavioral economics: Past, present, and future. In C. F. Camerer, G. Loewenstein, & M. Rabin (Eds.), *Advances in behavioral economics* (pp. 3–51). Princeton University Press: Princeton, NJ.

Cesarini, D., Lindqvist, E., Notowidigdo, M. J., & Östling, R. (2017). The effect of wealth on individual and household labor supply: Evidence from Swedish lotteries. *American Economic Review, 107*(12), 3917–3946. https://doi.org/10.1257/aer.20151589

Chandola, T., & Zhang, N. (2018). Re-employment, job quality, health and allostatic load biomarkers: Prospective evidence from the UK household longitudinal study. *International Journal of Epidemiology, 47*(1), 47–57. https://doi.org/10.1093/ije/dyx150

Charness, G., & Kuhn, P. (2011). Lab labor: What can labor economists learn from the lab? *Handbook of Labor Economics, 4*, 229–330. https://doi.org/10.1016/S0169-7218(11)00409-6

Chung, W., Ha, H., & Kim, B. (2016). Money transfer and birth weight: Evidence from the Alaska Permanent Fund Dividend. *Economic Inquiry, 54*(1), 576–590. https://doi.org/10.1111/ecin.12235

Cingano, F. (2014). *Trends in income inequality and its impact on economic growth* (OECD Social, Employment and Migration Working Papers No. 163). Paris: OECD Publishing. https://doi.org/10.1787/1815199X

Colombino, U. (2019). Is unconditional basic income a *viable* alternative to other social welfare measures?, *IZA World of Labor, 128v*2. https://doi.org/10.15185/izawol.128.v2

Costanza, R., & Patten, B. C. (1995). Defining and predicting sustainability. *Ecological Economics, 15*(3), 193–196. https://doi.org/10.1016/0921-8009(95)00048-8

CSRI. (2017). Global wealth report 2017. Zurich: Credit Suisse Research Institute. Accessed June 10, 2019, from https://static.poder360.com.br/2017/11/global-wealth-report-2017-en.pdf

Dalia Research. (2017). *The EU's growing support for basic income. Measuring the change in European support for basic income from April 2016 to March 2017*. Berlin: Dalia Research. Accessed June 10, 2019, from https://basicincome.org/wp-content/uploads/2017/05/DR-2017-survey.pdf

De Grauwe, P. (2017). *The limits of the market: The pendulum between government and market*. Oxford: Oxford University Press.

De Grauwe, P., & Polan, M. (2005). Globalization and social spending. *Pacific Economic Review, 10*(1), 105–123. https://doi.org/10.1111/j.1468-0106.2005.00263.x

De Wispelaere, J., & Stirton, L. (2018). The case against participation income – political, not merely administrative. *The Political Quarterly, 89*(2), 262–267. https://doi.org/10.1111/1467-923X.12513

Delsen, L. (1995). *Atypical employment: An international perspective: Causes, consequences and policy*. Groningen: Wolters-Noordhoff.

Delsen, L. (1997). A new concept of full employment. *Economic and Industrial Democracy, 18*(1), 119–135. https://doi.org/10.1177/0143831X97181007

Delsen, L. (2002). *Exit polder model? Socioeconomic changes in the Netherlands*. Westport, CT: Praeger Publishers.

Delsen, L. (2017). *Activation reform in the European welfare states and lessons from Dutch flexicurity* (IMR Working Paper NiCE17-02). Nijmegen: Nijmegen Center for Economics (NiCE), Institute for Management Research, Radboud University. https://doi.org/10.13140/RG.2.2.15051.28969

Delsen, L., van Gestel, N., & van Vugt, J. (2000). European integration: Current problems and future scenarios. In J. van Vugt & J. M. Peet (Eds.), *Social security and solidarity in European Union: Facts, evaluations, and perspectives* (pp. 223–253). Heidelberg: Physica.

Downes, A., & Lansley, S. (Eds.). (2018). *It's basic income: The global debate*. Bristol: Bristol University Press.

Dur, R., & van Lent, M. (2019). Socially useless jobs. *Industrial Relations. A Journal of Economy and Society, 58*(1), 3–16. https://doi.org/10.1111/irel.12227

Easterlin, R. A. (1974). Does economic growth improve the human lot? Some empirical evidence. In P. A. David & M. W. Reder (Eds.), *Nations and households in economic growth: Essays in honor of Moses Abramovitz* (pp. 89–125). New York: Academic Press. https://doi.org/10.1016/B978-0-12-205050-3.50008-7

Elster, J. (1986). Comment on Van der Veen and Van Parijs. *Theory and Society, 15*(5), 709–721. https://doi.org/10.1007/BF00239135

Eurofound. (2015). *Access to social benefits: Reducing non-take-up*. Luxembourg: Publications Office of the European Union.

Filer, R. K., Hamermesh, D. S., & Rees, A. E. (1996). *The economics of work and pay*. New York: Harper Collins.

Fischbacher, U., Gärter, S., & Fehr, E. (2001). Are people conditionally cooperative? Evidence from a public goods experiment. *Economic Letters, 71*(3), 397–404. https://doi.org/10.1016/S0165-1765(01)00394-9

Fisher, I. (1919). Economists in public service: Annual address of the President. *American Economic Review, 9*(1), 5–21. Accessed June 7, 2019, from http://www.jstor.org/stable/1813978

Fitoussi, J.-P., & Stiglitz, J. (2011). *On the measurement of social progress and well-being: Some further thoughts, Document du Travail 2011–19*. Paris: OFCE.

FitzRoy, F., & Jin, J. (2018). Basic income and a public job offer: Complementary policies to reduce poverty and unemployment. *Journal of Poverty and Social Justice, 26*(2), 191–206. https://doi.org/10.1332/175982718X15200701225179

Forget, E. (2011). *The town with no poverty. Using health administration data to revisit outcomes of a Canadian guaranteed annual income field experiment*. Winnipeg: University of Manitoba.

Frank, R. H. (1985). *Choosing the right pond*. Oxford: Oxford University Press.
Frank, R. H. (1997). The frame of reference as a public good. *The Economic Journal, 107*(445), 1832–1847. Accessed June 10, 2019, from https://www.jstor.org/stable/2957912
Frank, R. H. (2011). *The Darwin economy: Liberty, competition, and the common good*. Princeton, NJ: Princeton University Press.
Frey, C. B., & Osborne, M. A. (2013). *The future of employment: How susceptible are jobs to computerisation*. Oxford: University of Oxford.
Friedman, M. (1962). *Capitalism and freedom*. Chicago, IL: University of Chicago Press.
Gamel, C., Balsan, D., & Vero, J. (2006). The impact of basic income on the propensity to work: Theoretical issues and micro-econometric results. *The Journal of Socio-Economics, 35*(3), 476–497. https://doi.org/10.1016/j.socec.2005.11.025
Gerber, A. S., & Green, D. P. (2011). Field experiments and natural experiment. In R. E. Goodin (Ed.), *The Oxford handbook of political science*. Oxford: Oxford University Press. https://doi.org/10.1093/oxfordhb/9780199604456.013.0050
Gertler, P. J., Martinez, S. W., & Rubio-Codina, M. (2012). Investing cash transfers to raise long-term living standards. *American Economic Journal: Applied Economics, 4*(1), 164–192.
Goldsmith, S. (2010). *The Alaska Permanent Fund Dividend: A case study in implementation of a basic income guarantee*. Paper presented at the 13th Basic Income Earth Network Congress, Sao Paulo, Brazil. Accessed June 18, 2019, from https://scholarworks.alaska.edu/handle/11122/4170
Gottlieb, J. D., Townsend, R. R., & Xu, T. (2016). *Experimenting with entrepreneurship: The effects of job-protected leave* (NBER Working Paper 22446). Cambridge, MA: National Bureau of Economic Research.
Gough, I., & Meadowcroft, J. (2011). Decarbonising the welfare state. In J. S. Dryzek, R. B. Norgaard, & D. Schlosberg (Eds.), *The Oxford handbook of climate change and society* (pp. 490–503). Oxford: Oxford University Press.
Graeber, D. (2018). *Bullshit jobs: A theory*. New York: Simon and Schuster.
Graetz, M. J. (1979). Implementing a progressive consumption tax. *Harvard Law Review, 92*(8), 1575–1661. Accessed June 10, 2019, from https://www.jstor.org/stable/1340462
Groot, L. F. M. (1999). *Basic income and unemployment*. PhD Dissertation, Thela Thesis, Amsterdam.
Haigner, S., Höchtl, W., Jenewein, F. G., Schneider, F. G., & Wakolbinger, F. (2012). Keep on working: Unconditional basic income in the lab. *Basic Income Studies, 7*(1), 1–14. https://doi.org/10.1515/1932-0183.1230
Hall, P. A., & Gingerich, D. W. (2004). *Varieties of capitalism and institutional complementarities in the macroeconomy: An empirical analysis* (MPIfG Discussion Paper 04/5). Cologne: Max Planck Institute for the Study of Societies.
Hall, P. A., & Soskice, D. (Eds.). (2001). *Varieties of capitalism: The institutional foundations of comparative advantage*. Oxford: Oxford University Press.
Hanna, R., & Olken, B. A. (2018) *Universal basic incomes vs. targeted transfers: Anti-poverty programs in developing countries* (NBER Working Paper No. 24939). Cambridge, MA: National Bureau of Economic Research.
Hanushek, E. A. (1987). Non-labor-supply responses to the income maintenance experiments. In A. H. Munnell (Ed.), *Lessons from the income maintenance experiment* (pp. 106–130). Boston, MA: Federal Reserve Bank of Boston.
Harvey, P. (2006). The relative cost of UBI and NIT systems. *Basic Income Studies, 1*(2). https://doi.org/10.2202/1932-0183.1032
Hastings, T., & Heyes, J. (2016). Farewell to flexicurity? Austerity and labour policies in the European Union. *Economic and Industrial Democracy, 37*(1), 1–23. https://doi.org/10.1177/0143831X16633756
Haushofer, J., & Shapiro, J. (2016). The short-term impact of unconditional cash transfers to the poor: Experimental evidence from Kenya. *The Quarterly Journal of Economics, 131*(4), 1973–2042. https://doi.org/10.1093/qje/qjw025
Haushofer, J., & Shapiro, J. (2018). *The long-term impact of unconditional cash transfers: Experimental evidence from Kenya*. Accessed June 10, 2019, from http://jeremypshapiro.com/papers/Haushofer_Shapiro_UCT2_2018-01-30_paper_only.pdf

Haywood, L. (2014). *Bedingungsloses Grundeinkommen: eine ökonomische Perspektive, 33, DIW Roundup: Politik im Fokus*. Berlin: German Institute for Economic Research, DIW Berlin.

Hebst, D., & Mas, A. (2015). Peer effects on worker output in the laboratory generalize to the field. *Science, 350*(6260), 545–549. https://doi.org/10.1126/science.aac9555

Heckman, J. J., & Smith, J. A. (1995). Assessing the case for social experiments. *Journal of Economic Perspectives, 9*(2), 85–110. https://doi.org/10.1257/jep.9.2.85

Heckman, J. J., & Smith, J. A. (1996). Experimental and nonexperimental evaluation. In G. Schmid, J. O'Reilly, & K. Schömann (Eds.), *International handbook of labour market policy and evaluation* (pp. 37–88). Cheltenham: Edward Elgar.

Hohendanner, C., & Krug, G. (2018). *Does the impact of fixed-term contracts on health in Germany depend on "objective" job (in)security?* Accessed on June 10, 2019, from https://www.aiel.it/cms/cms-files/submission/all20170603161057.pdf

Hombert, J., Schoar, A., Sraer, D., & Thesmar, D. (2014). *Can unemployment insurance spur entrepreneurial activity?* (NBER Working Paper No. 20717). Cambridge, MA: National Bureau of Economic Research.

Hoynes, H. W., & Rothstein, J. (2019). *Universal basic income in the US and advanced countries* (NBER Working Paper No. 25538). Cambridge, MA: National Bureau of Economic Research.

Imbens, G. W., Rubin, D. B., & Sacerdote, B. I. (2001). Estimating the effect of unearned income on labor earnings, savings, and consumption: Evidence from a survey of lottery players. *American Economic Review, 91*(4), 778–794. https://doi.org/10.1257/aer.91.4.778

IMF. (2017). *Fiscal monitor: Tacking inequality*. Washington, DC: International Monetary Fund.

IMF. (2019). *World economic outlook: Growth slowdown, precarious recovery*. Washington, WC: International Monetary Fund.

ING. (2016, October). *Helicopter money: Loved but not spent*. ING International Survey special report.

Islam, N., & Colombino, U. (2018). *The case for NIT FT in Europe. An empirical optimal taxation exercise* (Working Paper Series 2018-08). Luxembourg Institute of Socio-Economic Research (LISER). https://doi.org/10.2139/ssrn.3183167

Jones, D.. & Marinescu, I. (2018). *The labor market impacts of universal and permanent cash transfers: Evidence from the Alaska Permanent Fund* (NBER Working Paper, No. 24312). Cambridge, MA: National Bureau of Economic Research.

Kangas, O., Jauhiainen, S., Simanainen, M., & Ylikännö, M. (eds.) (2019). *The basic income experiment 2017–2018 in Finland: Preliminary results*. Helsinki: Ministry of Social Affairs and Health. Accessed June 8, 2019, from http://julkaisut.valtioneuvosto.fi/handle/10024/161361

Kawagoe, T. (2009). *An experimental study of basic income guarantee*. Far East and South Asia meeting of the econometric society, 3–5 August, Tokyo, Japan.

Kelly, M. (2012). *Owning our future: The emerging ownership revolution*. Oakland: Berrett-Koehler.

Killingsworth, M. R. (1983). *Labor supply*. Cambridge: Cambridge University Press.

Killingsworth, M. R., & Heckman, J. J. (1986). Female labor supply: A survey. In O. Ashenfelter & R. Layard (Eds.), *Handbook of labor economics* (Vol. 1, pp. 103–204). Amsterdam: North-Holland.

Klosse, S., & Muysken, J. (2016). Curbing the labour market divide by fostering inclusive labour markets through a job guarantee. *Psychosociological Issues in Human Resource Management, 4*(2), 185–219. https://doi.org/10.22381/PIHRM4220168

Knight, K. W., Rosa, E. A., & Schor, J. B. (2013). Could working less reduce pressures on the environment? A cross-national panel analysis of OECD countries, 1970–2007. *Global Environmental Change, 23*(4), 691–700. https://doi.org/10.1016/j.gloenvcha.2013.02.017

Krehm, W. (2002). *Towards a non-autistic economy: A place at the table for society*. Toronto: COMER Publications.

Kuznets, S. (1937). *National income and capital formation, 1919–1935*. New York: NBER. Accessed June 10, 2019, from http://www.nber.org/chapters/c4231

Kuznets, S. (1955). Economic growth and income inequality. *American Economic Review, 45*(1), 1–28. Accessed June 10, 2019, from http://www.jstor.org/stable/1811581

Layard, R. (2005). *Happiness: Lessons from a new science*. London: Penguin.

Lockwood, B. B., Nathanson, C. G., & Weyl, E. G. (2017). Taxation and the allocation of talent. *Journal of Political Economy, 125*(5), 1635–1682. https://doi.org/10.1086/693393

Mankiw, N. G. (2010). Spreading the wealth around: Reflections inspired by Joe the plumber. *Eastern Economic Journal, 36*(3), 285–298. https://doi.org/10.1057/eej.2010.22

Mankiw, N. G., Weinzierl, M., & Yagan, D. (2009). Optimal taxation in theory and practice. *Journal of Economic Perspectives, 23*(4), 147–174. https://doi.org/10.1257/jep.23.4.147

Marinescu, I. (2018). *No strings attached: The behavioral effects of U.S. unconditional cash transfer programs* (NBER Working Paper No. 24337). Cambridge, MA: National Bureau of Economic Research.

Marx, A., & Peeters, H. (2004) *Win for life: An empirical exploration of the social consequences of introducing a basic income* (COMPASSS Working Paper WP2004-29). Accessed June 18, 2019, from http://www.compasss.org/wpseries/MarxPeeters2004.pdf

Marx, A., & Peeters, H. (2008). An unconditional basic income and labor supply: Results from a pilot study of lottery winners. *The Journal of Socio-Economics, 37*(4), 1636–1659. https://doi.org/10.1016/j.socec.2007.08.007

McGregor, J. M., & Pouw, N. (2019). Towards an economics of well-being. *Cambridge Journal of Economics, 41*(4), 1123–1142. https://doi.org/10.1093/cje/bew044

McKinsey Global Institute. (2017, December). Jobs lost, jobs gained: Workforce transitions in a time of automation.

Mirrlees, J. (1971). An exploration in the theory of optimal income taxation. *Review of Economic Studies, 38*(2), 175–208. https://doi.org/10.2307/2296779

Mitchell, W. F., & Muysken, J. (2010). Full employment abandoned: Shifting sands and policy failures. *International Journal of Public Policy, 5*(4), 295–313. https://doi.org/10.1504/IJPP.2010.032299

Mitchell, W. & Watts, M. (2004). *A comparison of the macroeconomic consequences of basic income and job guarantee schemes* (Working Paper No. 04-05). Callaghan: Centre of Full Employment and Equity, University of Newcastle. Accessed on June 8, 2019, from http://www.fullemployment.net/publications/wp/2004/04-05.pdf

NEF. (2009). *A bit rich: Calculating the real value to society of different professions*. London: New Economics Foundation. Accessed June 10 2019, from https://neweconomics.org/uploads/files/8c16eabdbadf83ca79_ojm6b0fzh.pdf

Nikiforos, M., Steinbaum, M., & Zezza, G. (2017). *Modeling the macroeconomic effects of a universal basic income*. New York: The Roosevelt Institute.

Noguera, J. A., & De Wispelaere, J. (2006). A plea for the use of laboratory experiments in basic income research. *Basic Income Studies, 1*(2), 1–8. https://doi.org/10.2202/1932-0183.1044

Northeastern University. (2018). *Optimism and anxiety: Views on the impact of artificial intelligence and higher education's response*. Boston. Accessed June 8, 2019, from https://www.northeastern.edu/gallup/pdf/OptimismAnxietyNortheasternGallup.pdf

OECD. (1998a). *The battle against exclusion: Social assistance in Australia, Finland, Sweden and the United Kingdom*. Paris: Organisation for Economic Co-operation and Development.

OECD. (1998b). *The battle against exclusion, Volume 2: Social assistance in Belgium, the Czech Republic, the Netherlands and Norway*. Paris: Organisation for Economic Co-operation and Development.

OECD. (2015). *In it together: Why less inequality benefits all*. Paris: OECD Publishing.

OECD. (2017). *Basic income as a policy option: Can it add up? Policy Brief on the future of work*. Paris: OECD Publishing.

OECD. (2018). *The future of social protection: What works for non-standard workers?* Paris: OECD Publishing. https://doi.org/10.1787/9789264306943-en

Okun, A. M. (1975). *Equality versus efficiency, the big trade-off*. The Brookings Institution: Washington, DC.

Olds, G. (2016, June). *Food stamp entrepreneurs* (Working Paper, No. 16-143). Harvard Business School.

Ostry, J. D., Berg, A., & Tsangarides, C. G. (2014). *Redistribution, inequality, and growth* (IMF Staff Discussion note, SDN 14/2). Washington, DC: International Monetary Fund.

Pech, W. J. (2010). Behavioral economics and the basic income guarantee. *Basic Income Studies, 5*(2), 12–28. https://doi.org/10.2202/1932-0183.1167

Pencavel, J. (1986). Labor supply of men: A survey. In O. Ashenfelter & R. Layard (Eds.), *Handbook of labor economics* (Vol. I, pp. 3–102). Amsterdam: North-Holland.

Piachaud, D. (2018). Basic income: Confusion, claims and choices. *Journal of Poverty and Social Justice, 26*(3), 299–314. https://doi.org/10.1332/175982718X15232797708173

Piasna, A. (2018). Scheduled to work hard: The relationship between non-standard working hours and work intensity among European workers (2005–2015). *Human Resource Management Journal, 28*(1), 167–181. https://doi.org/10.1111/1748-8583.12171

Piketty, T. (2014). *Capital in twenty-first century*. Cambridge: Belknap Press.

Piketty, T., Saez, E., & Stantcheva, S. (2014). Optimal taxation of top labor incomes: A tale of three elasticities. *American Economic Journal: Economic Policy, 6*(1), 230–271. https://doi.org/10.1257/pol.6.1.230

Pullinger, M. (2014). Working time reduction policy in a sustainable economy: Criteria and options for its design. *Ecological Economics, 113*, 11–19. https://doi.org/10.1016/j.ecolecon.2014.04.009

Raworth, K. (2017). *Doughnut-economics: Seven ways to think like a 21st-century economist*. London: Business Books.

Robbins, L. (1932). *An essay on the nature and significance of economic science*. London: Macmillan.

Robeyns, I. (2000). Hush money or emancipation fee. In R. van der Veen & L. Groot (Eds.), *Basic income on the agenda: Policy objectives and political chances* (pp. 121–136). Amsterdam: Amsterdam University Press.

Robins, P. K. (1985). Comparison of the labor supply findings from the four negative income tax experiments. *Journal of Human Resources, 20*(4), 567–582. https://doi.org/10.2307/145685

Rodrik, D. (1998). Why do more open economies have bigger governments? *Journal of Political Economy, 106*(5), 997–1032. https://doi.org/10.1086/250038

Rothschild, K. W. (2002). The absence of power in contemporary economic theory. *The Journal of Socio-Economics, 31*(5), 433–442. https://doi.org/10.1016/S1053-5357(02)00207-X

Rowlingson, K. (2011). *Does income inequality cause health and social problems?* Joseph Rowntree Foundation. Accessed June 10, 2019, from https://www.jrf.org.uk/report/does-income-inequality-cause-health-and-social-problems

Salehi-Isfahani, D., & Mostafavi-Dehzooei, M. H. (2018). Cash transfers and labor supply: Evidence from a large-scale program in Iran. *Journal of Development Economics, 135*, 349–367. https://doi.org/10.1016/j.jdeveco.2018.08.005

Schiller, B. R. (2007). *The economics of poverty and discrimination*. Upper Saddle River, NJ: Pearson/Prentice Hall.

Schmid, G., & Schömann, K. (1994). Institutional choice and flexible coordination. A socioeconomic evaluation of labor market policy in Europe. In G. Schmid (Ed.), *Labor market institutions in Europe* (pp. 9–57). New York: M. E. Sharpe.

Schor, J. (2005). Sustainable consumption and work time reduction. *Journal of Industrial Ecology, 9*(1–2), 37–50. https://doi.org/10.1162/1088198054084581

Schwellnus, C., Kappeler, A., & Pionnier, P.-A. (2017). *Decoupling of wages from productivity: Macro-level facts* (Economics Department Working Papers No. 1373). Paris: Organisation for Economic Co-operation and Development. https://doi.org/10.1787/18151973

Sinn, H. W. (1995). A theory of the welfare state. *Scandinavian Journal of Economics, 97*(4), 495–526. https://doi.org/10.2307/3440540

Sinn, H. W. (1996). Social insurance, incentives and risk taking. *International Tax and Public Finance, 3*(3), 259–280. https://doi.org/10.1007/BF00418944

Sommer, M. (2016). *A feasible basic income scheme for Germany: Effects on labor supply, poverty, and income inequality*. Berlin: Springer.

Stafford, F. (1986). Forestalling the demise of empirical economics: The role of microdata in labor economics research. In O. Ashenfelter & R. Layard (Eds.), *Handbook of labor economics* (Vol. I, pp. 387–423). Amsterdam: North-Holland.

Standing, G. (2017). *Basic income and how we can make it happen*. London: Pelican Books.

Steffens, N. K., Aslam, S. H., Peters, K., & Quiggin, J. (2018). Identity economics meets identity leadership: Exploring the consequences of elevated CEO pay. *The Leadership Quarterly.* https://doi.org/10.1016/j.leaqua.2018.10.001

Tinbergen, J. (1952). *On the theory of economic policy.* Amsterdam: North-Holland.

Titmuss, R. M. (1974). *Social policy: An introduction.* London: Allen & Unwin.

Torry, M. (2018). *Why we need a citizen's basic income.* Bristol: Policy Press.

Van Bavel, B. (2016). *The invisible hand? How market economies have emerged and declined since AD 500.* Oxford: Oxford University Press.

Van der Veen, R., & Groot, L. (Eds.). (2000). *Basic income on the agenda: Policy objectives and political chances.* Amsterdam: Amsterdam University Press.

Van Parijs, P., & Vanderborght, Y. (2017). *Basic income: A radical proposal for a free society and a sane economy.* Cambridge, MA: Harvard University Press.

Varian, H. R. (1980). Redistributive taxation as social insurance. *Journal of Public Economics, 14*(1), 49–68. https://doi.org/10.1016/0047-2727(80)90004-3

Virjo, I. (2006). A piece of the puzzle: A comment on the basic income experiment debate. *Basic Income Studies, 1*(2), 1–5. https://doi.org/10.2202/1932-0183.1045

Ward, B., & Dubois, R. (1972). *Only one earth: The care and maintenance of a small planet.* London: Penguin Books.

Widerquist, K. (2017, Oktober 17). Beyond trafficking and *slavery*: Basic income's third wave. *OpenDemocracy.* Accessed on June 10, 2019, from https://www.opendemocracy.net/en/beyond-trafficking-and-slavery/basic-income-s-third-wave/

Widerquist, K. (2018). *The devil's in the caveats: A critical analysis of basic income experiments for researchers, policymakers, and citizens.* Berkeley: Bepress. Accessed on June 10, 2019, from https://works.bepress.com/widerquist/86/

Widerquist, K., Noguera, J. A., Vanderborght, Y., & De Wispelaere, J. (Eds.). (2013). *Basic income: An anthology of contemporary research.* Chichester: Wiley.

Wilkinson, R. G., & Pickett, K. (2009). *The spirit level: Why more equal societies almost always do better.* London: Allen Lane.

Lei Delsen (1952) studied economics at the University of Groningen (the Netherlands) and received his Ph.D. in economics from the University of Maastricht (the Netherlands). He was a research fellow at the European Centre for Work and Society in Maastricht (1984–1987), and Assistant Professor at the Department of Applied Economics of the University of Nijmegen, the Netherlands (1987–2002). From 2003 to 2018 he was Associate Professor of Socio-Economic Policy, Department of Economics, Nijmegen School of Management, Radboud University, Nijmegen. He retired June 2018. He is a research fellow of NETSPAR (Network for Studies on Pensions, Aging and Retirement). His research deals with a number of topical European labour market problems and issues, including new forms of work, retirement from work, work-life balance, choices within pension schemes, responsible investment and the relationship between globalisation and the national welfare states. He is the author of *Atypical employment: An international perspective. Causes, consequences and policy* (Groningen: Wolters-Noordhoff, 1995) and *Exit polder model? Socioeconomic changes in the Netherlands* (Westport: Praeger, 2002). Articles include: A new concept of full employment, *Economic and Industrial Democracy* (1997); Choices within collective labour agreements *à la carte* in the Netherlands, *British Journal of Industrial Relations* (2006) (with J. Benders & J. Smits); Corporatism and economic performance: does it still work?, *Acta Politica* (2008) (with J. Woldendorp); Does the life course savings scheme have the potential to improve work-life balance?, *British Journal of Industrial Relations* (2009) (with J. Smits); Value matters or values matter? An analysis of heterogeneity in preferences for sustainable investments, *Journal of Sustainable Finance & Investment* (2019) (with A. Lehr).

Chapter 2
Individual Preferences for the Unconditional Basic Income in the European Union

Lei Delsen and Rutger Schilpzand

Abstract In representative democracies public opinions matter. In this chapter we analyse the preferences for an Unconditional Basic Income (UBI) among a large, representative sample of people in the 28 member states of the European Union (EU). The survey data were collected by online sampling on mobile devices in March 2017. We apply a multi-level ordered logit model and a fixed effects model. On average, almost three-quarters of the people in the EU stated to (probably) vote for the introduction of UBI, if there would be a referendum on introducing UBI. Half of the voters would like to see UBI being introduced after successful experiments in their own country or abroad; one third as soon as possible. The likelihood to vote in favour of UBI varies significantly between groups of people. The effect of awareness on preferences is inconclusive. The national macro-economic and welfare state contexts have significant effects. "It reduces anxiety about financial basic needs" is considered the most convincing argument for UBI. "It might encourage people to stop working" is considered the most convincing argument against UBI. The self-enhancement hypothesis is confirmed. The positive and negative effects of UBI on individual work choices balance out.

Keywords Public opinions · Stated preference survey · Unconditional basic income · Referendum · European Union

2.1 Introduction

This chapter presents analyses of the data of a unique 2017 European Union wide survey of public opinions on basic income collected by Dalia Research. We analyse the extent to which people in the European Union have preferences for an

---

L. Delsen (✉) · R. Schilpzand
Department of Economics, Institute for Management Research, Radboud University, Nijmegen, The Netherlands
e-mail: l.delsen@fm.ru.nl; ra.schilpzand@fm.ru.nl

© Springer Nature Switzerland AG 2019
L. Delsen (ed.), *Empirical Research on an Unconditional Basic Income in Europe*, Contributions to Economics, https://doi.org/10.1007/978-3-030-30044-9_2

Unconditional Basic Income (UBI), the extent to which such preferences differ across individuals and countries, and how such differences can be explained.

Survey data on the preferences for UBI, as well as on the behavioural consequences of UBI are very scarce. Most past and recent representative surveys on public opinions about UBI in the Organisation for Economic Co-operation and Development (OECD) area are single country surveys (e.g. Andersson & Kangas, 2002; Colombo, DeRocchi, Kurer, & Widmer, 2016; ING, 2018; Ipsos MORI, 2017; Kangas, Jauhiainen, Simanainen, & Ylikännö, 2019; Northeastern University, 2018; RSA, 2018; Splendid Research, 2018; Van Parijs & Vanderborght, 2017: 171–174). Until recently, there were no adequate cross-national surveys exploring individual preferences for UBI. The first survey of attitudes on UBI in the 28 member states of the European Union (EU) was conducted by Dalia Research in March 2016 (see https://daliaresearch.com/home/). In 2016, ING also surveyed almost 12,000 people in twelve European countries online, to investigate how people might actually behave in the event of 'helicopter money'[1] and what the economic effects might be (ING, 2016). In Round 8 (2016/2017), for the first time in the history of the European Social Survey (ESS), a set of welfare questions was included in the face-to-face survey on attitudes towards the introduction of a basic income. The survey was fielded in 23 countries: 21 European countries, of which 18 EU member states, and Russia and Israel (Meuleman et al., 2018).

All 36 OECD countries and all 28 EU member states are representative democracies. Knowledge about the attitudes of people towards UBI is a vital, still lacking ingredient to both the scientific and policy debate. Democracies require voters to have opinions about various issues. Preferences influence individuals' electoral choices, and hence impact public policy. Burstein's (2003) major conclusion in his review paper is that the impact of public opinion on public policy is substantial in democracies. Moreover, the impact of public opinion remains strong even when the activities of interest organisations, political parties and elites are taken into account. The knowledge of the preferences for UBI and what people believe about UBI (psychological feasibility) provides relevant information to establish the societal desirability as well as the political support (strategic feasibility) and hence the political feasibility, i.e. the achievability of UBI (De Wispelaere & Noguera, 2012). See Chap. 3 for the political feasibility of UBI in Europe. There, the feasibility of basic income policies in the 28 EU member states, as well as the various types of political feasibility and their interactions are analysed.

Survey data is well suited to provide insight in the reasons for individuals to support or oppose UBI, and also to ascertain public opinion within sub-groups, such as countries and age categories. The aim of this chapter is to explain differences in UBI preferences. Which individual and national factors are important drivers of UBI preferences?

---

[1] Based on a metaphor used by Nobel Laureate Milton Friedman five decades ago: "Let us suppose now that one day a helicopter flies over this community and drops an additional $1000 in bills from the sky, which is, of course, hastily collected by members of the community." (Friedman, 1969: 4).

The chapter is organised as follows. In Sect. 2.2, the dataset and method used to calculate the preferences for UBI are presented. In the result Sect. 2.3, first bivariate relationships are established, and some frequencies are presented and compared with earlier survey results. After that, the results of our multi-variate regression analyses are presented, explaining the support for UBI in the EU as a whole from personal characteristics, knowledge about UBI, changes in own individual work choices due to UBI, convincing arguments for and against UBI, including opinions about the fundability of UBI, the effects of UBI on solidarity, poverty risk, fairness, reciprocity, and the work choices of other people, and the national macro-economic and national welfare-state contexts. In the final Sect. 2.4 conclusions are drawn.

2.2 Data and Method

The survey data was collected by Dalia Research (see https://daliaresearch.com/home/) in March 2017. An online sampling on mobile devices (mobile phones, tablets, and computers) was used to measure the support for UBI in the EU. The sample of N = 11,021 was drawn across all 28 EU member states, taking current population distributions into account with regard to age (restricted to 14–65 years), gender and region/country. In order to obtain census representative results, the data were weighted based upon Eurostat statistics. The target weighting variables were age, gender, level of education (as defined by the International Standard Classification of Education (ISCED 2011) levels 0–2, 3–4, and 5–8), as well as the degree of urbanisation (rural and urban). A population composition weight adjustment is applied.

In Table 2.1 a comparison between the Dalia Research weighted descriptives and EU population is made. The differences can be regarded as negligible. An estimation of the overall design effect based on the weight adjustment was calculated by Dalia Research at 1.46 at the global level. Calculated for a sample of this size and considering the design effect, the margin of error would be ±1.1% at a confidence level of 95%. The design effect is the ratio of the actual variance to the variance expected with simple random sampling. The results of the basic income survey are representative of the European population as a whole.

The following definition of the UBI was used in the survey: "*A basic income is an income unconditionally paid by the government to every individual regardless of whether they work and irrespective of any other sources of income. It replaces other social security payments and is high enough to cover all basic needs (food, housing etc.).*" This definition of the UBI differs from the common definition used in the literature—obligation free cash benefit provided by the government, individual entitlement of all legal residents (see Delsen, Chap. 1): a specific income level—high enough to cover all basic needs—is added; no age differentiation and minimum requirements of nationality or residence are mentioned, and no explicit reference is made to how to finance, e.g. taxes, the UBI.

Table 2.1 Comparison of Dalia Research sample statistics and EU population statistics

	Total voters per category		EU statistics 2016[a]
	N	%	%
Total	10,080	100.00	100.00
Age categories			
14–25	1880	18.03	19.79
26–35	2129	20.39	19.22
36–45	2576	25.48	20.71
46–55	2238	23.39	21.53
56–65	1257	12.71	18.75
Gender			
Female	4898	49.70	48.86
Male	5182	50.30	51.14
Full-time job			
No	4236	45.78	48.82
Yes	5844	54.22	51.18
Education			
No formal[b]	229	2.77	
Some high school/secondary[b]	1705	23.08	26.5
High school or equivalent	4135	44.83	46.2
University or equivalent[b]	3699	26.14	27.3
Other/unanswered[b]	312	3.18	
Rural			
City	7314	74.41	77.86
Rural	2766	25.59	22.14
Country			
Austria	160	1.70	1.71
Belgium	209	2.23	2.22
Bulgaria	141	1.50	1.40
Croatia	88	0.88	0.82
Cyprus	18	0.18	0.17
Czech Republic	208	1.98	2.07
Denmark	108	1.03	1.12
Estonia	22	0.24	0.26
Finland	103	1.09	1.08
France	1122	11.97	13.06
Germany	1600	16.66	16.11
Greece	215	2.10	2.11
Hungary	206	2.06	1.93
Ireland	90	0.89	0.93
Italy	1225	12.18	11.89
Latvia	40	0.35	0.39
Lithuania	54	0.59	0.57
Luxembourg	14	0.11	0.11

(continued)

Table 2.1 (continued)

	Total voters per category		EU statistics 2016[a]
	N	%	%
Malta	12	0.10	0.09
Netherlands	322	3.47	3.33
Poland	939	7.71	7.44
Portugal	226	2.22	2.03
Romania	409	4.12	3.87
Slovakia	104	1.15	1.06
Slovenia	46	0.45	0.40
Spain	999	9.08	9.10
Sweden	265	1.87	1.93
United Kingdom	1135	12.10	12.81

Dalia research weighted observations used to calculate the percentages in the sample
[a]Source: Eurostat, year 2016, own calculations
[b]Eurostat combines these categories based on ISCED 2011 definition

The central survey question used for our research is: "*If there would be a referendum on introducing basic income today, how would you vote? (single choice)*

1. *I would vote for it*
2. *I would probably vote for it*
3. *I would probably vote against it*
4. *I would vote against it*
5. *I would not vote*".

To measure our dependent variable, the respondents' preferences for basic income, we use the recoded answers to this question to calculate the likelihood to vote in favour of UBI: I would vote for it (value 4), I would probably vote for it (value 3), I would probably vote against it (value 2), and I would vote against it (value 1). The option "5 I would not vote" was excluded. As a result, the number of respondents in our analyses dropped to $N = 10,080$.

The following background characteristics included in the survey are used as independent variables to explain differences in preferences for UBI: gender, age, formal education level, full-time job, degree of urbanisation, and country. The gender variable records whether respondents are male or female. Age is measured in years. Formal education is measured on a four-point scale: 1 no formal education, 2 some high school or secondary school education, 3 completed high school or secondary school education, and 4 completed university or equivalent degree. Full-time job concerns a dichotomised yes–no (1–0) question. The degree of urbanisation involves two choices: living in a city or in a rural area. Dummy variables are used for the 28 member states of the EU.

In addition to these background variables, independent variables measuring the extent to which respondents are familiar with UBI, when to introduce it, the effect of UBI on the individual's work choices, and their arguments for and against UBI are included in our analyses. The answers to the question "How familiar are you with the concept known as 'basic income'?" are recoded, ranging from 4 "I understand it fully", 3 "I know something about it", and 2 "I have heard just a little about it" to 1 "I have never heard about it".

The question on the preferred timing of introduction "At what point do you think your country should introduce the basic income?" offers five answers: "As soon as possible", "After successful experiments in their own country", "After successful experiments in other countries", "Not anytime in the near future", and "Never."

The question "What could be the most likely effect of basic income on your work choices? I would..." covers the following nine options: "...stop working", "...work less", "...do more volunteering work", "...spend more time with my family", "...look for a different job", "...work as a freelancer", "...gain additional skills", "A basic income would not affect my work choices", and "None of the above".

The two questions on arguments for and against UBI as well as the answer options were presented in randomised order. The multiple answer question "Which of the following arguments FOR the basic income do you find convincing? Choose all that apply." has seven answer choices: "It reduces anxiety about financing basic needs", "It creates more equality of opportunity", "It encourages financial independence and self-responsibility", "It increases solidarity, because it is funded by everyone", "It reduces bureaucracy and administrative expenses", "It increases appreciation for household work and volunteering", and "None of the above". The multiple answer question "Which of the following arguments AGAINST the basic income do you find convincing? Choose all that apply." also has seven response options: "It is impossible to finance", "It might encourage people to stop working", "Foreigners might come to my country and take advantage of the benefit", "It is against the principle of linking merit and reward", "Only the people who need it most should get something from the state", "It increases dependence on the state", and "None of the above".

Finally, we supplement the survey with country level context factors. In Europe, preferences for the state guaranteeing a minimum income protection, i.e. decent standard of living, decent housing and the state providing jobs for all are influenced by national context (Pfeifer, 2009). Her research shows that national unemployment levels are positively related to these preferences. The generosity of the welfare state, i.e. high total social expenditure and the attitudes towards the state guaranteeing a minimum income are negatively related. Lee (2018) shows, based on the ESS 2016 survey data, that support for UBI varies considerably between the European countries. In line with Pfeifer's (2009) study, she found that preferences for UBI are partly shaped by these national context factors: support for UBI is positively associated with national unemployment rates and negatively associated with national welfare state generosity. She concludes that the political feasibility of UBI is much higher in countries where households are economically insecure and government policies are inadequate. To examine the contextual determinants of the attitudes towards UBI we use national expenditures on social protection expressed in purchasing power standards (PPS)[2] per inhabitant in 2016 as a proxy for economic insecurity, and the national unemployment rates in 2016 as a proxy for job insecurity and the general climate of risks and insecurity, similar to Lee (2018). In addition to these social and economic risks, cultural values may also partly shape preferences for UBI. For the national differences in cultural values we use Geert Hofstede's cultural dimensions (Hofstede, Hofstede, & Minkov, 2010).

Different surveys may vary on a number of characteristics which may result in dissimilar outcomes. The accuracy and reliability of sample estimates mainly depend on the sample size and sample design. Surveys may exclude by design, because people are not part of the statistical population or by non-response, e.g. people on the margins of society. The latter was an important target group in past and recent natural UBI-related field experiments e.g. in the United States, Canada, Finland, Namibia and India (see Widerquist, 2005, 2018) and still is in the ongoing UBI-related natural field experiments in the Netherlands (see Muffels & Gielens, Chap. 5 and Betkó et al., Chap. 6) and the planned UBI pilot in Scotland (see Danson, Chap. 4). The Dalia Research sample deviates only negligibly compared to the statistical make-up of EU countries, see Table 2.1.

Based on a sample, one can only establish and assess preferences for UBI with a certain degree of statistical reliability, i.e. between confidence intervals. The estimated range of the values of a parameter depends on the quality of the measurement and the representativeness of the sample. The expressiveness of survey results is sometimes doubted. Surveys only measure stated intended behaviour, not actual observed behaviour after the introduction of UBI. Surveys may also lead to socially desirable answers by the respondents. This applies in particular to face-to-face interviews that are used, e.g. in the ESS survey. However, as the Dalia Research survey was conducted online, the greater degree of anonymity provides less socially desirable answers (Teppa & Vis, 2012), which is especially desirable given that our dependent variable concerns people's stated preferences for UBI. Moreover, money, i.e. the level of UBI is added to the central survey question. The latter also applies to the ESS survey on UBI. However, unlike the ESS survey, taxes to finance UBI are not explicitly mentioned in the definition. Framing and phrasing effects might occur (see Van Parijs & Vanderborght, 2017: 171–174). The size of the effect might not be as large in practice. Survey data for Finland and Sweden use different definitions and framing of UBI questions. In Sweden a large minority (44–46%) is in favour, while in Finland a large majority (59–76%) is in favour (Andersson & Kangas, 2002). However, the ESS survey, which uses another, but identical, definition for both countries, shows similar results: support for UBI in Sweden is 38% and 56% in Finland (Lee, 2018; Vlandas, 2018) indicating the effect of framing is limited. Moreover, despite differences in definitions and framing, as well as countries covered, surveys in Europe show—on average—that a majority (51–54%) is in favour or strongly in favour of UBI, or considers it a good idea. Only a small part

---

[2]PPS is a common currency used by Eurostat, the statistical office of the EU, to eliminate the differences in price levels between the EU countries allowing meaningful volume comparisons of national social security expenditure.

(14–15%) is strongly against UBI, or considers it a bad idea (Fitzgerald, Bottoni, & Swift, 2017; ING, 2016; Vlandas, 2018). This shows that different surveys on preferences for UBI produce rather similar results.

Van Parijs and Vanderborght (2017: 173) argue that although these surveys may be relevant to assessing the political prospects of a UBI, they are no more than snapshots of the opinions of the public that perhaps understood the idea but had scarcely thought about it. UBI is considered to be likely unfamiliar to the bulk of the respondents. Relevant here is that Dalia Research has conducted an EU wide UBI behaviour and attitudes survey twice. The familiarity with UBI increased from 58% of the Europeans in the survey of March 2016 to 63% of the Europeans in the March 2017 survey. The proportion of people (including non-voters) in the 28 EU countries supporting UBI increased from 64% in the 2016 survey to 68% in the 2017 survey. In both surveys almost one third (31%) of the respondents want their country to introduce UBI as soon as possible (Dalia Research, 2017). Note, however, that these two data sets are not fully comparable. Also, in the United States (US) survey results indicate an increasing trend in the support for UBI. In 2017, 48% was in support of a UBI programme for workers that are displaced by advances in artificial intelligence (AI) (Northeastern University, 2018). This Gallup poll of more than 3000 US adults also shows that 46% of those polled would be willing to pay higher personal taxes. And 80% would support a 'robot tax' for companies that benefit from AI to cover the costs of the UBI.

As the first step in our analysis, we provide descriptive results, i.e. bivariate results and some frequencies. However, the bivariate results do not give insight into the underlying preferences, because the independent variables used are related to each other. To get a better picture of the preferences of the different groups, we use multi-variate analyses. It discounts for overlapping explanations of preferences for or against UBI between correlated independent variables and expresses the net, i.e. *ceteris paribus*, effects of each independent variable, controlling for any other variable in the model. However, reverse causality, i.e. a two-way causal relationship, cannot be ruled out.

The second step consists of a regression analysis. The dependent variable consists of ordered categories, necessitating an analysis technique that allows several cut-off points to consecutively capture increasing probability without restraining the distance between the ordered options. We use two multi-variate regression analyses, a multi-level ordered logit model and a country fixed-effects variation. The survey has been conducted in multiple countries. The assumption of a completely random sample is too strict, indicated by an estimated survey design value higher than 1. A multi-level ordered logit model is used. This takes into account the interclass correlation between and within countries. We assume the effects to be similar across countries using a random intercept model. In addition, we show a fixed effects model to correct for any unmeasured heterogeneity that might correlate with the error term of the random effects.

2.3 Results

2.3.1 Descriptive Results: Bivariate Results and Frequencies

To calculate the EU-wide averages reported in this section we applied the design and populations weights mentioned in Sect. 2.2. Table 2.2 shows that almost three quarters (74.2%)—a large majority—of the voters indicated they would (probably) vote for UBI: "I would probably vote for it" (40.4%) is the biggest group of voters and with one third (33.8%) "I would vote for it" is the second largest group. A quarter (25.8%) of the voting respondents indicated they would (probably) vote against UBI: "I would probably vote against it" (16.0%), and "I would vote against it" (9.8%) is the smallest group. Not in Table 2.2, in the bigger EU countries a majority of voting respondents is in favour of UBI, i.e. vote for UBI plus probably vote for UBI. In decreasing order: Italy (81.0%), United Kingdom (UK) (76.6), Spain (76.3%), Germany (72.7%), Poland (71.5%), and France (69.1%). Hence, on balance the positive attitudes towards UBI are stronger than the negative attitudes. This indicates there is societal appeal and potential for UBI as well as political feasibility of UBI.

Our results show a more favourable opinion towards UBI in the EU than in the ESS, in which a slight majority (54%) is in favour (over 45%) or strongly in favour (about 9%) of UBI (Vlandas, 2018).[3] Our results also show more favourable attitudes than the 54% found by ING (2016).[4] These calculated averages are not fully comparable because they consist of different sets of European countries, different sampling from the statistical populations, and use dissimilar sample weights. Also, definitions, framing, and survey questions differ. For example, in the ESS questionnaire respondents were asked whether they are strongly against, against, in favour or strongly in favour of a basic income scheme. The following definition of basic income was used in the ESS questionnaire: "government pays everyone a monthly income to cover essential living costs that replaced many other social benefits. The purpose is to guarantee everyone a minimum standard of living, that everyone receives the same amount regardless of whether or not they are working and that people also keep the money they earn from work or other sources. The scheme itself is paid for by taxes."

Preferences for UBI may be different between socio-economic groups. ESS data clearly shows that in the EU the youngest (15–34 years) are most in favour of the UBI, and the oldest are least likely to be in favour. In Christian Democratic and Eastern Europe the support for UBI decreases with the age groups 15–34, 35–54 and 55–64, while in the Social Democratic countries and the UK and Ireland a U-shape is

---

[3]The Dalia Research survey total percentage is based on a combination of research and population weights. The percentages of the ESS are similarly calculated using a combination of design and population weights. See European Social Survey (2014, April 25). https://www.europeansocialsurvey.org/docs/methodology/ESS_weighting_data_1.pdf

[4]The internet-based ING International Survey (ING, 2016) only used country population size weights to calculate averages.

Table 2.2 Descriptive and bivariate statistics of all survey variables

	I would vote against it N	%	I would probably vote against It N	%	I would probably vote for it N	%	I would vote for it N	%	Total voters per category %[a]	Total non-voters per category N	%[a]
Total	1053	9.8	1668	16.0	4036	40.4	3323	33.8	100.0	941	100.0
Age categories											
14–25	157	7.1	309	16.2	822	43.7	592	33.1	18.0	321	32.2
26–35	234	10.4	376	17.6	841	39.7	678	32.4	20.4	200	20.9
36–45	276	9.7	430	15.6	1007	39.6	863	35.2	25.5	209	22.3
46–55	244	10.7	348	14.9	867	39.6	779	34.8	23.4	137	16.4
56–65	142	11.1	205	16.5	499	39.8	411	32.7	12.7	74	8.3
Gender											
Female	453	8.8	797	15.7	2062	41.9	1586	33.7	49.7	502	54.8
Male	600	10.7	871	16.4	1974	38.9	1737	34.0	50.3	439	45.2
Full-time job											
No	348	7.7	578	13.5	1751	41.2	1559	37.6	45.8	546	60.5
Yes	705	11.5	1090	18.2	2285	39.7	1764	30.6	54.2	395	39.5
Education											
No formal	22	7.7	42	14.9	75	38.7	90	38.8	2.8	69	8.4
Some high school/secondary	142	8.7	259	14.4	684	39.6	620	37.4	23.1	239	29.7
High school or equivalent	372	8.9	652	15.8	1739	42.1	1372	33.2	44.8	335	37.6
University or equivalent	490	12.6	671	18.5	1418	38.2	1120	30.7	26.1	205	15.4
Other/unanswered	27	8.4	44	11.9	120	41.4	121	38.4	3.2	93	9.0
Rural											
City	782	9.9	1196	15.9	2934	40.6	2402	33.7	74.4	667	72.3
Rural	271	9.5	472	16.5	1102	39.8	921	34.2	25.6	274	27.7

Effect										
Stop working	126	38.2	67	24.3	48	18.6	45	18.9	34	3.9
Work less	122	13.7	187	21.3	289	37.7	223	27.3	49	5.4
Do more volunteering work	25	4.1	100	13.7	357	48.0	272	34.2	39	4.2
Spend more time with my family	96	6.0	262	14.8	777	46.2	555	33.0	137	15.0
Look for a different job	39	6.6	118	21.2	215	39.0	173	33.3	36	4.2
Work as a freelancer	30	6.2	67	15.9	145	35.0	162	42.9	28	2.5
Gain additional skills	38	4.0	78	10.8	316	40.3	322	44.9	43	3.8
No effect	423	9.9	592	14.0	1576	39.9	1365	36.2	210	22.2
None of the above	154	16.5	197	22.5	313	37.4	206	23.6	365	38.8
Awareness										
I have never heard of it	141	13.3	170	16.5	360	36.1	325	34.2	325	36.4
I have heard just a little about it	223	8.9	484	20.3	1013	44.1	583	26.8	303	31.1
I know something about it	348	8.5	692	16.1	1887	46.3	1173	29.1	205	21.0
I understand it fully	341	11.2	322	11.6	776	29.0	1242	48.2	108	11.5
When to adopt										
As soon as possible	24	0.8	50	1.7	754	24.8	2349	72.7	94	11.0
After successful experiments in my country	48	1.3	332	9.5	2329	67.0	752	22.1	171	17.2
After successful experiments in other countries	121	7.2	500	31.5	786	50.3	168	11.0	251	24.4
Not anytime in the near future	406	30.9	670	53.7	144	12.2	42	3.2	184	20.9
Never	454	73.4	116	18.7	23	4.7	12	3.1	241	26.4
Arguments for										
It reduces anxiety about financing basic needs	245	4.3	617	10.9	2367	42.4	2273	42.4	283	27.1
It creates more equality of opportunity	113	2.5	384	8.7	1879	43.1	1951	45.8	239	25.4
It encourages financial independence and self-responsibility	97	3.0	293	8.7	1451	43.1	1526	45.2	152	15.3
It increases solidarity, because it is funded by everyone	81	3.1	257	9.1	1214	43.7	1243	44.1	151	16.2
It reduces bureaucracy and administrative expenses	98	4.2	274	11.8	921	42.1	943	41.9	120	13.0

(continued)

Table 2.2 (continued)

	I would vote against it N	%	I would probably vote against It N	%	I would probably vote for it N	%	I would vote for it N	%	Total voters per category %[a]	Total non-voters per category N	%[a]
It increases appreciation for household work and volunteering	116	3.3	327	10.4	1272	42.8	1288	43.5	29.9	156	16.3
None of the above	611	39.3	492	34.3	238	18.8	107	7.6	13.7	405	44.1
Arguments against											
It is impossible to finance	598	15.0	799	21.2	1406	38.4	902	25.5	34.9	239	25.2
It might encourage people to stop working	758	12.6	1038	17.7	2213	40.0	1593	29.7	54.6	305	30.9
Foreigners might come to my country and take advantage of the benefit	520	11.4	633	14.9	1594	39.3	1338	34.4	40.6	218	22.6
It is against the principle of linking merit and reward	530	20.2	660	25.5	838	34.7	463	19.7	23.5	161	15.7
Only the people who need it most should get something from the state	471	12.4	725	19.1	1367	39.7	988	28.8	35.3	233	24.2
It increases dependence on the state	476	14.0	586	18.0	1218	40.2	825	27.8	29.8	171	16.3
None of the above	56	6.1	102	11.3	318	34.3	473	48.3	9.8	345	36.9

[a]The percentages are per category, hence calculated in the column direction
Source: Dalia Research

recorded (Fitzgerald et al., 2017). In the Swiss 2016 referendum, the relationship between support for UBI and age was hump-shaped. Among the oldest age group (70+) support was the weakest (10%), followed by the youngest age group (18–29 years) (22%) and those 60–69 years old (25%) (Colombo et al., 2016). On average 4% of the respondents consider helicopter money a bad idea. It gradually increases with age from 18–24 years (12%) to 55–64 (17%) and 20% among those 65+ years (ING, 2016). The US survey data also shows that support for UBI decreases with age: from 54% in the age group 18–35 years to 38% among the 66 + years (Northeastern University, 2018). Our data does not show this age-related pattern. The highest support for UBI is also among the youngest 14–25 age category (76.8%), but is followed by 74.8% among the 36–45 years old; the lowest support for UBI is among those 26–35 years (72.1%) and 72.5% for the older 55–65 age category. The support of UBI by young people is partly related to their higher labour market risks; they are more likely to be in precarious work and to experience risk of poverty or social exclusion (Shanahan, Smith & Srinivasan, Chap. 3).

A UBI may have different implications for women and men. Women are generally more risk averse than men (see Booth & Nolen, 2012; Borghans, Heckman, Golsteyn, & Meijers, 2010; Dohmen et al., 2011; Kapteyn & Teppa, 2011). UBI reduces this economic risk. It is also expected that women are more in favour of UBI than men, because women have more to gain from UBI than men. UBI offers greater economic security, independence and empowers women. It will reduce the gender division of labour (Delsen, 1997; Haywood, 2014; Standing, 2017: 168; Torry, 2018: 58–59; Walter, 1989). Some feminists oppose this view. According to them, labour market activities—paid work—and financial independence are the road to emancipation. They consider UBI hush money, that tempers emancipation and sends women back home (Kawagoe, Chap. 8; Robeyns, 2000; Van Parijs & Vanderborght, 2017: 187–189; see also Widerquist, Noguera, Vanderborght, & De Wispelaere, 2013; 142–188). Based on ESS data, Fitzgerald et al. (2017) found that support for UBI by gender shows little difference, although there are some differences between groups of European countries: In Christian Democratic (f 48.0%, m 47.6%), Social Democratic (f 46.4% m 44.2%) and in Eastern Europe, with the highest support rates (f 69.7%, m 67.4%), females are more in favour than males, while in the UK and Ireland (f 48.6%, m 54.1%) and in Switzerland, with one of the lowest support rates (f 33.7%, m 35.7%), males are relatively more in favour of UBI. The Swiss 2016 referendum showed no significant gender differences in the support for UBI (Colombo et al., 2016). A Gallup poll of attitudes towards AI and its effect on their lives and work shows that female Americans (52%) are more in support of a UBI programme than males (43%) (Northeastern University, 2018). Our data show that more women (75.6%) would (probably) vote for UBI than men (72.9%).

Labour market status of the respondents may affect support for UBI. Full-timers may have less to win and more to lose (taxes) from the introduction of a UBI, relative to e.g. people without a job, people receiving various types of benefits and part-timers. On the one hand, unemployment benefit recipients may be in favour of a UBI because they face high marginal implicit tax rates, or because of the stringent job-search requirements. On the other hand, when social security benefit levels are high, they may be against the introduction of the less favourable UBI that covers basic needs replacing them. The ESS survey results show the highest support for UBI among social benefit recipients (66.0%) and respondents on unemployment benefits (65.0%), followed by wages/salaries earners (about 56.7%) and pensioners (52.8%). Support is lower among self-employed (49.5%) and farmers (48.1%), and is lowest for those whose main income source is capital gains, investments, savings, *etc.* (37.2%) (Vlandas, 2018). In the Swiss 2016 referendum, self-employed were most in support of UBI (36%), compared to the other categories of civil servants (26%) and employees (23%). These differences between professional groups are not statistically significant (Colombo et al., 2016). In line with the ESS results, our data shows that people with a full-time job are less (70.3%) in favour of UBI than non-full-timers (78.8%).

The ESS survey shows that support for UBI in Europe is rather stable for respondents with 8–15 years of education, falls thereafter and increases again for those with 19–20 years of education (Vlandas, 2018). On a seven-point scale for education level, support for UBI in Christian Democratic and Social Democratic countries shows a U-shape like relationship, Eastern Europe shows a more hump-shaped relationship with multiple peaks, and the UK and Ireland show multiple peaks (Fitzgerald et al., 2017). The Gallup survey in the US shows that higher educated (bachelor degree or higher) are less in favour of UBI (42%) than lower educated (less than bachelor degree) (51%) (Northeastern University, 2018). The Swiss 2016 referendum showed no significant differences between educational groups in the support for UBI (Colombo et al., 2016). Our data shows that support for UBI decreases with educational level, from 77.5% among people with no formal education to 68.9% among those with university or equivalent education.

In the June 2016 Swiss referendum on the introduction of a UBI of around €2255 a month per adult, and €564 per child, 23.1% voted in favour and 76.9% voted against. A post-ballot telephone survey of a sample (N = 1513) of the Swiss population shows that in rural areas (19%) significantly fewer people than in cities (32%) voted in favour of UBI (Colombo et al., 2016). These regional differences may be related to differences in economic and labour market conditions. Individuals in regions with higher poverty and unemployment rates and lower employment rates are likely to perceive more income and employment insecurity that translates into stronger public support for UBI. Eurostat data shows that in general poverty rates in cities are higher than in rural areas. In the EU the highest rate of risk of poverty or social exclusion is recorded among people living in rural areas (27.1%), followed by people living in cities (24.3%) and those living in towns and suburbs (22.3%). In 2017, the EU-28 unemployment rate in cities (8.4%) was somewhat higher than in towns and suburbs (7.7%) and in rural areas (6.8%), while there was little difference between EU-28 employment rates for rural areas (72.6%), towns and suburbs or cities (both 72.0%). Our bivariate data shows very little difference between rural areas (74.0%) and cities (74.3%) in voting (probably) in favour of UBI.

Labour market consequences of UBI is a major topic in the discussions on UBI. UBI may allow people to make a career move or to enter training or education. A UBI not only alleviates liquidity and credit constraints. When UBI is perceived as a

Table 2.3 Behaviour of respondents; effect of UBI on his/her own work choices (single choice) (percentage)

Effect	Females No.	%	Males No.	%	Total No.	%
Stop working	116	2.4	170	3.1	286	2.8
Work less	315	7.0	506	10.1	821	8.6
Do more volunteering work	348	7.5	406	8.1	754	7.8
Spend more time with my family	818	16.8	872	16.8	1690	16.8
Look for a different job	296	5.9	249	4.9	545	5.4
Work as a freelancer	207	4.0	197	3.8	404	3.9
Gain additional skills	395	7.2	359	6.8	754	7.0
No effect	1954	39.7	2002	37.7	3956	38.7
None of the above	449	9.6	421	8.6	870	9.1
Total	4898	100	5182	100	10,080	100

Source: Dalia Research

secure and steady source of income over time, risk-averse households will be more willing to invest in riskier but higher return activities (Forget, 2011; Gertler, Martinez, & Rubio-Codina, 2012; see also Füllbrunn, Delsen & Vyrastekova, Chap. 7). The UBI can be expected to help unleash entrepreneurship by buffering the potential self-employed against the risk of uncertainty and fluctuating income (Nooteboom, 1987). Over one third (38.7%) of the voting respondents indicated UBI will have no effect on their own work choices (see Table 2.3). 16.3% indicated it will have positive effects on their own labour market choices: "work as a free-lancer", i.e. becoming self-employed, "gain additional skills", i.e. investment in own human capital and "look for a different job", i.e. move to a more rewarding or suitable job. 24.6% indicated it will have socially desirable consequences ("more volunteering work" plus "spend more time with my family"), while only 11.4%—the smallest minority—indicated UBI will adversely affect their labour supply of those already working, i.e. "work less" plus "stop working". The latter applies only to employed people, and may be linked to the idea of people being lazy and to the negative connotation of work—people derive disutility from working and utility from leisure time—as assumed by main-stream economists in their dominant microeconomic theory. The *homo economicus*—the rational, free and independent individual—who is able to motivate their choice and to take responsibility, is considered to be the basic unity of the economy. People only work to be able to consume. Consumption is considered the ultimate goal of all economic activities. In this neoclassic framework, the labour supply effect depends on the consumption preferences of the individual employees. In response to a UBI, individuals who work a lot may increase labour supply, those who work only a little may decrease their labour supply and the unemployed may increase their labour supply (Gilroy, Heimann, & Schopf, 2013). UBI—non-labour income—induces employed people to reduce working time or leave the labour market, and the unemployed to stop seeking a job. However, the starting point that free time is pleasant and labour is unpleasant can be challenged. Moreover, people are no islands. Economic life cannot be divorced from social and cultural life. Economic transactions are embedded in a network of social relations between actors (Granovetter, 1985). The disincentive effect of UBI on labour supply may be compensated by the social and mental values attached to work, explaining why only 2.8% of the voting respondents indicated to stop working and 8.6% to work less. The disutility of work and the connected adverse effect of UBI on the supply of labour depend crucially on the level of intrinsic motivation and the quality of the present jobs. UBI reduces labour supply for those jobs for which people have no intrinsic motivation (bad jobs) and increases supply for jobs for which people have high intrinsic motivation (good jobs). The higher the UBI, the stronger the movement of people from bad to good jobs (Pech, 2010). Finally, 9.1% indicated none of the previous behavioural changes in work choices apply. This may suggest respondents being already in that 'right', i.e. the preferred position, or may concern respondents without a paid job. The marginal tax rate under UBI is zero. It replaces the 'old' high implicit marginal tax rate, i.e. high marginal deduction rates on additional income, because means-tested benefits, subsidies or remission of (municipal) taxes are reduced. Eliminating poverty and unemployment traps, UBI facilitates gaining additional skills and advancement of employees, it also makes it easier for individuals to return to work, and increases labour supply of inactive individuals, e.g. accept a (small) part-time job. Leisure is linked to the intrinsic motivation associated with the job. Intrinsic motivation is determined by e.g. social interaction, autonomy, and freedom (Gamel, Balsan, & Vero, 2006). UBI may contribute to freedom and autonomy, resulting in leisure indeed being perceived as an inferior good. In that case the employed continue working and the unemployed start looking for a job and start working. The impact of UBI on own work choices of US citizens shows similarity with the work choices of people in the EU: "spend more time with my family" and "get additional skill" and "work less" are the top three choices; "do more volunteering work", "look for different job", and "stop working" are the lowest ranked choices (Füllbrunn, Delsen & Vyrastekova, Chap. 7).

We can calculate the combined bivariate results of probably voting in favour and voting in favour and similarly, for probably voting against and voting against based on Table 2.2. The labour market effect of UBI differs considerably between those in favour and those against UBI. Voters against the UBI represent only a small group who would like to "Gain additional skills" (14.8%)". So, voters in favour are much more likely to "Gain additional skills" (85.2%). Interestingly, voters against the UBI are predominantly opting to "Stop working" (62.5%) if the UBI would be implemented. This is in stark contrast with those in favour (37.5%). Differences in intrinsic motivation and in the quality of the present job may explain this divide. Also an experienced suboptimal work-life balance may play a role.

It may be concluded that, on balance, the expected change in labour market behaviour does not seem to be that negative in the short term, and may even be positive in the longer term. However, the full on balance effect depends on the UBI scheme, including the level of the payment, the tax scheme, and the pre-existing social security, as well as on the quality and wage of the available jobs, the individual preferences for consumption, and perceptions and values (Gamel et al.,

2006; Gilroy et al., 2013; Groot, 1999: 135–143; Standing, 2017; Torry, 2018; Van Parijs & Vanderborght, 2017: 32–43).

Women have larger labour-supply elasticity than men, even after controlling for participation rates. Differences between countries are small (Evers, De Mooij, & Van Vuuren, 2008). The results of the four Negative Income Tax (NIT) field experiments in the US between 1968 and 1978, and during 1975–1978 in Canada, show that the work-disincentive effect is larger among women than among men (Burtless, 1986; Killingsworth, 1983: 392–408; Killingsworth & Heckman, 1986; Pencavel, 1986: 73–82; Robins, 1985; Widerquist, 2005). The NIT does not appear to have a pervasive effect on the work ethic of the low-income male population; in fact, most of the men do not respond at all (Moffitt, 1981). The negative effects of UBI (non-wage income) on work choices of women may be expected to be stronger than on those of men, because of weaker labour market attachment. However, our bivariate data indicate the opposite (see Table 2.3). The "no effect" on their own work choices between women (39.7%) and men (37.7%) is 2.0 percentage points. The positive effects of UBI on their own labour market choices is also stronger for females (17.1%) than for males (15.5%), while the adverse effect on their own labour supply is considerable smaller for females (9.4%) than for males (13.2%). Also unexpected, the socially desirable consequences of UBI are almost equal among men (24.9%) and women (24.3%). Our data do not confirm hush money. On the contrary: UBI does not send women back home; UBI will reduce the gender division of paid as well as unpaid work.

Table 2.2 shows about two thirds (65.7%) of the voting respondents is familiar with UBI. A quarter (25.1%) of the respondents indicated to fully understand the concept; 40.6% knows something about it. Over one third (34.3%) of the respondents indicated they never heard (10.2%) or heard only little (24.1%) of UBI. The familiarity with UBI increases the chance of being in favour of it. People who have never heard of it are less likely to be in favour of the UBI (70.3%), than if they understand it fully (77.2%). Unknown, unloved. However, the difference is not large, nor does it imply causation. Instead of awareness causing more support for UBI, reversed causality may apply; people who consider UBI more appealing may be more motivated to research and learn more about it.

Experience with referendums in Switzerland shows that women, young people, the uneducated and low-income earners are overrepresented among the non-voters (Leininger & Heyne, 2017; Linder, 2012). The Swiss 2016 referendum showed that both voters and non-voters were familiar with UBI, however, non-voters were less well informed than voters (Colombo et al., 2016). The Dalia Research non-voters that have never heard of UBI (36.4%) is much higher than voters (10.2%). Our data also shows overrepresentation of young people in the 14–25 year age group, people with no formal education, and those without a full-time job. Additionally, among women the proportion of non-voters is relatively high. The Heckman selection procedure (see Table 2.4) partially confirms this. The likelihood to vote is much lower in case you are young, not full-time employed and have a limited awareness of the UBI. The effect among women is insignificant. This is most likely because the gender effect is mediated by the full-time employment effect.

Table 2.4 Ordered probability to vote in favour of UBI in the European Union

	(1) Ordered probit	(2) Heckman ordered probit
Age	0.0181**	0.0183**
	(3.27)	(3.28)
Age*Age	−0.000221**	−0.000223**
	(−3.17)	(−3.18)
Male	0.0325	0.0330
	(1.39)	(1.41)
Full-time job	−0.152***	−0.150***
	(−5.83)	(−5.58)
Rural	0.0563*	0.0565*
	(2.08)	(2.09)
Education		
No formal	ref.	ref.
Some high school/secondary	−0.132	−0.132
	(−1.80)	(−1.80)
High school or equivalent	−0.152*	−0.152*
	(−2.11)	(−2.11)
University or equivalent	−0.264***	−0.264***
	(−3.56)	(−3.56)
Other/unanswered	−0.0659	−0.0657
	(−0.70)	(−0.70)
Awareness		
I have never heard of it	ref.	ref.
I have heard just a little about it	−0.153***	−0.144**
	(−3.55)	(−2.67)
I know something about it	−0.0802	−0.0671
	(−1.93)	(−1.06)
I understand it fully	0.181***	0.194**
	(4.01)	(2.93)
Effect on individual work choices		
Stop working	−0.542***	−0.542***
	(−8.59)	(−8.59)
Work less	−0.0522	−0.0522
	(−1.41)	(−1.42)
Do more volunteering work	0.0382	0.0382
	(0.98)	(0.98)
Spend more time with my family	0.101***	0.101***
	(3.52)	(3.52)
Look for a different job	−0.0301	−0.0301
	(−0.67)	(−0.67)
Work as a freelancer	0.190***	0.190***
	(3.51)	(3.51)

(continued)

2 Individual Preferences for the Unconditional Basic Income in the European Union

Table 2.4 (continued)

	(1) Ordered probit	(2) Heckman ordered probit
Gain additional skills	0.222***	0.221***
	(5.27)	(5.27)
No effect	0.188***	0.188***
	(8.32)	(8.32)
None of the above	−0.115**	−0.115**
	(−3.03)	(−3.03)
Arguments for		
It reduces anxiety about financing basic needs	0.430***	0.429***
	(16.04)	(16.04)
It creates more equality of opportunity	0.448***	0.448***
	(17.71)	(17.70)
It encourages financial independence and self-responsibility	0.269***	0.269***
	(10.35)	(10.35)
It increases solidarity, because it is funded by everyone	0.183***	0.183***
	(6.64)	(6.64)
It reduces bureaucracy and administrative expenses	0.0849**	0.0848**
	(2.91)	(2.91)
It increases appreciation for household work and volunteering	0.221***	0.221***
	(8.18)	(8.18)
None of the above	−0.668***	−0.668***
	(−15.43)	(−15.42)
Arguments against		
It is impossible to finance	−0.323***	−0.323***
	(−12.88)	(−12.88)
It might encourage people to stop working	−0.240***	−0.240***
	(−9.30)	(−9.30)
Foreigners might come to my country and take advantage of the benefit	0.0267	0.0267
	(1.08)	(1.08)
It is against the principle of linking merit and reward	−0.439***	−0.438***
	(−15.47)	(−15.47)
Only the people who need it most should get something from the state	−0.209***	−0.209***
	(−8.41)	(−8.41)
It increases dependence on the state	−0.195***	−0.194***
	(−7.30)	(−7.30)
None of the above	0.144**	0.144**
	(3.01)	(3.01)
cut1	−1.583***	−1.556***
	(−11.77)	(−9.25)
cut2	−0.678***	−0.651***
	(−5.08)	(−3.91)

(continued)

Table 2.4 (continued)

	(1) Ordered probit	(2) Heckman ordered probit
cut3	0.701***	0.728***
	(5.25)	(4.41)
atanhρ		0.0422
		(0.28)
Chance to vote		
Male		0.0619
		(1.72)
Full-time job		0.174***
		(4.58)
Rural		0.0215
		(0.53)
Awareness		
I have never heard of it		ref.
I have heard just a little about it		0.533***
		(10.94)
I know something about it		0.957***
		(19.25)
I understand it fully		1.000***
		(17.36)
Age		
14–25		−0.211***
		(−6.19)
26–35		−0.0551
		(−1.53)
36–45		−0.0182
		(−0.53)
46–55		0.129***
		(3.48)
56–65		0.155**
		(3.24)
Constant		0.337***
		(3.47)
Observations	10,080	11,021
Country Dummies	Yes	Yes
Wald test of independent equations probability		0.781

t statistics in parentheses
$*p < 0.05$, $**p < 0.01$, $***p < 0.001$
Source: Dalia Research

Voters and non-voters have different preferences for UBI. Non-voters are more negative about UBI, e.g. only 11.0% prefers UBI to be adopted "as soon as possible", while according to one quarter (26.4%) UBI should "Never" be introduced. Related to both the arguments for and the arguments against UBI and the most likely effect of UBI on their own work choices "None of the above" is the most frequent choice of non-voters. This could be because they have no opinion on UBI.

One third (33.1%) of the voting respondents think their country should introduce UBI "As soon as possible". Almost half of the voters (49.3%) still have to be convinced first. One third (33.8%) prefers an introduction of the UBI "After successful experiments in their own country", and 15.5% "After successful experiments in other countries". This not only indicates the preference for a well-considered introduction of UBI in Europe, but also the complementarity of experiments and surveys. It shows that the current and planned national field experiments in the Netherlands (see Muffels & Gielens, Chap. 5 and Betkó et al., Chap. 6) and Scotland (see Danson, Chap. 4) are desirable and useful; their results have policy relevance beyond the municipal; in regional, as well as national contexts. The established effects of these UBI experiments on social participation, health, well-being, poverty, labour supply, labour market mobility, entrepreneurship, as well as on school attendance, human capital, economic growth, and inflation are crucial for the support and political feasibility of UBI. "Not anytime in the near future" was indicated by 11.7%. Another, the smallest, minority (5.9%) is of the opinion that UBI should "Never" be adopted. Not shown in Table 2.2, cross-tabulation of preferences for the timing of the introduction of UBI are consistently distributed over the voting behaviour. "As soon as possible" is by far the most frequent choice by those in favour (71.9%); "after successful experiments in my own country" is by far the most frequent choice indicated by those probably in favour (56.1%); not soon is the most frequent answer chosen by respondents who indicated they would probably vote against (39.1%), and "Never" is the most frequent option among those who would vote against UBI (44.3%). However, correlation does not equal causation.

"It reduces anxiety about financial basic needs", i.e. the reduction of the poverty risk is considered the most convincing argument for the UBI (54.5%), followed by empowerment "It creates more equality of opportunity" (43.9%), and autonomy "It encourages financial independence and self-responsibility" (34.0%), "It increases appreciation for household work and volunteering" (29.9%), "It increases solidarity, because it is funded by everyone" (27.3%), and "It reduces bureaucracy and administrative expenses" (22.2%). These concern the desirability of UBI. Other convincing concerns which are not on the list is checked 13.7% of the time. Most of these (73.6%) are opposed to the UBI. The ranking of the arguments for UBI by US citizens is similar to the people in the EU (Füllbrunn, Delsen & Vyrastekova, Chap. 7).

If the voters for (the majority) and the voters against (the minority) had voted consistently, one would expect the frequencies of convincing arguments for UBI to be systematically higher than the frequencies of convincing arguments against. A high frequency of "None of the above" in the question on convincing arguments against and a lower frequency in the question on convincing arguments for UBI are also expected. However, this is not the case. The survey question focused on the 'quality' of the argument in general. This need not necessarily mean that the argument is convincing for the voter, for the question does not ask which of the following arguments against the basic income convince you. The results suggest that advocates of UBI are not unequivocally in favour. They may vote for UBI because they favour the concept, but are well aware that there are minuses. Inversely, voters against the UBI also show they are not unequivocally against. The frequency of "None of the above" for arguments against UBI is similar in voters for (48.3%) compared to "None of the above" for arguments in favour of UBI (39.3%). Hence, voters against UBI are aware of the benefits as well.

In the Swiss 2016 survey, a multiple answer question was used to establish the motives of the 'yes' and 'no' voters. Almost half (46%) of those with a favourable opinion did not aim at the actual introduction of UBI, but wanted to stimulate a discussion of what they thought was a good idea. For 30% of the yes-voters this was even the first mentioned motive. The next important motives were more social justice and less inequality (40%), mentioned first by 18% of the yes-voters, and criticism of the relationship between economy, society and freedom (37%), first mentioned by 16%. The latter mainly concerns the less than optimal work-life balance, and more freedom and autonomy over own life. For the no-voters, the two most mentioned motives by far, were the belief that such a UBI could not be financed (59%), for 30% of the no-voters this was the first mentioned motive, followed by the missing incentive to work: 56% and 22% (Colombo et al., 2016). It also shows that in response to the single choice question about arguments contra UBI, 22% of the yes-voters and 88% of the no-voters agree that UBI is not fundable; incentive to work would be lost (yes-voters 14%, no-voters 86%), being the only country to implement UBI would be detrimental (yes-voters 36%, no-voters 65%). The answers to the single choice question about arguments pro UBI shows that 89% of yes-voters and 25% of the no-voters agree that UBI enhances and promotes family work and voluntary work; 69% of the yes-voter and 13% of the no-voters think UBI can replace the present social security benefits without large extra costs, and respectively 78% and 18% agree that UBI may be a sensible solution for loss of jobs in the future due to digitalisation (Colombo et al., 2016).

Table 2.2 shows there are clear differences between the indicated effect of UBI on their own work choices and the expected effect of UBI on work choices of other people. People consider themselves morally superior to their fellow human beings, i.e. better than the average person, a phenomenon known as 'self-enhancement'. Other people are lazier than me (Standing, 2017: 165–167; Tapin & McKay, 2017). "It might encourage people to stop working", the disincentive to work, is considered the most convincing (highest frequency) argument against the UBI: 54.6%, followed by "Foreigners might come to my country and take advantage of the benefit" (40.6%). These two answers show the highest correlation. Both support the self-enhancement hypothesis, since it shows anxiety towards fellow members in the community who would stop working. The other arguments against UBI are "It is impossible to finance" (34.9%), "Only the people who need it most should get something from the state" (35.3%), "It increases dependence on the state" (29.8%), "It is against the principle linking merit and reward", i.e. against reciprocity and at odds with the current national welfare states (23.5%). "None of the above" is by far the least important argument against UBI (9.8%). The ranking of the arguments against UBI by US citizens is largely similar to the ranking by people in the EU; "stop working" is ranked first. Unlike in the EU where "immigration" is ranked second, in the US it is the lowest ranked argument against UBI. Self-enhancement is also confirmed by US survey data (Füllbrunn, Delsen & Vyrastekova, Chap. 7).

2.3.2 Results of Regression Analyses

The bivariate analysis provides overall insights but does not control for partial effects. For this reason, we apply a regression analysis. It allows an interpretation of partial effects of each variable. The regression results of the multi-level ordered logit model and the results of the country fixed effects model are largely the same: the same coefficients and the same significance levels are observed (see Table 2.5). This means that relaxing the assumption of unobserved heterogeneity most likely does not bias country level effects.

Fitzgerald et al. (2017)—based on ESS data—found in their logistic regression analysis that young people, unemployed people, those on lower incomes, and those feeling difficult on present income (negative feeling about income) and those in education tend to lend significantly more support to the UBI, across all countries. Additionally, their two control variables—"benefits only low income people" and "positive attitude toward immigration"—have a significant positive effect on the support for UBI. Survey results in Finland and Sweden show that young people are more enthusiastic about the basic income than old people (Andersson & Kangas, 2002). In our models, unlike these earlier results (decreasing or U-shaped), the likelihood to vote in favour of UBI has a hump-shaped relationship with age measured in years. The positive effect of age in favour of UBI levels off, as indicated by the negative coefficient of aged squared. The positive effect of age may be related to risk-averseness that increases significantly with age (see e.g. Dohmen et al., 2011; Kapteyn & Teppa, 2011). The timing of the implementation may also play a role. For some older people, the introduction of UBI may come 'too late' to make sense, for they will be retired by that time. In line with the ESS results, having a full-time job has a significant negative effect on voting in favour of UBI.

Like Fitzgerald et al. (2017) and Andersson and Kangas (2002), our analyses also do not confirm the gender effect. A respondent's religion and years of education do not appear to have a significant effect on levels of support for a basic income (Fitzgerald et al., 2017). In Finland and Sweden, support for UBI tends to diminish somewhat with the education level and more clearly with income (Andersson & Kangas, 2002). In the Swiss 2016 referendum, support for UBI was not significantly correlated with income levels (Colombo et al., 2016). Income and religion are not included in our data set. Related to education the bivariate results are confirmed: support for UBI decreases significantly with educational attainment.

Table 2.5 Multi-level models explaining the likelihood to vote in favour of UBI in the European Union

	(1) Random effects	(2) Fixed effects
Age	0.0302**	0.0308**
	(3.18)	(3.23)
Age*Age	−0.000376**	−0.000381**
	(−3.14)	(−3.18)
Male	0.0752	0.0755
	(1.88)	(1.89)
Full-time job	−0.264***	−0.263***
	(−5.93)	(−5.91)
Rural	0.0903	0.0927*
	(1.95)	(2.00)
Education		
No formal	ref.	ref.
Some high school/secondary	−0.266*	−0.258*
	(−2.05)	(−1.99)
High school or equivalent	−0.302*	−0.300*
	(−2.38)	(−2.36)
University or equivalent	−0.483***	−0.480***
	(−3.68)	(−3.66)
Other/unanswered	−0.135	−0.140
	(−0.81)	(−0.84)
Awareness		
I have never heard of it	ref.	ref.
I have heard just a little about it	−0.266***	−0.275***
	(−3.56)	(−3.66)
I know something about it	−0.158*	−0.167*
	(−2.20)	(−2.30)
I understand it fully	0.313***	0.305***
	(4.02)	(3.88)
Effect on individual work choices		
Stop working	−0.953***	−0.954***
	(−8.44)	(−8.44)
Work less	−0.0535	−0.0470
	(−0.83)	(−0.73)
Do more volunteering work	0.0619	0.0591
	(0.92)	(0.88)
Spend more time with my family	0.173***	0.173***
	(3.52)	(3.50)
Look for a different job	−0.0548	−0.0577
	(−0.70)	(−0.74)

(continued)

Table 2.5 (continued)

	(1) Random effects	(2) Fixed effects
Work as a freelancer	0.333***	0.334***
	(3.54)	(3.54)
Gain additional skills	0.373***	0.375***
	(5.20)	(5.22)
No effect	0.324***	0.323***
	(8.36)	(8.33)
None of the above	−0.205**	−0.206**
	(−3.14)	(−3.15)
Arguments for		
It reduces anxiety about financing basic needs	0.729***	0.729***
	(15.82)	(15.80)
It creates more equality of opportunity	0.755***	0.755***
	(17.39)	(17.37)
It encourages financial independence and self-responsibility	0.460***	0.454***
	(10.37)	(10.22)
It increases solidarity, because it is funded by everyone	0.305***	0.307***
	(6.49)	(6.51)
It reduces bureaucracy and administrative expenses	0.149**	0.146**
	(2.97)	(2.91)
It increases appreciation for household work and volunteering	0.360***	0.364***
	(7.79)	(7.87)
None of the above	−1.218***	−1.218***
	(−16.09)	(−16.07)
Arguments against		
It is impossible to finance	−0.556***	−0.556***
	(−12.93)	(−12.90)
It might encourage people to stop working	−0.421***	−0.419***
	(−9.52)	(−9.44)
Foreigners might come to my country and take advantage of the benefit	0.0327	0.0357
	(0.78)	(0.84)
It is against the principle of linking merit and reward	−0.763***	−0.758***
	(−15.65)	(−15.51)
Only the people who need it most should get something from the state	−0.360***	−0.362***
	(−8.45)	(−8.49)
It increases dependence on the state	−0.327***	−0.327***
	(−7.19)	(−7.19)
None of the above	0.240**	0.246**
	(2.90)	(2.96)
Macro level		
Expenditure on social protection (PPS) per inhabitant in 2016	−0.678**	
	(−2.87)	

(continued)

Table 2.5 (continued)

	(1) Random effects	(2) Fixed effects
Unemployment rates in 2016	0.0374**	
	(2.85)	
cut1	−2.669***	−2.850***
	(−9.93)	(−12.12)
cut2	−1.021***	−1.201***
	(−3.84)	(−5.18)
cut3	1.316***	1.141***
	(4.94)	(4.92)
Observations	10,080	10,080
Country dummies	No	Yes
McKelvey-Zavoina Pseudo R^2 fixed and random effects	0.389	0.383

t statistics in parentheses
*$p < 0.05$, **$p < 0.01$, ***$p < 0.001$
Source: Dalia Research

Fitzgerald et al. (2017) found that regions matter. People in towns/small cities as well as in suburbs are significantly less in favour of basic income relative to people in the country side. People in big cities are more favourable for UBI, but not significantly. In our data, the effect is more favourable for rural areas, but does not show a significant robust effect.

Awareness has a U-shaped effect. In contrast to the bivariate results, we see that if controlled for other influences the unknown, unloved hypothesis is not evident. While true for the most extreme cases "I have never heard of it" and "I understand it fully", the cases in between show a lower likelihood to vote in favour of the UBI. In Table 2.4, we show a two-stage approach to the voting behaviour of people, by including a Heckman selection procedure which takes the likelihood of voting if you are more informed into account. People who do not vote have an increasing chance to be uninformed of the UBI. If these non-voters would vote against the UBI, the U-shaped effect would turn into a positive effect, supporting the unknown, unloved hypothesis. However, if non-voters would vote in favour of the UBI, no relation between informed and voting behaviour would exist. Table 2.4 shows that although non-voters are less informed, the Heckman procedure does not show a substantial difference in the outcome of a possible referendum if non-voters would participate. Non-voters do not significantly change the outcome of the analysis. We find the results inconclusive to support or refute the unknown, unloved hypothesis. Therefore, even though reversed causality might play a part in the outcomes, its effect is insignificant.

The ordered probability to vote in favour of UBI (see Table 2.4) confirms this: awareness is relatively low among non-voter, non-full-timers. The 14–25 years age category is less likely to vote in favour of UBI. The non-voters in the older age categories (46–55 years and 55–65 years) are more likely to vote in favour.

The bivariate results of the effects of UBI on work choices of the individual respondent are partly confirmed by the regression analyses. The "stop working" option has a strong and highly significant negative effect on the voting behaviour in favour of UBI. It may be rational through the income and substitution effect. In line with the '*homo economicus*', self-selection of 'lazy' people may also apply. However, this negative effect may also be related to the quality of the current job. The negative effect of "work less" is not significant in the multi-level regressions. The negative sign may be related to little autonomy of employed people to reduce their individual working time, i.e. to start working part-time, the employees require permission of the employer (cf. Moffitt, 1981). In the bivariate results we find that women show more positive effects on labour market choices than men. For this reason we test the significance of this relationship. An additional interaction between men and the labour market effects of "stop working" and "work less" was negative but insignificant. Thus the expected sign was found; i.e. women are less likely to reduce working hours or stop altogether, but other effects mediate this mechanism.[5]

The work choice "spend more time with their family" is significantly positively related to the likelihood to vote in favour of UBI. This may be related to people not being fully satisfied with their current work-life balance. If that is the case, UBI is welfare enhancing. The positive effect of "do more volunteering work" is not significant in the multi-level regressions. Our analyses confirm that UBI is appreciated because it enables training and self-employment. "work as a freelancer", i.e. becoming a self-employed and "gain additional skills", i.e. investing in human capital, have a significant positive effect on the likelihood of voting in favour of UBI. UBI enables people to choose differently and may be efficiency and welfare enhancing. "Look for a different job" has a negative, but not significant coefficient. "No effect" on individual work choices is significantly positively related to voting in favour of UBI. UBI alleviates the risk of freelancers investing in new entrepreneurial ideas and those currently investing time and effort into learning additional skills. The significant positive relation of "No effect" may also indicate that the effect of UBI goes beyond the income and substitution effect, the choice between consumption and leisure, i.e. that work and UBI has meaning and value beyond the pecuniary one. The statistically negative effect of "None of the above" may concern benefit recipients and early retired people, as well as people without a job and people receiving various types of benefits. Moreover, as the definition of the UBI in the Dalia Research questionnaire includes a level high enough to cover all basic needs, UBI may imply a drop in the benefit level; for rational people the latter may be an incentive to start working, i.e. increase working hours, work more because of income and substitution effects. This may explain the negative effect on the voting in favour of UBI. Main-stream economics suggests that UBI encourages reduction of working time and leaving the labour market. The coefficients of various work choices on the

---

[5]Results not shown in the tables, but are available from the authors upon request.

individual level add up to zero.[6] The positive and negative effects balance out. Hence, adverse selection of UBI on the labour market is limited or not existing.

As expected, all convincing arguments for UBI are significantly positively related to voting in favour of UBI. The respondents answered consistently. However, our bivariate and multi-variate results differ. "It creates more equality of opportunity", i.e. fairness, is the strongest and the most significant argument for UBI, followed by "It reduces anxiety about financing basic needs", i.e. the reduction of the poverty risk. "None of the above" also shows a strong statistically significant relationship. The high negative coefficient cannot be explained by the extreme position that people who are against UBI choose this answer, but by advocates of UBI who are not unequivocally in favour.

Main-stream economics suggests there will be welfare immigration undermining the economic and political viability of a UBI scheme. All but one of the convincing arguments against UBI are consistently significantly negatively related to voting in favour of UBI. "Foreigners might come to my country and take advantage of the benefit" is the exception: this variable has a low positive not statistically significant coefficient. "It is against the principle of linking merit and reward", i.e. UBI is at odds with reciprocity, is the strongest and the most significant argument against UBI, followed by the disincentive effect on labour supply "It might encourage people to stop working". "None of the above" also is statistically significant. The positive coefficient can be explained by the fact that people who are in favour of UBI are more likely to choose none of the arguments against UBI.

Our analysis confirms the impact of national differences in the level of social and economic risks on preferences for UBI. Like Lee (2018), we find that the generosity of national welfare states, the level of social protection expenditure per inhabitants, has a significant negative influence on the likelihood of voting in favour of UBI. We also find that the national unemployment rates are significantly positively associated with the attitudes towards UBI. Cultural variables were insignificant if combined with social protection and unemployment. Most likely, if any cultural differences influence voting behaviour, they are mediated through institutional effects.[7]

There is no consensus in explanatory power calculations for (multi-level) ordered logit models, however, the McKelvey-Zavoina Pseudo R^2 is preferred over the alternatives (DeMaris, 2002). An adjusted calculation is used for the multi-level model (cf. Langer, 2017). Both estimated models explain roughly 39%. R-squared measures should, of course, never be interpreted as a one-to-one reflection of the strength of explanatory power of the causal effects in the population. Much may still be gained by future development of additional explanations, like political characteristics, social value orientations and beliefs for differences between people in their

---

[6]The work choices results do not have a natural reference category. Using effects coding allows the mean of the possibilities to be the reference category.

[7]Individualism vs. collectivism, power distance and indulgence vs. restraint significantly influence voting behaviour if added as individual national explanations. However, their significance disappears if combined with social protection and unemployment. Masculinity, uncertainty avoidance and long-term orientation had no effect. Regression results available from the authors upon request.

preferences for UBI. For instance, in the Nordic and Liberal countries people on the left are more supportive of UBI than people on the right. In Central and Eastern Europe the reverse applies. In Continental Europe, people on the left and right are equally supportive of UBI (Shanahan, Smith & Srinivasan, Chap. 3). The Swiss 2016 referendum showed the following statistically significant differences in the support for UBI: between the political outer left (49%) and the outer right (10%), between those in favour of a stronger state (40%) and those in favour of more market (deregulation) (14%), between those in favour of no income difference (35%) and those in favour of large income differences (16%), and between those who put little emphasis on full employment (32%) and people who put strong emphasis on full employment (19%) (Colombo et al., 2016).

2.4 Conclusions

On average, almost three-quarters of the people (age group 14–65) in the 28 EU member states stated to (probably) vote for the introduction of UBI if there would be a referendum on introducing UBI, indicating desirability of UBI. One third would like to see UBI being introduced as soon as possible; half after successful experiments in their own country or abroad. The effect of awareness on voting behaviour is inconclusive. The likelihood to vote in favour of UBI varies significantly between groups of people. The national macro-economic and welfare-state contexts have significant effects. "It might encourage people to stop working" is considered the most convincing argument against UBI. "It reduces anxiety about financial basic needs" is considered the most convincing argument for UBI. The self-enhancement hypothesis is confirmed. The positive and negative effects of UBI on individual work choices balance out.

Future research on the preferences for UBI could benefit by including additional personal characteristics, like primary occupation, income and wealth, as well as political characteristics and social value orientations and beliefs. There may be significant differences between the stated preferences and intentions expressed in the 2017 EU wide survey on UBI we used in our analyses, and the revealed preferences and outcomes in the future after the introduction of UBI.

References

Andersson, J. O., & Kangas, O. (2002). *Popular support for basic income in Sweden and Finland*. Paper for the BIEN 9th International Congress, Geneva, September 12–14.

Booth, A. L., & Nolen, P. (2012). Gender differences in risk behaviour: does nurture matter? *The Economic Journal, 122*, F36–F78. https://doi.org/10.1111/j.1468-0297.2011.02480.x

Borghans, L., Heckman, J. J., Golsteyn, B. H. H., & Meijers, H. (2010). Gender differences in risk aversion and ambiguity aversion. *Journal of the European Economic Association, 9*(2–3), 649–658. https://doi.org/10.1162/JEEA.2009.7.2-3.649

Burstein, P. (2003). The impact of public opinion on public policy: A review and an agenda. *Political Research Quarterly, 56*(1), 29–40. https://doi.org/10.1177/106591290305600103

Burtless, G. (1986). The work response to a guaranteed income: A survey of experimental evidence. In A. H. Munnell (Ed.), *Lessons from the income maintenance experiments* (pp. 22–52). Boston, MA: Federal Reserve Bank of Boston.

Colombo, C., DeRocchi, T., Kurer, T., & Widmer, T. (2016). *Analyse der eidgenössischen Abstimmung vom 5. Juni 2016, VOX-Analysen 121*. Genf/Zürich: gfs.bern and Institut für Politikwissenschaft der Universität Zürich.

Dalia Research. (2017). *The EU's growing support for basic income. Measuring the change in European support for basic income from April 2016 to March 2017*. Berlin: Dalia Research. Accessed June 10, 2019, from https://basicincome.org/wp-content/uploads/2017/05/DR-2017-survey.pdf

De Wispelaere, J., & Noguera, J. A. (2012). On the political feasibility of universal basic income: An analytic framework. In R. K. Caputo (Ed.), *Basic income guarantee and politics: International experiences and perspectives on the viability of income guarantee* (pp. 17–38). New York: Palgrave Macmillan.

Delsen, L. (1997, February). A new concept of full employment. *Economic and Industrial Democracy, 18*(1), 119–135. https://doi.org/10.1177/0143831X97181007

DeMaris, A. (2002). Explained variance in logistic regression: A Monte Carlo study of proposed measures. *Sociological Methods and Research, 31*(1), 27–74. https://doi.org/10.1177/0049124102031001002

Dohmen, T. H., Falk, A., Huffman, D., Sunde, U., Schupp, J., & Wagner, G. G. (2011). Individual risk attitudes: Measurements, determinants, and behavioural consequences. *Journal of the European Economic Association, 9*(3), 522–550. https://doi.org/10.1111/j.1542-4774.2011.01015.x

Evers, M., de Mooij, R., & Van Vuuren, D. (2008). The wage elasticity of labour supply: A synthesis of empirical estimates. *De Economist, 156*(1), 25–43. https://doi.org/10.1007/s10645-007-9080-z

Fitzgerald, R., Bottoni, G., & Swift, S. (2017). *The future of welfare: Basic income?* Accessed June 8, 2019, from http://citizensincome.org/wp-content/uploads/2017/11/European-Social-Survey-survey-on-Basic-Income.pdf

Forget, E. (2011). *The town with no poverty. Using health administration data to revisit outcomes of a Canadian guaranteed annual income field experiment*. Winnipeg: University of Manitoba.

Friedman, M. (1969). *The optimum quantity of money and other essays*. Chicago, IL: Aldine Publishing Company.

Gamel, C., Balsan, D., & Vero, J. (2006). The impact of basic income on the propensity to work: Theoretical issues and micro-econometric results. *The Journal of Socio-Economics, 35*(3), 476–497. https://doi.org/10.1016/j.socec.2005.11.025

Gertler, P. J., Martinez, S. W., & Rubio-Codina, M. (2012). Investing cash transfers to raise long-term living standards. *American Economic Journal: Applied Economics, 4*(1), 164–192. https://doi.org/10.1257/app.4.1.164

Gilroy, B. M., Heimann, A., & Schopf, M. (2013). Basic income and labour supply: The German case. *Basic Income Studies, 8*(1), 43–70. https://doi.org/10.1515/bis-2012-0009

Granovetter, M. S. (1985). Economic action and social structures. The problem of embeddedness. *American Journal of Sociology, 91*(3), 481–510.

Groot, L. F. M. (1999). *Basic income and unemployment*. Ph.D. Dissertation, Thela Thesis, Amsterdam.

Haywood, L. (2014). *Bedingungsloses Grundeinkommen: Eine ökonomische Perspektive, 33, DIW Roundup: Politik im Fokus*. Berlin: German Institute for Economic Research, DIW.

Hofstede, G., Hofstede, G. J., & Minkov, M. (2010). *Cultures and organizations: Software of the mind*. New York: McGraw-Hill.

ING. (2016, October). *Helicopter money: Loved but not spent*. ING special report.

ING. (2018). *Basisinkomen? Meerderheid ziet het eigenlijk niet zitten*. ING Financieel fit Barometer, Juli, ING Economisch Bureau.

Ipsos MORI. (2017, September 8). *Half of UK adults would support universal basic income in principle*. https://doi.org/10.1016/j.joep.2011.04.002.

Kangas, O., Jauhiainen, S., Simanainen, M., & Ylikännö, M. (Eds.). (2019). The basic income experiment 2017–2018 in Finland: Preliminary results. Helsinki: Ministry of Social Affairs and Health. Accessed June 8, 2019, from http://julkaisut.valtioneuvosto.fi/handle/10024/161361

Kapteyn, A., & Teppa, F. (2011). Subjective measures of risk aversion, fixed costs, and portfolio choice. *Journal of Economic Psychology, 32*(4), 564–580. https://doi.org/10.1016/j.joep.2011.04.002

Killingsworth, M. R. (1983). *Labor supply*. Cambridge: Cambridge University Press.

Killingsworth, M. R., & Heckman, J. J. (1986). Female labor supply: A survey. In O. Ashenfelter & R. Layard (Eds.), *Handbook of labor economics* (Vol. I, pp. 103–204). Amsterdam: North-Holland.

Langer, W. (2017). *How to assess the fit of multi-level logit models with Stata?* In: Meeting of the German Stata users group. Berlin: Humboldt University. https://doi.org/10.13140/rg.2.2.17570.32966

Lee, S. (2018). Attitudes toward universal basic income and welfare state in Europe: A research note. *Basic Income Studies, 13*(1), 1–9. https://doi.org/10.2139/ssrn.3209161

Leininger, A., & Heyne, L. (2017). How representative are referendums? Evidence from 20 years of Swiss referendums. *Electoral Studies, 48*, 84–97. https://doi.org/10.1016/j.electstud.2017.05.006

Linder, W. (2012). *Schweizerische Demokratie. Institutionen – Prozesse – Perspektiven*. Bern: Haupt.

Meuleman, B., van Oorschot, W., Baute, S., Delespaul, S., Gugushvili, D., Laenen, T., Roosma, F., & Rossetti, F. (2018, September). *The past, present and future of European welfare attitudes: Topline results from round 8 of the European Social Survey*. ESS Topline Results Series, Issue 8. Accessed June 8, 2019, from https://www.europeansocialsurvey.org/docs/findings/ESS8_toplines_issue_8_welfare.pdf

Moffitt, R. A. (1981, April 23–27). The negative income tax: Would it discourage work?. *Monthly Labor Review*.

Nooteboom, B. (1987). Basic income as a basis for small business. *International Small Business Journal, 5*(3), 10–18. https://doi.org/10.1177/026624268700500301

Northeastern University. (2018). *Optimism and anxiety: Views on the impact of artificial intelligence and higher education's response*, Boston. Accessed June 8, 2019, from https://www.northeastern.edu/gallup/pdf/OptimismAnxietyNortheasternGallup.pdf

Pech, W. J. (2010). Behavioral economics and the basic income guarantee. *Basic Income Studies, 5*(2), 12–28. https://doi.org/10.2202/1932-0183.1167

Pencavel, J. (1986). Labor supply of men: A survey. In O. Ashenfelter & R. Layard (Eds.), *Handbook of labor economics* (Vol. I, pp. 3–102). Amsterdam: North-Holland.

Pfeifer, M. (2009). Public opinion on state responsibility for minimum income protection: A comparison of 14 European countries. *Acta Sociologica, 52*(2), 117–134. https://doi.org/10.1177/0001699309104000

Robeyns, I. (2000). Hush money or emancipation fee? In R. van der Veen & L. Groot (Eds.), *Basic income on the agenda: Policy objectives and political chances* (pp. 121–136). Amsterdam: Amsterdam University Press.

Robins, P. K. (1985). Comparison of the labor supply findings from the four negative income tax experiments. *Journal of Human Resources, 20*(4), 567–582. https://doi.org/10.2307/145685

RSA. (2018). *Universal basic income survey*. London: The Royal Society for the encouragement of Arts, Manufactures and Commerce. Accessed June 8, 2019, from https://www.populus.co.uk/2018/08/more-than-twice-as-many-people-support-the-idea-of-a-basic-income-than-oppose-it/

Splendid Research. (2018). *Das bedingunslose Grundeinkommen. Eine repräsentativen Umfrage unter 1.024 Deutschen zu Ihrer Meinung zum bedingungslosen Grundeinkommen*. Hamburg: Splendid Research.

Standing, G. (2017). *Basic income and how we can make it happen*. London: Pelican Books.

Tapin, B. M., & McKay, R. T. (2017). The illusion of moral superiority. *Social Psychological and Personality Science, 8*(6), 623–631. https://doi.org/10.1177/1948550616673878

Teppa, F., & Vis, C. (2012). The CentERpanel and the DNB household survey: Methodological aspects. *DNB Occasional Studies, 10*(4), 1–53.

Torry, M. (2018). *Why we need a citizen's basic income*. Bristol: Policy Press.

Van Parijs, P., & Vanderborght, Y. (2017). *Basic income: A radical proposal for a free society and a sane economy*. Cambridge, MA: Harvard University Press.

Vlandas, T. (2018). *The politics of universal basic income (UBI)*. Accessed June 11, 2019, from http://blogs.lse.ac.uk/netuf/2018/03/07/the-politics-of-universal-basic-income-ubi/

Walter, T. (1989). *Basic income: Freedom from poverty, freedom to work*. London: Marion Boyars.

Widerquist, K. (2005). A failure to communicate: What (if anything) can we learn from the negative income tax experiments? *The Journal of Socio-Economics, 34*(1), 49–81. https://doi.org/10.1016/j.socec.2004.09.050

Widerquist, K. (2018). *The devil's in the caveats: A critical analysis of basic income experiments for researchers, policymakers, and citizens*. Berkeley: Bepress. Accessed June 8, 2019, from https://works.bepress.com/widerquist/86/

Widerquist, K., Noguera, J. A., Vanderborght, Y., & De Wispelaere, J. (Eds.). (2013). *Basic income: An anthology of contemporary research*. Chichester: Wiley.

Lei Delsen (1952) studied economics at the University of Groningen (the Netherlands) and received his Ph.D. in economics from the University of Maastricht (the Netherlands). He was a research fellow at the European Centre for Work and Society in Maastricht (1984–1987), and Assistant Professor at the Department of Applied Economics of the University of Nijmegen, the Netherlands (1987–2002). From 2003 to 2018 he was Associate Professor of Socio-Economic Policy, Department of Economics, Nijmegen School of Management, Radboud University, Nijmegen. He retired June 2018. He is a research fellow of NETSPAR (Network for Studies on Pensions, Aging and Retirement). His research deals with a number of topical European labour market problems and issues, including new forms of work, retirement from work, work-life balance, choices within pension schemes, responsible investment and the relationship between globalisation and the national welfare states. He is the author of *Atypical employment: An international perspective. Causes, consequences and policy* (Groningen: Wolters-Noordhoff, 1995) and *Exit polder model? Socioeconomic changes in the Netherlands* (Westport: Praeger, 2002). Articles include: A new concept of full employment, *Economic and Industrial Democracy* (1997); Choices within collective labour agreements à la carte in the Netherlands, *British Journal of Industrial Relations* (2006) (with J. Benders & J. Smits); Corporatism and economic performance: does it still work?, *Acta Politica* (2008) (with J. Woldendorp); Does the life course savings scheme have the potential to improve work-life balance?, *British Journal of Industrial Relations* (2009) (with J. Smits); Value matters or values matter? An analysis of heterogeneity in preferences for sustainable investments, *Journal of Sustainable Finance & Investment* (2019) (with A. Lehr).

Rutger Schilpzand (1984) studied Economics (2008–2013) and Law (2008–2014) at Radboud University in Nijmegen and is currently working on his Ph.D. in International Economics. His research concerns the effect culture has on aspects of economic growth, i.e. how inequality, poverty and economic growth develop over time; the deviations in long-run economic growth; and cultural influences on growth resilience.

Chapter 3
Is a Basic Income Feasible in Europe?

Genevieve Shanahan, Mark Smith, and Priya Srinivasan

Abstract A basic income policy, whereby individuals receive unconditional, regular payments regardless of their income, wealth or economic activity, has been a long-held goal for many. Increasing discussions among a variety of stakeholders and evidence of concrete actions in many European states suggest its time may have come. Yet there is also resistance, and the feasibility of such a policy is subject to significant constraints, both in terms of implementation and achievement of desired outcomes. We use data on campaigns, political support and pilot studies from a variety of sources to assess the likely feasibility of a basic income policy in the European Union. The emerging pilots and other concrete actions suggest that there have been important, if fragile, steps forward. We suggest that while discussion and public statements of support are still a long way from a realisable basic income policy, the pressures for radical and innovative reforms of the welfare state mean that basic income will remain a relevant solution for elements of current and future labour market challenges.

Keywords Types of political feasibility · Operationalisation of basic income · Basic income policy · Welfare and labour market regimes · European Union

3.1 Introduction

At times, basic income appears to be a policy of the current Zeitgeist. Across the European Union (EU), and indeed the world, it is possible to observe green shoots of basic income policies, debates and campaigns. Indeed, today basic income is adopted by many mainstream political parties, academics and other leaders from politics and business (Heller, 2018). This after many years of less-prominent research and campaigning (Standing, 2011). It is now possible to point to concrete examples of field-level experimentation in Finland and the Netherlands (Kangas,

---

G. Shanahan · M. Smith (✉) · P. Srinivasan
Grenoble Ecole de Management, Université Grenoble Alpes ComUE, Grenoble, France
e-mail: Genevieve.Shanahan@grenoble-em.com; Mark.Smith@grenoble-em.com

2016; Muffels & Gielens, Chap. 5), and plans for pilot studies in a number of EU member states, including Germany, Spain and Scotland (Brooks, 2017; Danson, Chap. 4). Furthermore, the 2018 Council of Europe resolution 2197 provides pan-national impetus to the basic income 'cause' (CoE, 2018). On the other hand, these actors are not necessarily working with a common definition of a basic income and other political developments point to limits and resistance to such policies. For example, its rejection by the European Parliament (Valero, 2017), the result of the 2016 referendum in Switzerland (Colombo, DeRocchi, Kurer, & Widmer, 2016) and a large number of EU countries with limited or no concrete actions.

The increasing prominence of basic income in public debates in recent years might suggest that implementation of such a policy has become more feasible than it once was. In the 1990s and 2000s, advocates generally believed that the best hope for the introduction of a basic income would be by the back door, "embedded in more piecemeal income-maintenance schemes targeting specific vulnerable groups rather than universal coverage" (Caputo, 2012: 5). By 2016, by contrast, close to half the population in most countries included in the European Social Survey expressed support for a basic income policy (Fitzgerald, 2017).

Survey data collected by Dalia Research in 2017 show that, on average, almost three-quarters of people in the 28 EU member states indicate that they would (probably) vote for the introduction of a basic income if it were put to a referendum (see Delsen & Schilpzand, Chap. 2).

However, with increasing political debate and research exposure of basic income policies comes greater scrutiny of pilot study results. A more sober prognosis has emerged from some political analyses of implementation and experimentation. De Wispelaere, Halmetoja, and Pulkka (2018: 15), for instance, conclude their evaluation of the Finnish basic income experiment on a pessimistic note, arguing that "recent interest in basic income experimentation may amount to little more than a glitch in a remarkably stable policy landscape focused on labour market activation".

In this chapter, we explore the feasibility of basic income policies in the EU in light of their apparent popularity, yet simultaneous challenges of gaining adequate support and resources for implementation. Recent proposals and pilot studies notably fall short of *universal* basic income, in that they tend to target certain populations or vulnerable groups. Nevertheless, we include these initiatives in our analysis since, in contrast to more conventional welfare-state transfers, these proposals emphasise unconditionality. Thus, in this chapter we use the term unconditional basic income (UBI), rather than universal, since the unconditionality of the income is the core feature that sets such policies apart from other means-tested or insurance-based transfers that predominate in most welfare regimes.

This chapter is structured as follows. Following this introduction, Sect. 3.2 considers support for UBI within different institutional contexts and how we conceptualised feasibility for a policy which remains at an early stage of development. Section 3.3 discusses our methodological approach to the analysis of feasibility across the EU and our use of data from the Basic Income Earth Network (BIEN). Section 3.4 presents our analysis along the four dimensions of feasibility outlined by De Wispelaere and Noguera (2012)—strategic feasibility, institutional feasibility, psychological feasibility, and behavioural feasibility. Finally, Sect. 3.5 discusses our findings and their implications for both the feasibility of UBI policies and the analysis of these initiatives in European labour markets.

3.2 Policy Feasibility and Basic Income

Relatively broad public support for UBI is reflected in data from the European Social Survey, which measures attitudes across European countries (Fig. 3.1). Here, the share of respondents in favour or strongly in favour of having a UBI scheme in their country exceeds 50% in thirteen of the eighteen EU countries for which we have data (Fitzgerald, 2017; Lee, 2018). Respondents were given a standardised and relatively detailed description of a UBI scheme in order to ensure a common understanding.[1] Support hardly varies by gender, with 53.7% of men in favour or strongly in favour compared to 54.7% women, on average across the surveyed countries (European Social Survey, 2016). By contrast, Europe-wide Dalia Research survey data suggest that more women (75.6%) would (probably) vote for UBI than men (72.9%) (Delsen & Schilpzand, Chap. 2).

The EES 2016 results show that there is no clear relationship between support and existing welfare state or political regimes. For instance, we find strong support among proponents of UBI in Finland, while in Sweden the support is at the lower end of the distribution (see Fig. 3.1). Similarly, continental European countries such as Belgium and Germany find themselves at opposite ends of the distribution. The top three supporting countries are member states of the EU from the former Eastern bloc—Lithuania, Hungary and Slovenia—but support is more muted amongst other members of this group, such as Estonia and the Czech Republic.

Yet in spite of relatively widespread public support for a UBI policy from both sides of the political divide, and other stakeholders, the actual details and feasibility of such an innovative welfare state reform is a more nuanced topic. Indeed, one key issue for the political feasibility of a UBI is often presented as a core strength—the fact that it can draw support from diverse political orientations. De Wispelaere (2016) calls this the problem of persistent political division, whereby superficially aligned support for UBI obscures crucial disagreements over the specifics of the model to be adopted. These disagreements are often rooted in distinct framings of the

---

[1] Respondents to the European Social Survey (ESS) wave 8 were presented with a description of a basic income scheme that included the following elements: (a) "the government pays everyone a monthly income to cover essential living costs"; (b) "it replaces many other social benefits"; (c) "the purpose is to guarantee everyone a minimum standard of living"; (d) "everyone receives the same amount regardless of whether or not they are working"; (e) "people also keep the money they earn from work or other sources"; and (f) "this scheme is paid for by taxes". They were then asked if, overall, they would be against or in favour of having this scheme in their country with the following options: strongly against, against, in favour; strongly in favour; don't know (European Social Survey, 2016).

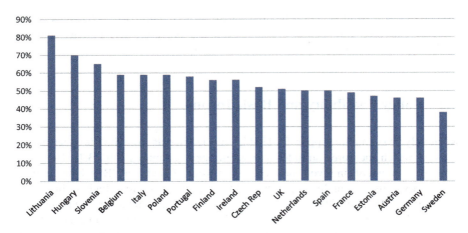

Fig. 3.1 Public support for a UBI policy in Europe by country (2016) (Note: % of population in favour or strongly in favour of having a UBI scheme in their country)
Source: European Social Survey (2016), Lee (2018), and Fitzgerald (2017)

purpose of a UBI. Perkiö (2019: 10) identifies the most prominent of these frames, with UBI being variously conceived as "a tool to incentivise work and other activities" (the 'activity' frame), "a way to improve the income level or income security of deprived groups" (the 'subsistence' frame), "a policy to correct systemic flaws in social protection" (the 'systemic reform' frame), a way to "improve the fulfilment of social rights" (the 'rights' frame), or "necessary because of the dearth of traditional forms of employment" (the 'transformation of work' frame).

In his report ahead of the Finnish partial UBI experiment, Olli Kangas, one of the pilot's leading designers, foregrounded the transformation of work frame, suggesting that a full UBI could be seen "as an instrument that would help to reduce the supply of labour and in this way allow more equal distribution of work and wealth and provide people with participatory opportunities outside paid work" (Kangas, 2016: 19). Yet the implementation of the experiment ultimately aligned much more with the activation frame, such that a "basic income is now largely perceived as a tool to promote labour market reintegration in Finland" (De Wispelaere et al., 2018: 17). Furthermore, De Wispelaere and Noguera warn, not all political support is equally valuable. While various political actors across the EU are incorporating UBI proposals or trials into their platforms, effective support is only that which comes from powerful actors capable of engaging in "the necessary political action to build a sustainable coalition around the policy" (De Wispelaere & Noguera, 2012: 22). The endorsements offered by politically marginal actors are classed as 'cheap', to the extent that they are unable to back them up with resources and action. Worse, political support can even be costly for the UBI cause where the support of a controversial actor dissuades others from endorsing the same policy.

We can thus see that a number of obstacles and risks arise on UBI's road towards political feasibility (De Wispelaere, 2016; Noguera & De Wispelaere, 2006; Torry, 2014;

Widerquist, 2005). First, the actual implementation of UBI may be blocked by the inability of advocating parties to agree on substantive policy design. That is, UBI may be straightforwardly politically infeasible with no agreement on the detail. Second, in an attempt to achieve agreement, the enacted UBI policy may be diluted such that it fails to achieve any one of its intended ends. Third, and most risky for those promoting inclusion, the political negotiation may become dominated by parties motivated by the potential for UBI to serve neoliberal or nationalist ends, rendering the policy a tool of oppression. As a result, research on political feasibility—and specifically the interaction between its various component types (Torry, 2014)—is necessary to assist in the navigation of these political opportunities and threats.

De Wispelaere and Noguera offer a useful analytical framework for evaluating the political feasibility of UBI, where feasibility is broadly understood as concerning a state in which "the background conditions are such that there is a reasonable probability of the policy becoming actualized in the foreseeable future" (De Wispelaere & Noguera, 2012: 17). This matrix provides a useful delineation between four types of feasibility, based on the dimensions of agency and constraints identified as particularly central to feasibility.

In terms of agency, it is possible to distinguish discrete and diffuse variants. Discrete agency is the agency of identifiable political actors whose interests, capacities and intentions can, at least in principle, be specifically identified and addressed in order to effect desired change. Diffuse agency, by contrast, is that wielded by large collectives, such as the electorate, whose choices are much more difficult to directly influence.

In terms of constraints, the relevant distinction can be understood as that between prospective and retrospective constraints. Prospective constraints, according to the authors, are those "that affect the probability of a policy being instituted," whereas retrospective constraints are those "that affect both the functioning and resilience of a policy once instituted" (De Wispelaere & Noguera, 2012: 20). Of course, *predictions* regarding retrospective constraints—in our case, the effects UBI will have once instituted—themselves constitute one type of prospective constraint to be overcome if UBI is to be accepted and enacted.

The four types of political feasibility then follow from the interaction of these dimensions (see Table 3.1). Strategic feasibility asks whether identifiable political actors can be mobilised to support a given policy. Institutional feasibility addresses the question of whether the policy would achieve its stated aims within the existing policy framework, or whether that framework would first need to be modified (this includes what is sometimes termed 'financial feasibility' concerning the economic effects of a UBI within a given tax and welfare regime (see, for example, Torry, 2014). Psychological feasibility concerns whether the general public supports or can be persuaded to support the policy. Finally, behavioural feasibility asks whether the behavioural incentives the policy establishes would cohere with its aims, or undermine the policy's viability.

Naturally, the four types of feasibility influence and are influenced by one another. In a democratic society, strategic feasibility depends on psychological feasibility—that is, political actors support policies at least in part on the basis of

Table 3.1 A feasibility framework for a UBI in Europe

	Prospective constraints	Retrospective constraints
Discrete agency	*Strategic feasibility*: stated support from key political actors in the form of commitments, participation in platforms supporting UBI and/or support for pilot schemes	*Institutional feasibility*: likely fit of a UBI policy with existing welfare regimes and existing income transfers, including likely distributional effects
Diffuse agency	*Psychological feasibility*: overall support as measured by surveys, referenda or other instruments for capturing public opinion	*Behavioural feasibility*: the extent to which elements of a UBI policy adhere to the stated goals and achieve desired outcomes

Source: Authors' adaptation of De Wispelaere and Noguera (2012)

support for that policy amongst the general public (on the psychological and political feasibility of UBI in the EU see also Delsen & Schilpzand, Chap. 2). It seems clear, additionally, that both the strategic and psychological feasibility of UBI are at least partially grounded in the policy's expected consequences.

UBI experiments can be understood as providing information about a given UBI proposal's likely behavioural and institutional feasibility (that is, the viability of the policy once implemented), which is then used to inform public and political opinion regarding that proposal, and UBI more generally (that is, UBI's achievability in terms of public and strategic feasibility).

It is possible to build upon this framework to develop a conceptualisation of feasibility of UBI specifically, outlining indicators of each feasibility type. In Table 3.1 we elaborate these feasibilities. For strategic feasibility, components include actions by various political actors that may act as proof of support for a UBI policy. Institutional feasibility could be assessed in terms of the fit between proposed measures and the existing welfare and labour market regimes within the nation state. Psychological feasibility would include the extent of public support as measured by voting patterns and/or survey data. For behavioural feasibility, it would be important to consider the details of UBI policy proposals in relation to their (likely) impacts upon labour market participants. For instance, Muffels & Gielens (Chap. 5) offer a review of the four types of feasibility in the context of local UBI-related experiments in the Netherlands. The objective of the agreed feasibility studies of the introduction of UBI in Scotland is also to establish these feasibility types (see Danson, Chap. 4).

In addition, this disaggregation of indicators of feasibility helps us to identify relatively more or less advanced aspects of UBI's political feasibility, as well as points of contradiction. However, the early stages of even the most advanced UBI initiatives means that collecting such data to analyse the feasibility of UBI is challenging. While De Wispelaere and Noguera (2012) allow us to conceptualise whether and what type of UBI policy would be feasible, the available data sources, particularly in countries with embryonic UBI campaigns, present a methodological challenge.

3.3 Methodology

Comparative analysis of policy making across nations is often difficult given the variation in institutional contexts (Clasen & Siegel, 2007). Such analysis becomes even more challenging with regards to embryonic policy proposals whose details are not yet fully and clearly articulated, and are subject to change in response to feasibility appraisals and pilot studies. Nevertheless, it remains important to analyse existing proposals and experiments to understand the current state of UBI feasibility and propose potential routes forward. To this end, we evaluate and analyse the proposals and experiments that have emerged over the past 3 years within the EU.

The Basic Income Earth Network (BIEN) was our primary source for a working definition of UBI, and for information on policy proposals across European countries. We chose to focus on BIEN as it is the most prominent and long-running international organisation focused on debating the concept of UBI, having been founded in 1986. These debates take place at the BIEN biannual conferences and in the pages of its academic journal, *Basic Income Studies*. Additionally, BIEN's Basic Income News service serves as a repository of information about public debate of and policy proposals relating to UBI.

To catalogue relevant policy proposals, then, we searched the Basic Income News archives for stories regarding each of the 28 EU countries published between January 2016 and March 2019. As Basic Income News aims to provide updates every time a policy is proposed, amended, or rejected, this website helped us to construct a timeline of each proposal. Additionally, the fact that Basic Income News relies on a network of 'country experts' means that the relevant political context is cited in many cases. In this way, we made use of the Basic Income News team's aggregation and filtering of news, related to UBI from around the world, to establish our initial database of proposals. We then supplemented this information by conducting more widespread internet searches for news and articles related to the cited proposals. In this way, we were able to triangulate, corroborate and complete the details taken from Basic Income News.

In our analysis of the completeness of each proposed policy, we relied on the definition put forth by BIEN: that is, that a UBI is "a periodic cash payment unconditionally delivered to all on an individual basis, without means-test or work requirement" (Basic Income Earth Network, 2015). Given that this is BIEN's official definition, we take these elements to be broadly agreed upon by those leading the concept of UBI. Furthermore this definition corresponds with other definitions from leading proponents of UBI, such as Van Parijs (1992).

Our analysis demonstrates that many policy proposals exclude one or more of the elements of this definition, often in the name of strategic and/or institutional feasibility. Nevertheless, our review adopted an inclusive approach to the initiatives and it seemed important to pay attention to these deviations in our assessment of the feasibility of UBI in the European context. We thus scored each proposal according to the number of elements of the BIEN definition it maintains. In categorising initiatives we considered six core elements of UBI that operationalise our definition:

- Periodicity of payment: the income is paid at regular intervals (for example every month), rather than as a once-off grant;
- Format: it is paid in an appropriate medium of exchange, allowing those who receive it to decide what they spend it on. It is not, therefore, paid either in kind (such as food or services) or in vouchers dedicated to a specific use;
- Payment level: it is paid on an individual basis and not, for instance, to households.
- Coverage: it is paid to all residents, not only e.g. citizens;
- Income conditionality: no means test is applied;
- Work conditionality: no conditions related to willingness work or other requirements are applied.

Given the importance of the institutional feasibility dimension, furthermore, we classified UBI policy proposals according to the existing welfare regime of the country in question. A UBI policy would replace a substantial part of the prevailing welfare regime, particularly unemployment benefits, and so it is important to evaluate the proposals in light of the distance between the existing welfare regimes and a full UBI scheme. There is considerable debate around the categorisation of welfare regimes (for example Esping-Andersen, 1990; Ferrera, 1996), which are beyond the scope of this chapter. Thus, we decide to adopt a typology that integrates welfare and labour market regimes, given that UBI operates at the nexus of the labour market and welfare policy, and because this typology captures all EU countries with UBI proposals, projects or pilot schemes: Continental Europe (Austria (AT), Belgium (BE), France (FR), Germany (DE) and Luxembourg (LU)), Central Eastern Europe (Bulgaria (BG), Croatia (CR), Czech Republic (CZ), Estonia (EE), Hungary (HU), Latvia (LV), Lithuania (LT), Poland (PL), Romania (RO), Slovenia (SI) and Slovakia (SK)), the Nordic countries (Denmark (DK), Finland (FI), the Netherlands (NL) and Sweden (S)), the Southern Europe (Cyprus (CY), Greece (GR), Italy (IT), Malta (MT), Portugal (PT) and Spain (ES)), and the Liberal countries (the United Kingdom (UK) and Ireland (IE)). In the literature there is some consistency among researchers adopting these approaches in their categorisation of welfare and labour market regimes as Nordic, Continental, Mediterranean, Liberal and Central Eastern Europe groupings (for example Eamets et al., 2015; Hemerijck, 2013; Russell, Leschke, & Smith, 2019; Stovicek & Turrini, 2012).

3.4 Analysing Feasibility

In this section we develop the analysis of feasibility within different European national contexts using the De Wispelaere and Noguera's (2012) framework of political feasibility types—institutional feasibility, strategic feasibility, psychological feasibility, and behavioural feasibility (see also Table 3.1). This decomposition of basic income initiatives permits the analysis of various elements of policy development in the broadest sense, while capturing the prospective nature of most basic income policies. By comparison with welfare and labour market institutions in economies like the United States, existing European welfare state regimes have some supportive elements that might be considered compatible with a basic income—for example, regular transfers, the presence of some non-means tested or unconditional payments, and more generous funding levels. However, the operationalised components of a full basic income scheme would nevertheless require a significant change in the functioning of much of the modern welfare state.

3.4.1 Institutional Feasibility

To begin, we plot each basic income proposal and initiative according to its degree of development and welfare/labour market regime. Each of the initiatives recorded over the 3-year period analysed from the BIEN data, and corroborated with other sources, was categorised within one of four levels: firstly, the top level where we found concrete evidence of a pilot or advanced plans ('+'); secondly, evidence of proposals for a pilot, adoption by political parties/candidates or high-profile events ('~'); thirdly, low-key events without national or regional organisation ('−'); and, finally, EU member states with no results ('0').

These initial results demonstrate that there is some evidence of variation in the compatibility of institutional settings and basic income across welfare regimes. As we might expect, based on their more generously-funded welfare regimes and egalitarian principles, we find that the Nordic countries all demonstrate some evidence of pilot studies or advanced actions in relation to basic income. In line with Lee (2018), these data confirm that while those countries with the least generous income security models in their welfare regime have high public support for basic income policies (Fig. 3.1), they also have fewer developed policy initiatives. Indeed, the majority of Central and Eastern European countries have no measures under discussion according to the data. Furthermore, regression analyses show that, in the EU, support for UBI is positively associated with national unemployment rates and negatively associated with the generosity of the national welfare state regime. The influence of cultural differences on support for UBI is mediated through institutional effects (Delsen & Schilpzand, Chap. 2).

Half of the EU member states have a pilot or advance plans adopted by politicians, while ten countries have no UBI initiatives (see Table 3.2). In contrast to the groupings of Nordic, Central and Eastern European countries at each end of the policy development spectrum, we observe that the Continental European countries are distributed across all four categories. In 2017, France appeared to be pioneering UBI amongst this group, with the policy acting as a key platform for the Socialist Party's presidential candidate, Benoît Hamon (Williamson, 2017), and subject to feasibility studies in multiple départements (Barthet, 2018). More recent pilot study developments under the 'HartzPlus' initiative, due to commence in early 2019, means that Germany has the more developed policy initiative of this group (HartzPlus, 2019). On the other hand, all of the larger Southern European states

Table 3.2 Basic income initiatives by stage of development in 28 EU member states, January 2016–March 2019

	+	~	−	0
Nordic countries	FI (Kela) NL (Weten Wat Werkt)	DK, SE		
Central & Eastern Europe		EE, SI	RO, HU, CR	CZ, BG, PO, SK, LV, LT
Continental Europe	DE (HartzPlus)	AT	FR	BE, LU
Southern Europe	ES (B-Mincome)	IT, GR, PT		CY, MT
Liberal countries		UK (Scotland), IE		

Note: + = pilot or advanced plans; ~ = pilot proposals, adoption by political parties or candidates, or high-profile events; − = low-key events; 0 = no results
Source: Authors' analysis of BIEN data

have strong evidence of concrete activity in the basic income arena (with Spain's B-Mincome experiment the most developed initiative here). This possibly reflects concerns around exclusion and the lack of a social safety net—particularly for young people (Smith et al., 2018). It is important to note that the liberal model, usually dominated by the UK, is only placed on the more-developed end of the distribution thanks to the advanced progress of the Scottish Citizens Basic Income feasibility study (see Danson, Chap. 4).

3.4.2 Strategic Feasibility

The next step of the analysis is to consider each of the six operationalised elements of the basic income definition—payment level, inclusiveness, payment periodicity, payment format, work conditionality and income conditionality. Given the heterogeneous status of initiatives around basic income, the available information is by definition incomplete and the analysis often pertains only to policy proposals, with the exception of pilots or well-developed plans for pilot studies. Nevertheless, analysis of the BIEN data provides relatively complete information on the key elements of fifteen policy initiatives, even if these are sometimes far from implementation. These elements are summarised in Table 3.3.

Payment Level The payment of a UBI to individuals, rather than households, is a key principle of any UBI policy. Indeed, rights derived at the household level have been found to create inequalities (Lewis, 1992). For example, the possibility to transfer tax allowances or leave arrangements within households often reinforces existing gendered working patterns and gender inequalities (Smith & Villa, 2012). Analysis of the propositions and initiatives across countries in Table 3.3 demonstrates that the majority of proposals comply with this individualised requirement (for those thirteen countries for which we have information). The main exceptions

Table 3.3 Elements of basic income initiatives in 28 EU member states, January 2016–March 2019

	Nordic countries	Continental Europe	Central & Eastern Europe	Liberal countries	Southern Europe
1. Payment level					
Individual payment	DK, FI, SE, NL	AT, DE, FR	EE	IE	ES
Household		FR			IT, ES
No information				UK (Scotland)	GR
2. Inclusiveness					
Paid to all residents	DK	AT	EE	IE	ES, PT
Partial (age or income)	FI, NL, SE	FR		UK (Scotland)	IT, GR
No information		DE			ES
3. Payment periodicity					
Weekly or monthly	DK, SE, NL, FI	FR, DE, AT	EE	IE	IT, ES
No information				UK (Scotland)	PT, GR
4. Payment format					
Electronic	DK, FI	AT, FR, DE,	EE	IE	
No information	SE, NL			UK (Scotland)	ES, PT, GR, IT
5. Work conditionality					
No requirements	DK, FI, SE, NL	AT, DE, FR	EE	UK (Scotland)	ES
No information				IE	IT, GR
6. Income conditionality					
No requirements	DK, FI, SE, NL	AT, DE, FR	EE	IE	ES
Means tested	NL	FR			ES, IT
No information				UK (Scotland)	GR

Note: No policy proposals available for review for Bulgaria, Croatia, Cyprus, Czech Republic, Hungary, Latvia, Lithuania, Poland, Romania, Slovakia, Slovenia, Belgium, Luxembourg or Malta. In the case of Spain, two initiatives were analysed: Barcelona's B-Mincome and a 2016 Catalonian proposal
Source: Authors' analysis of BIEN data

are in France and Italy where options for declaration and payment at the household level were included in the proposals.

Periodicity Another key feature of UBI is the regularity of payment, i.e. that it is not a lump-sum payment but a regular income. This requirement is evidenced in all fourteen of the proposals for which we have information. Given the regularity of many welfare-state transfers this core requirement of a UBI appears to be feasible and coherent with existing institutional arrangements of European welfare regimes.

Payment Format Another important feature of UBI is that recipients are free to choose how to spend it. Thus, the payments are made in cash or to a bank account, rather than in vouchers, food stamps or another form of payment in kind where the recipient is restricted in their purchases. As with the regularity of payments element, this requirement is in line with many welfare-state transfers in modern European welfare regimes. We find that all countries for which we have the details include electronic bank transfers in their proposals and UBI experiments. At a pragmatic level, such payments are also more straightforward administratively (Arcarons, Pañella, & Mèlich, 2014; Torry, 2014; though for limitations to the administrative ease of a UBI, see also De Wispelaere & Stirton, 2012, 2013, 2018).

Work Conditionality Two key conditionality features are central to UBI initiatives—that there is no requirement to work and payments are not conditional on income or wealth. For the first condition, we find that in all the proposals for which we have adequate data there are no work requirements and no requirement to demonstrate a willingness to work. This condition breaks with many existing welfare regimes, which require willingness to work or proof of active job-search for receipt of certain transfers.

Income Conditionality Similarly, UBI is defined by a lack of conditionality regarding income or wealth, meaning that it does not involve means testing. Our results in this regard are more heterogeneous. Proposals in several countries—the Netherlands, France, Italy and one of two Spanish proposals—include some conditions related to recipients' income. In the case of the Netherlands, conditionality was applied to one of the control groups in the experiment (see also Muffels & Gielens, Chap. 5). In the case of France, the 2017 presidential candidate, Benoît Hamon, ultimately proposed focusing a UBI on young people from poorer households. Furthermore, prior to its suspension in 2018, changes were made to the Finnish partial UBI experiment that led to the introduction of payment restrictions for those accepting part-time jobs or starting their own ventures.

Inclusiveness Second to the non-conditionality requirements, inclusion or population coverage is perhaps the most significant hurdle for any UBI policy. Here we find greater divergence among the policies proposed and discussed as compared to the other dimensions. Only six of the fifteen proposals included all residents. The majority of UBI proposals and experiments included some kind of targeting, such as towards young people, benefit recipients or poor households. These differences with regard to inclusion are at least partly based on differences in predicted behavioural effects (behavioural feasibility) and public support (psychological feasibility).

3.4.3 Psychological Feasibility

As we have seen above, public support for UBI is rather high according to the comparative data of the 2016 European Social Survey (see Fig. 3.1) and Delsen and Schilpzand (Chap. 2). Although support tends to be stronger in countries with the least developed actions (Lee, 2018)—notably the member states of Central and Eastern Europe—overall the support ranges from just under 40% of the public in Sweden to almost 80% in Lithuania. Comparing these data with our findings regarding policy proposals, we can see that support exists both in countries with active policy actions regarding UBI (such as Finland) and those with less developed actions (for example Poland, Belgium)—suggesting support for both actual proposals and the UBI concept in the absence of concrete plans.

In Table 3.4 we explore these data further. Since young people are one of the groups hardest hit by changes on the labour market and the threats often identified as justifications for measures to promote greater security, such as a UBI (O'Reilly, Leschke, Ortlieb, Seeleib-Kaiser, & Villa, 2018; Smith & Shanahan, 2018), it is perhaps unsurprising that support is generally higher among this age group. This greater level of support among 15- to 34-year-olds holds for all country groupings for which we have data. Nevertheless, the gradient of support with age is not steep and the older age groups demonstrate support that is no more than ten percentage points lower than that of the youngest. By contrast, 2017 survey data from Dalia Research show that in the EU, the likelihood to vote in favour of UBI has a hump-shaped relationship with age measured in years (Delsen & Schilpzand, Chap. 2).

One of the unique characteristics of UBI policies is the support that they can draw from both sides of the political divide. While we may question the definitions used by campaigners from diverse standpoints, in the ESS data presented in Table 3.4

Table 3.4 Public support for basic income policy in Europe

	Continental Europe (%)	Nordic countries (%)	Central & Eastern Europe (%)	Liberal countries (%)
Age group				
15–34	53	50	73	61
35–54	45	44	68	49
55–64	44	46	63	50
65+	46	41	66	43
Political affiliation				
Left	45	52	62	58
Centre	56	48	69	51
Right	45	38	67	38
Total (unweighted)	50	48	62	54

Note: Political affiliation measured on a 10-point scale: 0–4 = left; 5 = centre; 6–10 = right. See footnote 1 for details of methodology
Source: European Social Survey (2016) and Fitzgerald (2017); data for Southern European countries are unavailable

each respondent was shown a standardised definition. These data thus demonstrate that this consistent support exists even with a common definition. Individuals who identify themselves as right-leaning tend to record lower support than their left-leaning counterparts overall, but this trend is reversed in the Central and Eastern European countries. Similarly, those on the left in Continental countries demonstrate the same level of support as those on the right, and it is the centre ground that here shows the highest level of support.

3.4.4 Behavioural Feasibility

In considering measures for the analysis of behavioural feasibility we encounter two key difficulties in relation to UBI: first, the scant evidence from concrete experiments, and second, the fact that the policy is claimed by adherents of different, and often incompatible, visions for society, with differing aims regarding its behavioural effects. This is especially clear in the case of the Finnish study, which was constructed to measure only the potential labour activation effects, and thereby ignores other reasons for UBI support, such as the explicit aim to reduce working hours and valorise unpaid work (Kangas, 2016; Perkiö, 2019).

Existing field studies can tell us a limited amount regarding UBI's potential effects on different labour market groups, but the lack of long-term studies means we can extrapolate little. For example, the fact that existing studies suggest people do not generally give up work in response to receiving a UBI (Forget, 2011; Martinelli, 2017; Salehi-Isfahani & Mostafavi-Dehzooei, 2018) does not mean that they would not do so under a long-term UBI programme, which could shape adaptive preferences (Cholbi, 2018).

Agent-based modelling offers the potential for useful, fine-grained predictions of various labour-market groups' behavioural responses to UBI in advance of expensive trials (De Wispelaere & Noguera, 2012: 31). Yet this area of research is as-yet too young to have produced meaningful results. In the meantime, we can perhaps draw some tentative conclusions from existing field studies and hypotheses based on survey data regarding the potential impact of UBI on different groups (see, for instance, Delsen & Schilpzand, Chap. 3). This consideration by labour market sub-group is important since psychological feasibility, and evidence from existing proposals, demonstrates that groups such as the young may be priorities. Similarly, concern for the gendered effects of a UBI demonstrates the risk of unintended behavioural consequences (Gheaus, 2008; Robeyns, 2000).

For those currently receiving unemployment benefits, it is argued that UBI might in fact have positive effects on work participation, by smoothing effective marginal tax rates, thereby "lowering the very high rates affecting people on low incomes who currently lose welfare support if they earn more" (Sandbu, 2016). In this way, UBI could effectively mitigate existing welfare traps that discourage job take-up and help close the gap between 'work rich' and 'work poor' individuals and households.

For young people, a UBI might be attractive as a means to support the search for and establishment of a meaningful career, facilitating professional exploration and skills development or training. Young people today form a substantial part of the so-called 'precariat' (Bidadanure, 2013)—this is defined by insecurity in income and employment, compounded by an absence of support from communities in times of need alongside a lack of benefits from the state or accrued via employment histories through company benefits or private benefits (Standing, 2011). By providing a secure and solid income floor, a UBI could better enable young people to make strategic choices for their long-term careers, rather than short-term subsistence.

With regard to caregivers, UBI might be thought of as a way to support and valorise care work "as a form of worthwhile but non-commodifiable activity" (Baker, 2008). Furthermore, a UBI that is paid to individuals rather than households would offer some financial independence to those caregivers, disproportionately women, who find themselves otherwise financially dependent and thus vulnerable to violence and exploitation (Schulz, 2017; Zelleke, 2008). On the other hand, others see a risk that a UBI might further entrench the gendered distribution of care work, encouraging female caregivers to further withdraw from the labour market (Gheaus, 2008; Robeyns, 2000). A UBI might thus be understood as a necessary, but insufficient, condition for realising the universal caregiver ideal (Elgarte, 2008; Robeyns, 2001; Zelleke, 2008).

These potential behavioural implications will increase psychological and strategic feasibility to the extent that they align with, or are perceived to align with, outcomes desired by the public at large and relevant political actors. More experimentation is necessary, however, to provide persuasive evidence for these outcomes. This might include both field and laboratory experiments (Noguera & De Wispelaere, 2006; Füllbrunn, Delsen & Vyrastekova, Chap. 7), as well as complementary survey data to gauge likely behavioural outcomes. For proponents of UBI, additionally, further advocacy work is necessary to perform this conversion from behavioural to psychological, strategic and, thereby, political feasibility writ large.

3.5 Conclusion

In this chapter, we addressed the question of how it is that UBI policies remain so far from implementation, despite their relatively high public support. We used data from the 2016 European Social Survey and policy proposals in EU countries from the past 3 years to analyse the current state of UBI's feasibility along four dimensions proposed by De Wispelaere and Noguera (2012)—strategic feasibility, institutional feasibility, psychological feasibility, and behavioural feasibility. The available data and the embryonic state of much UBI policy means that we find the question of the feasibility of UBI in Europe is not easy to answer.

The behavioural feasibility of UBI illustrates the challenge from both a methodical and political perspective. For example, it might be argued that, in terms of behavioural implications, a UBI is highly feasible as the existing evidence suggests negligible work participation effects (Forget, 2011; Martinelli, 2017; Salehi-Isfahani & Mostafavi-Dehzooei, 2018; Delsen & Schilpzand, Chap. 3), which align well with the prevailing political commitments of European governments. Yet the evidence is not yet concrete, ongoing experiments have yet to come to fruition, and the long-term effects of UBI policies are as-yet completely unknown.

Furthermore, a number of distinct feasibility pathways towards UBI have been proposed, which will each elicit quite different feedback dynamics between the feasibilities presented here. As noted by Torry (2014), overall political feasibility likely relies on a sufficient level of each type, and one feasibility type may require the prior achievement of others, drawing analogy to a relay race. The evidence presented in this chapter shows that one route towards a UBI would be to begin with a partial policy, at a level below subsistence, and increase over time (Kangas, 2016; Lansley & Reed, 2019). This could offer the advantage of immediate universal coverage (facilitating psychological feasibility) and provide time to gradually adapt existing welfare regimes (facilitating institutional feasibility). Yet the potentially modest short-term effects (limited behavioural feasibility) might in turn render such an approach unattractive for proponents and other political actors (limiting strategic feasibility). By contrast, a route that begins by offering a full UBI to specific population segments generally viewed as 'deserving' (as suggested by Torry, 2014) might be more behaviourally, strategically and psychologically feasible, but could run the risk of stalling in the attempt to progress to universal coverage due to the limited psychological feasibility of expanding to more controversial or less 'deserving' population segments (for instance, regarding UBI as a potential migration pull factor, see Scharpf, 2000). Further research might thus fruitfully evaluate and compare various pathways towards UBI using the feasibility typology mobilised here.

Importantly, given the heterogeneity of policy proposals and initiatives we find among EU countries regarding institutional contexts and types of public support, such feasibility assessments would need to be sensitive to the specific institutional context of each state. This is especially important given the EU's limited appetite for Europe-wide legislation regarding income support, as evidenced by its stance towards intervention on minimum wage (Fernández-Macías & Vacas-Soriano, 2016). Equally, even where EU institutions are more active, for example in attempts to reduce the gender pay gap, variations in implementation within different national contexts remain important in determining outcomes (Smith, 2012). Thus, prospects for a feasible UBI may advance more effectively as national and regional administrations push forward with experiments and pilots. Indeed, it may well be that different routes will be appropriate to different institutional contexts according to specific labour market challenges, governance structures and the maturity of the UBI debates.

Nevertheless, the underlying labour market and welfare pressures for a UBI, which help explain the interest in the policy from across the political spectrum, remain relevant. Concerns in European countries around the consequences of increasing inequalities in both income and security (Standing, 2011), availability of quality jobs (Pallier, 2019) and the consequences of new forms of work will each exert pressure for more innovative policy responses (O'Reilly et al., 2018). Furthermore, the anticipated consequences of technological advances, artificial intelligence and other innovations are likely to threaten both the quality and quantity of employment and provide an additional imperative for policy-makers to innovate in order to address the conventional challenges of labour market change (Pallier, 2019). While it is clear that a UBI is not a panacea for inequalities (Smith & Shanahan, 2018) and does not come without its own risks of unintended consequences (Gheaus, 2008), the evidence presented in this chapter demonstrates widespread support and signs of feasibility in a number of European contexts.

References

Arcarons, J., Pañella, D. R., & Mèlich, L. T. (2014). Feasibility of financing a basic income. *Basic Income Studies, 9*(1–2), 79–93. https://doi.org/10.1515/bis-2014-0005

Baker, J. (2008). All things considered, should feminists embrace basic income? *Basic Income Studies, 3*(3), 12–31. https://doi.org/10.2202/1932-0183.1129

Barthet, E. (2018, June 6). Revenu de base: treize départements français veulent tenter l'aventure. *Le Monde*. Retrieved October 6, 2019, from https://www.lemonde.fr/emploi/article/2018/06/06/solidarite-treize-departements-veulent-experimenter-le-revenu-de-base_5310230_1698637.html

Basic Income Earth Network. (2015). *About basic income*. Retrieved October 6, 2019, from https://basicincome.org/basic-income/

Bidadanure, J. (2013). The precariat, intergenerational justice and universal basic income. *Global Discourse, 3*(3–4), 554–560. https://doi.org/10.1080/23269995.2014.898531

Brooks, L. (2017, December 25). Scotland united in curiosity as councils trial universal basic income. *The Guardian*. Retrieved October 6, 2019, from https://www.theguardian.com/uk-news/2017/dec/25/scotland-universal-basic-income-councils-pilot-scheme

Caputo, R. K. (2012). *Basic income guarantee and politics: International experiences and perspectives on the viability of income guarantee*. New York: Palgrave Macmillan.

Cholbi, M. (2018). *The desire for work as an adaptive preference*. Autonomy Institute. Retrieved October 6, 2019, from http://www.autonomyinstitute.org/wp-content/uploads/2018/07/The-Desire-For-Work-As-An-Adaptive-Preference-V2-.pdf

Clasen, J., & Siegel, N. A. (2007). Comparative welfare state analysis and the 'dependant variable problem'. In J. Clasen & N. A. Siegel (Eds.), *Investigating welfare state change: The 'dependant variable problem' in comparative analysis* (pp. 3–12). Cheltenham: Edward Elgar.

Colombo, C., DeRocchi, T., Kurer, T., & Widmer, T. (2016). *Analyse der eidgenössischen Abstimmung vom 5. Juni 2016*, VOX-Analysen 121. Genf/Zürich: gfs.bern and Institut für Politikwissenschaft der Universität Zürich.

Council of Europe. (2018). *The case for a basic citizenship income* (Resolution 2197). Retrieved October 6, 2019, from http://assembly.coe.int/nw/xml/XRef/Xref-XML2HTML-en.asp?fileid=24429

De Wispelaere, J. (2016). The struggle for strategy: On the politics of the basic income Proposal. *Politics, 36*(2), 131–141. https://doi.org/10.1111/1467-9256.12102

De Wispelaere, J., Halmetoja, A., & Pulkka, V. V. (2018). The rise (and fall) of the basic income experiment in Finland. *CESifo Forum, 19*(3), 15–19.

De Wispelaere, J., & Noguera, J. A. (2012). On the political feasibility of universal basic income: An analytic framework. In R. K. Caputo (Ed.), *Basic income guarantee and politics: International experiences and perspectives on the viability of income guarantee* (pp. 17–38). New York: Palgrave Macmillan.

De Wispelaere, J., & Stirton, L. (2012). A disarmingly simple idea? Practical bottlenecks in the implementation of a universal basic income. *International Social Security Review, 65*(2), 103–121. https://doi.org/10.1111/j.1468-246X.2012.01430.x

De Wispelaere, J., & Stirton, L. (2013). The politics of unconditional basic income: Bringing bureaucracy back in. *Political Studies, 61*(4), 915–932. https://doi.org/10.1111/j.1467-9248.2012.01004.x

De Wispelaere, J., & Stirton, L. (2018). The case against participation income—political, not merely administrative. *The Political Quarterly, 89*(2), 262–267. https://doi.org/10.1111/1467-923X.12513

Eamets, R., Beblavý, M., Bheemaiah, K., Finn, M., Humal, K., Leschke, J., et al. (2015). *Report mapping flexicurity performance in the face of the crisis: Key indicators and drivers of youth unemployment* (STYLE Working Papers, WP10.1). CROME, University of Brighton. Retrieved October 6, 2019, from http://www.style-research.eu/publications/working-papers/

Elgarte, J. M. (2008). Basic income and the gendered division of labour. *Basic Income Studies, 3*(3). https://doi.org/10.2202/1932-0183.1136

Esping-Andersen, G. (1990). *The three worlds of welfare capitalism*. Cambridge: Polity Press.

European Social Survey. (2016). *ESS8—2016 documentation report*. Retrieved October 6, 2019, from https://www.europeansocialsurvey.org/docs/round8/survey/ESS8_data_documentation_report_e02_1.pdf

Fernández-Macías, E., & Vacas-Soriano, C. (2016). A coordinated European Union minimum wage policy? *European Journal of Industrial Relations, 22*(2), 97–113. https://doi.org/10.1177/0959680115610725

Ferrera, M. (1996). The 'southern model' of welfare in social Europe. *Journal of European Social Policy, 6*(1), 17–37. https://doi.org/10.1177/095892879600600102

Fitzgerald, R. (2017, November 17). Survey reveals young people more likely to support universal basic income, but it's not a left-right thing. *The Conversation*. Retrieved October 6, 2019, from https://theconversation.com/survey-reveals-young-people-more-likely-to-support-universal-basic-income-but-its-not-a-left-right-thing-87554

Forget, E. (2011). The town with no poverty: The health effects of a Canadian guaranteed annual income field experiment. *Canadian Public Policy, 37*(3), 283–305. https://doi.org/10.3138/cpp.37.3.283

Gheaus, A. (2008). Basic income, gender justice and the costs of gender-symmetrical lifestyles. *Basic Income Studies, 3*(3). https://doi.org/10.2202/1932-0183.1134

HartzPlus. (2019). *Sanction-free: Another perspective on our welfare system*. Retrieved October 6, 2019, from https://hartz-plus.de/english

Heller, N. (2018, July 2). Who really stands to win from universal basic income? It has enthusiasts on both the left and the right. Maybe that's the giveaway. *The New Yorker*. Retrieved October 6, 2019, from https://www.newyorker.com/

Hemerijck, A. (2013). *Changing welfare states*. Oxford: Oxford University Press.

Kangas, O. (2016). *From idea to experiment: Report on universal basic income experiment in Finland* (Working Papers 106). Helsinki: Social Insurance Institution of Finland (Kela). Retrieved October 6, 2019, from http://hdl.handle.net/10138/167728

Lansley, S., & Reed, H. (2019). *Basic income for all: From desirability to feasibility*. London: Compass. Retrieved October 6, 2019, from http://www.compassonline.org.uk/publications/basic-income-for-all-from-desirability-to-feasibility/

Lee, S. (2018). Attitudes toward universal basic income and welfare state in Europe: A research note. *Basic Income Studies, 13*(1), 1–9. https://doi.org/10.2139/ssrn.3209161

Lewis, J. (1992). Gender and the development of welfare regimes. *Journal of European Social Policy, 2*(3), 159–173. https://doi.org/10.1177/095892879200200301

Martinelli, L. (2017). *Exploring the distributional and work incentive effects of plausible illustrative basic income schemes*. Bath: Institute for Policy Research. Retrieved October 6, 2019, from http://www.bath.ac.uk/publications/exploring-the-distributional-work-incentive-effects-of-plausible-illustrative-basic-income-schemes/attachments/Luke_WP2_Web.pdf

Noguera, J., & De Wispelaere, J. (2006). A plea for the use of laboratory experiments in basic income research. *Basic Income Studies, 1*(2), 1–8. https://doi.org/10.2202/1932-0183.1044

O'Reilly, J., Leschke, J., Ortlieb, R., Seeleib-Kaiser, M., & Villa, P. (2018). *Youth labor in transition*. Oxford: Oxford University Press.

Pallier, B. (2019, June 7). The political consequences of technological change. *Sciences Po*. Retrieved October 6, 2019, from www.sciencespo.fr/news/news/the-political-consequences-of-technological-change/4186

Perkiö, J. (2019). From rights to activation: The evolution of the idea of basic income in the Finnish political debate, 1980–2016. *Journal of Social Policy*, 1–22. https://doi.org/10.1017/S0047279418000867

Robeyns, I. (2000). Hush money or emancipation fee? A gender analysis of basic income. In R. van der Veen & L. Groot (Eds.), *Basic income on the agenda: Policy objectives and political chances* (pp. 121–136). Amsterdam: Amsterdam University Press.

Robeyns, I. (2001). Will a basic income do justice to women? *Analyse & Kritik, 23*(1), 88–105. https://doi.org/10.1515/auk-2001-0108

Russell, H., Leschke, J., & Smith, M. (2019). Balancing flexibility and security in Europe? The impact of unemployment on young peoples' subjective well-being. *European Journal of Industrial Relations*. https://doi.org/10.1177/0959680119840570

Salehi-Isfahani, D., & Mostafavi-Dehzooei, M. H. (2018). Cash transfers and labor supply: Evidence from a large-scale program in Iran. *Journal of Development Economics, 135*, 349–367. https://doi.org/10.1016/j.jdeveco.2018.08.005

Sandbu, M. (2016, July 22). Free lunch: Radically misunderstood. *The Financial Times*. Retrieved October 6, 2019, from https://www.ft.com/content/92ad59c2-4f5d-11e6-88c5-db83e98a590a

Scharpf, F. W. (2000). Basic income and social Europe. In R. van der Veen & L. Groot (Eds.), *Basic income on the agenda: Policy objectives and political chances* (pp. 155–160). Amsterdam: Amsterdam University Press.

Schulz, P. (2017). Universal basic income in a feminist perspective and gender analysis. *Global Social Policy, 17*(1), 89–92. https://doi.org/10.1177/1468018116686503

Smith, M. (2012). Social regulation of the gender pay gap in the EU. *European Journal of Industrial Relations, 18*(4), 365–380. https://doi.org/10.1177/0959680112465931

Smith, M., Leschke, J., Russell, H., & Villa, P. (2018). Stressed economies, distressed policies, and distraught young people. In J. O'Reilly, J. Leschke, R. Ortlieb, M. Seeleib-Kaiser, & P. Villa (Eds.), *Youth labor in transition. Inequalities, Mobility, and Policies in Europe* (pp. 104–131). Oxford: Oxford University Press.

Smith, M., & Shanahan, G. (2018). Do young people want Universal Basic Income? In J. O'Reilly, C. Moyart, T. Nazio, & M. Smith (Eds.), *Youth employment: STYLE handbook*. Bristol: Policy Press.

Smith, M., & Villa, P. (2012). Gender equality and the evolution of the Europe 2020 strategy. In R. Blanpain (Ed.), *Labour markets, industrial relations and human resources management: From recession to recovery* (pp. 3–23). Alphen aan den Rijn: Kluwer Law International.

Standing, G. (2011). *The precariat: The new dangerous class*. London: Bloomsbury Academic.

Stovicek, K., & Turrini, A. (2012, May). *Benchmarking unemployment benefit systems* (Economic Papers 454). Brussels: European Commission.

Torry, M. (2014). *A basic income is feasible: But what do we mean by 'feasible'?* Paper for the BIEN Congress, 27–29 June, Montreal. Retrieved October 6, 2019, from http://www.basicincome.org/bien/pdf/montreal2014/BIEN2014_Torry.pdf

Valero, J. (2017, February 16). Parliament plenary rejects universal basic income. *EurActiv*. Retrieved October 6, 2019, from https://www.euractiv.com/section/economy-jobs/news/parliament-plenary-rejects-universal-basic-income/

Van Parijs, P. (1992). *Arguing for basic income: Ethical foundations for a radical reform.* London: Verso.

Widerquist, K. (2005). A failure to communicate: What (if anything) can we learn from the negative income tax experiments? *Journal of Socio-Economics, 34*(1), 49–81. https://doi.org/10.1016/j.socec.2004.09.050

Williamson, L. (2017, January 24). France's Benoit Hamon rouses Socialists with basic income plan. *BCC News.* Retrieved from https://www.bbc.com/news/world-europe-38723219.

Zelleke, A. (2008). Institutionalizing the universal caretaker through a basic income? *Basic Income Studies, 3*(3). https://doi.org/10.2202/1932-0183.1133

Genevieve Shanahan (1990) studied Philosophy (2008–2014) at University College Cork and University College London (M. Phil Stud). She is currently working on her Ph.D. in the field of Organisation Studies at the Grenoble Ecole de Management, where her dissertation concerns the ways in which technology enables and impedes genuine democratic functioning in work and alternative organisations. She has research interests in Unconditional Basic Income, post-work society, platform work, cooperatives and social enterprises.

Mark Smith (1971) is Professor of Human Resource Management at Grenoble Ecole de Management, France. He previously worked at Manchester Business School. His interests focus on labour market outcomes of individuals and organisations with a particular interest in the role of gender and age. He has carried out research work for a number of European and national institutions and has authored or co-authored many books, book chapters and journal articles. He publishes regularly in the media about his research and the management of business schools. His most recent books include *Youth Employment* (with J. O'Reilly, C. Moyart, & T. Nazio (Cambridge: Policy Press, 2018), *Gender and the European Labour Market* (with F. Bettio & J. Plantenga (London: Routledge, 2013) and *Business Ethics* (with P. O'Sullivan & M. Esposito (London: Routledge, 2012).

Priya Srinivasan (1974) completed her Masters in Human Resource Management from the University of Mumbai in 2007 and has more than ten years' experience in management and human resource management roles in the corporate sector. Since moving to France she has worked as a part-time research assistant and career counsellor at Grenoble Ecole de Management, France. Her main areas of interest are well-being at work, gender, diversity and culture, and she aims to start doctoral studies in 2019. She has a co-authored book chapter on women in top management in France (with K. Zhuk & M. Smith) (Basingstoke: Palgrave McMillan, 2012).

Chapter 4
Exploring Benefits and Costs: Challenges of Implementing Citizen's Basic Income in Scotland

Michael Wlliam Danson

Abstract Faced with extremely high levels of poverty and inequality, four local authorities in Scotland are proposing to introduce pilot Unconditional Basic Income (UBI) schemes in their respective areas. Much of civic society in Scotland is supporting the implementation of these experiments to explore different UBI models, consider how they might be funded and assess public approval. The Scottish Government has established funding to undertake studies into the possible pilot schemes, in particular to evaluate their political, financial, behavioural, psychological and institutional feasibilities. UBI is also being promoted by key agencies such as CBINS (Citizen's Basic Income Network Scotland). This chapter suggests the main driver for these UBI pilots is the alleviation of poverty and inequality and discusses how these schemes and subsequently a Scotland-wide basic income might address the inequalities that generate poor living standards for many. After noting poverty is embedded amongst those dependent on welfare benefits through long-term illness, disability, unemployment, lone parenthood, the chapter confirms that most in poverty are in working households, while most self-employed also have low standards of living. The major barrier to introducing any UBI in Scotland, however, is argued to be the opposition of the Conservative UK Government and its Treasury, social protection and tax departments; independence would allow a Scotland-wide scheme to be introduced without these particular constraints.

Keywords Unconditional basic income · Poverty · Experiments · Scotland · Local government · Partnership

---

M. W. Danson
School of Social Sciences, Heriot-Watt University, Edinburgh, Scotland
e-mail: m.danson@hw.ac.uk

4.1 Introduction

There are differing reasons and rationales for arguing for the introduction of a citizen's basic income, as is demonstrated by the contrasting chapters in this volume. From a historical analysis of the origins and promotion of the concept, a range of economic, moral, religious, political and other justifications have been offered from sometimes contrasting and contradictory philosophical positions (see Delsen, Chap. 1). Following from this, the proponents in any particular context may be motivated by conditions and challenges specific to their community or beliefs. For many in Scotland involved in campaigning for an Unconditional Basic Income (UBI), the alleviation of poverty is the over-riding factor; four local authorities have themselves shown some interest in examining whether a UBI could contribute to addressing poverty. Others are now waiting on the outcome of their analyses and experiments to gauge whether this should be adopted more widely. There are three significant organisations driving discussions and debates advocating that a UBI should be within the basket of policies and interventions to address high levels of income poverty and inequality across Scotland: the four local authorities (Edinburgh, Fife, Glasgow, North Ayrshire) working in partnership to test the feasibility of UBI by introducing pilots in each of their areas, the RSA (Royal Society for the encouragement of Arts, Manufactures and Commerce) and CBINS (Citizen's Basic Income Network Scotland) whose mission is "to advance research and public education about the economic and social effects of Citizen's Basic Income." ... "A Basic Income (BI), (Citizen's Income, Citizen's Basic Income or Universal Grant) is an unconditional, non-withdrawable income for every individual as a right of citizenship" (CBINS, 2018). It is a right for everyone, every citizen whether man, woman or child, and is exempt from tax. The aim of CBINS is to educate the general public, opinion-formers and decision makers about the potential desirability and feasibility of UBI schemes. It recognises that while the concept is simple, implementation is both complex and technical (Atkinson, 1995; Miller, 2017; Reed & Lansley, 2016; Standing, 2017; Torry, 2015, 2018). Consistent, with the approach of most other commentators, CBINS accepts there is not one optimal UBI scheme. However, it undertakes advocacy workshops and training as "the better informed the public, the more likely they are to persuade decision-makers to establish a suitable basic income scheme for the benefit of everyone" (CBINS, 2018).

The pursuit of a more informed population and electorate by the RSA has its foundations in similar areas. Their 2018 publication 'Realising Basic Income Experiments in the UK' followed from evidence that the current social security system was "ineffective in enhancing motivations to work, leading to increased destitution, harmful to mental and physical health, with insufficient support for individuals" (Young, 2018: 3). This is complemented by a number of reports, including by the National Audit Office (NAO) (2018), which has highlighted the financial hardship caused by the progressive introduction of 'Universal Credit' (the new combined welfare benefit that is meant to simplify and replace most other mainstream payments for the unemployed, disabled, poor, etc.).

The leadership being shown by the officers and politicians of the four local government authorities who are assessing the feasibility of UBI schemes in their areas both complements and reinforces the impression that there is growing interest and support in Scotland. Their prime reasons for applying UBI mirror the sentiments of CBINS and the RSA, as evidenced in their recent joint press release on receiving funding for the feasibility studies: "Fife, North Ayrshire, City of Edinburgh and Glasgow City Councils are working together with NHS Health Scotland and the Improvement Service (the public agency that works with local councils and their partners to improve health and wellbeing through community leadership, strong local governance and the delivery of high quality, efficient local services) to explore the feasibility of pilots in their areas with the aims of reducing poverty and inequality and a possible route to a fairer and simpler welfare system" (Basic Income Scotland, 2018). As these organisations—the four councils being those who have selected UBI as a route worth exploring and the others being those public bodies dedicated to excellence in well-being and public administration—are partnering in these various initiatives and in others that support the development of intelligence, advocacy and the practicalities of implementation, it confirms that Scotland is a seed bed for policy innovation and activation. As such, it underscores the need to describe and analyse these attempts at introducing a new approach to reducing endemic poverty, disparity and uneven development.

Many would suggest that Scotland has a more communitarian tradition than England, with a greater tendency to encourage and support interventions of universalism and social cohesion (see, for discussion, Danson, McAlpine, Spicker, & Sullivan, 2013; Haydecker, 2010; Hetherington, 2018; Mooney & O'Sullivan, 2015). Such perceptions and sentiments, almost regardless of their strength or degree of difference, have driven experimentation and looking outward towards alternative and more inclusive models of social policy and welfare (for example, Mooney & O'Sullivan, 2015). The continuing cross-party support for universal benefits and services in Scotland, in contrast to the populist dialogue in England and Westminster, suggests that building solidarity across communities, generations and citizens through a UBI potentially has much traction as a national paradigm (Calhoun, 2018). As will be argued below, the broad foundations in support of the UBI experiments, of using the Scottish budget to mitigate some of the austerity cuts in benefits (Fraser, 2019; Mooney & O'Sullivan, 2015; O'Hara, 2019) and of similar interventions and initiatives are consistent with this evolving difference in attitudes north and south of the border.

This chapter is structured to explore the context to this pursuit of UBI as a contribution to alleviating poverty and inequality in the next Sect. 4.2. This is followed in Sect. 4.3 by a review of the literature and theory of the potential role of UBI in combatting and overcoming such social ills. Section 4.4 introduces and assesses the development of UBI in Scotland, expanding on the agencies, dialogues and recent developments. This leads into a discussion of the feasibility studies and their scope, considering the attitude and stance of different political levels and departments in Sect. 4.5. This necessarily leads onto an exploration of the constraints, barriers and budgets that confront those who are endeavouring to launch the pilot experiments over the next few years in Sect. 4.6. Section 4.7 offers a brief summary of what a UBI might look like if it was effective across Scotland today, noting that under devolution with many fiscal, revenue and expenditure powers reserved to the UK Government this must be illustrative only. And, given this constitutional state, in Sect. 4.8 the conclusions so far are presented finally.

4.2 Context: Poverty and Inequality

Britain is reportedly the fifth largest economy in the world and one of the richest (World Economic Forum, 2018). Yet, UK and European statistics reveal deep levels of poverty and inequality that mark it out as significantly different as a society from the rest of Northern and Western Europe, and indeed much of the 'developed world' (Elliott & Atkinson, 2012). Official data from UK Government agencies reveal that, after housing costs were controlled for, in 2015/2016, 1,050,000 people (20%) were living in poverty in Scotland; of these, 260,000 were children, 650,000 were 'working age' adults and 140,000 were pensioners (Scottish Government, 2018a). These represented, respectively, over a quarter of all children in Scotland (26%), a fifth of 'working age' adults (20%), and 13% of pensioners. The total in relative poverty, which compares individual and household incomes with the levels of income nationally, declined from 25% of the population, after housing costs, in 2000/2001 to 16% in 2011/2012 but has been on the rise since to 20%. Absolute poverty, which adjusts for inflation, has continued to fall from 33% (1988/1989) to 18% (2015/2016) but now shows signs of rising also (Scottish Government, 2018a). The most recent comparative data (Tables 4.1 and 4.2) show that the UK continues to have poverty rates worse than the EU average and Scotland is slightly better than the other countries within the UK (with different definitions applying for these two sets of data). While 'inequality' encompasses differences in wealth within society, poverty tends to be considered in terms of differences in income and in the capacity to live a decent life. Much of the discourse on poverty, and so on income poverty, therefore informs the case for UBI although arguments for longer term restructuring of society and the economy rest more on wealth distribution.

Over the 5 years between 2011 and 2015, one in nine people in Scotland were always in poverty, so that 11% faced persistent poverty in this supposedly rich country (Scottish Government, 2018a). These data are especially important as they capture these extraordinary depths of poverty which are endemic to the UK system and also reveal the high degree of inequality in the economy. Each of these characteristics of the 'Anglo Saxon' welfare system, common in many ways across the UK and North America, contrast markedly with the Nordic and other systems of social security in Northern and Western Europe. It should be noted that Scotland's poor fare relatively better than in the rest of the UK; the Scottish Government mitigates some of the worst effects of the UK welfare system directly in tempering cuts to some social security payments while other public services are delivered

Table 4.1 At-risk-of-poverty rate in Europe by poverty threshold—EU-SILC

Country	Percent	Country	Percent
Czechia	9.1	Malta	16.8
Finland	11.5	European Union	16.9
Norway	12.3	*United Kingdom*	17.0
Denmark	12.4	Portugal	18.3
Slovakia	12.4	Luxembourg	18.7
Netherlands	13.2	Croatia	20.0
France	13.3	Greece	20.2
Slovenia	13.3	Italy	20.3
Hungary	13.4	Estonia	21.0
Austria	14.4	Spain	21.6
Poland	15.0	Latvia	22.1
Ireland	15.6	North Macedonia	22.2
Cyprus	15.7	Lithuania	22.9
Sweden	15.8	Bulgaria	23.4
Belgium	15.9	Romania	23.6
Germany	16.1	Serbia	25.7

Source: European Union Statistics on Income and Living Conditions (EU-SILC). https://bit.ly/2J3jZh5
United Kingdom in Italics—As the text is discussing the levels of poverty in the UK and this draws attention to its position relative to the EU and to the other member states

Table 4.2 Poverty rates across the UK, after housing costs (AHC)

Percentage (3-year average)	England	Wales	Scotland	Northern Ireland
1994/1995 to 1996/1997	24.62	27.01	23.56	
1995/1996 to 1997/1998	24.58	27.37	23.39	
1996/1997 to 1998/1999	24.69	26.51	23.25	
1997/1998 to 1999/2000	24.26	26.05	23.09	
1998/1999 to 2000/2001	23.74	25.25	23.77	
1999/2000 to 2001/2002	23.11	25.12	23.67	
2000/2001 to 2002/2003	22.55	24.43	23.10	
2001/2002 to 2003/2004	22.04	23.80	21.69	
2002/2003 to 2004/2005	21.37	22.54	20.63	20.29
2003/2004 to 2005/2006	21.16	22.03	19.66	20.30
2004/2005 to 2006/2007	21.60	22.21	19.11	19.70
2005/2006 to 2007/2008	22.32	23.87	18.99	19.72
2006/2007 to 2008/2009	22.70	23.04	18.78	19.37
2007/2008 to 2009/2010	22.63	22.99	18.88	20.51
2008/2009 to 2010/2011	22.16	21.91	18.38	20.47
2009/2010 to 2011/2012	21.69	22.72	17.58	21.44
2010/2011 to 2012/2013	21.24	23.14	17.64	20.40
2011/2012 to 2013/2014	21.23	22.72	17.82	20.67
2012/2013 to 2014/2015	21.31	22.69	18.28	20.75
2013/2014 to 2015/2016	21.57	23.45	18.57	20.32
2014/2015 to 2016/2017	21.96	23.67	19.05	19.85

Source: https://www.gov.uk/government/statistics/households-below-average-income-199495-to-201617

without charge compared with England, e.g. eye tests, dental treatments, medical prescriptions, university fees.

Even without Brexit and all its, as yet unknown, consequences, the renowned and well-regarded Institute of Fiscal Studies is forecasting a worsening of the position at least until 2021/2022 (Hood & Waters, 2017). Children's poverty in particular is expected to increase across the UK from 29% in 2014/2015 to 36%. For working age non-parents there will be no change, staying around 17.5% over this period, and there will be slight increases in poverty for pensioners from 14 to 15%. The reasons behind these depressing forecasts are that low income households with children are very dependent on social security benefits. The continuing austerity programme: welfare benefit freeze with real falls in the value of social protection payments, policies such as the limit of welfare support to two children (unless, extraordinarily for a modern democracy, if the mother can demonstrate subsequent children were born as a result of rape), cuts to public services, and so on, all hit the incomes of the poorest and of these families especially hard (Hood & Waters, 2017; Scottish Government, 2018a). Correspondingly, these vulnerable families gain the least from earnings growth as their benefits are progressively withdrawn and wages at the lower end of the jobs market have been more sticky than at the middle and top (Standing, 2014; Torry, 2018).[1]

Following on from this latter point, and countering the notion and mantra that Britain's approach is 'to make work pay' by ensuring that people and their families are always better off in employment than on benefits, 64% of working age adults and an incredible 70% of children are in working households where at least one member has a job. They are earning their poverty. Further, the withdrawal rate—the effective marginal rate of 'tax' on their family earnings at these lower ends of the labour market—are much higher than those faced by the highest paid and the wealthiest. Looking at the latest estimates applying consistent data from across the UK they suggest that, on a moving average basis, while poverty amongst all working age adults in 1998/2001 to 2014/2017 is anticipated to have been around 19–20%, the proportion of those in work has increased from 48 to 59% (Hood & Waters, 2017). This absolute worsening position is explained by inflation—especially in transport and other essentials—hitting lower income groups hardest and so the numbers and rates of working poor are increasing.

The parallel mantra to 'making work pay' has been the encouragement to improve your own position by being more entrepreneurial and enterprising (Galloway, Danson, Richards, Sang, & Stirzaker, 2016). Indeed, there has been a large increase in the number of 'entrepreneurs' in recent years, almost doubling as a proportion of the active labour force. However, the significant successes in raising the business birth rate in Scotland and across the UK can be explained largely by significant increases in businesses—registered and unregistered—where there were no employees: that is, by a significant rise in the numbers of self-employed (Galloway

---

[1]This disproportional wage growth at the top applies to most OECD countries (Schwellnus, Kappeler, & Pionnier, Schwellnus, Kappeler, & Pionnier, 2017).

et al., 2016). Evidence drawn from various sources and based on official Government data reveal many self-employed workers earn less than the national minimum wage and it is estimated that over three-quarters are in income poverty. Further, the self-employed are not entitled to statutory sick pay, maternity or paternity pay, paid holidays, training support, and will be reliant on the state and their own savings in retirement. As with the employed workforce, but with these additional costs of living, there are reasons to examine whether and how a UBI would improve the living standards of the poorest in the community.

These data drawn from different official sources and from reputable bodies confirm that there are deep, intractable and worsening levels of poverty in the UK, including Scotland, with the working poor often facing significant barriers or indeed no apparent way out of their deprivation. Significant structural issues have been apparent and developing with the UK economy and labour market for several decades (Elliott & Atkinson, 2012) with most of the growth in employment being at or around the national minimum wage level (Standing, 2014), so that the case for considering alternative forms of lifting those in work and on benefits above the poverty line is needed. A race towards an economy based on low wages-low productivity-low investment cannot lead to a sustainable future, rather Britain's destiny is 'Going South' (Elliott & Atkinson, 2012). Proponents of UBI argue it offers the potential of both raising the living standards of poorer working families (this will be discussed below) and of improving the economic performance of the country overall. Also, it follows that a key element of such changes is to improve the bargaining power of the low paid and so indirectly address market failures.

The challenges faced in raising the profile of endemic and widespread poverty amongst the poorest in society is not just a matter of gaining access to the labour market, therefore. Nevertheless, children are far less likely to be in poverty if someone in the household works full-time, at 12%, compared with part-time work only, 35%, or where no one is working where 61% are below the poverty line (White, 2017). Addressing the family position of those dependent on benefits is a priority, as argued elsewhere (Danson et al., 2013; Danson, McKay, & Sullivan, 2015; Mooney, McKendrick, Scott, Dickie, & McHardy, 2016). Research and statistics from comparative studies across the social democratic countries closest to the UK demonstrate quite starkly how the British regime penalises those who cannot work through disability or illness, redundancy or lack of demand (Drejer, Freundt, Hansen, & Straubinger, 2010; Lindsay & Houston, 2013). In a study of the 'net replacement ratio' (unemployment payments for those losing their jobs) across seven countries around the North Sea, those in the UK who formerly earned half the average wage, could expect less than a quarter of their pre-unemployment income in social security benefits. Other systems paid between 60% and 90% of previous earnings. Other comparisons were from 12% in the UK to 50–74% in other systems (average wage), 9% against 37–57% (1.5 times average wage) and 6% compared with 35–45% of former income for those on double average wages previously. Research from the OECD presents similar comparisons of low replacement rates for all family groups under different former earnings (OECD, 2017). Yet, with employment rates higher than most of the UK's near neighbours and so with lower unemployment rates, total public spending on social protection as a percent of GDP is below everywhere in Northern and Western Europe: the UK welfare system is ungenerous both collectively and at the level of the individual and household (Sinfield, 2011).

As well as needing to raise the level of out-of-work benefits for the unemployed and those otherwise inactive, the additional challenges and costs of living faced by the disabled, long-term sick, lone parents, old and carers must be recognised and addressed in any system which aims to ensure at least minimum levels of social security for citizens. Because of the issues of stigmatisation and other reasons for underclaiming (Danson et al., 2013; Lindsay & Houston, 2013), a citizen's basic income offers a means to overcome some but not all the constraints that these vulnerable groups must face. Exploring the role of UBI in providing a floor income for all is discussed in later sections, after an initial appreciation of the costs of the current welfare state.

According to Sinfield (2011): "Why some affluent Western democracies maintain substantial poverty and others are more egalitarian and accomplish low levels of poverty" (quoting Brady, 2009: 166) "can be explained in terms of the relative funding of their respective welfare states." Consistent with the analysis offered here, he reveals that only Estonia, out of 24 European countries, has more poverty among the unemployed than the UK. He continues, "Only seven countries have higher rates of poverty among those in work; and when poverty among all those aged 18–64 years is considered, only six EU countries are worse: yet the UK is one of the richest nations" (Sinfield, applying Eurostat, 2010).

Research by McKnight, Duque, and Rucci (2018) has shown how "relative income poverty rates tend to be higher when income inequality is higher and this suggests that increases in income inequality are associated with increases in relative income poverty rates." As a major contributor to poverty, therefore, it is imperative that policies to reduce poverty focus on addressing high levels of economic inequality in the UK. The depths and persistence of poverty and inequality, in and out of work, that characterises the economy and society of the UK, and applies as forcibly in Scotland, has created an added driver for considering the potential role of a citizen's basic income as a component of policy change.

4.3 A Role for a Universal Basic Income?

As the previous Sect. 4.2 has indicated, the reasons for increasing poverty and inequality in Scotland are low wages and incomes from work and self-employment; persistent, precarious work; disability, poor health, unpaid caring responsibilities, lone parenthood; low out-of-work benefits, which have been falling in real value; the complexity of the social protection system, exacerbated by stigmatisation; and high marginal withdrawal rates. All these factors have deepening and scarring effects throughout working and then retired life, and these have macro-economic impacts as they transmit individual problems for health and well-being through to the wider economy with restraints on productivity, depressed tax revenues, and further demands on public services. The proponents of a citizen's basic income argue that it would address many of these ills directly by raising the incomes of the poorest at source.

There are a number of justifications offered for a UBI and include reference to such diverse rationales as human rights, ownership of a nation's assets, the basis of national wealth, and solidarity. As Basic Income Earth Network (BIEN) and CBINS cofounder Annie Miller (2017) has catalogued: "Everyone has the right to a standard of living adequate for the health and well-being of himself and of his family, including food, clothing, housing and medical care and necessary social services, and the right to security in the event of unemployment, sickness, disability, widowhood, old age or other lack of livelihood in circumstances beyond his control." This quote is Article 25 (1) of the Universal Declaration of Human Rights, adopted by the General Assembly of the United Nations on 10 December 1945. "Thomas Paine, 1797, argued that the land and natural resources belong to the people. Since land has been appropriated for private use, the owners owe a rent to the whole excluded population." Continuing to seat the arguments for UBI within the economics discipline, she continues: "A 2005 World Bank study concluded that most of a nation's wealth derives from intangible capital; that is, from human capital and the quality of institutions, especially the rule of law. The wealthier the nation, the more this is so." And, considering 'institutions' in their economic and sociological sense of informal institutions such as customs, or stable, valued, and recurring patterns of behaviour as well as formal organisations of e.g. government, they are important in determining the behaviour of individuals and as structures and mechanisms of society and social order (Hamilton & Liu, 2013). They belong to all citizens, therefore, and, as intangible assets, the wealth the nation derives from them should be for all. As private wealth is dependent upon this, it is argued (Miller, 2017; Standing, 2017) that all citizens should be rewarded with an effective dividend of this generated wealth, distributed in the form of a UBI (Standing, 2017 calls this the 'social dividend', following its introduction by the economists George Cole (1935: 234–235) and James Meade (1972) in the 1930s; from that era, the 1943 proposal by the Liberal MP Juliet Rhys-Williams is close to the citizen's income described here).

This reasoning confirms that solidarity is an essential pre-condition for the generation of private wealth and so supports the introduction of UBI as a recognition of what all are due, but also establishes that all are dependent on many others in society to reinforce and protect the institutions that underpin societal wealth and well-being. In the words of poet John Donne (1624) "No man is an island." Individual decisions and actions affect other people, and this interdependence means citizens are mutually responsible for each other.

Arguments and theoretical frameworks from social sciences for introducing a UBI have been offered and captured by Miller (2017), Torry (2015, 2018), Standing (2017), Van Parijs and Vanderborght (2017) and others. Several of these, as well as many other sources, make the case for a UBI in terms of addressing poverty and inequality, but their rationales have also been evolving over time to reflect and react to new challenges. These include the rise of the precariat (Standing, 2011) and artificial intelligence (AI), where such strange bedfellows as the billionaires Richard

Branson and Elon Musk have become advocates (some suggest many jobs are threatened by AI and so UBI offers financial security without work, while Mark Zuckerberg argues entrepreneurship is inspired by UBI—see Füllbrunn, Delsen & Vyrastekova, Chap. 7) alongside Muhammad Yunus, the 2006 Peace Nobel Prize laureate and founder of the Grameen Bank.[2]

Within the Scottish context, Miller (2017) has referred to the inter-generational dimensions of income, wealth and equality, highlighting the values engraved on the Scottish mace in the Scottish Parliament: 'wisdom, justice, compassion and integrity', which she argues would be complemented by a UBI scheme to "transform our society from one of fear and despair to one of compassion, justice, trust and hope".

While there have been a number of field experiments and pilot UBI schemes introduced around Europe and the world, as demonstrated and discussed by Delsen in Chap. 1 (and in the collections of such bodies as BIEN, Citizens Basic Income Trust (CBIT)[3]), in the remainder of this chapter the focus will be on the activities and arguments for a Scottish Citizen's Basic Income to address the issues of poverty and inequality described here. Further, although it is a radical alternative to the current social security system, designed for the conditions and economy of the nation in the twenty-first century, it is still in harmony with the objectives of the UK post-World War II Beveridge Plan to rid society of the five 'giant evils': want, disease, ignorance, squalor and idleness. Armstrong (2017) has demonstrated that these may not only be undefeated, but are actually gaining in strength in the UK. The failure of the existing welfare state to eradicate or reverse the waves of these 'evils' again supports the imperative of establishing a new relationship between the state, society and its citizens. The campaigning organisations in Scotland (CBINS, RSA and the pilot local authorities) are convinced that UBI is an essential component of such a new paradigm. However, a "BI could not be claimed as a cure for all of society's ills, but it is a necessary, though not sufficient, condition for a better society" (Miller, 2017). 'Better' here goes beyond a narrow economistic definition of 'more', as this does not necessarily address issues of equity and distribution fairness.

Pulling together the threat from AI and unpaid robots to levels of effective macro-economic demand in the economy (the arguments of Branson and Musk, for instance), the depressing impact on take home pay from the rise of the low paying employment for the precariat and consequently on states' tax revenues, there are strong economic drivers for reconsidering how citizens' disposable incomes can be raised to alleviate poverty on the one hand, and to ensure that there is sufficient consumer spending for a buoyant market place on the other. UBI seems to have entered the centre stage for advocates from across the spectrum, making it all the more important to evaluate the forms and conditions for any proposed UBI scheme.

---

[2]https://www.cnbc.com/2018/02/20/richard-branson-a-i-will-make-universal-basic-income-necessary.html, https://www.cnbc.com/2018/06/18/elon-musk-automated-jobs-could-make-ubi-cash-handouts-necessary.html, and https://basicincome.org/news/2018/07/india-muhammad-yunus-says-its-time-to-introduce-basic-income/

[3]https://basicincome.org/research/research-depository/, http://citizensincome.org/research-analysis/

4.4 Basic Income in Scotland

To recap the Scottish context within the UK: with almost the highest levels of inequality across the OECD, living standards have been falling for many through austerity measures and stagnant real wages. Tax revenues have not only been held down by the moves to low income self-employment and other precarious work, but for many years the rich have been hiding their incomes and wealth in tax havens, often under British protection, as revealed by the disclosures of the 'Paradise and Panama Papers'. Britain has the lowest levels of out-of-work benefits in Northern and Western Europe: both relative to average incomes and in absolute numbers, so that in sum there is the lowest aggregate spending on social protection/security as a proportion of GDP across these countries.

Britain's long-run low levels of growth mean it is 'Going South' and Brexit is expected to lead to further downgrades. All these factors have impacts on and are impacted by low productivity compared with these competitor economies. Traditional Keynesian strategic interventions to come out of a recession have been abandoned by successive Westminster parties and governments who have pursued a neoliberal agenda for the last three decades and more, with the race to reassert some nineteenth century nostalgic trade domination: a chimera based on poverty wages and worsening employment conditions.

In England, reforms to the National Health Service through charging for essential medical prescriptions has led to the costs of administering the system being greater than even the charge imposed; so there is no contribution to meeting the costs of the drugs themselves. More generally, the much-heralded reforms to social security have seen spiralling costs which outstrip any planned 'savings' (e.g. according to the National Audit Office, 2018 the new Universal Credit "is not value for money now, and that its future value for money is unproven"). Further changes to the welfare state along these lines will increase hardship, waste money and deepen poverty, according to all the evidence presented here. Against that record of neoliberal charging and privatisation of public services, and obviously with a different political discourse and much more social democratic and communitarian tradition in Scotland, authorities have decided it is time for a radical look at alternatives and at Citizen's Basic Income in particular.

The case for a UBI in Scotland has been made by the lead research and advocacy organisations CBINS and RSA, as outlined earlier. The poverty and inequality scourge that has continued to inflict injustice, health and well-being costs on many has meant an increasing questioning over the failure of the national (UK) state to offer prospects of an end to low incomes, hopelessness and despair (Spicker, 2011). In detailed analyses of the system, he has concluded that: "Poverty is not the moral, cultural or social problem of a permanently excluded underclass, but an economic risk that affects everyone" (Spicker, 2002). Foreshadowing some of the arguments for a UBI, where anyone can fall into poverty, he continued that: "The purpose of the welfare state should not be to target programmes more carefully on 'the poor', but to ensure that there is a general framework of resources, services and opportunities which are adequate for people's needs, and can be used by everyone", reiterating the Beveridge vision of the welfare state as about more than the 'poor' alone.

In a review of Spicker's (2011) book, BIEN suggests[4] that it "would be perfectly fair to describe his book as a sustained argument for a partial Citizen's Income". Based in Scotland he joins a number of those involved in promoting, advocating, working towards the adoption of a Citizen's Basic Income, though he and some other critics remain sceptical of the concept and proposals. The landscape in which this debate and discourse is being conducted is of poverty and inequality, but also of a Government and Parliament in Scotland with some powers over public expenditure, including some in the areas of social security (see e.g. Spicker, 2018 for an attempt to describe some of these in what is an evolving and confusing situation of transfer of some powers, but reservation of many to the UK Westminster Government and administration; see also Scottish Government (2018b).

While child poverty is above 10% in almost all parts of Scotland, and generally in excess of 20%, the highest rates are in Glasgow and surrounding old industrial areas. In 2017, in the City of Glasgow local authority area, the largest city, over a third of young people lived in low income households (34.3%); North Ayrshire recorded almost 30% (29.3%); in the old coalfield area of Fife one quarter (24.5%) were in poverty (End Child Poverty, 2018). Within these local government areas, concentrations of over 35% were to be found in significant parts of the towns and cities, while even in the capital Edinburgh many communities experienced rates above 30%. Considering another proxy for many of the components of living standards and quality of life, the Scottish Government (2016) offers estimates of the percentage of households in relative poverty in Scottish local authorities which confirm that Glasgow, Fife and North Ayrshire are all above the average for the country, while Edinburgh displays a wider range of incomes than the norm, suggesting relative poverty alongside riches for some. On the income domain of the comprehensive Scottish Index of Multiple Deprivation (SIMD), one area of Edinburgh is ranked the worst in the country out of 6976 data zones and another at 24, North Ayrshire and Fife both have proportionately high representation in the worst 1% on this key indicator but Glasgow dominates this as with most such statistics with half of the worst 0.5%.

Other research and statistics (Beatty & Fothergill, 2016a, 2016b, 2017) confirm that there is pressing and apparently intransigent suffering from poverty, income and wealth inequality across these four local government areas. Faced with continuing austerity cuts, forecasts from the Institute of Fiscal Studies (Hood and Waters, 2017) and Beatty and Fothergill (2016b) respectively of further and deepening hardship, of relative and absolute falls in incomes due to Brexit and stagnating levels of economic performance, these local authorities have been exploring their common interests in reducing poverty and tackling inequality. In particular they have been coordinating an approach that would examine the role that a basic income might play, applying principles of partnership working and community engagement.

These discussions and developments have been informed by their own officers and interests of some of their elected members, but also by CBINS, RSA, the

---

[4]https://basicincome.org/news/2012/06/review-paul-spicker-how-social-security-works-an-introduction-to-benefits-in-britain/

National Health Service in Scotland, Scottish Government expertise, academics and intelligence and advice from BIEN, CBIT, and others.[5] The construction of the case for exploring the feasibility of experiments or pilots in the four areas has also built upon the work of long-term advocates of UBI specifically in Scotland, and Annie Miller (2017) and the late Professor Ailsa McKay (2005, 2007). Across the political spectrum, organisations such as Reform Scotland (2017) have welcomed these moves; Ronnie Cowan, MP, Scottish National Party (SNP) led a debate in Westminster Hall on UBI in October 2016, the Reid Foundation and Common Weal have both promoted it from the Left; the Scottish Green Party have long supported UBI.[6] A Cross-Party Group has been created in the Scottish Parliament: "To examine the options for a basic income as a policy for reform of the current social security system in Scotland, including, where appropriate, its potential sources of funding", drawing membership from the Scottish National Party, Scottish Labour and the Scottish Greens, representing 91 of the 128 Members of the Scottish Parliament (MSPs).

After extensive public consultations, there was a joint manifesto commitment by the SNP and Labour parties in Fife Council to identify a town in Fife in which to test out a pilot of UBI. This was advised by a good level of public awareness of the concept of basic income in the region, with more than half of the population sample saying that they know something about it, or understand it fully. Of local people expressing a preference, over 62% were in favour of a trial being undertaken in Fife (Fife Council Research, 2016).[7] North Ayrshire Council was driven by its Community Planning Partnership's 'Fair for All Strategy' which aims to reduce inequalities to pursue a radical initiative to address poverty and is focused on UBI as a way forward. Glasgow City Council was informed by the city's Glasgow Poverty Leadership Panel (PLP) to join the Scottish UBI partnership, with the Labour Councillor Matt Kerr to the fore in promoting this approach. Finally, the City of Edinburgh Council, as part of the wider poverty and inequality reduction agenda, resolved to work with the other local authorities to develop and evaluate UBI proposals for their areas.

4.5 Feasibility Studies and Scope

With this interest and support for at least a set of pilots so emphatic in Scotland, the Scottish Parliament Social Security Committee held an evidence session on UBI on March 9, 2017. As well as exploring the concept, the Committee investigated the feasibility of introducing a UBI in Scotland. Reflecting the concerns expressed in

---

[5] See https://basicincome.scot/whats-happening-scotland/ for a list of partners and others involved.
[6] https://www.theyworkforyou.com/whall/?id=2016-09-14a.419.0, http://reidfoundation.org/wp-content/uploads/2014/03/InPlaceOfAnxiety.pdf, https://www.commonspace.scot/tags/basic-income, https://greens.scot/news/green-policy-of-basic-income-progresses-in-scotland
[7] The 2016 European Social Survey data shows support for UBI in the UK is 51% and 56% in Ireland (Lee, 2018). See also Delsen & Schilpzand, Chap. 2.

other commentaries, matters considered included "what level of UBI is sufficient, how it could be funded and whether it could work in Scotland based on the current devolved powers?" (Scottish Parliament, 2017a, 2017b). All four authorities presented written evidence, and representatives from the main bodies advocating UBI in Scotland appeared in person to expand on their own written evidence (available along with the Parliament's own research, Social Security Committee (2017b)). The Committee determined to maintain a watching brief on how the pilots were progressing and to identify what assistance and support the pilot authorities might require from the Scottish and UK Governments.

Around the same time, a briefing on UBI was prepared by the Scottish Government officers for the First Minister and this presented an objective evaluation of the possibilities and constraints within the UK constitutional position of Scotland to be considered in preparing pilots and implementation (Scottish Government, 2017). This encouraged the First Minister to suggest she was "both interested in UBI and sceptical of some of the claims made around its impact—but because of that I believe it's right to test those claims and to properly explore whether there could be a role for UBI in our social-security system" (Sturgeon, 2018). Therefore, the Scottish Government announced support for the local authorities to plan and prepare feasibility studies for their respective pilots (Scottish Government, 2018c).

The funding for these feasibility studies was on the official basis that UBI is "recognised as a radical form of social assistance which advocates of the concept suggest has the ability to tackle deeply ingrained social inequalities" (Scottish Government, 2018c: 2), confirming that the Government considered this initiative as being about poverty, justice and inequality. The conditions to be met by the proposals were for each pilot or pilot partnership to produce two briefing papers: the first by end of September 2019 (nature of proposed pilot; the research questions; likely costs; benefits of pilot; proposed sources of funding); the second by end of March 2020 (set out full details of the ethical, legislative, financial and practical implementation of the pilot; and findings were to be shared to establish an evidence base for Scotland.

In reality, the four pilot authorities submitted a joint proposal which was subsequently funded. This joint approach was characteristic of the partnership working that typifies economic and social development in Scotland (Danson & Lloyd, 2012). Internally, across and between organisations, there has been much joint ownership, collaboration and cooperation with sharing of information, intelligence and resources. CBINS, Carnegie UK Trust, RSA, and Improvement Service (established to support Councils, elected members and Community Planning Partnerships) have been in discussions, meetings and events with Councils, local community activists, and academics. Sometimes these meetings have been under the auspices of the Scottish Basic Income Pilot Steering Group—(of representatives from the four local authority councils supported by NHS Health Scotland and the Improvement Service which aims to steer the development of the feasibility and pilot stages of UBI in Scotland) to progress the pilots for Scotland. As noted earlier, other groups have been showing interest, including all political parties, except for the Conservatives, a few maverick members apart; as will be seen later, this is significant in limiting developments. Beyond these mainstream interests, the Chamber of Commerce, Scottish Trade Union Congress, the local authorities' collective body for Scotland (CoSLA), the Big Lottery Fund Scotland and the Child Poverty Action Group have engaged with this development and discussions around UBI in Scotland.

Five key feasibility study objectives have been identified and agreed by the sponsors and authorities, with answers to be pursued on whether the introduction of UBI would have: political feasibility, i.e. broad support for proceeding with and implementing a pilot of UBI?; financial feasibility, i.e. would it be possible to finance a UBI? Would implementation impose financial losses on households/individuals?; psychological feasibility, i.e. is the idea of a UBI readily understood and seen to be beneficial by the community?; behavioural feasibility, i.e. whether UBI works for households and individuals once it is implemented?; and, institutional feasibility. i.e. would there be institutional support for a pilot from a range of organisations? including the practicalities of how a pilot will be funded/administered, and illustrating/understanding the benefits of a UBI. The initial work by Fife Council suggested that these are both pertinent questions and, where appropriate, the population is fairly knowledgeable and has sufficient awareness to be able to respond. On the political feasibility of UBI in the 28 EU member states see Shanahan, Smith and Srinivasan (Chap. 3).

Complementing this, new staff are being recruited and research capacity retained to support the preparation of the feasibility studies and pilots. The key elements of the feasibility plan were drawn up to:

- Develop a common framework for UBI pilots in Scotland, using an evidence-informed logic model of UBI which sets out the theory of change and what outcomes might be expected from the introduction of a UBI;
- Develop specific research questions—tested through a local pilot, or explored through engagement sessions, and use these to inform and develop design options for local pilots and test hypotheses about the impact of a UBI (different local authority areas may look to explore different aspects in their local work);
- Explore behavioural effects and macro-economic impact of UBI;
- Learn from international pilots;
- Engage with key stakeholders, including elected members, national agencies including Department of Work and Pensions (DWP) and HM Revenue and Customs (HMRC);
- Explore different design options and levels of financing. Explore and identify sources of funding, and practical issues of implementation, such as eligibility, and payment mechanisms;
- Develop an evaluation framework, and an evaluability assessment;
- Deliver community engagement/partner/other stakeholder workshops.

These are proposed with the intentions to develop policy and delivery options for piloting UBI in Scotland that can be implemented given current political and economic constraints, to agree on model(s) for the pilots across local authorities to recommend to the Scottish Government, and to develop an evaluation plan for the pilots that will answer the priority research and policy questions around the feasibility and impact of the policy and to plan any baseline measurement, research governance and ethical approval. The key elements in successful delivery embrace the notion that it should be possible for each pilot area to develop different models of a UBI pilot linked to their area, potentially focusing on specific groups (i.e. families, care leavers, lone parents, health-related) or specific geographies (i.e. town, locality, neighbourhood). Further, to promote and encourage acceptance and approval, at least for the pilot stages, community engagement would be used to test out and explore findings. The planned schedule for the feasibility study and pilots is:

- Phase 1 (months 1–6): March 2018 to August 2018
- Phase 2 (months 7–12): September 2018 to March 2019
- Phase 3 (months 13–18): April 2019 to September 2019
- Phase 4 (months 18–24): October 2019 to March 2020
  - Baseline data collected
  - Full data collection and analysis agreed
  - Progress report/full business case for pilots to Scottish Government (March 2020).

With the key decision then to be made: are funding and delivery mechanisms in place? Interpreting this timeline confirms that, contrary to the expectations of many commentators and citizens, nothing of the implementation will start in practice until 2020 at the earliest. Pilots will then run for 2 years, and, with evaluation and recommendations to follow with political decisions on adoption of a UBI model contingent on these, it would be the mid-2020s before a full implementation could be envisaged across Scotland. A significant reason for this cautious approach is twofold: for any pilot it will be essential to gain necessary support to influence the future of national policy; the role of the Department of Work and Pensions (DWP), HM Revenue and Customs (HMRC), HM Treasury and the NHS will be vital in the design and implementation of UBI pilots. While the former is inserted to satisfy the requirements of the Scottish Government to determine affordability, sustainability and the approval of the population, the latter highlights that UK Government departments must be integral to the conception, implementation and funding of the pilots. Without cooperation from the UK Government, there are significant concerns on all elements of the pilots' feasibility and evaluation, and this brings the constitutional arrangements to the very core of the development of these experiments.

4.6 Constraints, Barriers and Budgets

The critical questions raised whenever a UBI trial is being proposed revolve around who will benefit and who will pay, and these sit within wider discourses on public expenditure and taxes. In the specific Scottish case and the four pilot authorities in particular, this requires an exploration of who funds the Scottish and local government budgets, what is the role of the UK Treasury, what is known about the peculiar form of devolution and fiscal federalism in the UK as it applies to Scotland uniquely. This means understanding the complex and evolving roles, powers and jurisdictions of the UK and Scottish governments, parliaments, authorities, departments, and other bodies, and how they interact. The Scottish Parliament and Government have some devolved powers over elements of the tax system, welfare state and social security, but many others remain reserved to the UK Westminster Parliament and Government. And, complicating all these considerations, all the ramifications of Brexit and what form it will take, its implications, etc. are altering the very political, social and economic landscape in unplanned and unanticipated ways.

In a recent debate in the UK Parliament, it was not contested that the people of Scotland are sovereign, which contrasts with the English perspective that sovereignty lies with Parliament. The consequences of that constitutional difference is but one of many that are usually not appreciated in London, and these may have a bearing on many aspects of plans to implement even a localised UBI pilot. Even though Scotland is considered by some to have a very powerful Parliament, all the devolution of revenue powers still means the majority of taxes raised in Scotland (57.9%) remain under UK control (Scottish Government, 2018d). Recent devolution over some elements of income taxes has increased tax raising powers from under a fifth (19.9%) to almost a third of total revenues (32.4%), with a further 9.7% assigned from UK-administered VAT. Powers over many property taxes had already been given back to the Scottish Parliament. There are greater powers over spending which has increased recently from 59.1 to 63% of direct public expenditure in Scotland.

However, and of most relevance to the UBI proposals, spending on social spending (which includes social security, pensions) is the largest element of public expenditure in Scotland at about £24 billion in 2016–2017. The most recent data show the highest element of social benefit spending is state pensions (41.6%), then other DWP (UK Department of Work and Pensions: 31.2%), and a set of other UK benefits—HMRC (the tax department), child benefit, tax credits, and universal credit which account for 15.8%; housing benefits (9.3%); and finally the Scottish Government social security benefit responsibilities amount to a mere 2.1% (mostly ameliorating some of the more iniquitous parts of UK legislation). Therefore, almost all social protection spending, eligibility criteria, administration and rule-setting remain under the management of UK Westminster departments, and so under the political control of the UK Conservative Government, which, as noted above, is opposed to UBI.

Under the Scotland Act 2016, from the developments discussed above, it is estimated that in 2016–2017 with the substantial devolution of income tax, the total of devolved and assigned taxes would have accounted for about 38% of non-North Sea Scottish revenue. However, and critical for considering introducing a realistic comprehensive UBI experiment, only 'non-saving non-dividend income tax liabilities' were devolved; Westminster continues to set various elements of the income tax system anyway, but also retains all control over non-wage and salary liabilities.

In summary, much social protection—benefits and pensions—remains under UK Government control and for many of the poorest and elderly this would be replaced by a UBI in any pilot. The UK Government is not in favour of UBI, and the Conservatives in Scotland are not in favour of the pilots or the concept of UBI in any form. On the payment of UBI in any experiment, therefore, there is a major obstacle to progress with the obstruction of the UK Government central; traditionally, it has also been the case that the DWP has resisted any other degree of experimentation at a sub-national (i.e. within a part of the UK) level, with 'full employment initiatives' in Glasgow and some English cities blocked in the 1990s, for instance. Paying for UBI pilots requires a revenue stream, and yet much tax raising is reserved under UK Government control. In terms of using UBI as a tool for redistribution, the local authorities would want to tax income from all earnings, including savings and investments. Again, the opposition of HMRC and the Treasury to loss of control over their respective empires is a barrier to a full UBI pilot being implemented in Scotland.

Briefly: DWP, Treasury, HMRC are all critical to longer term plans for UBI in Scotland and the rest of the UK if there was interest (and local campaign and advocacy organisations in many cities and towns in England and Wales suggest there is). Additionally, they are all important for pilot schemes if these are to be comprehensive regarding assessing the behaviour of taxpayers, workers, entrepreneurs, citizens. These are perhaps the reasons behind the constant criticism from right-wing politicians of the proposed pilots on the grounds that they cannot evaluate such factors; omitting, of course, that it is their own Westminster government that is ensuring this is the case. This raises the prospect that only partial pilots can be launched, tracing the behaviours of poor citizens in the main.

There are further issues to be addressed regarding how to tax local citizens, if a pilot is to be tested for affordability by seeking revenue funding from the local population at least to some extent. Nevertheless, while assessing these revenue-raising features of one side of piloting the introduction of a UBI scheme will be limited, modelling and reference to past literatures and experiments can contribute to anticipating behavioural changes. Identifying these sources of intelligence on likely impacts is being undertaken by CBINS and partners (RSA, BIEN, CBIT, etc.) and it is an objective of the feasibility studies. To facilitate informed analysis and debate over the implementation of a UBI in Scotland, to hone arguments to counter the criticisms of sceptics and opponents, and to improve the levels of knowledge and understanding about the issues raised by the constraints and barriers, funding has been supplied by a consortium of Scottish universities (SUII, the Scottish Universities Insight Institute) to organise a series of workshops in autumn 2018. The ones responsible for organising these workshops are academics—led by the author of this chapter—in collaboration with CBINS—which he also chairs—RSA and others. This project is aiming to facilitate multi-disciplinary and cross-sector learning about UBI, development, implementation and evaluation of UBI pilots in Scotland, with toolkits and evaluation guidance co-produced for critical assessment, new UBI-related research, and a multi-disciplinary and cross-sector Scottish UBI network to support learning and inform future policy and practice.

Scottish and international researchers, policymakers, practitioners and citizens are being brought together to critically explore rationales, requirements and consequences of UBI in Scotland, focusing on how UBI interacts with key socio-economic issues. These workshops will be focused through initial scoping papers on human rights and equality, especially gender, age and disability, caring, affordable housing, and employment and entrepreneurship. These individual workshops will generate briefing papers and other outputs, and all will be subject to a final concluding event to consider evaluation and modelling methodologies, incorporating economists—micro- and macro-modellers, public policy analysts, and other impact technicians. Project inputs and outputs will be disseminated by CBINS and SUII to wider practice and research communities across Scotland and internationally.

4.7 Some Illustrative Examples

The pilots being proposed as yet require work on their locations, coverage, forms and details, hence the agenda for the feasibility studies stage. While the operation of the pilots will be informative for authorities, the public and academics as to the concept, challenges and engagement, it will allow hypotheses to be tested regarding the attitudes to and behavioural effects of different levels of UBI and different types and levels of financing. Depending on the model UBI schemes undertaken, there will be issues over whether they are voluntary or compulsory and with concerns over changes in benefits if moving outwith the location, with security of pensions and other 'passported' payments, allowances and credits, especially when these are dealt with by different agencies. Indeed, this raises again the importance of effective and agreed inter-agency partnership working with UK Government departments, as means-tested elements of tax and social security benefits will interact with automatic entitlement to UBI (see Muffels & Gielens, Chap. 5 and Betkó et al., Chap. 6, on how these issues of selection bias are dealt with in the Dutch experiments). As any pilot would seek not to make anyone worse off by participating in the experiment, those who would pay higher taxes in a full implementation would be protected from this; so the behavioural impacts on the better off of this element of a UBI scheme cannot be measured directly.

Longitudinal surveying of those involved in the pilots, whether citizens or administrators, staff with health or employment agencies, etc. will allow some assessment of the impacts of UBI on incomes, expenditures, choices, education and training, employment and enterprise, health and well-being, caring and cared for and so forth. With reasonable assumptions from labour economics and research on participation, withdrawal rates, and incentives and disincentives, modelling using the computable general equilibrium macro-economic model of the Fraser of Allander Institute at Strathclyde University should allow some estimation of UBI effects on both sides of the market. This would facilitate exploring whether the low paid on precarious jobs are empowered to seek better rewarded positions with UBI or the higher paid discouraged from pursuing promotions or working overtime.

Some of the suggestions for evaluation suites from within the Scottish Basic Income Pilot Steering Group have focused on applying Randomised Control Trials (RCT) or saturation samples (see Widerquist, 2018 for a review of some of the analytical issues); some scepticism is in order here as the pilots will be targeted on communities selected for their particular characteristics and therefore not 'random', while voluntary participation and not making any citizen worse off means that there is no control over the population (cf. Muffels & Gielens, Chap. 5). Other techniques (such as the Triple I tool, dark logic modelling, plausible theory and agent based modelling) similarly owe their origins to medical and agriculture sciences where controlled trials only have to account for a limited set of active factors; this is clearly very different from the case of a village or town, care-leaving group with their individual, household and many other variables impacting on their lifestyle attitudes, choices and behaviours. Beyond these constraints on the research parameters, the evaluations cannot be universal for the population of a community as not all members will join or stay with the pilot, undoubtedly biasing the sample and the transferability of outcomes.

Other longer-term effects of the introduction of a UBI will not be apparent within the 2 years of a UBI pilot, or the impacts will be outwith the immediate location as boundary effects apply; these include changes in the demand for labour—to contrast with the supply side and to reflect possible improvements in human capital and greater empowerment of low paid workers, changes in productivity, wages and prices, average profit rates for businesses, new companies moving into deprived areas, investment in the local economy and workforce (Miller, 2017).

Considering the net costs of implementing a UBI at the local level, it has been suggested the funds to be distributed locally would be balanced by a series of financial and other savings: from the social security benefits and pensions being replaced; from the simplified and less-intrusive administration, with reduced fraud and error; through reductions in many personal and associated tax allowances, creating increased income tax revenues; while the indirect cost of poverty on the NHS, personal social services, poverty alleviation programmes, and on the criminal justice system would all be reduced. Further discussions and transfer of powers would also allow new thresholds and increased income tax rates to raise extra revenues, Scotland could also introduce new taxes such as land value tax (to capture some of the worth of the very large land holdings of the rich, which are presently mainly untaxed), tourism and sales taxes, etc.

With cooperation of the UK tax and benefit authorities, most of these would be achievable within the powers of the Scottish Government. Besides these, at the UK level UBI could be made more affordable by significant campaigns to reduce illegal tax evasion and reduce legal tax avoidance by closing many tax loopholes. With many absentee wealth holders and others relying on investment and savings income, devolving taxes on non-wage income and on capital would broaden the tax base within Scotland. This latter change would be more significant if AI and robots reduce employment as anticipated.

In launching pilot UBIs, it will be important for local authorities to at least be able to demonstrate where funds could be identified to make the scheme affordable. Put against the aggregate UBI payments made to all citizens under each pilot, these potential sources would allow calculations to be made of the sum of net transfers—the total amount that net taxpayers transfer to net recipients. Although the pilot authorities have not made specific proposals of the rates for their UBI schemes, Annie Miller (2017) has offered these suggestions based at the Scottish level with flat income tax rates (see Table 4.3). These are illustrative only, but demonstrate the sorts of rates that might be affordable under certain assumptions

4 Exploring Benefits and Costs: Challenges of Implementing...

Table 4.3 Illustrative UBI schemes to match a floor and two poverty benchmarks for Scotland, 2017–2018

Scotland's mean income per head of population in 2015 (latest available figure) was £ 392.40 per week	Means tested benefits	A FLOOR: MTB levels 2017–2018	Intermediate UBI scheme A	UBI B	UBI C	Official EU poverty benchmark AHC 2014–2015	MIS poverty benchmark AHC 2016
Amounts for:							
Pensioner (aged 65+)		159.35	160.00	157.00	165.00	140.59/101.81	165.15
Working age (25–64)		73.10	100.00	125.60	150.00	140.59/101.81	177.99
£ per week							
Young adult (16–24)		57.90	100.00	125.60	150.00	140.59/101.81	177.99
Premium for parent with child		0.00	0.00	31.40	30.00	0.00	0.00
Each cared for child (aged 0–15)		84.29/66.87	65.00	62.80	90.00	101.81/48.48	92.00
UBI levels as proportions of UK's mean income per head in 2015:							
Pensioner			0.4077	0.4001	0.4205		
Working age			0.2548	0.3201	0.3823		
Young adult			0.2548	0.3201	0.3823		
Premium for parent with child			0.0000	0.0800	0.0765		
Each cared for child			0.1656	0.1600	0.2294		
HOUSEHOLD CONFIGURATIONS: £ per week			Total UBI payments to household				
Pensioner, single	Pension	159.35	160.00	157.00	165.00	140.59	165.15
Pensioner, couple	Credit	243.25	320.00	314.00	330.00	242.40	240.45
Working age, single	JSA/	73.10	100.00	125.60	150.00	140.59	177.99
Working age, couple	ESA	114.85	200.00	251.20	300.00	242.40	304.25
Young adult		57.90	100.00	125.60	150.00	140.59/101.81	177.99

(continued)

Table 4.3 (continued)

Scotland's mean income per head of population in 2015 (latest available figure) was £ 392.40 per week	Means tested benefits	A FLOOR: MTB levels 2017–2018	Intermediate UBI scheme A	UBI B	UBI C	Official EU poverty benchmark AHC 2014–2015	MIS poverty benchmark AHC 2016
Lone parent + toddler	JSA/ESA CB, CTC	157.39	165.00	219.80	270.00	189.07	270.48
Lone parent + pre-school + primary-school child		224.26	230.00	282.60	360.00	237.55	344.62
Lone parent + pre-school + primary-school + secondary-school child		291.13	295.00	345.40	450.00	339.36	452.98
Couple + toddler	JSA/ESA CB, CTC	199.14	265.00	345.40	420.00	290.88	348.66
Couple + pre-school + primary-school child		266.01	330.00	408.20	510.00	339.36	422.41
Couple + pre-school + primary-school child + secondary-school child		332.88	395.00	471.00	600.00	441.17	540.63
Couple + four children		399.75	460.00	533.80	690.00	489.65	589.08
Flat tax rate required in restructured inc tax system; plus MARGIN of 0.0590 gives the flat tax rate required for TOTAL COST OF SOCIAL SECURITY			0.2694 0.3284	0.3167 0.3757	0.3716 0.4306		
TOTAL TAX RATE with earnings/income disregard			–	0.4183	0.4713		

Source: Adapted from Miller (2017) and offered here with her kind permission

MTBs means-tested benefits, *AHC* after housing costs have been deducted, *MIS* minimum income standards, *inc* income. Sec secondary school child, *JSA* Jobseeker's allowance, *ESA* employment and Support allowance, *CB* child benefit, *CTC* child tax credit

and introduced over time. The illustrative flat tax rates in this model range between 27 and 47% and are based upon certain assumptions about the tax base/coverage, tax allowances, who are defined as 'citizens', and so forth; these are either controlled by Westminster or subject to change induced by other tax changes. Other models have been proposed by, for example, Torry (2018), Martinelli (2017) and Reed and Lansley (2016). Martinelli in particular offers a set of comparator levels of UBI with associated costs.

4.8 Conclusions So Far

UBI has a long social science history: "A certain small income, sufficient for necessities, should be secured for all, whether they work or not" (Russell, 1918). Atkinson captured many arguments in his 1995 book, followed by the volume by Widerquist, Noguera, Vanderborght, and De Wispelaere (2013). This international research has been developing the rationale and theoretical underpinnings further led by Van Parijs (2004), Wright (2004) and Standing (2017).

The global reach of the concept has led to pilots in North America, Kenya and India, for instance, but with context and duration consistently stressed as important in their evaluations and transferability. As well as the seminal works above, these experiments have been discussed in *Basic Income Studies* and other journals covering three key areas: ethics and rationale, analysis of funding, implementation options and viability, and impact and learning from the pilot schemes. A wide consensus across Scotland supports the proposal for pilot studies to assess the effectiveness, affordability and potential impacts of a UBI scheme. This endorsement reflects the Scottish partnership approach to social and economic initiatives, which has been the model for developing innovative policy interventions collaboratively, between agencies in systems of multi-governance and has become the template across the European Union (Danson & Lloyd, 2012).

Alleviating poverty and inequality in a more effective, inclusive and universal way has been the dominant driver in Scotland for considering piloting and implementing a UBI for all. The key features of a UBI in Scotland are accepted across most advocates and supporters: a cash transfer payment based on the individual is universal, unconditional, non-selective (except by age) and is not means-tested. It is delivered regularly and automatically to all who qualify. It is for everyone, and is tax-exempt.

Informed by the work of CBINS, RSA, BIEN, CBIT and others, and the learning of the officers in local authorities, Scottish government and health services, the feasibility studies should progress the proposed schemes and identify a series of experiments that complement and contribute wider knowledge and understanding of the practice and challenges for rolling a full Citizen's Basic Income across Scotland. The particular form of devolved and reserved fiscal and expenditure powers available to the Scottish Parliament and Government makes introduction of all but small pilots problematic, and this is exacerbated by the strong opposition of the UK Conservative party and administration to the very concept of UBI.

Overall it can be expected that the Scottish local pilots will proceed to implementation, focusing on specific constituencies suffering from poverty and isolation: an old mining village in Fife, those who have been cared for by the state, etc. The lessons learned, the evaluations and modelling all add to the growing bank of knowledge of the immediate impacts of a UBI. That full implementation is not anticipated before the mid-2020s will disappoint many proponents of this radical alternative to the current social security and protection system, impatient to see an end to a welfare state that relies on sanctions, penalties, heavy administrative burdens and paperwork for client and department alike. The cross-party support for universal benefits and services in Scotland is increasingly contrasting with the rhetoric from the UK Government and Parliament, so that UBI as a means of inclusion and solidarity across communities, generations and citizens has more opportunities for adoption in Scotland.

Brexit and the independence movement, of course, are defining the social, economic and political environment in Scotland and the UK presently, and will continue to do so for years to come. While there are no realistic prospects of major changes in the political atmosphere or party agendas at Westminster, the Labour Party has expressed interest in UBI and so joins the SNP, Greens and Plaid Cymru in the UK Parliament in wanting to explore UBI as a potential policy alternative. As all the indications are that Labour would rely on these other parties for a working majority, the Scottish pilots may become more important over time, either as intelligence for a UK intervention or as the prototype for an independent Scotland. Interesting times.

Acknowledgements Thanks are due to Lei Delsen for his comments and feedback which have improved the chapter significantly.

References

Armstrong, S. (2017, October 10). Want, disease, ignorance, squalor and idleness: Are Beveridge's five evils back? *The Guardian*. Retrieved October 6, 2019, from https://www.theguardian.com/society/2017/oct/10/beveridge-five-evils-welfare-state

Atkinson, A. (1995). *Public economics in action: The basic income/flat tax proposal*. Oxford: Oxford University Press.

Basic Income Scotland. (2018). *Green light for basic income pilot*. Retrieved October 6, 2019, from http://basicincome.scot/2018/05/24/green-light-for-basic-income-pilot-thanks-to-successful-funding-bid/

Beatty, C., & Fothergill, S. (2016a). *Jobs, welfare and austerity: How the destruction of industrial Britain casts a shadow over present-day public finances*. Sheffield: Centre for Regional, Economic and Social Research, Sheffield Hallam University. Retrieved October 6, 2019, https://www4.shu.ac.uk/research/cresr/sites/shu.ac.uk/files/cresr30th-jobs-welfare-austerity.pdf

Beatty, C., & Fothergill, S. (2016b). *The impact on Scotland of the new welfare reforms.* Sheffield: Sheffield Hallam University. Retrieved October 6, 2019, from https://www4.shu.ac.uk/research/cresr/sites/shu.ac.uk/files/impact-scotland-new-welfare-reform.pdf

Beatty, C., & Fothergill, S. (2017). The long shadow of industrial Britain's demise. *Regions, 308*(4), 5–8. https://doi.org/10.1080/13673882.2017.11958667

Brady, D. (2009). *Rich democracies poor societies: How politics explain poverty.* Oxford: Oxford University Press.

Calhoun, C. (2018). Populism, nationalism and Brexit. In W. Outhwaite (Ed.), *Brexit: Sociological responses* (pp. 57–76). Cambridge: Anthem Press.

CBINS. (2018). *Who are CBINS?* Citizen's Basic Income Network Scotland. Retrieved October 6, 2019, from https://cbin.scot/who-are-cbins/

Cole, G. (1935). *Principles of economic planning.* London: Macmillan.

Danson, M., & Lloyd, G. (2012). Devolution, institutions, and organisations: Changing models of regional development agencies. *Environment and Planning C: Politics and Space, 30*(1), 78–94. https://doi.org/10.1068/c1145r

Danson, M., McAlpine, R., Spicker, P., & Sullivan, W. (2013). *The case for universalism: An assessment of the evidence on the effectiveness and efficiency of the universal welfare state.* Biggar: Jimmy Reid Foundation. Retrieved October 6, 2019, from http://reidfoundation.org/portfolio/the-case-for-universalism-an-assessment-of-the-evidence-on-the-effectiveness-and-efficiency-of-the-universal-welfare-state/

Danson, M., McKay, A., & Sullivan, W. (2015). Supporting Britain's workless—An international perspective. *Social Policy and Administration, 49*(2), 277–298. https://doi.org/10.1111/spol.12123

Donne, J. (1624). No man is an island. In Devotions upon emergent occasions and severall steps in my sickness - Meditation XVII. https://www.scottishpoetrylibrary.org.uk/poem/no-man-is-an-island/

Drejer, T., Freundt, A., Hansen, H., & Straubinger, S. G. (2010). *Net replacement rates for unemployed in 7 European countries* (CWS Working Paper No. 1). Centre for Welfare State Research, Odense, University of Southern Denmark.

Elliott, L., & Atkinson, D. (2012). *Going south: Why Britain will have a third world economy by 2014.* Basingstoke: Palgrave Macmillan.

End Child Poverty. (2018). Retrieved October 6, 2019, from http://www.endchildpoverty.org.uk/poverty-in-your-area-2018/

Eurostat. (2010). *Table 1, In-work poverty in the EU.* Luxembourg: European Commission.

Fife Council Research. (2016). *Basic income.* Glenrothes: Fife Council.

Fraser, G. (2019, January 4). Scottish Government cash to 'mitigate UK welfare cuts'. *Holyrood.* Retrieved October 6, 2019, from https://www.holyrood.com/articles/news/scottish-government-cash-mitigate-uk-welfare-cuts

Galloway, L., Danson, M., Richards, J., Sang, J. K., & Stirzaker, R. (2016). *In-work poverty and enterprise: Self-employment and business ownership as contexts of poverty.* Edinburgh: Heriot-Watt University.

Hamilton, K., & Liu, G. (2013). *Human capital, tangible wealth, and the intangible capital residual* (Policy Research Working Paper No. 6391). Washington, DC: World Bank. Retrieved October 6, 2019, from https://openknowledge.worldbank.org/handle/10986/13176

Haydecker, R. (2010). Public policy in Scotland after devolution: Convergence or divergence. *POLIS Journal, 3*(Winter), 1–52.

Hetherington, P. (2018, May 7). Will Scotland lead the way for cradle-to-grave care in the UK? *The Guardian.* Retrieved October 6, 2019, from https://www.theguardian.com/uk-news/2018/may/07/scotland-lead-way-cradle-grave-care-uk-devolved-tax-increase

Hood, A., & Waters, T. (2017). *Living standards, poverty and inequality in the UK: 2017–18 to 2021–22.* London: Institute of Fiscal Studies. Retrieved October 6, 2019, from https://www.ifs.org.uk/publications/10028

Lee, S. (2018). Attitudes toward universal basic income and welfare state in Europe: A research note. *Basic Income Studies, 13*(1), 1–9. https://doi.org/10.1515/bis-2018-0002

Lindsay, C., & Houston, D. (Eds.). (2013). *Disability benefits, welfare reform and employment policy*. Basingstoke: Palgrave.

Martinelli, L. (2017). *Assessing the case for a universal basic income in the UK* (IPR Policy Brief). University of Bath. Retrieved October 6, 2019, from https://www.bath.ac.uk/publications/assessing-the-case-for-a-universal-basic-income-in-the-uk/attachments/basic_income_policy_brief.pdf

McKay, A. (2005). *The future of social security policy: Women, work and a citizen's basic income*. London: Routledge.

McKay, A. (2007). Why a citizens' basic income? A question of gender equality or gender bias. *Work, Employment & Society, 21*(2), 337–348. https://doi.org/10.1177/0950017007076643

McKnight, A., Duque, M., & Rucci, M. (2018). *Double trouble: A review of the relationship between UK poverty and economic inequality* (Oxfam Policy and Practice Working Paper). Retrieved October 6, 2019, from https://policy-practice.oxfam.org.uk/publications/double-trouble-a-review-of-the-relationship-between-uk-poverty-and-economic-ine-620373

Meade, J. (1972). Poverty in the welfare state. *Oxford Economic Papers, 24*(3), 289–326. https://doi.org/10.1093/oxfordjournals.oep.a041224

Miller, A. (2017). *A basic income handbook*. Edinburgh: Luath Press.

Mooney, G., McKendrick, J., Scott, G., Dickie, P., & McHardy, F. (Eds.). (2016). *Poverty in Scotland 2016: Tools for transformation*. London: Child Poverty Action Group.

Mooney, G., & O'Sullivan, P. (2015). The impact of the Scottish Independence Referendum on devolution and governance in the United Kingdom. *Knowledge Exchange Seminar Series*. Retrieved October 6, 2019, from http://www.niassembly.gov.uk/globalassets/documents/raise/knowledge_exchange/briefing_papers/mooneyosullivankesspaper1.pdf

National Audit Office (NAO). (2018). *Rolling out universal credit*. London. Retrieved October 6, 2019, from https://www.nao.org.uk/report/rolling-out-universal-credit/

O'Hara, B. (2019, March 4). Statement to house. *House of Commons Hansard*, Column 762, Volume 655. Retrieved October 6, 2019, from https://hansard.parliament.uk/commons/2019-03-04/debates/1E3A4E87-E2BC-4C53-98D5-E4497A48722D/SocialSecurity

OECD. (2017). *Net replacement rates for six family types: Initial phase of unemployment. During the initial phase of unemployment, 2001–2015*. Retrieved October 6, 2019, from http://www.oecd.org/els/benefits-and-wages-statistics.htm

Reed, H., & Lansley, S. (2016). Universal basic income: An idea whose time has come? *Compass*. Retrieved October 6, 2019, from https://www.compassonline.org.uk/wp-content/uploads/2016/05/UniversalBasicIncomeByCompass-Spreads.pdf

Reform Scotland. (2017). *Basic income guarantee*. Edinburgh. Retrieved October 6, 2019, from https://reformscotland.com/wp-content/uploads/2017/12/basic-income-briefing.pdf

Russell, B. (1918). *Proposed roads to freedom: Socialism, anarchism, and syndicalism*. London: George Allen & Unwin.

Schwellnus, C., Kappeler, A., & Pionnier, P.-A. (2017). *The decoupling of median wages from productivity in OECD countries* (Economics Department Working Papers No. 1373). Paris: Organisation for Economic Co-operation and Development.

Scottish Government. (2016). *SIMD 2016 ranks and domain ranks. The Scottish index of multiple deprivation*. Edinburgh. Retrieved October 6, 2019, from https://www.gov.scot/Topics/Statistics/SIMD

Scottish Government. (2017). *First minister—Briefing on citizens basic income*. Edinburgh. Retrieved October 6, 2019, from https://beta.gov.scot/binaries/content/documents/govscot/publications/foi-eir-release/2017/10/foi-17-02092/documents/74d4a6fc-9d26-4263-98f8-e1accd50a648/74d4a6fc-9d26-4263-98f8-e1accd50a648/govscot:document/?inline=true/

Scottish Government. (2018a). *Poverty in Scotland*. Edinburgh. Retrieved October 6, 2019, from https://www.gov.scot/Topics/Statistics/Browse/Social-Welfare/IncomePoverty

Scottish Government. (2018b). *Social security for Scotland*. Edinburgh. Retrieved October 6, 2019, from https://www.gov.scot/Resource/0053/00538245.pdf

Scottish Government. (2018c). *Citizens basic income. Feasibility studies fund. Application for funding.* Edinburgh. Retrieved October 6, 2019, from https://basicincome.scot/wp-content/uploads/sites/75/2018/04/CBI-fund-application-290318-PUBLIC.pdf

Scottish Government. (2018d). *Scotland's budget documents 2018–19: Budget (Scotland) bill supporting document for the year ending 31 March 2019.* Edinburgh. Retrieved October 6, 2019, from https://www.gov.scot/Resource/0053/00530618.pdf

Scottish Parliament Social Security Committee. (2017a). *Citizen's income. Evidence.* Edinburgh. Retrieved October 6, 2019, from http://www.parliament.scot/parliamentarybusiness/CurrentCommittees/103211.aspx

Scottish Parliament Social Security Committee. (2017b). *Official report: Session 5.* Edinburgh. Retrieved October 6, 2019, from http://www.parliament.scot/parliamentarybusiness/report.aspx?r=10836&mode=pdf

Sinfield, A. (2011). *Whose welfare state now? A whose economy seminar paper.* Oxfam. Retrieved October 6, 2019, from https://policy-practice.oxfam.org.uk/publications/whose-welfare-state-now-146174

Spicker, P. (2002). *Poverty and the welfare state: Dispelling the myths.* London: Catalyst.

Spicker, P. (2011). *How social security works: An introduction to benefits in Britain.* Bristol: Policy Press.

Spicker, P. (2018). *Social policy blog.* Retrieved October 6, 2019, from http://www.spicker.uk/social-policy/uk.htm

Standing, G. (2011). *The precariat.* London: Bloomsbury Academic.

Standing, G. (2014). *A precariat charter: From denizens to citizens.* London: Bloomsbury Academic.

Standing, G. (2017). *Basic income: And how we can make it happen.* London: Pelican/Penguin.

Sturgeon, N. (2018, May 31). Why basic income is worth a serious look. *The Economist.* Retrieved October 6, 2019, from https://www.economist.com/open-future/2018/05/31/why-universal-basic-income-is-worth-a-serious-look

Torry, M. (2015). *101 Reasons for a citizen's income: Arguments for giving everyone some money.* Bristol: Bristol University Press.

Torry, M. (2018). *Why we need a citizen's basic income.* Bristol: Policy Press.

Van Parijs, P. (2004). Basic income: A simple and powerful idea for the twenty-first century. *Politics & Society, 32*(1), 7–39. https://doi.org/10.1177/0032329203261095

Van Parijs, P., & Vanderborght, Y. (2017). *Basic income: A radical proposal for a free society and a sane sconomy.* Cambridge: Harvard University Press.

White, A. (2017). *Poverty statistics 2015/16.* Retrieved October 6, 2019, from https://www.gov.scot/Topics/Statistics/Browse/Social-Welfare/IncomePoverty

Widerquist, K. (2018). *The devil's in the caveats: A critical analysis of basic income experiments for researchers, policymakers, and citizens.* Berkeley: Bepress. Retrieved October 6, 2019, from https://works.bepress.com/widerquist/86/

Widerquist, K., Noguera, J. A., Vanderborght, Y., & De Wispelaere, J. (Eds.). (2013). *Basic income: An anthology of contemporary research.* Chichester: Wiley-Blackwell.

World Economic Forum. (2018). *The world's biggest economies in 2018.* Retrieved October 6, 2019, from https://www.weforum.org/agenda/2018/04/the-worlds-biggest-economies-in-2018/

Wright, E. O. (2004). Basic income, stakeholder grants, and class analysis. *Politics & Society, 32*(1), 79–87. https://doi.org/10.1177/0032329203261099

Young, C. (2018). *Realising basic income experiments in the UK: A typology and toolkit of basic income design and delivery.* London: Royal Society for the encouragement of Arts, Manufactures and Commerce.

Michael Wlliam Danson (1953) was born in Inverness, Scotland and studied economics and statistics at the University of Aberdeen (M.A. Hons) and in 2014 received a DLitt for his work on *Regional Economic Development and Regional Development Agencies* from the University of the West of Scotland. He was a senior research fellow in Social and Economic Research at the University of Glasgow (1978–1985), senior economist in Chief Executive's Department, Strathclyde Regional Council (1985–1988), lecturer/senior lecturer/reader/professor at the Department of Economic Management (1988–2005) and Associate Dean of Research (2005–2012) University of West of Scotland, he is professor of enterprise policy and director of doctoral programmes at the School of Social Sciences, Heriot-Watt University. His research is on urban, rural and regional economic development, publishing on economic impacts and evaluations of poverty and inequality, early onset dementia, micro brewing and micro distilling, Gaelic, Kawaski disease, and taxation. He has published in international journals including *Urban Studies, Regional Studies, Environment & Planning, European Planning Studies,* he has 16 edited books and undertaken research for OECD, European Commission, national and international governments, parliaments and agencies.

Chapter 5
Job Search, Employment Capabilities and Well-being of People on Welfare in the Dutch 'Participation Income' Experiments

Ruud Muffels and Erwin Gielens

Abstract The chapter discusses the history, design and first empirical findings of Dutch local RCT (Randomised Controlled Trial) experiments with participation income which are currently implemented in 11 cities. The emergence of these local experiments can be viewed as reflecting an ongoing shift in Dutch social policy from a classical 'stick and carrot' or workfare approach of social welfare, to a social investment and capacitating approach. The empirical analyses discuss the methodology and outcomes on job search, employment chances and work capabilities, and the health and well-being of some 1500 participants using survey and municipal administrative data. We perform LCA (Latent Class Analysis) to provide a profile of the participants of the experiments and estimate (binary logit regression) their exit probabilities into paid work. In the end we formulate some expectations and conclusions about the meaning and effects of these participation income experiments in the Netherlands for people's employment, health and well-being situation, and their wider implications for social policy, notably with a view to a social investment and capacitating approach.

Keywords Participation income · Randomised controlled trial experiments · Job search · Employment chances · Capabilities · Social investment · Binary logit · Latent class analysis

R. Muffels (✉)
ReflecT/Tranzo, Tilburg University, Tilburg, The Netherlands
e-mail: ruud.j.muffels@uvt.nl

E. Gielens
Department of Sociology, Tilburg University, Tilburg, The Netherlands
e-mail: E.E.C.Gielens@uvt.nl

5.1 Introduction

Many more countries than ever before currently show interest in the ideas of a participation or basic income, and are preparing or even implementing local or national experiments, but with varying levels of success (like in the United States, Canada, Scotland, Finland, Switzerland, Italy, the Netherlands and France) (see also Chap. 1). The chapter discusses the history, design and first empirical findings of Dutch local RCT (Randomised Controlled Trial) experiments with participation income, which were implemented in the fall of 2017 in 11 cities. These experiments have strong similarities with participation income (Atkinson, 1996) and basic income approaches to social policy (cf. Groot, Muffels, & Verlaat, 2019). Section 5.2 discusses why the emergence of these local experiments might be viewed as an 'innovative attempt' to shift Dutch social policy-making into a social investment and capacitating approach, admitting though that these attempts are still in its infancy (Hemerijck, 2013, 2017). For that reason Morel, Palier, and Palme (2012) have called it an emerging policy paradigm. Notably, in the recent economic crisis, under the influence of austerity macro-economic policies to reduce government budget deficits, social policy seems to have returned to the neoliberal market-oriented welfare paradigm. Work-first and workfare principles are reinforced through a stronger monitoring and tightening of benefit access conditions, cuts in unemployment and disability benefit levels, and duration and stricter law enforcement, especially for youngsters and school-leavers on social assistance. Stronger law enforcement occurred notably with respect to social assistance beneficiaries' application obligations and reintegration duties (Delsen, 2017; Hemerijck, 2017; Soentken, van Hooren, & Rice, 2017). This also means that classical activation policies that are vested on 'making work pay' are still dominant. Social investment policies that create participation and integration opportunities by pro-actively investing in people's capacities or 'capabilities' (Hemerijck, 2017; Sen, 2004, 2009) are therefore still in their infancy.

Policy-makers at community level, however, start to realise that traditional policy instruments, e.g. monetary incentives, are, apart from being costly in implementation, also not necessarily effective, and for this reason they show mounting interest in alternative approaches inspired by new behavioural insights to policy-making and the testing of these policies in the field. The basic income initiatives and local Participation Act (*Participatiewet*) experiments can be viewed as a way to test these behavioural policies and the interventions needed to influence behaviour. Therefore, in Sect. 5.3 the design and content of these experiments which were launched in 11 municipalities in 2017 are explained in more detail. Then, in the second part (Sect. 5.4) we switch to the empirical analyses of the research. The focus is on the outcomes of the first participants' survey which was held as part of the research that was set up as a classical RCT (Randomised Controlled Trial) experimental design. The first survey fits into a longitudinal research design with three survey waves during the 2 years of experimenting. The three panel waves are aimed at collecting information on a broad set of chosen outcome measures, such as reintegration into work, social participation, health, well-being and self-management. We report on the Latent Class Analyses (LCA) performed on the first survey in the various municipalities. Participants were grouped based on motivation, job-search behaviour and capabilities. We aim to profile the beneficiaries on social welfare in these cities and how these profiles relate to perceived health and living conditions. After that (in Sect. 5.5), we report on the analysis of the employment chances of the participants by calculating the actual exit probabilities into paid and unpaid work of those who were entitled to a social assistance benefit in the 2-year period before the experiment started, that is June 2016 to June 2018. These exit probabilities are calculated by a logit regression model in which we include a number of variables, which are known to be important determinants for people's employment opportunities and capabilities, such as gender and age, ethnicity, education level, duration in unemployment, household composition, etc. The findings show huge inequality in employment chances among the welfare recipients and between the various latent classes. In the concluding Sect. 5.6 we formulate some expectations and conclusions about the impact these trust or participation income experiments are likely to have on participants' employment chances, their capabilities, their health, well-being and the wider implications for welfare state policies.

5.2 The Road to a Social Investment and Capacitating Approach[1]

According to many welfare state observers, the post-war welfare state evolution in Europe was marked by three stages (Hemerijck, 2013; Pierson, Castles, & Naumann, 2014). The first stage, up to the 1970s, was featured by innovation and expansion, in which citizens were granted comprehensive social rights. Universal rights and countercyclical welfare spending based on Keynesian demand management principles were considered salient for adjustment to recessions and employment. The second stage, during the 1980s and early 1990s, followed after inflationary pressures, caused by wage rises beyond productivity levels, mass unemployment, 'deadlock corporatism' (Hemerijck, 2013) and sluggish growth. It can be characterised as the period of contraction by way of fiscal austerity and retrenchment policies. It was also the era of monetary, supply-side economics to suppress inflation and to free markets from their collective regulation, by reducing the role of the state in favour of the market. This was done through cost-containment (retrenchment policies), privatisation (shifting responsibility from the state to the citizen) and deregulation (for example, reducing labour market rigidity through more lenient employment protection). A similar evolution took place in the Dutch welfare state, resembling the institutional set-up that follows from the mainstream economists' paradigm, oriented at weak coordination, low employment protection, 'stick and carrot' type of

---

[1]The section is based on Groot, Muffels and Verlaat (2019).

unemployment insurance and workfare oriented labour market policies (Delsen, 2002; Hemerijck, 2013). Social policies at local level resembled this neoliberal policy, while embracing the 'stick and carrot' approach and maintaining strong access conditions to social assistance benefits especially. The neoliberal shift became manifest in reforms in social insurance (cutbacks in benefits, shortening of duration, tightening of access-conditions, and so on) and activating labour market policy through 'make work pay' policies (in-work benefits, tax deductions, wage subsidies), combined with stimulating social pacts to barter wage restraint to reduce inflationary pressures for employment sharing (working-time flexibility and parental leave schemes, and so on). In 1993, according to Hemerijck, since the mid-1990s, a third stage set in of what he calls the 'social investment' welfare state (Hemerijck, 2013). The term 'social investment' refers to a welfare state that is pro-active or 'enabling' in creating integration and participation opportunities to its citizens and notably to the disadvantaged (see also Maydell et al., 2006; Morel et al., 2012). The theoretical underpinning of this third stage in the development of the welfare state is according to Hemerijck (2017) associated with inclusive growth and inclusive societies' concepts, which stress the adverse consequences of the widening of the inequality gap between insiders and outsiders on the labour market. Hemerijck (2017) also refers to the transitional labour market approach of Günther Schmid ('making transitions pay'), flexicurity principles (the nexus of promoting flexibilisation while safeguarding employment and income security) and Sen's capability theory to theoretically underpin the 'capacitating' approach (Schmid & Gazier, 2002; Sen, 2004, 2009). Especially Sen's capability approach might be used in this respect for defining a value-based concept of sustainable employment being one of the outcome measures chosen (van der Klink et al., 2016). In Sen's approach, work should reflect the values people consider important for their lives, such as autonomy and free choice, meaning and recognition, and security and trust. We believe that these ideas might provide new avenues to social policy, while they all have the focus on social investment in common. In our view, behavioural economics insights and psychological motivation theories also need to be added to provide a behavioural perspective to this third stage of welfare state policy evolution (Deci & Ryan, 1985; Fehr & Schmidt, 2003). These two theoretical strands, combined with the social investment approach and Sen's capability theory, constituted the theoretical underpinnings of the Dutch local experiments in the Participation Act. The third stage in the welfare state development went parallel with shifting public support for workfare and unconditional basic income (UBI). In 1993, workfare was supported by 59% of the population, whereas 65% of the population was opposed to basic income (cf. Delsen, 2002). Based on evidence from the 2016 European Social Survey, that picture seems to have changed: half of the Dutch population supports UBI (Lee, 2018).

Due to the wake of the economic crisis in 2008, the underlying shift in the Netherlands to a 'capacitating' approach of social policy has not disappeared. However, as argued earlier, it has encountered stronger barriers to its further evolvement, due to the mentioned austerity policies during the crisis that significantly reduced the available budgets for reintegration policies, notably at the local level. The Dutch welfare system is in the welfare regime literature conceived as a hybrid case that is strongly vested on its own corporatist and liberal roots (Goodin, Headey, Muffels, & Dirven, 1999). Dutch activation policies that were implemented since the mid-1990s are still strongly vested on the workfare principle and a 'stick and carrot' approach to activation (see also Delsen, 2011, 2017). This means that even though we believe that the Netherlands are on their way to implement elements of the investment and capacitating approach, this will only gradually and not fully replace the workfare principles on which the system is grounded. The basic income debate has not been influential during the crisis years up to 2015, after which the Netherlands recovered from the economic crisis and became one of the fastest growing economies in the EU. From 2015 on, when the decentralisation of the Participation Act was implemented, for various reasons already explained, the debate on basic income exhibited a revival. The launching of the local experiments with alternative implementation practices of the Participation Act received a lot of media exposure, and this gave further impetus to the debate. On the feasibility of UBI policies in the 28 EU member states see Shanahan, Smith and Srinivasan (Chap. 3).

The social investment approach hinges according to Hemerijck (2017) on three major welfare functions: stocks (raising the quality of human capital), flows (easing life-course transitions) and buffers (maintaining strong minimum-income protection). The capacitating approach therefore also implies a shift from 'making work pay' policies (workfare) to 'making transitions pay' (enabling to act). The latter 'make transitions pay' approach entails investments in people's endowments and capabilities (human capital; opportunities) that equip people with more options to choose and act (easing transitions) or do the things which one has reason to value for their own lives. This is pursued not by penalising, but by capacitating and addressing people's 'intrinsic motivation' through rewarding self-initiative and creating opportunities to act. Providing opportunities to people which match their capacities and talents is much more effective in the long run (improved job matches) even though it not necessarily aligns immediately with workfare principles to quickly reintegrate the unemployed into full-time paid work. In this way people are endowed with more 'free choice' and personal autonomy, which might also mean that there is more room for risk-taking and personal autonomy or self-management. For policy-making, the shift to social investment and 'enabling' would therefore also imply the pursue of social values such as personal autonomy and free choice, but also reciprocity and trust (Muffels, 2014). The build-up of relations of trust in policy activation practices allegedly pays off in the form of skills upgrading, improved job matches and productivity gains, but also in improving people's health and subjective well-being.

5.3 Design and Ideas of the RCT-Experiments

5.3.1 Implementation of the Dutch Experiments and the Research

As of January 1, 2015, the implementation of the Social Assistance Law became decentralised to the municipalities and its name changed into the Participation Act. According to the new Participation Act, the various already existing obligations, such as the obligation to regularly apply for available jobs and to accept job offers selected by the municipality (application and reintegration obligation), were reinforced and became stricter. According to the new law, the welfare recipients now got an even more strict duty to accept work, even if it does not fit their skills or occupational background (reintegration obligation). Another change is that recipients must be willing to commute up to 3 h. However, probably the most significant change is that under the new law, the municipality specifies what welfare recipients have to do in return for keeping their benefits, varying from volunteer work to insertion into local societal activities (in Dutch *'Tegenprestatie'*). Failure to fulfill these obligations under this *quid pro quo* requirement may result in a reduction of the benefit. This is also the case when the beneficiary's efforts to regain work are judged unsatisfactory, or when he/she does not obey to the strict access conditions and rules (cf. Groot et al., 2019). These stricter requirements had very little success in getting people back to work, for which reason the municipalities requested the Government to allow them to experiment with alternative ways of supervision and reintegration. As of February, 2017, a new Article 83 of the Participation Act came into force. Six municipalities (Utrecht, Tilburg, Groningen, Deventer, Nijmegen and Wageningen) were then admitted to experiment according to this new Article 83 in the Participation Act. Another five municipalities: Amsterdam, Apeldoorn, Epe, Oss and Geldrop-Mierlo, used the existing room in the Participation Act to reform their implementation practices (not-Article 83 municipalities in Table 5.1). The not-Article 83 municipalities were allowed to relax the strict obligations and to pursue intensive tailor-made support following the rules of the Participation Act. However, they are not able to relax the strict withdrawal rules of additional earnings, which is only allowed for municipalities which are formally admitted to experiment according to Article 83. Nine out of 11 municipalities have finished the recruiting of participants for their experiment after they started in the fall of 2017. On the Nijmegen experiment see Betkó et al., Chap. 6. The municipalities of Utrecht and Amsterdam, but also Geldrop-Mierlo, started later in mid-2018. At the end of 2018, a total of more than 3500 social assistance beneficiaries were already participating in these experiments. In the end, more than 5000 welfare recipients are likely to be participating, consisting of about 8% of the target population of social assistance beneficiaries in the ten ongoing experiments. Table 5.1 gives an overview of the number of participants in these local experiments.

In our view, the social assistance experiments in the Netherlands can be seen as a way to shift local social policy practices into a social investment or 'capacitating'

Table 5.1 Social assistance (SA) (target) population and participants of the Dutch trust experiments (Article 83 and Not-Article 83 municipalities)

Municipalities			Participants	
	SA population	Target population	Application	Realisation
Article 83 municipalities				
Tilburg	8200	6000	800	703
Wageningen	800	800	300	408
Deventer	3117	3117	1000	553
Utrecht	12,500	8100	900	780
Nijmegen	8000	5000	400	270
Groningen	11,000	8744	700	891
Subtotal	43,617	31,761	4100	3625
Not-Article 83 municipalities				
Apeldoorn/Epe	4300	3425	540	495
Oss	2225	1500	300	300
Geldrop-Mierlo	890	890	90	50
Amsterdam	42,000	42,000	750	750
Subtotal	48,525	46,925	1590	1545
Total	93,032	79,576	5780	5220

approach, even though they are yet in their infancy, and workfare policies are still mainstream. The experiments give more room to the municipalities for experimenting with tailor-made, integrated, demand-oriented and intensive mediation policies (although Article 83 requirements are rather strict and do not provide much space for experimenting, e.g. by relaxing the earnings withdrawal rules). The experiments aim to relax the rather strict 'workfare-based' rules and obligations. Following Sen's ideas, the relaxation of the obligations in these experiments should give the participants more room and time (free choice) to pursue goals that people consider best for their lives. The strict monitoring of the rules and obligations are conceived as reflecting distrust, whereas these ideas underlying the experiments are based on the assumption that building up trust through supporting and coaching people, and by creating integration and participation opportunities is likely to be more effective in the longer run. The aim of the various experiments is also to improve the motivation and capabilities of the citizen to take up one's own responsibility (self-management) for achieving the things in life they consider important.

5.3.2 Underlying Policy Theory: Ideas and Insights

The local municipalities needed to formulate the underlying 'policy theory' and the theoretical underpinnings in detail in the application form of the experiment to be accepted under the heading of the experimentation Article 83. The hypotheses and assumptions underlying the local experiments were also asked for in detail.

All municipalities formulated such a policy theory which was grounded on five insights from a wide range of literatures, and which formed their theoretical underpinnings:

- The first insight concerns recent findings on the impact of poverty on people's mind-set. Research in this relatively new field of study by Mani, Mullainathan, Shafir, and Zhao (2013) and Mullainathan and Shafir (2013) demonstrates that (financial) scarcity and poverty stress reduces people's cognitive resources. Assuming that financial scarcity and compliance activities consume large parts of claimants' cognitive resources, little is left for other important and cognitively challenging tasks, such as job search;
- The second insight from behavioural economics concerns the role of implicit values underlying welfare state institutions and practices for behaviour, such as reciprocity and trust. Reciprocity means that individuals reward favours (positive reciprocity), while taking revenge when being harmed (negative reciprocity) (Fehr & Schmidt, 2003). Negative incentives such as the benefit sanctions in social welfare systems might not be the best way to induce cooperative and compliant behaviour. Experimental economics also showed that people, in response to received trust, tend to be extra motivated to put more effort in their task, and by doing so reward the trustor. Trust in this way generates feelings of positive reciprocity and therewith sustained effort and increased productivity (Bohnet, Frey, & Huck, 2001);
- The third insight stems from psychological motivation theories and refers to the observation that extrinsic incentives can crowd out intrinsic motivation (Frey & Jegen, 2001). Self-determination theory (Deci & Ryan, 1985) suggests that intrinsically motivated people engage in an activity because they find it enjoyable and interesting, and because of that show more behavioural effectiveness, persistence and enhanced well-being (Ryan, Kuhl, & Deci, 1997) . The theory also states that putting trust in people generates feelings of 'self-efficacy' with salient effects on job search and sustainable employment. Previous research also shows that one can effectively strengthen intrinsic motivation by, amongst others, conveying the activity as choice rather than as control;
- The last insight also pertains to 'free choice' and refers to Sen's capability theory. According to Sen, capabilities are the choices people are offered to do the things they consider important for their own lives (referring to people's 'intrinsic motivation'). This way people are offered opportunities which fit their motivation and which improve their personal autonomy and self-confidence, while enhancing their well-being (Sen, 2004, 2009). As argued earlier, Sen's capability approach is very well suited to construct a value-based measure for sustainable employment (van der Klink et al., 2016).

These insights shaped the design of the experiments and the definition of the treatment groups. Inspiration for these behavioural insights as a tool for social policy-making can be found in Nobel laureate Richard Thaler's ideas on nudging; encouraging people to behave in their broad self-interest (Thaler & Sunstein, 2008).

As explained before, similar insights also constituted the theoretical underpinnings of the third 'social investment' stage in the evolution of welfare state policies.

(Dis)similarities with Basic Income

The local experiments are called trust experiments, for the initial idea was to render people more trust by exempting them from the standard application and re-integration obligations. Below we give some more detail on these experiments:

- In all experiments a shift takes place from sanctioning and penalising the efforts of the clients (by way of sanctioning and benefit cuts) to rewarding effort. Finding work, even if it is for a small number of weekly hours, is rewarded with a higher income by reducing the withdrawal rate at which earnings are subtracted from the benefit, from the current 75% in the first 6 months and 100% with longer durations of stay in social assistance, to 50% for the entire two-year experimenting period. This feature resembles the features of a basic income scheme, notably of a Negative Income Tax (NIT), according to which the basic income is gradually taxed away and returns zero at a certain income threshold. The income threshold in all local experiments is implicitly set at 120% of the social assistance level, because people are allowed to earn additionally a maximum of € 200 per month, which is 20% of the basic social assistance allowance of a single person;
- The focus is on safeguarding a more or less unconditional right on a minimum income and rewarding people's own efforts and initiatives, whereby the reintegration is not limited to paid full-time work only, but allows for a broader range of social integration measures and outcomes (bridge and part-time employment, education, self-management, well-being, health and social participation). The unconditionality of the income support breaks with the conditionality in the Participation Act, even though reciprocity, defined by the expectation that clients need to be motivated to participate in the experiment and to engage in participation activities, is still the leading principle in all experiments;
- Most cities acknowledge that some sort of reciprocity is needed, but that this can take different forms, such as the client showing its own-initiative, own-responsibility and efforts in improving his/her chances for work or social integration. In their view, unconditionality is not a reward for laziness, but a different way of activating the client and for creating opportunities for integration. This way of tailor-made supervision and coaching tunes better with scientific insights in behavioural economics and psychological motivation theories, and also seems to mirror a mature relationship between government and citizen, based on trust and common interests. Even though the reciprocity principle is maintained, the more relaxed way of monitoring clients and the willingness to keep trust in the client that he or she is not misusing the welfare benefit resembles the basic features of a basic income schemes to some extent;
- All cities express the importance of performing evaluation research to assess the effects of the various treatments in the local experiments: not only on employment, also on social integration, health, human capital and capabilities, objective and subjective well-being, and quality of life outcomes. The expectation is that the new treatment of social assistance claimants will also especially improve the

motivation, health and well-being of the beneficiaries to resemble the expected salient outcomes of basic income experiments again on these indicators, as is also illustrated in evaluation research of NIT experiments in the United States and Canada in the 1970s (cf. Groot, 2004).

5.3.3 The Design of the Local Experiments; The Various Treatments

The various treatments in the design of the local experiments differ to some extent. Essentially, they all want to examine the effects of four separate treatments:

1. *The self-management and exemption group.* Participants are expected to help themselves in re-entry to work. The idea is that beneficiaries need to learn how to help themselves through acting pro-actively and with confidence, that is, through self-management. The participants are exempted from the existing application and re-integration obligations. They might (Tilburg, Nijmegen, Groningen, Deventer, Utrecht and Wageningen) or might not (Amsterdam, Apeldoorn/Epe, Oss, Geldrop-Mierlo) be subject to the reduced withdrawal rate of earnings. In Tilburg, participants may get an additional exit premium of € 2400 when the recipient exit the benefit through finding full-time paid work;
2. *The earnings release group.* The additional earnings of participants, when they are able to find paid work, will be withheld from the benefit at a rate of 50%, instead of 75 or 100% in the standard case. This group is hence rewarded for their attempts to find work and earn a living through working;
3. *The tailor-made supervision group.* Participants get extra support through tailor-made supervision and intensive mediation. They have contact with their (work) coach or contact person at the municipality office more frequently, and the treatment of the client is demand-driven instead of supply-driven, *i.e.* the wishes and expectations of the client are leading for the content of the treatment;
4. *The standard treatment group.* Participants in this group get the standard treatment as was conducted in the period before the experiments started. They are, of course, subject to the existing strict application and re-integration obligations.

The Dutch local experiments are not shaped according to an unconditional basic income (UBI) for everyone, but according to a guaranteed minimum or less conditional participation income for low income people on social welfare. They are also rather different from the NIT experiments in the United States and Canada in the late 1960s and early 1970s (cf. Groot, 2004). There are some similarities though, e.g. with respect to the chosen experimental RCT (Randomised Controlled Trial) design and the choice of the treatment groups, notably the earnings release treatment group (cf. Groot et al., 2019).

5.3.4 Evaluation Research of the RCT-Experiments

The 11 local experiments are all designed as RCT-experiments, which means that the social assistance beneficiaries are randomly assigned to the four treatment groups. Respondents sign an agreement with the social assistance office, in which they commit themselves to actively participate in the research by filling in the three survey questionnaires over the two-year period. They also need to declare to positively cooperate with the municipality and to actively engage in the specific treatment they are randomly assigned to. This means that the participants have no unconditional right on a minimum guarantee as in an UBI scheme, because at least a weak form of reciprocity is assumed in the design of the experiments.

Surveys will be held among the participants to assess the effects of the experiment with a view to the broad set of outcome measures chosen. Even though the primary aim of the national government of these local experiments is to increase the number of people fully exiting out of the social welfare benefit through reintegration into full-time paid work, for the municipalities the experiments are also considered a success when they contribute to improving the social participation of their clients and/or their health and well-being. Hence, the range of outcome measures to be taken into consideration by the municipalities is broader than exit into paid work only. The process evaluation contains a questionnaire on the mediation process of the individual respondent to be filled in by the case-workers. In addition, at regular occasions (every 6–9 months) focus group meetings are held with the project leader(s) and the case-workers about their experiences with the renewed treatment (in total three or four meetings).

5.3.4.1 Methodology: Data and Outcome Measures

The experiments in the four cities started in October 2017. After 9 months, as shown in Table 5.1, the achieved number of social assistance beneficiaries actually participating in these experiments appears to be 1800 out of a target population of 1900 initially. The total number of participants in all experiments will in the end be about 5200. The participant samples in the four municipalities appear to be fairly representative for their targeted social assistance population. Not all beneficiaries are selected. People living in institutions are excluded, as well as people with a full disability benefit (*Wet Werk en Inkomen naar Arbeidsvermogen*, WIA). People over 64 and migrants who are not able to speak or understand Dutch are also excluded from the experiment. In Tilburg and Nijmegen, the youngsters up to 27 years of age were not allowed to be part of the experiment, because they are subject to a dedicated reintegration programme which would interfere with the treatments in the experiment. In the other two cities, youngsters are allowed to participate and are even overrepresented, whereas the older beneficiaries are underrepresented. The low-educated are slightly underrepresented in all cities. Selection bias in the city of Nijmegen experiment is addressed in detail by Betkó et al. in Chap. 6.

Participant surveys are to be held three times over the two-yearly experimentation period. This will enable us to assess the longer-term treatment effects. The data for the analyses in this chapter are derived from the first survey that was taken during the period October 2017–September 2018. The number of participants and survey respondents is shown in Table 5.1.

The first participant questionnaire contains some 40 questions covering the following topics: subjective health, subjective well-being, perception of one's capabilities, self-efficacy and self-confidence, social trust, institutional trust, work attitudes, job-search behaviour, disability, social participation, social networks, opinions on support by the municipality and the financial situation. The first survey was held during or shortly after the first meeting of the case-worker with the social welfare recipient who has declared to be willing to take part in the experiment. Participants are allowed to fill in the questionnaire at home before the first talk with the case-worker when they wish to do so. Those who indicated that they are unable to fill in the online questionnaire are allowed to fill in a paper questionnaire. Only a very small minority (less than 3%) did that.

5.3.4.2 Outcome Measures

The outcome measures were, as much as possible, defined in correspondence with the international standard classifications. Entry into paid work is translated here as the likelihood of obtaining a job with as many hours as needed to escape from social assistance. A definition of sustainable employment is less straightforward, because sustainability might be defined in terms of security or stability of work, or in terms of people's fitness to the job. In Sect. 5.2 we already referred to Sen's capability concept that can be used to define a value-based measure of sustainable employability. In the questionnaire we included a list of seven capability indicators aimed at measuring this concept. The definitions for subjective well-being use the standard zero to ten scale of people's judgement about the level of satisfaction with life. In addition, people's level of happiness is asked for and people's perception of their meaning of life (Diener, Suh, Lucas, & Smith, 1999; Veenhoven, 1996). The definition of health is standard and subjective while making a distinction between physical and mental health. For a complete list we refer to Tables 5.2 and 5.3, in

Table 5.2 Operationalisation of the health and well-being measures (acronyms and brief questionnaire wording)

Societal activities		Physical limitations		Mental limitations	
CHCA	Care for children		Health issues	PERS	Personal problems
STUD	Study	HDCAP	Handicap	REL	Relation problems
VOL	Volunteer work	PDISA	Partly disabled	DEBT	Debts
		ADDDR	Addicted to drugs/ alcohol	ADDGA	Addicted to gaming
		PHEA	Physical health issues	MHEA	Mental health issues
		PREGN	Pregnant		

5 Job Search, Employment Capabilities and Well-being of People on...

Table 5.3 Operationalisation of the other outcome measures

Concept	Variable	Label	Min	Max
Capabilities		Things which are considered important in life but which one currently does not have or can do	1	5
	CAP1	To do the things for which one got an education or training	1	5
	CAP2	To learn new things in life	1	5
	CAP3	Co-participation in say in work or life	1	5
	CAP4	Having good contacts with other people	1	5
	CAP5	To set one's own goals/targets	1	5
	CAP6	Have sufficient income	1	5
	CAP7	Meaningful contribution to the life of others	1	5
Subjective well-being	SWB1	Satisfied with current living situation	0	10
	SWB2	Do you consider the things you do in life meaningful?	0	10
	SWB3	Did you feel happy the last couple of weeks	1	5
Self-Efficacy	SE1	I can find paid work if put effort in it	1	5
	SE2	I will find work in the future	1	5
	SE3	I can make a good impression if I want to	1	5
	SE4	I can find a job that fits my experience and education	1	5
Participation	SOCP	Feel myself part of society	0	10
Social trust	STRUST	Most people can be trusted	0	10
Societal activities	HRLCA	Hours per week spent to care for relatives	0	60
	HVOL	Hours per week spent to volunteer work	0	60
	HEDU	Hours per week spent to education/training	0	60
	HCHCA	Hours per week spent to care for children	0	60
Material deprivation		Cannot afford the things I consider a necessity		
	DEP1	One time a day eating vegetables or fruit		1
	DEP2	One meal a day with meat, chicken or fish		1
	DEP3	Two pairs of shoes		1
	DEP4	Laptop or desktop computer		1
	DEP5	Leisure activities outside the family		1
	DEP6	To celebrate special occasions		1
	DEP7	Once a year going on holidays abroad		1
	DEP8	Replacement of worn-out furniture		1
	DEP9	Replacement of housing amenities		1
	DEP10	Replacement of clothes		1
	DEP11	Once a month going out for a dinner		1
	DEP12	Regularly participating in leisure activities		1
	DEP13	Access to internet		1
	DEP14	Make use of public transport facilities		1
Poverty	FSIT	What is the financial situation of your household? (have to use my savings, have to make debts, can just make ends meet, can save a little, can save a lot)	1–5	

which most operationalisations of the variables in the participants' first survey of the four Dutch social assistance experiments are listed.

5.4 Research Questions and Empirical Analyses of the First Survey Data

The second part of the chapter deals with the analyses of the first participants' survey in four out of the 11 municipalities: Apeldoorn, Oss, Tilburg and Wageningen. Two research questions were formulated. One question on the differences in motivation, job-search behaviour and the capabilities of welfare recipients, and how that translates into specific outcomes as shown in various participants' profiles (Latent Class Analysis). The other question on the inequality of (re)employment probabilities between welfare recipients with different levels of education and years of stay in social assistance (binary logit regression).

5.4.1 Latent Class Analysis: Profiling of Participants of Four Dutch Experiments

In the first step of the analysis, we aim at researching the behavioural responses of these welfare recipients to their situation, in particular their job-search behaviour and how that translates into a specific profile of their health and living conditions. The theoretical framework stems from Sen's capability theory, behavioural economics and motivational psychology. It departs from the distinction between what people want to achieve as shown through their motivation and job-search behaviour, and what they in reality can achieve given their capabilities and the opportunities they have or the barriers they face. With respect to the first research question, the hypothesis to be tested is that the motivation, job-search behaviour and abilities of welfare recipients (what they want to achieve and what they can achieve) differ, due to differences in their work experience, skills, and duration of stay in social assistance. We therefore selected a number of, in our view, important indicators of their search behaviour and abilities, and applied an LCA (Latent Class Analysis) to get a better picture of these differences. In the second step we examined to what extent these differences in search behaviour and abilities translate into unequal health and living conditions. The chosen indicators are listed in Table 5.4.

In Table 5.5, the outcomes of the LCA estimations for the four municipalities are shown. The analyses were performed on the 1474 completed questionnaires by September 1, 2018.

Table 5.6 presents more detail on the scores on each of the variables included in the analyses, *i.e.* the differences in job search and perceived employment chances of the participants in the four cities.

5 Job Search, Employment Capabilities and Well-being of People on... 123

Table 5.4 Operationalisation of indicators of motivation and abilities regarding paid work

What people want: job-search behaviour	What people can: abilities and barriers to work
Number of job applied for in the last 4 weeks	Can start with a paid job within 2 weeks of time
Actively searching for a job for at least 1 h a week	Reasons for not being able to start within 2 weeks of time disability:
Want to search for a paid job in near future	Cannot start due to mental health problems Cannot start due to physically impairments Cannot start due to participation in volunteer work, care for children or study for more than 24 h a week

Source: Muffels and van der Klink (2017)

Table 5.5 Profiles of survey respondents participating in four Dutch trust experiments: results of LCA model estimations (N = 1474)

Indicators	Passive, work-unfit (ph)	Passive, work-unfit (mh)	Passive, work-fit	Active, work-fit	Total
Apeldoorn/Epe					
N =	63	142	62	173	440
%	14.32	32.27	14.09	39.32	100.00
Oss					
N =	75	38		135	248
%	30.24	15.32		54.44	100.00
Tilburg					
N =	141	163	43	160	507
%	27.81	32.15	8.48	31.56	100.00
Wageningen					
N =	93	67		119	279
%	33.33	24.01		42.65	100.00

ph physical health issues, *mh* mental health issues
Source: Data from first participants' survey by September 1, 2018

In the four cities about 75% (Tilburg, Oss) to 85% (Apeldoorn/Epe, Wageningen) of the participants on July 1, 2018 had completed the first survey. In all municipalities the number of latent classes that best describes the various patterns in search behaviour and abilities is either three (Wageningen, Oss) or four (Apeldoorn/Epe, Tilburg).

The cluster of 'work-fit' participants are either still actively searching for a job, or are discouraged and not searching anymore because they accepted that they are unable to fulfil the requirements of the labour market. In Wageningen and Oss, about 42–54% of the participants belong to the first active, work-fit category, in Tilburg and Apeldoorn/Epe this is only one third (32%) to 39% (see Table 5.5). A substantial part (25–30%) of this active, work-fit category, however, still faces health problems; either physical or mental ones. The mirror image is that the share of passive, work-unfit people is rather large in these four cities, ranging from 45 to 67% of the

Table 5.6 Job search and perceived employment chances of the participants in four of the Dutch trust experiments

Indicators	Cluster 1	Cluster 2	Cluster 3	Cluster 4	All clusters
Apeldoorn/Epe	*Passive, work-unfit (ph)*	*Passive, work-unfit (mh)*	*Passive, work-fit*	*Active, work-fit*	*All*
Applying for jobs (%)	1.6	4.9	19.4	100.0	43.9
Active searching (%)	11.1	12.0	27.4	100.0	48.6
Can start within 2 weeks (%)	30.2	56.3	77.4	85.5	67.0
Want to search for job next 4 weeks (%)	15.9	0.0	100.0	78.6	47.3
Perception being unfit for work (%)	87.3	73.9	46.8	29.5	54.5
Physically work-unfit (%)	100.0	0.0	0.0	22.0	23.0
Mentally work-unfit (%)	0.0	42.3	14.5	12.7	20.7
Participating ($\geq$ 24 hours a week) in care or education (%)	39.7	47.9	48.4	41.6	44.3
N =	63	142	62	173	440
Percent	14	32	14	39	100
Oss	*Passive, work-unfit (ph)*	*Passive, work-unfit (mh)*		*Active, work-fit*	*Total*
Applying for jobs (%)	0.00	15.79		80.74	46.37
Actively searching for a job (%)	0.00	23.68		96.30	56.05
Want to search for a job next 4 months (%)	24.00	5.26		64.44	43.15
Can start with a paid job within 2 weeks of time (%)	84.00	7.89		97.04	79.44
Perception of disability (%)	62.67	97.37		24.44	47.18
Physical health problems (%)	34.67	0.00		22.96	22.98
Mental health problems (%)	29.33	100.00		23.70	37.10
Cannot start work for alternative activities (%)	25.33	42.11		28.89	29.84
N =	75	38		135	248
Percent	30.24	15.32		54.44	100
Tilburg	*Passive, work-unfit (ph)*	*Passive, work-unfit (mh)*	*Passive, work-fit*	*Active, work-fit*	*Total*
Applying for jobs (%)	0.00	0.00	2.33	73.75	23.47
Actively searching for a job (%)	0.00	9.20	0.00	96.25	33.33
Want to search for a job next 4 months (%)	0.00	9.20	100.00	58.75	29.98
Can start with a paid job within 2 weeks of time (%)	46.81	43.56	60.47	91.25	60.95
Perception of disability (%)	56.03	83.44	44.19	27.50	54.83
Physical health problems (%)	56.03	0.00	51.16	22.50	27.02

(continued)

Table 5.6 (continued)

Indicators	Cluster 1	Cluster 2	Cluster 3	Cluster 4	All clusters
Mental health problems (%)	0.00	100.00	0.00	25.63	40.24
Cannot start work for alternative activities (%)	48.94	41.72	44.19	48.13	45.96
N =	141	163	43	160	507
Percent	27.81	32.15	8.48	31.56	100
Wageningen	*Passive, low work-fit*	*Passive, work-unfit (mh)*		*Active, work-fit*	*Total*
Applying for jobs (%)	0.00	1.49		68.07	29.39
Actively searching for a job (%)	0.00	5.97		96.64	42.65
Want to search for a job next 4 months (%)	54.84	44.78		90.76	67.74
Can start with a paid job within 2 weeks of time (%)	32.26	17.91		63.03	41.94
Physical health problems (%)	44.09	0.00		18.49	22.58
Mental health problems (%)	0.00	100.00		21.01	32.97
Perception of disability (%)	44.09	79.10		31.09	46.95
Cannot start work for alternative activities (%)	45.16	26.87		42.86	39.78
N =	93	67		119	279
Percent	33.33	24.01		42.65	100

ph Physical health issues, *mh* Mental health issues
Source: Participants' first survey October 2017–September 2018

participants' population under scrutiny. A rather large fraction of the participants in the experiments faces physical and mental health issues (57% in Wageningen and 60% in Tilburg).

An obvious explanation for these different outcomes across the municipalities is not easily found, but it might be that the locally coloured reintegration policies of the municipalities in particular play a role here. We might presume that a more activating and supporting policy approach in Wageningen and Oss, compared with a more distant 'stick and carrot' approach in Tilburg and Apeldoorn/Epe, might have played a part for their better performance in re-inserting people into the labour market. The profiles of the population of participants in all four municipalities show a rather gloomy picture about the labour market opportunities of people enrolled in social welfare programmes.

The hypothesis on the large differences between welfare recipients in what they want and what they in reality can achieve seems herewith to be confirmed. The latent-class-model solution that fitted the data best in the four cities seems fairly robust with respect to how sensitive it is to changes in the selected indicators and in the sample composition. The LCA-solution found in the various cities is technically sound, because there is a very good fit according to the various fit indices (p-value;

Table 5.7 Fit indices for the LCA model estimations in four Dutch trust experiments

Fit indices	Tilburg	Apeldoorn/Epe	Wageningen	Oss
N clusters	4	4	3	3
p-value	0.000	0.030	0.004	0.006
Dissimilarity index	0.261	0.266	0.364	0.413
Classification error	0.017	0.015	0.019	0.035
R^2 standard	0.961	0.962	0.949	0.898
BIC	4655.055	4077.483	2677.367	2336.233
Log likelihood	−2219.000	−1932.223	−1265.478	−1099.199
Robust estimation se	Yes	Yes	Yes	Yes
N =	507	440	279	248

Source: Data from first participants' survey by September 1, 2018

log-likelihood ratio and Bayesian Information Criterion (BIC)) and there is a strong distinction between the classes, while the number of classification errors in the data is small (no more than 4%). The analyses are carried out with Latent Gold 5.1. Table 5.7 shows the results.

5.4.2 Inequality of Outcomes: Self-efficacy, Health and Well-being

In the second step we tried to find out to what extent the differences in what people want and can achieve also translate into high inequality of people's health and living conditions across the latent classes. Apart from a high level of inequality, we also expect a poor level of health and living conditions overall (indicated by low well-being, high level of deprivation and lack of free choice or capabilities). This is important, because the aims of the municipalities with the experiments are, apart from improving the welfare recipients' labour market chances, to improve their health and living conditions. For the municipalities, these outcome measures determine the level of success or failure of the experiments. Figure 5.1 shows the outcome profiles disaggregated by the various LCA clusters. The following outcome measures are used: the perception of self-efficacy, the perceived level of social participation, one's subjective health, the perception of one's own fitness for work, the subjective well-being (the average of life-satisfaction, happiness and meaning of life), the perception of one's opportunities or capabilities (based on seven indicators), and the number of people out of poverty and out of material deprivation (x out of 10).

Figure 5.1 shows that the two work-unfit clusters (the red and blue lines) perform worse with respect to most of the outcome measures, except for the number of people out of poverty which is about six to seven out of ten. That means that 30–40% of the participants consider themselves poor (defined as cannot make ends meet) in all

5 Job Search, Employment Capabilities and Well-being of People on...

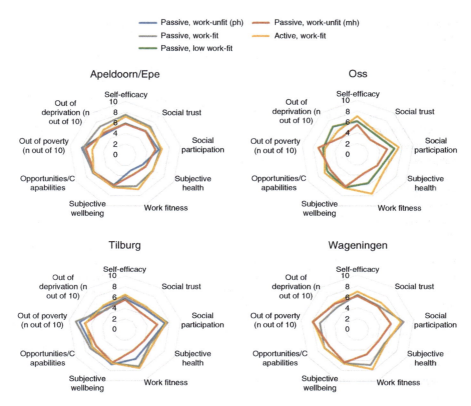

Fig. 5.1 Inequality of outcomes across latent clusters of welfare recipients partaking in Dutch trust experiments

clusters in all municipalities. The two groups perform worse, especially with respect to the perception of their self-efficacy, the level of social trust, the level of social participation and the perceived level of capabilities. The achievements on these latter indicators are rather low; at or below six on a scale of zero to ten. In Table 5.8 more detail is given on the scores on these outcome measures, *i.e.* the inequality in outcomes across the three or four clusters in the four municipalities.

5.5 Inequality of Access to Employment

The second research question deals with the inequality of access to employment across the social assistance population. Due to the short period of experimentation to date, we cannot present reliable figures on the impact of the various treatments on exit into employment yet. The results will become available after the two-year period of experimentation, at the end of 2019 or early 2020. We will then be able to view the

Table 5.8 Perceived living conditions at the first survey based on the various outcome measures by LCA cluster

Apeldoorn/Epe	Passive, work-unfit (ph)	Passive, work-unfit (mh)	Passive, work-fit	Active, work-fit	Total
Self-efficacy	5.88	5.79	7.53	7.21	6.61
Social trust	5.65	5.68	6.98	6.59	6.22
Social participation	6.06	5.51	6.40	6.73	6.19
Subjective health	3.56	4.31	5.77	5.71	4.96
Work fitness	3.03	3.94	6.10	6.83	5.25
Subjective well-being	5.94	6.07	6.28	6.40	6.21
Opportunities/ capabilities	6.50	6.41	6.72	6.50	6.50
Out of (n out of 10)	7.9	7.2	7.6	6	7.9
Out of deprivation (n out of 10)	5.20	5.60	6.90	6.00	5.90
N =	63	142	62	173	440
Percent	14	32	14	39	100
Oss	Passive, low work-fit	Passive, work-unfit (mh)		Active, work-fit	Total
Self-efficacy	6.21	5.54		7.08	6.58
Social trust	4.83	3.53		5.37	4.92
Social participation	6.60	5.38		7.45	6.87
Subjective health	4.80	4.05		5.54	5.09
Work fitness	5.58	3.62		7.71	6.43
Subjective well-being	6.39	6.31		6.59	6.49
Opportunities/ capabilities	6.20	5.57		6.71	6.39
Out of poverty (n out of 10)	6.30	7.04		5.92	6.20
Out of deprivation (n out of 10)	6.67	4.21		5.48	5.65
N =	75	38		135	248
Percent	30.24	15.32		54.44	100
Tilburg	Passive, work-unfit (ph)	Passive, work-unfit (mh)	Passive, work-fit	Active, work-fit	
Self-efficacy	5.86	5.54	6.29	6.51	6.00
Social trust	5.25	4.23	5.56	5.63	5.06
Social participation	7.15	5.78	7.70	7.45	6.85
Subjective health	4.87	3.95	5.16	5.71	4.86
Work fitness	5.73	4.12	7.23	7.62	5.93
Subjective well-being	6.85	6.45	6.62	6.62	6.63
Opportunities/ capabilities	6.65	5.96	7.01	6.54	6.43

(continued)

Table 5.8 (continued)

Apeldoorn/Epe	Passive, work-unfit (ph)	Passive, work-unfit (mh)	Passive, work-fit	Active, work-fit	Total
Out of poverty (n out of 10)	8.09	7.23	8.89	7.06	7.55
Out of deprivation (n out of 10)	5.60	5.09	4.88	5.88	5.46
N =	141	163	43	160	507
Percent	27.81	32.15	8.48	31.56	100
Wageningen	*Passive, low work-fit*	*Passive, work-unfit (mh)*		*Active, work-fit*	*Total*
Self-efficacy	6.38	6.19		6.95	6.58
Social trust	5.70	5.61		6.42	5.98
Social participation	8.26	5.91		7.79	7.49
Subjective health	5.29	4.21		5.61	5.17
Work fitness	6.83	4.75		7.66	6.68
Subjective well-being	6.56	6.38		6.63	6.55
Opportunities/capabilities	6.71	5.79		6.67	6.47
Out of poverty (n out of 10)	6.71	7.89		7.80	7.47
Out of deprivation (n out of 10)	5.38	6.12		6.22	5.91
N =	93	67		119	279
Percent	33.33	24.01		42.65	100

ph Physical health issues, *mh* Mental health issues
Source: Participants' first survey October 2017–September 2018

effects of the treatments on exit into paid work, but also on social participation, self-management, well-being and health. However, for the period during which we collected data at the municipalities, stretching from the beginning of 2015 to July 2018, we are able to calculate the actual and theoretical exit probabilities into paid work for the beneficiaries of social assistance, including the participants of the local experiments in the various treatments for the years 2016–2018. Since the experiment will last for 2 years, we present the calculated 2-year exit probabilities into paid work in this section.

5.5.1 Administrative Data

The administrative files of the municipalities have been used to calculate the actual and theoretical yearly exit probability into paid work. The exit chances are likely to improve over time, due to the alternative treatment in the experiment. In the next

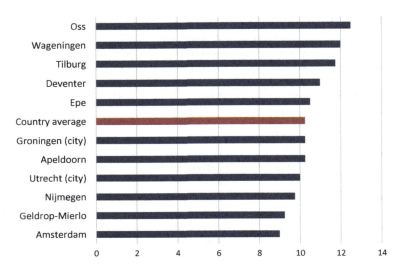

Fig. 5.2 Yearly (actual) exit probabilities for 11 Dutch cities in % of total population on January 1 moving out from social assistance into a paid job, 2016–2018

stage of the research, the actual exit chances will be compared with the theoretical ones in the beginning.

To calculate these exit probabilities, all people who are receiving a social assistance benefit and who are registered at the municipal social assistance offices since January 2015 to August 2018 are selected. The exit probabilities are known to be rather small. From the administrative Statistics Netherlands (*Centraal Bureau voor de Statistiek*, CBS) files, the exit probabilities into paid work between 2016 and 2018 are calculated for the 11 cities currently experimenting, including the four cities that are included in the analysis here (see Fig. 5.2). The average exit probability for these experimenting cities was just over 10% per year in the period 2016–2018, but varying a lot across cities, as well as across subgroups of welfare recipients. The lowest exit rates were found in the cities of Amsterdam, Geldrop-Mierlo and Nijmegen, and the highest in Tilburg, Wageningen and Oss. These are the actual exit rates into paid work. The municipal data show that the average benefit duration is about 2 years, but with very long spells in all cities. The longest spell was found in Oss with 39 years.

In the third step, theoretical exit probabilities are calculated by estimating a binary logit regression model on exit into paid work (robust estimation), in which the duration of the spell was included as one of the regressors. In addition, a number of control variables were added to correct for composition effects and selective non-response such as for age and age squared, gender, education level, ethnicity, having a minimum level of qualification for the labour market, the household situation (single *vs.* married) and the housing situation (renter or owner). A few variables were added indicating the support practices of the municipality, such as

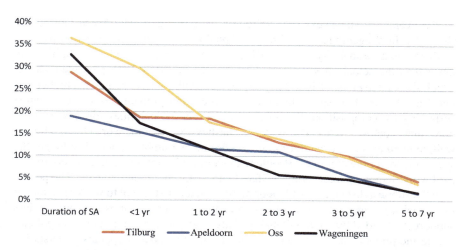

Fig. 5.3 Predicted exit probabilities of social assistance beneficiaries by benefit (SA) duration, June 1, 2016–June 1, 2018 in four experimenting cities. Source: Municipal BUS (social assistance benefit statistics) data 2015–2018

whether people are receiving services for support in handling debts,[2] or whether they get a loan, or whether they are sanctioned and benefits are reduced. Eventually, a variable was included indicating the distance to the labour market as estimated by the case-worker. In some cities this scale is called a 'stepladder' or a 'customer profile'. In practice, it is a scale ranging from 1 to 6; 1 indicates a socially excluded person with very poor chances to find a job in due time, and 6 indicates a short distance to the labour market and a high likelihood to find paid work on short notice. The model estimations show that age and age squared (younger and older people are less likely to find work), education level (having a starter qualification or not), gender, the household situation (single or couple), spell duration, and the labour market distance scale contributed most to the explanatory power of the model. The people who entered social assistance before June 1, 2016 and either stayed or left for accepting work after June 1, 2016 up to June 1, 2018 (for Tilburg July 1) were then selected.[3] This way it was possible to examine exit probabilities for a period of 2 years, which is also the period of experimenting. In Fig. 5.3 the calculated exit probabilities are plotted by the duration of the allowance spells. Figures are shown for the four cities Tilburg, Oss, Apeldoorn/Epe and Wageningen.

---

[2] According to the Natural Persons *Debt Restructuring* Act (*Wet schuldsanering natuurlijke personen*, Wsnp) Dutch municipalities are obliged to help their residents with problematic debts. The main objective of the Wsnp is to offer (financial) perspective to individuals in a desperate financial situation as a result of debts.

[3] We used the period of June 1, 2016 to June 1, 2018 even though we had data up to September 1. The reason is that the data are administratively corrected by the municipality on a two monthly basis.

The average predicted exit probability for this 2-year period is 15% in Tilburg and Oss, 14% in Wageningen and 9.8% in Apeldoorn/Epe, which means an average predicted exit probability of 5–7.5% per year. The predicted probabilities are lower than the actual rates from the CBS figures for 2016–2018 presented earlier, which show an average of 10% per year. Oss and Tilburg have somewhat higher exit rates, notably at short spell durations. The predicted probabilities decrease when correcting for composition differences, notably the probabilities for shorter durations, that is below 2 years. The evidence clarifies how poor the work chances for the welfare recipients are, even during this economic favourable period. The longer the spells, the lower the exit rates. People with short spells are much more likely to find paid work than people receiving welfare benefits for more than 2 years. The people with the shortest distance to the labour market are the first to exit to work. The longer the social assistance spell lasts, the poorer the job opportunities are, but the less support is provided by the municipality. This might be due to retrenchment policies during the previous crisis, because of which the municipality appears understaffed and primarily provides support to the better equipped ('creaming off').

5.5.2 Skill Level

Exit probabilities are much lower for people with a minimum level of education. To be accepted as a candidate for job applications one needs a so-called starter or minimum qualification level, which is set at a particular level of professional education. People having these minimum qualifications are much more likely to find work, notably at spell durations up to 5–7 years in Oss and for all durations in Apeldoorn/Epe.[4] With longer durations the advantage disappears in Oss, but not in Apeldoorn/Epe (Fig. 5.4).

5.5.3 Exit Chances of Participants

At the start of the experiment, the exit chances are likely to be similar between the various treatment groups due to the random assignment procedure. Because of selective response and the *a priori* exclusion of particular groups (people in institutions, 65+, fully disabled, homeless, lack of proficiency in Dutch), the exit probabilities may differ between participants and non-participants. In Table 5.9 these two groups are compared for the four cities mentioned earlier: Apeldoorn/Epe, Oss and Wageningen. The exit chances are, after correction for composition differences, even

---

[4]In the administrative social assistance data for the four cities no education information is available for Tilburg and Wageningen.

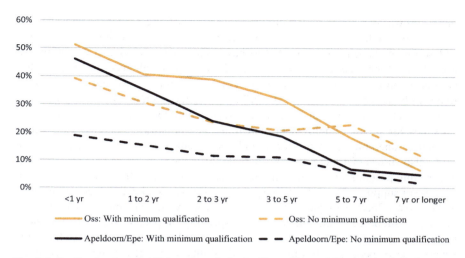

Fig. 5.4 Predicted exit probabilities of people in Apeldoorn/Epe and Oss moving in before June 1, 2016 and exit after June 1, 2016 by having a minimum education level or not. Source: Municipal BUS (social assistance benefit statistics) data 2015–2018

Table 5.9 Predicted exit probabilities of experiment participants, non-participants and withdrawals for the period between June 1, 2016 and June 1, 2018 in Apeldoorn/Epe, Oss, Tilburg and Wageningen

	Not-Article 83		Article 83 experiments	
Population	Apeldoorn/Epe (%)	Oss (%)	Tilburg (%)	Wageningen (%)
Participants	9.86	17.00	13.64	10.1
Non-participants	10.30	15.00	14.99	10.03
Withdrawals	11.52	17.00	12.55	2.4
Total	10.29	15.00	14.78	10.0
N =	3174	1503	5024	907

Source: Municipal BUS (social assistance benefit statistics) data 2015–2018

smaller for participants than for non-participants in Apeldoorn/Epe and Tilburg but slightly higher for participants in Oss.

5.5.4 Expected Effects of the Interventions

The aim of the experiments is to improve the effectiveness of the social assistance scheme. This means not only to improve the exit chances to work, but also to increase the level of social participation, health and well-being. Before the start of the experiments, a literature review (covering the economic and psychological literature) was conducted to explore the broad range of effects that the interventions implemented in the experiment (earnings release, intensive tailor-made supervision and self-management) are expected to have. The study shows that the effects of activating labour market policies averaged 11.5% over all medium-term studies (12–24 months), whereas the average percentage for experimental research is found to be much lower, 5.6%. The effects show the average effects of assistance in job search, work creation in the public sector, monitoring and control/sanctions, subsidies for private employment, and training. The study concerns both people entitled to unemployment insurance and people entitled to social assistance. The study also shows that there are considerable differences in the calculated effects of counselling programmes, depending on the type of research, but also depending on the type of support offered. Intensive guidance towards work and job coaching seem to be most effective in guiding people into paid work, *i.e.* more effective than training or support in searching for work. Especially for people with a large distance to the labour market, intensive mediation is needed and more effective. Intensive supervision of people with a psychiatric disability works effectively to lead these people to work, according to international research (Bond, Drake, & Luciano, 2015; Card, Kluve, & Weber, 2010, 2015; Marshall et al., 2014). The effects of this intervention are greater than the effects of the regular workfare interventions mentioned above, and vary between 10 and 25% (on average 15%). It was therefore assumed that the experiments will yield an absolute increase of the employment rate between 5 and 10% (for the exemption and earnings release treatment) to 15–25% (for the treatment of tailor-intensive supervision). This would imply that the treatments would at maximum create an additional effect on the exit chances into work of about 10%. In the experiments 10% is assumed, which is considered a very ambitious, but still realistic, target (see Muffels & van der Klink, 2017). This means that if the current exit rate is on average 15% over a period of 2 years, then the rate will rise to 25% due to the interventions. For the other outcome measures no strict targets were set. Recent research by Bigotta, Bonoli, Fossati, Lalive, and Oesch (2018) on a similar Swiss RCT-experiment (Lausanne), which also lasted for 2 years (2015–2017) with intensive tailor-made mediation, shows an effect of 9% over the 2 years period, indicating that the presumed 10% for the Dutch experiments might be feasible.

5.6 Conclusions and Discussion

In this chapter, it is argued that the launching of a variety of local participation income experiments in 11 Dutch cities in 2017 can be explained by three main factors: a paradigm shift towards social investment policies, a matured societal debate on basic income, and new behavioural insights in welfare state policy-making (nudging) which provide a different perspective on the reintegration of disadvantaged people in society. The local experiments have some similarities with the basic income ideas, which potentially provides new avenues for social policy-making (Atkinson, 1996; Van Parijs, 2004). These avenues resemble the contended third stage in welfare state policy to render people more personal autonomy, to build up trust, and to enable people to participate in society by providing opportunities and 'free choice'. The term 'social investment' or inclusive society has been used pertaining to such a welfare state that is pro-active and 'enabling'. The term 'trust experiments' illustrates the wish of the municipalities to depart from the workfare or 'stick and carrot' approach and to reform the treatment practices so as to build-up trust and providing 'free choice' to people, instead of primarily distrusting people by strict monitoring and sanctioning practices. Insights from behavioural economics, Sen's capability approach, and psychological motivation theories suggest that investing in personal autonomy, trust and intrinsic motivation might pay-off in terms of people's performance, their health and subjective well-being.

The municipalities themselves have formulated a wider range of goals than reintegration into work only. The experiments are also seen as a success when positive outcomes on health, self-management and well-being are achieved. In the second part of the chapter the focus shifted to the empirical analyses, using administrative and participants' survey data gathered in the four municipalities. In this way, a clear picture could be obtained of the large differences in job-search behaviour and the capabilities of welfare recipients, and of the inequality in access to employment, health and well-being outcomes across that population. Latent class analyses were performed to distinguish more or less homogenous groups.

The outcomes show that the employment opportunities of most welfare recipients are poor due to limitations they have concerning completed education, language skills and notably health, because of which many are unfit for the offered jobs. Three to four latent classes or groups can be distinguished in these cities. Two groups are still active in searching, but have serious health problems, whereas the other one or two groups are passive, and disappointed or discouraged about their opportunities. The work-unfit perform worse with respect to health, well-being, self-efficacy, and social participation on all outcome measures. The findings call for innovative policies, in which not people's inability to work is stressed, but in which opportunities and free choices are created by investments in people's skills and abilities. The findings show that the first hypothesis on the large differences between the welfare recipients in what they want and what they in reality can achieve is to be confirmed. It was also shown that this leads to a very high level of inequality across social welfare recipients in capabilities and opportunities, in health and well-being, and in living conditions in general (income, poverty, deprivation). In a next step, we calculated theoretical exit probabilities into paid work while correcting for selective response and composition differences. The exit probabilities turned out to be very low for most groups, most notably for the low-educated and people with long social assistance spells. The hypothesis on the large inequality in outcomes due to differences in motivation, behaviour and capabilities is therewith also confirmed with respect to employment chances. The chapter eventually sets out that the experiments may mark an irreversible shift in welfare state policy-making. As innovative attempts to move from conditional social assistance to less or unconditional participation or basic income (NIT) are becoming more prominent, the experiments resemble a policy perspective that might be a more aligned and appropriate response to the underlying societal dynamics. Such a policy might be better equipped to resolve the challenges of rising inequality and dualisation of the labour market with the aim of improving trust, free choice and personal autonomy, and creating wider opportunities to disadvantaged people.

References

Atkinson, A. B. (1996). The case for a participation income. *Political Quarterly, 67*(1), 67–70. https://doi.org/10.1111/j.1467-923X.1996.tb01568.x

Bigotta, M., Bonoli, G., Fossati, F., Lalive, R., & Oesch, D. (2018). *Helping social assistance recipients find jobs: Evidence from a controlled trial* (ESPANet working paper, University of Lausanne, Switzerland)

Bohnet, I., Frey, B. S., & Huck, S. (2001). More order with less law: On contract enforcement, trust and crowding. *The American Political Science Review, 95*(1), 131–144. Retrieved June 8, 2019, from https://www.jstor.org/stable/3117633

Bond, G. R., Drake, R. E., & Luciano, A. (2015). Employment and educational outcomes in early intervention programs for early psychosis: A systematic review. *Epidemiology and Psychiatric Sciences, 24*(5), 446–457. https://doi.org/10.1017/S2045796014000419

Card, D., Kluve, J., & Weber, A. (2010). Active labour market policy evaluations: A meta-analysis. *The Economic Journal, 120*(November), F452–F477. https://doi.org/10.1111/j.1468-0297.2010.02387.x

Card, D., Kluve, J., & Weber, A. (2015). *What works? A meta analysis of recent active labor market program evaluations* (IZA Discussion Paper No. 9236). Bonn: Institute for the Study of Labor

Deci, E. L., & Ryan, R. M. (1985). *Intrinsic motivation and self-determination in human behavior*. New York: Plenum.

Delsen, L. (2002). *Exit polder model. Socioeconomic changes in The Netherlands*. Westport: Praeger.

Delsen, L. (2011). *Welfare state reform in the Netherlands: 1982–2003* (IMR Working Paper NiCE11–01). Nijmegen Center for Economics (NiCE), Institute for Management Research, Nijmegen: Radboud University. Retrieved June 8, 2019, from https://www.researchgate.net/publication/308504724_Welfare_state_reform_in_the_Netherlands_1982-2003

Delsen, L. (2017). *Activation reform in the European welfare states and lessons from Dutch flexicurity* (IMR Working Paper NiCE17–02). Nijmegen Center for Economics (NiCE), Institute for Management Research, Nijmegen: Radboud University. Retrieved June 8, 2019, from https://www.researchgate.net/publication/319007835_Activation_reform_in_the_European_welfare_states_and_lessons_from_Dutch_flexicurity

Diener, E., Suh, E. M., Lucas, R. E., & Smith, H. L. (1999). Subjective well-being: Three decades of progress. *Psychological Bulletin, 125*(2), 276–302. https://doi.org/10.1037/0033-2909.125.2.276

Fehr, E. & Schmidt, K. M. (2003). Theories of fairness and reciprocity: Evidence and economic applications. In: M. Dewatripont, L. P. Hansen & S. J. Turnovsky (eds.) *Advances in economics and econometrics*, Econometric Society, Eighth World Congress (Vol. 1, pp 208–257).

Frey, B. S., & Jegen, R. (2001). Motivation crowding theory. *Journal of Economic Surveys, 15*(5), 589–611. https://doi.org/10.1111/1467-6419.00150

Goodin, R. E., Headey, B., Muffels, R., & Dirven, H.-J. (1999). *The real worlds of welfare capitalism.* Cambridge: Cambridge University Press.

Groot, L. (2004). *Basic income, compensatory justice and unemployment.* Boston: Kluwer.

Groot, L., Muffels, R. J., & Verlaat, T. (2019). Welfare states' social investment strategies and the emergence of Dutch experiments on a minimum income guarantee. *Social Policy & Society, 18* (2), 277–287. https://doi.org/10.1017/S1474746418000283

Hemerijck, A. (2013). *Changing welfare states.* Oxford: Oxford University Press.

Hemerijck, A. (Ed.). (2017). *The uses of social investment.* Oxford: Oxford University Press.

Lee, S. (2018). Attitudes toward universal basic income and welfare state in Europe: A research note. *Basic Income Studies, 13*(1), 1–9. https://doi.org/10.2139/ssrn.3209161

Mani, A., Mullainathan, S., Shafir, E., & Zhao, J. (2013). Poverty impedes cognitive function. *Science, 341*(6149), 976–980. https://doi.org/10.1126/science.1238041

Marshall, T., Goldberg, R. W., Braude, L., Dougherty, R. H., Daniels, A. S., Sushmita Shoma Ghose, E. D., et al. (2014). Supported employment: Assessing the evidence. *Psychiatric Services, 65*(1), 16–27. https://doi.org/10.1176/appi.ps.201300262

Maydell, v. B., Borchardt, K., Henke, K.-D., Leitner, R., Muffels, R., Quante, M., et al. (2006). *Enabling social Europe.* Berlin: Springer.

Morel, N., Palier, B., & Palme, J. (2012). *Towards a social investment welfare state? Ideas, policies and challenges.* Bristol: The Policy Press.

Muffels, R. (2014). Berghman's social security definition: Challenging the goals and values of welfare states. In W. Oorschot, H. Peeter, & K. Boos (Eds.), *Invisible social security revisited. Essays in honour of Jos Berghman* (pp. 109–126). Tielt: Lannoo Publishers.

Muffels, R., & Van der Klink, J. (2017). *Offerte vertrouwensexperimenten Apeldoorn, Oss, Renkum, Epe en Geldrop-Mierlo: Onderzoekdesign en kostenraming onderzoek.* Tilburg: Tilburg University. 10 mei.

Mullainathan, S., & Shafir, E. (2013). *Scarcity – The true cost of not having enough.* London: Penguin Books.

Pierson, C., Castles, F. G., & Naumann, I. K. (2014). *The welfare state reader.* Cambridge: Polity Press.

Ryan, R. M., Kuhl, J., & Deci, E. L. (1997). Nature and autonomy: An organizational view of social and neurobiological aspects of self-regulation in behavior and development. *Development and Psychopathology, 9*(4), 701–728. https://doi.org/10.1017/S0954579497001405

Schmid, G., & Gazier, B. (Eds.). (2002). *The dynamics of full employment. Social integration through transitional labour markets.* Cheltenham: Edward Elgar.

Sen, A. K. (2004). Capabilities, lists, and public reason: Continuing the conversation. *Feminist Economics, 10*(3), 77–80. https://doi.org/10.1080/1354570042000315163

Sen, A. K. (2009). *The idea of justice.* London: Allen Lane.

Soentken, M., van Hooren, F., & Rice, D. (2017). The impact of social investment reforms on income and activation in the Netherlands. In A. Hemerijck (Ed.), *The uses of social investment* (pp. 235–243). Oxford: Oxford University Press.

Thaler, R. H., & Sunstein, C. R. (2008). *Nudge: Improving decisions about health, wealth, and happiness.* New Haven: Yale University Press.

van der Klink, J. J., Bültmann, U., Burdorf, A., Schaufeli, W. B., Zijlstra, F. R., Abma, F. I., et al. (2016). Sustainable employability—definition, conceptualization, and implications: A perspective based on the capability approach. *Scandinavian Journal of Work Environment & Health, 42* (1), 71–79. https://doi.org/10.5271/sjweh.3531

Van Parijs, P. (2004). Basic income: A simple and powerful idea for the twenty-first century. *Politics and Society, 32*(1), 7–39. https://doi.org/10.1177/0032329203261095

Veenhoven, R. (1996). Developments in satisfaction-research. *Social Indicators Research, 37*(1), 1–46. https://doi.org/10.1007/BF00300268

Ruud Muffels (M.A. economics, Tilburg) is Professor of Socio-Economics (chair in labour market and social security) at Tranzo, the Center for Care and Wellbeing and the Department of Sociology of Tilburg University. Before, he was Director of Reflect—a Research Institute on Flexicurity and Labour Market Dynamics at Tilburg University. He is also a research fellow at NETSPAR, the network for research on ageing, and a fellow at research institutes in Berlin (DIW) and Bonn (IZA). His primary interests concern labour market dynamics, income and poverty, comparative welfare state analysis and socio-economic policy. He has published more than 300 papers in a wide range of economic, sociological and interdisciplinary journals (*Proceedings of the American National Academy of Sciences* (PNAS), *Journal of the Royal Statistical Society, Journal of European Social Policy, Social Policy & Society, PLoS One, Journal of Occupational and Environmental Medicine, Journal of Sociological Methodology, Work Employment and Society, Journal of Population Economics, Social Indicators Research, Journal of Public Policy, Acta Sociologica, LABOUR*, and others) and in a large number of international academic volumes. Most recent one is *Flexibility and employment security in Europe: Labour markets in transition* (Cheltenham: Edward Elgar (2008). Earlier books are *Enabling social Europe* (with B. von Maydell & R. Leitner (Berlin: Springer-Verlag, 2006), *Social exclusion in European welfare states* (with P. Tsakloglou & D. Mayes (Cheltenham: Edward Elgar, 2002) and *The real worlds of welfare capitalism* (with Robert E. Goodin & Bruce Headey (Cambridge: Cambridge University Press, 1999).

Erwin Gielens (1991) studied Sociology in Tilburg (2013–2016), completed a research master program cum laude (2016–2018) and has just started working to obtain his Ph.D. (2018) with a talent grant. His main interests lie in welfare state development, welfare attitudes and media studies. His project aims to unravel the basic income debate. He published an essay on policy feedback in *Sociology Magazine*, questioning the link between social policy and stigmatisation. He also co-authored a recent publication in the *International Journal of Social Welfare* on how deservingness cues are interpreted differently according to one's ideology.

Chapter 6
The Who and the Why? Selection Bias in an Unconditional Basic Income Inspired Social Assistance Experiment

János Betkó, Niels Spierings, Maurice Gesthuizen, and Peer Scheepers

Abstract It is well documented that it is important to take selection effects into account when analysing social experiments. A Randomised Controlled Trial (RCT) design usually prevents selection bias, but not when participation is voluntary. Despite the abundance of literature on the existence of selection bias, few studies provide in-depth insights on how these selection effects take place in practice, and what causes different groups to be over—or under-represented. Nijmegen is one of a number of Dutch municipalities that conduct an experiment with the social assistance system, loosely inspired by the Universal Basic Income (UBI). Participants receive their allowance with less conditions, and get the opportunity to earn additional income. In this chapter, selection effects are tested, using registry data of participants and all non-participants in the population. In addition, qualitative data are used to interpret the selection effects we find. Several characteristics turned out to increase or decrease participation: education, country of origin, being single, having an exemption of the obligation to work, and part-time work providing additional income. Further, we propose that stress is an important deterrent for people to participate in an experiment like this, even when the experiment is aimed at (among others) stress reduction, like the one in Nijmegen.

Keywords Social assistance · UBI-related experiment · Selection bias · Mixed methods · Randomised controlled trial

6.1 Introduction and Research Question

In recent years, at several places in the world, the concept of the Universal Basic Income (UBI) has (re)gained a foothold in political, academic and public debates. It has become increasingly popular for a number of reasons, among them:

J. Betkó (✉) · N. Spierings · M. Gesthuizen · P. Scheepers
Radboud Social Cultural Research, Radboud University, Nijmegen, The Netherlands
e-mail: j.betko@nijmegen.nl; n.spierings@maw.ru.nl; m.gesthuizen@maw.ru.nl; p.scheepers@maw.ru.nl

dissatisfaction with the current social security system and the stress it causes for the people depending on it, (anxiety about) the disappearance of low skilled jobs due to automatisation and robotisation, the success of 'direct cash transfers' in development aid, and a wish to tackle inequality and reduce poverty.[1] This renewed interest has led to (the preparation of) a number of social experiments across the globe (*e.g.* in Finland, Stockton (USA), Ontario (Canada),[2] and Scotland (UK)) (see Danson, Chap. 4), with either the basic income, or basic income-inspired social security policies. In the Netherlands, a number of local experiments have been initiated, including one by the municipality of Nijmegen (see Muffels & Gielens, Chap. 5).

This experiment in Nijmegen has the form of a Randomised Controlled Trial (RCT). RCTs are sometimes considered the 'gold standard' of social experiments (see for example: Smith, 2000: 1; Kluve, 2010), or are at least the preferred method (Campbell & Stanley, 1963; Shadish, Cook, & Campbell, 2002). That does not mean that this approach is without disadvantages. On the contrary: numerous publications point to the dangers and deficiencies of the RCT design. Mentioned, for example, are the ethical and political controversies regarding the random distribution of people over treatment and control groups (Heckman & Smith, 1995; Smith, 2000), as well as the difficulty to generalise to a wider population (Shadish et al., 2002) . The methodological literature also rightfully stresses the danger of biases in (social) experimental designs. Among them are selection bias, reporting bias, attrition bias, performance bias (Higgins & Green, 2011), substitution bias, drop-out bias (Heckman, Hohmann, Smith, & Khoo, 2000; Heckman & Smith, 1995), and randomisation bias (Heckman & Smith, 1995).

The Nijmegen experiment sheds light on how and to what degree some of these issues play a role. We focus on selection effects, which mainly consist of selection bias, but also involve to a lesser extent other biases (this is further elaborated on in Sect. 6.3). Like the comparable experiments that are currently conducted in the Netherlands, as well as some in other countries across the globe, it is based on voluntary participation.[3] This is legitimate from an ethical point of view, *i.e.* not to experiment on people against their wishes. Unfortunately though, this voluntariness causes the issue of selection bias to recur. It is known that voluntary participation influences the generalisability of the outcomes (Greenberg & Shroder, 2004). Based on general insights from the social sciences, we know that outcomes of a social experiment differ between societal groups (see *e.g.* Inglehart, 1997; Klandermans, 1984). This is likely to influence groups' willingness to participate, as people realise they have more or less to gain from an experiment.

---

[1] An overview of these arguments can be found for example in Bregman (2014), the same line of argumentation can be found in the proposals by local politicians, *e.g.* Westerveld (2015) for Nijmegen.

[2] Ontario's basic income pilot will end on March 31, 2019 (Jeffords, 2018; https://globalnews.ca/news/4422214/ontario-basic-income-pilot-end/). The Finnish basic income experiment has ended on December 31, 2018 (see De Wispelaere, Halmetoja, & Pulkka, 2018).

[3] For example, the Ontario experiment was based on voluntary participation as well.

Starting from the notion that it is methodologically plausible that biases can occur, in this study we formulate general expectations along which lines (like social groups and people's characteristics) they may occur. In the current methodological literature on social experiments, there is to the best of our knowledge little reference made to specific empirical studies or results regarding the characteristics of people along which biases are found. Our study explicitly theorises and tests which selection biases are found in the Nijmegen experiment, and how strong those biases are. We are able to contribute to the research in this field, due to the large amount and variety of data we have collected. Not only do we have extended registry data on the participants, but also on the entire target group.[4] In addition to that, we use qualitative data dealing with reasons for participation and dropping out. This enables us not only to (statistically) test if selection effects occur, like on gender, age, country of birth, household composition and characteristics related to the social allowance, but the mixed method approach also enables us to further explain why some of these effects occur. Thus, the Nijmegen experiment functions as a 'case study' for how these biases turn out in practice: in the specific setting of a social experiment on social assistance based on elements of the UBI, in which participation is voluntary and which is partly aimed at labour market activation of participants. While relevant for social experiments in general, our analysis bares specific relevance for the local social assistance experiments in the Netherlands and UBI-related experiments around the world. The local experiments we conduct in the Netherlands are mentioned among 'the experiments with the basic income' in both media (*e.g.* Boffey, 2015; Hamilton, 2016) and academia (*e.g.* Groot, Muffels, & Verlaat, 2019; Standing, 2017) (and for which this book is a testimony). As the results of these experiments, whatever they may be, will get drawn into that international debate, it is important they are interpreted correctly, and this can only be done if biases are taken into account.

The research question that will be answered in this chapter is: which factors contribute to people participating, or not participating, in the experiment with social assistance, as it is held in Nijmegen? The specific factors we will zoom in on are standard socio-economic and demographic characteristics, and characteristics related to the social assistance allowance.

Below in Sect. 6.2, we will first give some context relevant to the experiment. In Sect. 6.3, we will discuss the theory on which the experimental design is based. It shows that some of these theoretical grounds and treatments are expected to make the experimental policy have a stronger than average effect on only a subset of the social welfare population. Combining this logic with more general social science theories, we will formulate a number of hypotheses on the socio-economic and demographic characteristics for which we expect an over—and under-representation in this UBI-based social experiment. In Sect. 6.4 and Sect. 6.5 we subsequently discuss the methodological set up of this study and present the results. Finally, in the

---

[4] Mainly the data in the registry of the *WerkBedrijf* (the local reintegration organisation) and the data of the department *Zorg & Inkomen* (Care & Income) of the municipality.

closing Sect. 6.6, we will get back to the larger implication of our results, also for other social experiments.

6.2 Context

Some background of the social system in the Netherlands is necessary to understand the experiment's set-up and the possible selection effects. With the term 'social assistance', we refer to the final safety net of the Dutch welfare state: the Participation Act (*Participatiewet*).[5] Municipalities are fully financially responsible for the implementation of the Participation Act. If a person loses her job, they will not have to fall back immediately to social assistance. First, there is the more generous salary related unemployment benefit (Unemployment Act, *Werkloosheidswet, WW*). For the first 2 months the unemployment benefit is 75% of the last earned wage. After those 2 months it is 70% of the last earned wage. Only when this expires—after a number of months (with a maximum of 38 months) based on the age of the dismissed person and on the years that person had a paid job—they will receive a social assistance benefit. Next to unemployment, people receive social assistance, for example, after a divorce, after graduating without being able to find employment, or after being granted a refugee status. Social assistance is aimed to be high enough to keep somebody out of poverty. For a single person, it amounts to € 1025.55 per month (70% of the legal minimum wage). For couples, it amounts to the minimum wage, which is € 1465.07.[6] In general, to stay above the poverty line, people on social assistance also need to make use of national and local anti-poverty arrangements (*e.g.* national tax allowances to compensate for rental or health insurance costs, local compensations for necessities that cannot be provided for in another way, or local contributions to children from poor families so they can participate in sports or cultural activities). The existence of a legally guaranteed minimum income does not imply that poverty according to this standard does not exist in the Netherlands. Not everybody who is entitled to assistance or an anti-poverty arrangement receives it. The number of poor citizens is higher than the number of welfare benefits.[7] The risk of poverty and long-term poverty is highest among social assistance recipients. The poverty rate among social assistance recipients lies between 40–45% (Delsen, 2016). Dutch municipalities operate a policy income limit between 110% and 130% of the guaranteed minimum income.

The Participation Act came into effect on January 1, 2015, replacing the former social assistance act (WWB). It represented a (further) shift from 'welfare' to

---

[5] All Dutch laws can be found at the website wetten.overheid.nl

[6] These amounts are for 2019.

[7] The central poverty line of the Netherlands Institute for Social Research (*Sociaal en Cultureel Planbureau*, SCP) (for a single person € 1063 in 2014) is based on having an income which is 'not much but sufficient' and includes what is considered necessary to eat, live, buy clothes and take part in social activities.

'workfare', and from collective solidarity to individual responsibility (Delsen, 2016). It drew quite some criticism, from politicians, municipalities and civil society (*e.g.* Tinnemans, 2014; Vliegenthart, 2016). Among others, people thought the act too bureaucratic, too strict, and operating too much from a paradigm of distrust. In combination with the other regulations concerning taxes and local subsidies, the entire social security system was also considered to be too complex.

In the period before the Participation Act came into effect, the UBI was put on the (political) agenda, among others due to a popular journalistic publication in Dutch on the subject (Bregman, 2014).[8] Consequently, critics of the Participation Act also looked at the UBI as a potential solution to a number of problems they had with the act. They thought a UBI, or a UBI-inspired social assistance, could reduce bureaucracy and the complexity of the welfare state—a salient issue for many citizens on social assistance (*e.g.* lower-educated people), and reduce poverty and stress among people depending on social assistance (Boffey, 2015; Ranshuijsen & Westerveld, 2015; Westerveld, 2015). Thus the goals of the Nijmegen experiment are manifold. By changing the welfare regime to an approach based on trust and the capabilities of people on social assistance, they are expected to have an easier time finding a job (either full-time, part-time or self-employed), are expected to be healthier and happier, experience less stress, be less poor and to participate more in society.

The experimentation Article 83 of the Participation Act (see Muffels & Gielens, Chap. 5) allows municipalities to divert from the act on a number of issues for a limited time, to experiment with the goal of improving the effectiveness of the act. Importantly, however, municipalities need permission from the central government to do so. Without going into great detail in the wishes of all municipalities that expressed interest, the objections of the national government to several experimental proposals, the negotiations and the restrictions put on the experiment by the Ministry of Social Affairs,[9] the end result was that only a limited number of municipalities were allowed to depart from the act. Two deviations are allowed: one with the obligation that people on social assistance have to look for a job, and the second with the restrictions for people on social assistance to earn money in addition to receiving social assistance.[10] If municipalities chose to experiment with the (abolishment of the) obligation to look for work, the national government set the condition that they also had to experiment with a more 'strict' regime.

The municipality of Nijmegen chose[11] to experiment both with increasing the opportunity to earn money from work, and with relieving the participants from the

---

[8]This was later also internationally released as 'Utopia for realists'.

[9]For those interested, Betkó (2018) gives an overview of this, and the broader context – it is only available in Dutch though.

[10]Under normal rules, a person on social allowance is allowed to keep 25% of money earned through work, up to a maximum of € 200 per month, for a maximum of 6 months. In the experiment, participants are allowed to keep 50%, up to a maximum of € 200 per month, for the entire duration of the experiment which is 22 months.

[11]The city council voted for the proposal to experiment with a large majority.

obligation to look for work (and all obligations that are related to that). Thus it was obliged to experiment with a stricter regime as well. The required stricter regime did pose some problems in the design of the experiment.[12] As participation was supposed to be voluntary, a very strict regime would not make participation very appealing (and likely to contribute to selection bias). Therefore, the municipality of Nijmegen, the local reintegration organisation (*WerkBedrijf Rijk van Nijmegen*, hereafter: WerkBedrijf)[13] and the involved researchers from the Radboud University (us), designed an approach specifically for this experiment. It had a relative high frequency of obligatory contact moments for all participants, while still catering as much as possible to the wishes and capabilities of the participants in that treatment. The chosen method consisted of a combination of group meetings, where people could meet and learn from each other; coaching on life and job skills; and giving participants maximum freedom in choosing their goals (full-time work, part-time work, volunteering, or self-employment). This in combination with the desired training or support needed to reach these goals. In Sect. 6.4.1 the design is described in more detail.

6.3 Theoretical Background and Hypotheses

Our theoretical expectations are built on two theoretical frameworks. We begin with theory on biases in social experiments, which we will connect to theories on the impact of the experiment's treatments. Taking these together, we formulate why we expect certain groups of people on social assistance (not) to be interested in applying for the experiment and thus which selection effects might be expected. The premise is here that people who have more to gain (financially or otherwise) are more likely to participate.

6.3.1 Social Experiments and Selection Bias

Important for our study is what is exactly meant by 'selection bias'. A useful definition is given in the Cochrane Handbook for Systematic Reviews of Interventions: "Selection bias refers to systematic differences between baseline characteristics of the groups that are compared" (Higgins & Green, 2011: Section 8.4.1). The idea of an RCT is that, due to the random allocation of people over the groups, selection bias is adequately taken care of. However, in (social) experiments like ours, where participation is voluntarily, there are two groups to begin with: one with

---

[12]In Nijmegen, as well as in the other municipalities that held similar experiments.

[13]The Werkbedrijf is engaged in job placement and reintegration. It is an administrative-regional association of municipalities, social partners (employers and trade unions) and the UWV (*Uitvoeringsinstituut Werknemersverzekeringen*; Employee Insurance Agency).

people who want to participate, and one with the rest of the population. Within the group of participants, there should be no selection bias between treatment(s) and control. But if one wants to generalise effects to the whole population, which usually will be the case, selection bias rears its head once more, as has been documented in the literature on social experiments (Heckman & Smith, 1995). Heckman and Smith argue further that the question which factors affect the decision to apply for or participate in an experiment (*e.g.* advertising, local labour markets, income, ethnic background, and gender) is often not answered in RCTs.

In addition to selection bias, there is another bias that needs to be addressed when discussing selection effects: drop-out or attrition bias. Drop-out bias (*e.g.* Heckman et al., 2000) happens when not all participants (fully) complete the treatment. Particularly those in the control groups have fewer incentives to stay in. Some might even drop out before the actual start of the experiment, which leads to a selection effect.[14]

In this chapter, we compare the full target population with the people who start the experiment. Thus, we collect empirical evidence on the overall effects of selection bias and early-on drop-out bias (that occurs between the application for the experiment and the start of it). In other words, our study sets out to contribute to filling the gap in the empirical knowledge on these biases.

6.3.2 Why the Experiment Should Work and Thus Holds Appeal

The two treatments in the Nijmegen experiment are expected to have positive effects on the participants, and thus to appeal to people to participate in the experiment. At the same time, the treatment effects might differ according to people's characteristics, which is also likely to translate to the appeal.

The expectations regarding the treatment are for the most part theoretically grounded in the behavioural sciences and in behavioural economics. Over the past decades, we have seen an increasing realisation, not only in the social sciences but also in the economic discipline, that people do not solely make rational choices, and are no '*homo economicus*' (see *e.g.* Sen, 1977; Thaler & Sunstein, 2008; Tversky & Kahneman, 1981). Many choices are made under the influence of social and psychological processes. It is the combination of both rational choice and such behavioural processes that we focus on.

We assume the economic, rational-choice mechanism to be relevant as people are being allowed to keep part of their earnings besides their allowance (thus increasing their income), and this can triggers them to work in (part-time) jobs that might not be

---

[14]This could also be seen as a specific form of randomisation bias, where participants in a specific group (often the control group) are participating less in the data gathering (Smith, 2000). In this case, the randomisation process leads to selective drop out; to perceive this process is more important than the exact labelling, be it drop-out or randomisation bias.

worth the effort in the existing means-tested social assistance system. As a consequence, such activities should increase their social capital (*e.g.* social network and skills) as well as their human capital (*e.g.* work experience and knowledge), which increases their value on the labour market, helping them to find full-time employment and increasing the likelihood of ending their dependency of social assistance. Indeed, people who have a part-time job next to their allowance find it easier to escape social assistance by means of work (Divosa, 2015). It is important to note that, while we use the term 'part-time' here, this also applies to people with short periods of full-time work. If somebody works full-time, usually one is not eligible for an allowance. If somebody works full-time for a (very) short period, for instance one or 2 weeks, the principle is the same as for someone who works part-time. When the monthly income is lower than a social assistance allowance, one is eligible and the income from work is deducted from the allowance (when not meeting the conditions as described in footnote 11).

From behavioural theories we use several concepts. For instance, Fehr and Gächter (2000) described the concept of reciprocity. The theory states how, driven by reciprocity, people make an effort, even against their own interest, to reward those who approach them in a positive way and punish those that approach them negatively. We translated this into a more positive, trust-based approach in the experiment, which is expected to yield better results than the usual approach (as described in Sect. 6.2), which is prompted by distrust (see also Muffels & Gielens, Chap. 5). Moreover, in behavioural literature there is a growing strand focussing on the effects of poverty on stress, and stress on poverty. It suggests a downward spiral feedback loop. Poverty leads to increased stress and reduces mental bandwidth. This in turn can decrease people's willingness to engage in activities they perceive as risky (risk aversion) and increase time discounting (the tendency not to perceive positive effects or rewards in the future). It can also lead to a decrease of self-control and willpower. In turn, this impairs people's decision-making and reduces their cognitive bandwidth, thus making it more difficult to escape from poverty (Haushofer & Fehr, 2014; Moynihan, Herd, & Harvey, 2014; Mullainathan & Shafir, 2013; van Geuns, 2013). In our experiment, this is incorporated in different ways. First, the opportunity to increase their income with part-time work can reduce financial scarcity and the accompanying stress. Second, and arguably more importantly, the stress of being subject to a large number of rules and regulations should be reduced. Both for participants who get the first treatment, in which they are exempted from the obligation to re-integrate (*i.e.* apply for jobs), and for those who receive the second treatment, in which they get coached towards a self-selected goal. In short, all these behavioural mechanisms should contribute to participants of the treatment experiencing a higher degree of autonomy and lower burden compared to the regular rules.

Summarised, we expect the treatments to have positive effects on employment, income, participation, well-being and health. This is because the treatments enable the participants to make more of their own choices (instead of the local government making the choices for them), empower them in finding a job or other activity besides their social assistance allowance and give them the opportunity to earn a modest amount of money besides their allowance. Both these mechanics could reduce the stress participants experience, which in turn could lead to other positive effects.

By and large, these are evidently also reasons why the experiment is interesting for participants. Even though they are most likely not familiar with a concept like bandwidth, we clearly communicated that there would be fewer rules, more freedom, and more opportunities to keep a bit of money. At the core of this reasoning we thus have two incentives reflecting the different theoretical schools discussed above: the *economic incentive*—from rational-choice based theory—that people are able to earn more money, and the *psychological incentive*—based on behavioural theories—that participants are given more autonomy and freedom and the expectation that the extra trust that the local government gives them will be repaid in a reciprocal way.

6.3.3 Expectations on Likelihood to Participate

From these core mechanisms discussed above we can now derive expectations on which different groups of people are (more) likely to participate in the experiment than others, and thus which biases in participation we can expect. Given data availability and general social science theories, we will focus on three groups of characteristics that will act as independent variables: individual factors, like gender, education and age; characteristics of the household people live in, like the presence of children; and a characteristic directly linked to the social assistance situation and history of the potential participant, like the number of years somebody received social assistance.

Individual Factors
First, there is little reason to expect that the rational-economic factors differ between men and women. The behaviour aspect does, however, relate to average gender differences. Several studies have shown that women are more chronically stressed and experience more minor stressors, also considering similar life events (Matud, 2004; *cf.* Deater-Deckard & Scarr, 1996). Such higher stress perceptions might cause more incentives to participate, as one of the treatments implies fewer rules. And even though our second treatment increases the intensity of support, its focus on group sessions and coaching might actually increase women's likelihood to participate as well, since prior research has shown that solutions for stress are more directed towards social support (Ptacek, Smith, & Dodge, 1994). On the other hand, one could argue that women more often take care of children, and have less opportunity to engage in part-time work. This is controlled for, since we include household composition (including the presence of children) as a variable. In short, the experiment's predicted impact of stress reduction can be expected to particularly appeal to women:

H1: Women are more likely to participate in the social assistance experiment than men.

Regarding age, we expect that the older the individuals, the less likely it will be that they apply for the experiment, because of more limited economic incentives. In the current labour market, it is harder to find a job for older people. Especially the group that is 55+ has a difficult time getting a job (CBS, 2017; Lötters et al., 2013). So, for these people, there is less chance to benefit from the possibility to earn an extra bit of money. Older people's economic expectations in this respect might be substantiated by their experiences with the municipality of Nijmegen. Local government has neither the budget nor the personnel capacity to help all people on social assistance to find a job. Older people are referred to the WerkBedrijf for additional support less often than younger people (possibly because it is reasoned younger people have more chance to benefit from a re-integration trajectory into the labour market). This also means that part of this older group has less behavioural reasons to participate. In practice, they are already left alone by the municipality and its obligations. To summarise:

H2: The older people on social assistance are, the less likely they are to participate in the experiment.

According to the human capital theory, education is a form of human capital that adds skills and thus increases chances on the labour market (Becker, 1964). In addition, an educational degree functions as a signal for potential employers on a person's productivity, ability and trainability (Arum & Shavit, 1995; Spence, 1973). This leads to the assumption that, in general, the higher people are educated, the easier it is to find a (part-time) job. Higher-educated people are thus more likely to benefit from the possibility to generate extra income in this way. Furthermore, literature shows that the higher people are educated, the more they value their autonomy (Inglehart, 1997). Based on this a positive effect might be expected:

H3: The higher people are educated, the more likely they are to participate in the experiment.

As for country of birth, we expect that it is easier for people who are born in the Netherlands to find a part-time job than for others who are not born in the Netherlands, possibly due to experiences with labour market discrimination (*e.g.* Van Doorn, Scheepers, & Dagevos, 2013). So as a group, people born in the Netherlands have a stronger economic incentive compared to people born in other countries (both Western as non-Western). Moreover, these non-Dutch groups will also be less likely to participate, for the practical reason that all the recruitment has been in Dutch, and not all individuals in these groups are proficient in the Dutch language.[15]

H4: People born in the Netherlands are more likely to participate in the experiment.

Household-Related Factors

Due to the way the tax laws work in the Netherlands, single parents usually have more opportunities to have a small income besides an allowance. Without going into

---

[15]See Sect. 6.4.1 for reasons behind this choice in design.

detail of tax exemption regulations, we can say in general that several tax allowances depend on income. The higher the income, the lower the tax allowances.[16] Specifically for single parents, the income threshold is higher (they can earn more money before losing tax allowances). Thus the economic incentive to participate is stronger. Then again, in addition to our core theoretical mechanisms, we should realise that single parents spend a lot of time caring for their child(ren). Living on a social minimum income, they do not have opportunities to get relief through (for example) extra childcare or hiring a cleaner. These considerations of practical nature would lead to the expectation that single parents are less likely to participate. So for the group of single parents, there are contradicting expectations. Of course, the possibility exists that both effects occur, and they cancel each other out. Because we expect to find effects on the specific sub category 'single parents', we use it as the reference category in our logistic regression model.

H5a: Single parents are more likely to participate in the experiment.
H5b: Single parents are less likely to participate in the experiment.

A specific household type is the group of so-called 'costs sharers' (*kostendelers*). The Participation Act states that when several people who are not family[17] live together at the same address, they will—per person—receive a lower social assistance allowance,[18] since they can share necessary costs, like the costs for housing. Because of the lower allowance they get and the way that interacts with taxation law (cost sharers have a lower income, and are thus less or not at all hindered by income thresholds for tax allowances), it is more beneficial for them to complement their allowance with an income from a (part-time) job. This gives this group a relatively bigger economic incentive to participate in the experiment. On the other hand, in the category 'miscellaneous', we have reasons to assume that the people who are costs sharers are not the most promising to find a job. The fact that somebody is unable to sustain a housing unit on his or her own, suggests that something is not going well, beyond having to live on social assistance. After all, the social allowance should be high enough to enable living in an apartment or house (whether or not from a social housing corporation). As with single parents, we have contradictory expectations, and similarly, we will formulate both of them. Again, effects might cancel each other out.

H6a: People who are costs sharers are more likely to participate in the experiment.
H6b: People who are costs sharers are less likely to participate in the experiment.

---

[16]This only goes for the national tax allowances. On the local level, the municipality of Nijmegen considers a person on social assistance as eligible for local arrangements.

[17]And (thus) neither a 'couple'.

[18]Single person 70%; two persons each 50%, total 100%; 3 persons 43.33% each, total 130%; 4 persons 40% each, total 160%; 5 persons 38% each, total 190%, *etc.*

Individuals' Allowance Situation and History

The first category of allowance characteristics is the number of years somebody received social assistance. For them, the same mechanism is relevant as for people of age. The longer people receive an allowance, the less chance they have in the (current) labour market (decreasing their likelihood of participating according to rational-choice theory), and in practice there is less chance they are sent to the WerkBedrijf for re-integration. Often, with no recent working experience, the chance of obtaining a part-time job is relatively small. In practice, a part of this group is not bothered by the municipality with re-integration obligations.

H7: The longer people receive social assistance, the less likely they are to participate in the experiment.

The second category of allowance characteristics is whether somebody has an exemption from the obligation to work. In general, people only get such an exemption for a weighty reason, such as (temporarily) not being able to work due to a medical reason. Therefore, from a rational-choice perspective it is logical that for a large part of the group with an exemption, the economic incentive is not there. In addition, the obligations of these people differ from the people without an exemption. They already have more autonomy due to fewer obligations. So, also from the behavioural perspective they have fewer reasons to participate.

H8: People with an exemption from the obligation to work are less likely to participate in the experiment.

Finally, there are people who earn money in addition to their allowance. Under normal rules, these people have to hand in all of the money they earn (or more correctly: their allowance is reduced with the amount of money they earn). The exception is the first 6 months somebody earns additional income: in this period, people are allowed to keep 25%, up to € 200. In the experiment, people are allowed to keep 50% of what they earn, up to € 200. For people who already had an additional income, the economic incentive is thus much stronger than for the average person on social assistance. After all, if these people are randomly designated to one of the treatment groups, they will have an increase in income without having to change their behaviour (they are already working).

H9: People who already earned money next to their allowance before the experiment, are more likely to participate in the experiment.

In Table 6.1 we summarise our expectations.

Table 6.1 Summary of demographic, household and allowance factors explaining biases in participation in the Nijmegen social assistance experiment

Individual	Household	Allowance
Gender (f+)	**Household composition (single / couple/single parent /couple with children): Single parent (+) or (−)**	*Number of years on social assistance (−)*
Age (−)	**Costs sharing (+) or (−)**	*Exemption from obligation to work (−)*
Education (+)		**Receives an income additional to the allowance (+)**
Country of birth (NL+)		

Note: *italics* if related to behavioural theory, **bold** if related to rational choice theory, ***bold italics*** if both

6.4 Data and Methods

6.4.1 Case: The Nijmegen Experiment

In the Nijmegen UBI-inspired experiment people had to apply to participate. After the close of the registration, we randomised participants proportionally over three different groups of which the applicants knew the content before applying: two treatment groups and one control group. Participants in the first treatment group were allowed to keep more money when earning an income besides their social allowance payment *and* were relieved from all obligations requiring them to look for work. Participants in the second treatment group were allowed to keep more money when earning an income besides their social allowance payment *and* got intensive (group) coaching to help them reach the goals they set for themselves. The second treatment is the 'strict' group (as described in Sect. 6.2). However, eventual results for this treatment should be interpreted carefully as our strict regime does not favour the stick over the carrot, which 'strict' might suggest. The treatment involves a human centred, social and empowering regime, based on personal choice and autonomy, with an obligatory component. This is also relevant for our study. The experiment is designed to be appealing to everybody, so it should not lead to selection bias (which the inclusion of a heavy-handed treatment might). The people in the control group were treated in exactly the same way as before the experiment, but will participate in a survey four times, spread out over 3 years. For this they receive a modest gift voucher once a year, to prevent drop-out. The survey is conducted using Computer Assisted Personal Interviewing (CAPI). The execution of these interviews is done by a commercial research bureau,[19] that is hired for this job.

The choice for combination treatments was not made from a purely academic perspective. As described in the methodological literature on social experiments, it is

---

[19] Labyrinth Onderzoek & Advies, Utrecht.

common that practical, institutional and political factors influence experimental designs (Heckman & Smith, 1995; Shadish et al., 2002). This also applies to the Nijmegen experiment. The combination of treatments is an example of this. From a pure academic perspective, separate treatments would have been more logical. But combining them resembled the most the alternative treatment the municipal council asked for in their proposals.

It is worth noting that not all people on social allowance were eligible for the experiment. There were a number of national and local criteria that led to exclusion from the experiment, some legal and some practical. They are described in Box 6.1 (see also Muffels & Gielens, Chap. 5). As an example, we excluded people under 27 because they are by law excluded from any possibility to earn income next to the allowance, not even in an experiment. Thus the experiment would appeal less to them, and including them would introduce a specific selection bias and complicate the analysis.

Box 6.1 Reasons for Exclusion from Nijmegen Social Assistance Experiment

Age under 27 at the start of the experiment.
Reaching retirement age before the end of the experiment.
Exceptionally vulnerable people in a specific register (*doelgroepenregister*).
History of violence against public servants.
Already participating in an intensive job-trajectory (with commitments to a third party (employer), or one that was bound to lead to result on short notice.

For people to participate, the experiment not only had to be appealing, but they also had to know about its existence. To reach a broad and large group of potential participants, a wide range of recruitment instruments was used. The most important ones are given in Box 6.2. Important to note here—particularly given our research question—is that advertisement was only in Dutch. Consequently, we expect a selection bias in terms of ethnicity, as among the people on social assistance there are those who do not speak Dutch. This choice was made given the disproportional costs of translating the surveys used in this project in a valid way, as well as the practical impossibility of multi-language group sessions.

Box 6.2 Means of Recruitment of Participants for Nijmegen Social Assistance Experiment

A 3 minute animation video, spread through social media and shown in city offices.
A number of meetings in different parts of town, where a presentation on the experiment was given. People could ask questions and immediately apply. The meetings were announced in various ways, including in letters and through social media.

(continued)

> **Box 6.2** (continued)
>
> Posters and flyers, among others at city offices, the reintegration organisation, and civil organisations.
> A personal letter, with a flyer, sent to everybody.
> Advertisement through social media.
> Information in (digital) newsletters.
> People were told about the experiment in personal contacts with employees of the social assistance department and the regional reintegration organisation.
> Advertisement in local media.
> Press release sent to local media.
> During the moment where people on social assistance are obliged to hand in a monthly required form, there were civil servants on the floor of the city office to tell them about the experiment. People could enroll on the spot.

The official start of the experiment was on December 1, 2017. To increase the number of participants, people on social assistance were given a second chance to register, and on April 1, 2018 another group joined.[20] The enlistment procedure was by and large the same as the original one, only more modest. However, this time three groups of people got a personal letter, stressing that the experiment could be of particular interest to them. These groups were people not yet on social assistance during the former advertisement campaign, people who turned 27 since then, and people who already had a part-time job.

6.4.2 Data and Models

This study is based on both quantitative and qualitative data. The main source consist of registration data from the municipality of Nijmegen on its habitants who are on social assistance. These data include a wealth of information, among others on gender, age, household composition, time on social assistance, education, country of birth, ethnicity, the neighbourhood where people live, whether somebody earns money in addition to the social assistance, and special circumstances (like living in an institution, or being homeless). We connected the data file of all social assistance recipients with the data file containing the participants of the experiment. This allows us to compare participants with non-participants on these background characteristics.

In total, there are about 7500–8000 social assistance allowances in Nijmegen, of which approximately 1000 are payments to couples.[21] Adding together all the people who were on social assistance on either December 1, 2017 or on April 1, 2019, and

---

[20] The experiment ends on October 1, 2019.

[21] This might seem quite a wide range, but it is good to keep in mind that the number of people on social assistance is never stable; people enter and exit the scheme every day. For example, both the

after applying the exclusion criteria for the experiment (see Sect. 6.2),[22] approximately 6010 people remained. These constitute the target population, of whom 258 started the experiment in the first wave, and 66 in the second, leading to 324 participants in this study and 5686 non-participants. If a participant exits social assistance, and enters again during the period of the experiment, they enter the experimental treatment again instead of the normal one.

Our outcome is dichotomous: participates or not. That is why we use logistic regression models, in which a positive coefficient indicates that a group of people is over-represented in our experiment and a negative coefficient indicates under-representation. In addition, we use a Chi-square in combination with a Cramer's V to measure the association between participation in the experiment and the relevant independent variables bivariately as a first step.

6.4.3 Operationalisations

Gender is measured as either male or female. Age is recoded into four categories: 27–34, 35–44, 45–54 and 55–64. Education is recoded into four standard categories on highest completed education: basic, lower secondary, higher secondary, and tertiary education. Unfortunately, for over 40% of the people education is categorised as "unknown" in the municipal administration.[23] We included this as a separate category. Country of birth is measured in three categories[24]: the Netherlands, another Western country, or a non-Western country. Household composition is measured in four variabilities: alone (no children), single parent, couple (no children), or couple with children. Costs sharing is measured as a simple yes or no. The time somebody received social assistance is measured in years since last entry, divided in the following variabilities: less than a year, between one and 3 years, and longer than 3 years.[25] This only refers to current social assistance spell. Whether somebody has an exemption from the obligation to work is measured in three categories: no exemption, partial exemption and a full exemption. The variable "Has an income next to the allowance" is measured in euro's. For this

---

entire population of people on social assistance and the target population for this experiment differed at the time of the first and the second wave (December 2017 and March 2018).

[22]We are not able to do this fully. For example, the assessment on whether or not the re-integration trajectory an applicant was already receiving was a barrier for participation, was done on a case by case basis by a professional. It was not done based on a list of criteria that could be used to reduce our population.

[23]In the evaluation of the experiment, we will be able to use data of Statistics Netherlands (*Centraal Bureau voor de Statistiek*, CBS) instead of the municipality, which is much more accurate.

[24]Following the definition of Statistics Netherlands.

[25]This is based on the experience the municipality has with social assistance duration. Under 1 year, people have reasonable chance to find a job. Between 1 and 3 years, it gets more difficult, and once somebody is on social assistance for longer than 3 years, the chance of leaving it due to finding a job is very small.

analysis we recoded it as a simple yes or no, 'yes' meaning any amount of income in 2017 until December 1, the starting date of the experiment. The descriptive statistics for these variables are shown in Table 6.2.

6.4.4 Qualitative Data

In addition to the quantitative data, we use qualitative data that indicate reasons as to why people chose to participate, chose not to, and chose to drop out after applying. We use these to verify and further interpret the results of the quantitative analyses. They can shed light on whether the mechanisms at work fit the theoretical mechanisms, and whether they can help to explain unexpected results and reveal additional processes.

We have two sources of qualitative data that give us valuable insights in the motives of potential participants. First, we interviewed three civil servants of the municipality of Nijmegen who were responsible for the recruitment. They spoke to hundreds of people on social assistance, who came to hand in their monthly form (see under Sect. 6.2) about participating in the experiment. Thus they have a good overview on the reasons why people did or did not want to participate in the experiment. Second, the research bureau that conducted the survey for testing the treatment effects administrated the reasons given for not filling out the survey by applicants; in total 44 applicants refused to cooperate in the survey, for various reasons.[26]

6.5 Results

The results of our analyses are presented in Tables 6.3 and 6.4. The bivariate analyses are shown in Table 6.3 and the multivariate logistic regression models are presented in Table 6.4. Table 6.5 contains the summary of the biases in our sample. Our main conclusions are based on the full logistic model (Table 6.4, Model 3). The other models and bivariate analysis are used to establish what overall differences exist between the sample and the target population and to which factor they can be ascribed. By comparing the different logistic regression models, we can see what proportion is explained by the different characteristics (by comparing the Nagelkerke R^2) and how characteristics that seem to be relevant at first sight are explained (away) by other characteristics, indicating spurious relationships.

As for the qualitative data, we analysed whether findings were mentioned by multiple sources (either by more recruiters, or by a recruiter and in the information provided by the research bureau), and the importance given to the findings (for

---

[26]The transcripts of the interview and the documents provided by the research bureau can be consulted at request. For this, contact the authors.

Table 6.2 Descriptive statistics of explanatory variables in the Nijmegen social assistance experiment

Variable	N	Mean/ percentage	Minimum	Maximum	St. dev.
Gender	6010				
Male	2969	49.4			
Female	3041	50.6			
Age (years)	6010	46.27	27	64	10.24
27–34	1043	17.4			
35–44	1498	24.9			
45–54	1942	32.3			
55–64	1527	25.4			
Education	6010				
Primary	1130	18.8			
Low secondary	1057	17.6			
High secondary	835	13.9			
Tertiary	545	9.1			
Unknown	2443	40.6			
Country of birth	6010				
Netherlands	3382	56.3			
Other Western	310	5.2			
Non-Western	2318	38.6			
Household situation	6010	67.1			
Single, no children	4034	18.5			
Single with children	1109	5.7			
Couple, no children	340	8.8			
Couple with children	527				
Cost sharer	6010				
Yes	519	8.6			
No	5491	91.4			
Time on social assistance (years)	6010	[a]	0	21[a]	[a]
Less than 1 year	891	14.8			
Between 1 and 3 years	1791	29.8			
More than 3 years	3328	55.4			
Exemption from the obligation to work					
No exemption	3502	58.3			
Partial exemption	331	5.5			
Full exemption	2177	36.2			
Income from work					
Yes	713	11.9			
No	5297	88.1			
Amount (€)	737	3586.58	10	14,925.00	3367.17

Source: Register data Nijmegen municipal administration (December 2017, April 2018)
[a]Due to administrative reasons, the maximum duration registered is 21 years, making the mean, maximum and standard deviation scores unreliable

Table 6.3 Likelihood to participate and not to participate in the Nijmegen social assistance experiment, Chi square and Cramer's V

	Does not participate (N = 5686)		Participates (N = 324)		Chi^2	P	Cr-V
	Number	Percentage	Number	Percentage			
Individual characteristics							
Gender					1.07		0.01
Male	2818	49.6	151	46.6			
Female	2868	50.4	173	53.4			
Age					12.48	**	0.05
27–34	972	17.1	71	21.9			
35–44	1420	25.0	78	24.1			
45–54	1826	32.1	116	35.8			
55–64	1468	25.8	59	18.2			
Education					64.32	**	0.10
Primary	1107	19.5	23	7.1			
Lower secondary	1026	18.0	31	9.6			
Higher secondary	762	13.4	73	22.5			
Tertiary	509	9.0	36	11.1			
Unknown	2282	40.1	161	49.7			
Country of birth					39.85	**	0.08
Netherlands	3145	55.3	237	73.1			
Non-Western	2243	39.4	75	23.1			
Western	298	5.2	12	3.7			
Household characteristics							
Household composition					26.42	**	0.07
Single no kids	3801	66.8	233	71.9			
Single parent	1036	18.2	73	22.5			
Couple with kids	510	9.0	17	5.2			
Couple no kids	339	6.0	1	0.3			
Costs sharing					4.98	*	0.03
Costs sharer	502	8.8	17	5.2			
No costs sharer	5184	91.2	307	94.8			
Allowance characteristics							
Duration allowance					23.75	**	0.06
Less than a year	829	14.6	62	19.1			
Between 1-3 years	1666	29.3	125	38.6			
More than 3 years	3191	56.1	137	42.3			
Exemption from obligation to work					33.60	**	0.08
No exemption	3272	57.5	232	71.0			

(continued)

Table 6.3 (continued)

	Does not participate (N = 5686)		Participates (N = 324)		Chi²	P	Cr-V
	Number	Percentage	Number	Percentage			
Partial exemption	306	5.4	25	7.7			
Full exemption	2108	37.1	95	21.3			
Income					255.89	**	0.21
No income	5102	89.7	195	60.2			
Income	584	10.3	129	39.8			

** $p < 0.01$, * $p < 0.05$, ~ $p < 0.10$
Source: Register data Nijmegen municipal administration (December 2017, April 2018)

example: was something mentioned as 'an important reason' by a recruiter, or was something relatively often a drop—out cause in the document from the research bureau). When we came across unexpected findings we reread the qualitative material from that perspective to see whether it offered clues to explain that particular finding.

6.5.1 Individual Characteristics

The first demographic characteristic, a person's gender, has no statistically significant relationship with the likelihood of participation in any of the models. There is thus no indication that selection bias based on gender takes place and H1 is rejected. Similarly, we find no final significant relationship in the logistic models for age, leading to the rejection of H2. Age is statistically significant in the bivariate analysis, where notably people in the oldest age category show a decreased chance of participation, but this is cancelled when controlled for other variables. One recruiter stressed that younger people participated relatively more to earn extra income, and older people opted relatively more for a less restrictive approach.

Education in itself, our third individual characteristic, shows a statistically significant impact in all analyses. Tables 6.3 and 6.4 show that especially people in the two lowest educated categories have lower likelihoods to participate in the experiment. Those with higher secondary and tertiary education are more likely to participate. It is remarkable that the tertiary educated participate slightly less than the higher secondary educated. This might be related to another important result for education: the people of whom the educational level is missing in the municipal registration are also more likely to participate. Overall, these results lead to support for H3. The recruiters also observed that education plays a role in participation; higher-educated people were more interested. One elaborated that the higher-educated people were generally more motivated by the increased autonomy and decreased regulations, while lower-educated participants were generally more interested in the opportunity to earn extra income (similar to what was observed concerning 'age'). These insights suggest that the selection bias on education is

6 The Who and the Why? Selection Bias in an Unconditional Basic Income... 159

Table 6.4 Likelihood of participation in the Nijmegen experiment, logistic regressions with individual, household and allowance characteristics, N = 6010

	Model 1		Model 2		Model 3	
	B	Sig.	B	Sig.	B	Sig.
Individual characteristics						
Gender						
Male	Ref.		Ref.		Ref.	
Female	0.15		−0.04		0.01	
Age						
27–34	Ref.		Ref.		Ref.	
35–44	−0.12		−0.15		−0.05	
45–54	0.06		0.07		0.19	
55–64	−0.43	*	−0.35	~	−0.09	
Education						
Primary	Ref.		Ref.		Ref.	
Lower secondary	0.12		0.07		0.13	
Higher secondary	1.29	**	1.23	**	1.16	**
Tertiary	1.07	**	1.03	**	0.96	**
Unknown	1.05	**	1.00	**	0.88	**
Country of birth						
Netherlands	Ref.		Ref.		Ref.	
Non-Western	−0.75	**	−0.69	**	−0.68	**
Western	−0.63	**	−0.62	*	−0.58	*
Household characteristics						
Household composition						
Single parent			Ref.		Ref.	
Single no kids			−0.14		−0.03	
Couple no kids			−2.88	**	−3.14	**
Couple with kids			−0.46		−0.66	*
Cost sharing						
No cost sharing			Ref.		Ref.	
Cost sharing			−0.54	*	−0.41	
Allowance characteristics						
Duration allowance						
More than 3 years					Ref.	
Less than a year					0.04	
Between 1-3 years					−0.12	
Exemption from obligation to work						
No exemption					Ref.	
Full exemption					−0.45	**
Partial exemption					0.32	
Income						
No income					Ref.	

(continued)

Table 6.4 (continued)

	Model 1		Model 2		Model 3	
	B	Sig.	B	Sig.	B	Sig.
Income					1.72	**
Intercept	−3.42	**	−6.01	**	−6.61	**
−2 log likelihood	2407.34		2377.40		2196.23	
Nagelkerke R^2	0.06		0.07		0.15	

** $p < 0.01$, * $p < 0.05$, ~ $p < 0.10$
Source: Register data Nijmegen municipal administration (December 2017, April 2018)

Table 6.5 Summary of statistical significance ($p < 0.05$) of variables explaining differences between participants and non-participants in the Nijmegen social assistance experiment

Variable	Chi-square	Multivariate regression (Model 3)	Effect	Matches expectation?
Gender (female)	No	No		No
Age	Yes	No		No
Education	Yes	Yes	+	Yes
Country of birth	Yes	Yes	NL: +	Yes
Household composition	Yes	Yes	Single kids > single no kids > couple kids > couple no kids	Partial
Costs sharing	Yes	No		No
Duration	Yes	No		No
Exemption	Yes	Yes	−	Yes
Additional income	Yes	Yes	+	Yes

(at least partly) caused by the higher-educated people's wish to have more autonomy, which corresponds with the theory used to derive hypothesis 3 (Inglehart, 1997). This would mean that different mechanisms appeal to differently educated people.

Country of birth is significant in both analyses as well. People who are born in the Netherlands are more likely to participate in the experiment, while people born in other countries are less likely to do so. For Western countries, this effect is only weakly significant ($p < 0.1$). H4 is accepted. We expected this among others due to the language barrier, and this is supported by the qualitative data. One recruiter mentioned language as a deterrent for participation, and the document from the research bureau explicitly mentioned it as a reason for dropping out in four cases. Language seems a crucial part in explaining why both non-Western and Western people born abroad participated less.

6.5.2 Household Characteristics

The household characteristics show mixed results. Model 3 in Table 6.4 shows that the composition of the household is a significant factor in participation. We had contradictory expectations, either single parents would participate more compared to all other categories (H5a) due to increased possibilities to gather additional income, or participate less (H5b) due to not having the time to engage in an experiment. The results show something else. Single parents indeed have a significanty higher likelihood to participate compared to couples (with and without kids), but hardly differ compared to singles without kids. The dividing line is between singles and couples. Further, it is noticeable that couples without kids are very unlikely to participate, even compared with other couples. All this leads to the rejection of H5b, and the partial acceptance of H5a (though it is the question if our assumptions on why single parents are more likely to participate can hold).

We also tested the role of costs sharing (*i.e.* people sharing a household without being a couple, and receiving a lower per person social assistance allowance, given their opportunity to share costs). We had contradictory expectations, having good reasons to assume both over-and under-representation. Without controlling for other factors, costs sharers have a significantly lower likelihood to participate as is shown in Table 6.3. In the multivariate model 3 it is still negative, but no longer significant, indicating that the expected selection bias is absent. Both H6a and H6b are rejected.

6.5.3 Allowance Characteristics

Our last cluster of factors focuses on the characteristics of people's allowance. A longer duration of the allowance decreases the likelihood to participate according to the bivariate model (Table 6.3). In the logistic models (Table 6.4) though, the significance of this duration effect disappears. Overall, we reject H7.

Exemption from the obligation does have an effect. In the full logistic model the effect of a full exemption is highly significant and decreases the likelihood to participate. We therefore accept H8. In line with the theory behind our hypothesis and the importance of economic reasoning, a number of people expressed disinterest in the experiment to recruiters, due to their exemption from the obligation to work. Given the prominence of the possibility to earn money next to the allowance, they felt the experiment was not for them (being unable to work).

Lastly, having an income has a significant effect on the likelihood to participate in all analyses. People with an additional income were far more likely to participate. H9 is supported.

6.5.4 Additional Findings in the Qualitative Data

Regarding the general mechanisms, all three recruiters stressed that the possibility to earn extra income was the most mentioned reason for participation. However, one recruiter expressed that a number of people chose not to participate, because of uncertainty about the interaction between additional income and tax allowances. Likewise, people in a debt-restructuring programme[27] were less interested, since they are not allowed to keep extra income. Two recruiters mentioned people were willing to participate in the experiment because of the option to do more on own initiative and have less interference from the municipality when looking for a job. Here we see that the (behavioural) motivation for more autonomy plays a role in people's decision to participate.

In addition, there is one related mechanism for not participating that is mentioned by all three recruiters. Many people on social assistance indicated they were not able to cope with the pressure of participating. They were scared of the changes it would bring, and thus did not participate. Similarly, the research bureau recorded that five people dropped out, due to too high psychological and emotional pressure. While stress reduction is a sub-mechanism that is expected to help people improve in other areas and was one of the goals of the experiment (Westerveld, 2015), actual stress also appeared to be a barrier to participate and thus a cause for bias. When testing the impact of the treatment in later studies, this means that there is some selection bias on the dependent variable that is likely to lead to underestimating the actual effect (King, Keohane, & Verba, 1994).

Finally, the qualitative interviews highlighted other additional factors that influenced participation, and in some cases might have led to a selection bias. First, as for reasons to participate, some people mentioned that the option to quit the experiment at any time they wanted was conditional for their participation, though not a reason for participating in itself. It suggests that conducting social experiments in which participants are not allowed to quit before its ending could lead to selection bias (likely from people who highly value autonomy and prefer fewer restrictions). Some participants were particularly interested because of the intensive treatment, wanting the coaching, and even the obligatory meetings as an extra motivation for themselves to get active. Also, one recruiter mentioned that it was easier to recruit people with whom there was already a personal connection. Additionally, some people were aware of the original aim of the experiment, the local basic income, and wanted to participate because they support that idea.[28] All these

---

[27]According to the Natural Persons Debt Restructuring Act (*Wet schuldsanering natuurlijke personen*, Wsnp) Dutch municipalities are obliged to help their residents with problematic debts. The main objective of the Wsnp is to offer (financial) perspective to individuals in a desperate financial situation as a result of debts.

[28]Survey data show that advocates of UBI may vote for the introduction of UBI because they favour the concept and want to stimulate the discussion, but are well aware that there are downsides too (see Delsen & Schilpzand, Chap. 3).

arguments indicate that socio-ideological motivations can also foster participation, but the frequency in which they came up is limited, and thus are not expected to have a lot of effect on the outcome of the experiment.

Second, additional reasons to refuse participation were mentioned as well: distrust towards the (local) government, bad experiences in the past with reintegration services, and principled objection to randomisation. In the Nijmegen case, the ethical objections against randomisation in an RCT were not brought up by policy-makers and politicians, as literature suggests, (*e.g.* Greenberg & Shroder, 2004; Heckman & Smith, 1995; Smith, 2000), but only by some potential participants themselves. Also, some people gave the impression of not being interested in making an effort, and preferring to stay out of sight. Altogether, these reasons together suggest that the unmotivated might be under-represented, and (highly) motivated are somewhat over-represented—the latter particularly so in the second treatment group (as participants could decide to drop out to 'escape' from obligatory meetings).

6.5.5 Overall Results

Overall, our statistical analyses show that all three clusters of factors matter, but not all variables of each cluster. As summarised in Table 6.5, we found that in comparing participants and non-participants, we should take into account education level, country of birth, household composition, exemption from the obligation to work and additional income. The most substantial effects were found for education, household composition (for 'couple no kids') and additional income. Most effects found were in line with our expectations, but only in about half of the factors we found a significant effect.

6.6 Conclusion and Discussion

6.6.1 Conclusion

The question guiding this chapter was "which factors contribute to people participating, or not participating, in the experiment with social assistance, as it is held in Nijmegen?" Answering this question sheds more empirical light on selection effects in social experiments, as well as on its causes, which we were able to do due to the registry data on the entire target population combined with a mixed methods approach. We formulated multiple hypotheses based on rational-choice theory and insights from behavioural science. Our empirical analyses show no significant differences between the participants and the target population regarding gender, age, costs sharing and the time somebody has an allowance.

The other five hypotheses yield significant results, although only four of them are fully confirmed. Higher-educated people (hypothesis 3) and people being born in the Netherlands (hypothesis 4) are significantly more likely to participate. Having a full exemption for the obligations regarding reintegration reduces the likelihood to participate. The composition of the household plays a significant role, but not exactly in the way we anticipated. Based on the theoretical mechanisms, we expected effects on single parents. Even though we found single parents significantly more likely to participate than couples (with and without kids), the main difference was between singles (also the ones without kids) and couples. This leads to the rejection of H5b and the partial acceptance of H5a. In addition, it is remarkable that couples without kids are very unlikely to participate. The reason for this, and for under-representation of couples in general, might be an interesting topic for further research. It has been noticed before that unemployment tends to come in couples (Ultee, Dessens, & Jansen, 1988), maybe the mechanisms behind that can offer some explanation. Finally, a relatively strong significant effect was found for people who already had an income before the experiment (hypothesis 9). This was to be expected: the rational-choice mechanism works most directly and visibly for this group. People who did not have an income yet, even if they would have above average gains from finding a part-time job, still needed to get that job to enjoy this advantage. People who already had income only needed to subscribe (and be lucky enough not to be randomised into the control group) to have a significant increase of income.

From that perspective, we could argue that participation in the experiment is on the low side. With so much to gain and nothing to lose, it is remarkable that over 80% with a registered income does not bother to participate. This might be due to what is known of how reciprocity functions: negative reciprocity is generally stronger than positive (Fehr & Gächter, 2000). People who feel they are unjustly disadvantaged by the government might not want to cooperate (in an experiment conducted by that government) even if it is in their own interest. Indeed, potential participants approached by recruiters mentioned the unwillingness to participate, caused by earlier bad experiences with a branch of government, or a general lack of trust therein.[29] Another concept that might shed light on the relative modest participation of people who already had an income is that of 'administrative burden' (Moynihan et al., 2014) . In their study, Moynihan and colleagues show how administrative hurdles that seem small, can have big effects on the individuals affected by them. This can lead to refraining from participating in a programme advantageous to them. Part of this concept is the fact that people tend to overvalue their *status quo*, even against an objectively superior situation. Other authors have also noted that bureaucratic procedures and (lacking) information about eligibility are hurdles when applying to welfare support (Renema & Lubbers, 2018). All this is an important reminder that, although personal material gain (as put forward by the rational-choice model) is a strong motive, it is far from all-explaining.

---

[29]One recruiter mentioned people had bad experiences with additional income. Having income in addition to an allowance is something that notoriously often goes wrong. This can lead to people losing their allowance, or having to repay tax allowances over a year after receiving them. For people on the subsistence minimum, this has grave consequences. It is not farfetched to assume that people who have experienced this once, will not be very eager to participate in an experiment with additional income.

Based on the overall results, we can draw the conclusion that the effects of selection bias are not that strong. The correlations (Cramer's V, in Table 6.3) are all rather weak, except the one for 'income'. However, that one score is still weak in conventional terms. At the same time, laying bare for which factors bias occurs is important for analysing and interpreting the results of the experiment, even if the bias is weak. It does not only help to interpret the generalisability of the differences between control and treatment groups, but also informs which control variables should be included in multivariate analyses when researching the differences between the developments among the target population and the treatment groups.

One unexpected, but important result is the effect of stress on participation, which was shown by the qualitative data. As described earlier, stress reduction among this group was one of the reasons politicians started this experiment, and stress reduction plays an important role in the mechanisms. This very same stress is also a reason for people not to participate and to drop out. In hindsight, we could have anticipated this. We approached 'stress' as something negative that could be alleviated by the experiment, and thus as a reason for people to participate. However, the literature also shows that this same stress impedes people's ability to make long term decisions (in their own interest). In that sense, this outcome is logical.

6.6.2 Limitations

The premises in this chapter are that selection effects are determined by what people have to gain by participating, either financially or otherwise (through gaining more autonomy, or stress relief). One could argue that there are other mechanisms that contribute to participating in an RCT experiment. Maybe this group participates more often in general in experiments, regardless of the specific contents. There are studies that analyse participation in questionnaires (*e.g.* Suchman & McCandless, 1940) and laboratory experiments (*e.g.* Slonim, Wang, Garbarino, & Merrett, 2013). To the best of our knowledge there is no similar research for RCTs. Moreover, we cannot simply assume that selection effects in replying to questionnaires (for instance: higher educated people participate more, Suchman and McCandless (1940)) or participating in short laboratory experiments (people who volunteer more often participate more, Slonim et al. (2013)) also take place in an intensive social experiment that takes almost 2 years. At the same time, we cannot rule out that there exist similar effects for RCTs. In some ways, this could even be expected. Though we have people participating who are homeless or institutionalised, it is conceivable that these are not represented according to the weight of their category. The very reclusive people, who hardly leave their house or do not open their mail, are obviously more difficult to reach. Another (somewhat related) consideration is whether the selection effects we find are not partly due to the mechanism of comprehension of the experiment. Higher educated people probably understand the experiment (and the opportunities it offers) better than lower educated ones, and people born in the Netherlands will on average understand it better than people born in other countries. This could play a role, no doubt. On the other hand, everything possible has been done in the recruitment to make the experiment as accessible as possible: personal contact, communication in an easy understandable language, animated movies and presentations throughout the city for those who are less literate. The relative small sizes of the selection effects indicate that this was at least partially successful. If (some) categories of people who are (on average) worse off (and have less chance to improve their situation) are indeed under-represented, we might overestimate the effect of the treatments when generalising the effects to the target group. On the other hand, the people on social assistance who are on the verge of getting a job could be under-represented (since they would have left the system before the start of the experiment). So it is hard to say something definite on the effects of these unobservable characteristics (which is a good example of the problem with external validity in RCTs).

6.6.3 Contributions to Science and Policy

In this study, we have empirically shown a number of selection effects in our experiment. We conclude that the selection effects in our social experiment can be traced back mostly to selection bias, and to a lesser extent to drop-out bias. The statistical data revealed the presence of selection bias, and the qualitative data confirms drop-out bias. Heckman and Smith (1995) mention that little is known about the effects of (among others) gender, ethnic background and advertisement in social experiments. Our experiment has addressed both gender and ethnic background (through country of origin), and sheds light on advertisement due to the attention we have given the recruitment processes. We assume advertisement plays a role in limiting the selection effects on the one hand, and due to the language used in the recruitment of participants on the other. In addition to these results, we have identified a number of other factors that can play a role in participating (or not) in an RCT through our interviews with recruiters; further research might show how relevant these are.

Our experiment also gives insight into the question whether rational-choice or behavioural concepts (most noticeably reciprocity (Fehr & Gächter, 2000)), the effects caused by stress related to poverty (Haushofer & Fehr, 2014; van Geuns, 2013) and bandwidth (Mullainathan & Shafir, 2013) are decisive in these selection effects. The outcome is that based on our results, we cannot conclude one mechanism is supported more over the other. The effect found for education and exemption can be explained by both mechanisms, and the role of country of origin adds practical expectations regarding selection effects to the story (the recruitment procedure was in Dutch only). The impact of income provides considerable support for the rational-choice mechanism, while the qualitative data underscore the importance of stress and behavioural arguments as well. We suppose that the two mechanisms are complementary. The different mechanisms might sometimes partly balance each other out, as they motivate groups of people at different ends of the scale. To illustrate, younger and lower-educated people seem to be mostly interested in earning extra income, while older and higher-educated people are more interested in autonomy and a less restrictive regime. As for the rational-choice argument: it is crucial that people understand their advantage. Not all people might understand that, or underestimate it. People have to be aware of the rationality of a choice to be able to be motivated by it.

This study's results are also relevant for policy-makers, among others exactly because of this possible lack of understanding people seem to have on what they have to gain. The results for costs sharers and single parents have particular implications for local policy. Based on rational-choice arguments, both groups were expected to participate more, which was not the case (at least: the overrepresentation of singles in general does not seem to imply that specific single *parents* are more likely to participate, and for the reasons we assumed). This suggests a lack of awareness of the possibilities. If a municipal government, such as the Nijmegen one, wants to stimulate their inhabitants on social assistance allowance to earn an income in addition to the allowance—and thus cost the municipality less money—it has to make sure those financial and non-financial advantages are known by and understandable for these people. Even if it is only the normal policy of being allowed to keep 25% of additional earnings.

The negative effect of stress on participation also has implications for our experiment, and similar social experiments (including those related to the UBI) based on voluntary participation in the Netherlands and worldwide. A group that is supposed to have specific advantages from the treatments (that is: people who experience stress due to the social assistance system) is most likely underrepresented due to selection bias and drop-out bias. When this is the case, the effects of the treatments could be substantially underestimated. Both researchers and policy-makers who want to experiment with social assistance policy should be well aware of this.

Acknowledgements This project was possible due to the municipality of Nijmegen, which instigated, organised and funded the experiment; the European Commission, who generously contributed by means of an ESF-SITS grant; and the Ministry of Social Affairs (SZW), who gave permission to deviate from the Participation Act and provided assistance in practical ways.

References

Arum, R., & Shavit, Y. (1995). Secondary vocational education and the transition from school to work. *Sociology of Education, 68*(3), 187–204. https://doi.org/10.2307/2112684

Becker, G. S. (1964). *Human capital: A theoretical and empirical analysis, with special reference to education*. New York: Columbia University Press.

Betkó, J. G. (2018). Het Nijmeegse experiment met de Participatiewet. *Sociaal Bestek, 80*(3), 34–36. https://doi.org/10.1007/s41196-018-0070-2

Boffey, D. (2015) Dutch city plans to pay citizens a 'basic income', and greens say it could work in the UK, the Guardian, 26 December. Retrieved June 8, 2019, from https://www.theguardian.com

Bregman, R. (2014). *Gratis geld voor iedereen*. Amsterdam: De Correspondent.

Campbell, D. T., & Stanley, J. C. (1963). Experimental and quasi-experimental designs for research. In N. L. Gage (Ed.), *Handbook of research on teaching* (pp. 171–246). Boston: Houghton Mifflin.

CBS. (2017) *55-plussers minder snel aan de slag dan jongere groepen*. Retrieved June 8, 2019 from www.cbs.nl

De Wispelaere, J., Halmetoja, A., & Pulkka, V.-V. (2018). The rise (and fall) of the basic income experiment in Finland. *CESifo Forum, 3*(19), 15–18.

Deater-Deckard, K., & Scarr, S. (1996). Parenting stress among dual-earner mothers and fathers: Are there gender differences? *Journal of Family Psychology, 10*(1), 45–59. https://doi.org/10.1037/0893-3200.10.1.45

Delsen, L. (2016) *The realisation of the participation society*. Welfare state reform in the Netherlands: 2010–2015, IMR Working Paper NiCE16-02, Nijmegen center for economics (NiCE), institute for management research, Nijmegen: Radboud University. Retrieved June 8, 2019, from https://www.researchgate.net/publication/305083246_The_realisation_of_the_participation_society_Welfare_state_reform_in_the_Netherlands_2010-2015

Divosa. (2015). Divosa-monitor factsheet (2015-II): Parttime werk in de bijstand. Retrieved June 8, 2019, from https://www.divosa.nl/sites/default/files/publicatie_bestanden/20150630_factsheet_parttime_werk_in_de_bijstand.pdf

Fehr, E., & Gächter, S. (2000). Fairness and retaliation: The economics of reciprocity. *The Journal of Economic Perspectives, 14*(3), 159–181. https://doi.org/10.2139/ssrn.229149

Greenberg, D. H., & Shroder, M. (2004). *The digest of social experiments*. The Urban Institute: Washington, DC.

Groot, L., Muffels, R. J., & Verlaat, T. (2019). Welfare states' social investment strategies and the emergence of Dutch experiments on a minimum income guarantee. *Social Policy & Society, 18*(2), 277–287. https://doi.org/10.1017/S1474746418000283

Hamilton, T. B. (2016) The Netherlands' upcoming money-for-nothing experiment, The Atlantic, Retrieved June 8, 2019, from https://www.theatlantic.com

Haushofer, J., & Fehr, E. (2014). On the psychology of poverty. *Science, 344*(6186), 862–867. https://doi.org/10.1126/science.1232491

Heckman, J. J., & Smith, J. A. (1995). Assessing the case for social experiments. *The Journal of Economic Perspectives, 9*(2), 85–110. https://doi.org/10.1257/jep.9.2.85

Heckman, J., Hohmann, N., Smith, J., & Khoo, M. (2000). Substitution and dropout bias in social experiments: A study of an influential social experiment. *Quarterly Journal of Economics, 115*(2), 651–694. https://doi.org/10.1162/003355300554764

Higgins, J. P. T, Green, S. (2011). Cochrane handbook for systematic reviews of interventions. Version 5.1.0 [updated March 2011]. The Cochrane collaboration. Retrieved June 13, 2019, from www.handbook.cochrane.org

Inglehart, R. (1997). *Modernization and postmodernization: Cultural, economic, and political change in 43 societies*. Princeton: Princeton University Press.

Jeffords, S. (2018, 31 August). March 2019 to mark end of Ontario's basic income pilot. *Global News*. Retrieved June 8, 2019, from https://globalnews.ca

King, G., Keohane, R. O., & Verba, S. (1994). *Designing social inquiry: Scientific inference in qualitative research*. Princeton: Princeton University Press.

Klandermans, B. (1984). Mobilization and participation: Social-psychological expansisons of resource mobilization theory. *American Sociological Review, 49*(5), 583–600. https://doi.org/10.2307/2095417

Kluve, J. (2010). The effectiveness of European active labor market programs. *Labour Economics, 17*(6), 904–918. https://doi.org/10.1016/j.labeco.2010.02.004

Lötters, F., Carlier, B., Bakker, B., Borgers, N., Schuring, M., & Burdorf, A. (2013). The influence of perceived health on labour participation among long term unemployed. *Journal of Occupational Rehabilitation, 23*(2), 300–308. https://doi.org/10.1007/s10926-012-9398-5

Matud, M. P. (2004). Gender differences in stress and coping styles. *Personality and Individual Differences, 37*(7), 1401–1415. https://doi.org/10.1016/j.paid.2004.01.010

Moynihan, D., Herd, P., & Harvey, H. (2014). Administrative burden: Learning, psychological, and compliance costs in citizen-state interactions. *Journal of Public Administration Research and Theory, 25*(1), 43–69. https://doi.org/10.1093/jopart/muu009

Mullainathan, S., & Shafir, E. (2013). *Scarcity: Why having too little means so much*. New York: Times BooksMacmillan.

Ptacek, J. T., Smith, R. E., & Dodge, K. L. (1994). Gender differences in coping with stress: When stressor and appraisals do not differ. *Personality and Social Psychology Bulletin, 20*(4), 421–430. https://doi.org/10.1177/0146167294204009

Ranshuijsen, A., & Westerveld, E. (2015, 27 January). Durf lokaal experiment met basisinkomen aan. *De Gelderlander*.

Renema, J. A., & Lubbers, M. (2018). Welfare-based income among immigrants in the Netherlands: Differences in social and human capital. *Journal of Immigrant and Refugee Studies, 17*(2), 1–24. https://doi.org/10.1080/15562948.2017.1420276

Sen, A. K. (1977). Rational fools: A critique of the behavioral foundations of economic theory. *Philosophy & Public Affairs, 6*(4), 317–344. Retrieved June 8, 2019, from http://www.jstor.org/stable/2264946

Shadish, W. R., Cook, T. D., & Campbell, D. T. (2002). *Experimental and quasi-experimental designs for generalized causal inference*. Boston: Houghton Mifflin.

Slonim, R., Wang, C., Garbarino, E., & Merrett, D. (2013). Opting-in: Participation bias in economic experiments. *Journal of Economic Behavior and Organization, 90*, 43–70. https://doi.org/10.1016/j.jebo.2013.03.013

Smith, J. A. (2000). *A critical survey of empirical methods for evaluating active labor market policies, Department of Economics Research Reports 2000-6*. London (ON): Department of Economics, University of Western Ontario.

Spence, M. (1973). Job market signaling. *Quarterly Journal of Economics, 87*(3), 355–374.

Standing, G. (2017). *Basic income and how we can make it happen*. London: Pelican Books.

Suchman, E. A., & McCandless, B. (1940). Who answers questionnaires? *The Journal of Applied Psychology, 24*(6), 758–769. https://doi.org/10.1037/h0063437

Thaler, R. H., & Sunstein, C. R. (2008). *Nudge: Improving decisions about health, wealth, and happiness*. New Haven: Yale University Press.

Tinnemans, W. (2014). Participatiewet wordt een drama, *Sociale Vraagstukken*. Retrieved June 8, 2019, from www.socialevraagstukken.nl

Tversky, A., & Kahneman, D. (1981). The framing of decisions and the psychology of choice. *Science, 211*(4481), 453–458. https://doi.org/10.1126/science.7455683

Ultee, W., Dessens, J., & Jansen, W. (1988). Why does unemployment come in couples? An analysis of (un)employment and (non)employment homogamy tables for Canada, the Netherlands and the United States in the 1980's. *European Sociological Review, 4*(2), 111–122. https://doi.org/10.1093/oxfordjournals.esr.a036471

Van Doorn, M., Scheepers, P., & Dagevos, J. (2013). Explaining the integration paradox among small immigrant groups in the Netherlands. *Journal of Immigration and Integration, 14*(2), 381–400. https://doi.org/10.1007/s12134-012-0244-6

van Geuns, R. (2013). *Every picture tells a story. Armoede: Een gedifferentieerd verschijnsel*. Amsterdam: Amsterdam University Press.

Vliegenthart, A. (2016). Versoepel tegenprestatie en kostdelersnorm. *Sociale Vraagstukken*. Retrieved June 8, 2019, from www.socialevraagstukken.nl

Westerveld, E. (2015). *Motie: Experimenteer met vertrouwen*. Retrieved June 8, 2019, from https://nijmegen.groenlinks.nl/

János Betkó (1980) works for the municipality of Nijmegen. He is the project manager of the basic income-related social experiment in Nijmegen. As an external Ph.D. student he conducts a large part of the research on the effects of the experiments. The hope is that this construction increases the chance that any new insights that are gained through research will be put into policy. He wrote about the policy context in which the Nijmegen experiment came into being and how it was organised (Een effectieve en sociale bijstand: het Nijmeegse experiment, *Sociaal Bestek*, 2018). He was educated as an historian, not a social scientist, so he is still suffering from a modest culture shock, mainly related to having to do stuff involving numbers.

Niels Spierings (1983) is Assistant Professor in Political Sociology at Radboud University (Nijmegen, the Netherlands). His research interests include labour market participation, trust, political attitudes, and ethnic and gender inequalities. He also has a keen interest in quantitative and qualitative research methods, mixed methods more particularly. On these different topics and approaches he has published several monographs, as well as in a wide ride range of international peer-reviewed journals, including *Social Forces, Research in Social Stratification and Mobility, European Sociological Review*, and *World Development*.

Maurice Gesthuizen (1977) is an Assistant Professor in the Department of Sociology at Radboud University (Nijmegen, the Netherlands). His major research interests include educational inequality, economic vulnerability, social capital, and their interrelations. He has published widely on these subjects in international scientific journals.

Peer Scheepers is Professor of Comparative Methodology at the Department of Sociology, Faculty of Social Sciences, Radboud University (Nijmegen, the Netherlands). He has developed research lines on social cohesion and has extensively published (>400 contributions) in (inter-)national journals on inclusion versus exclusion of (ethnic and sexual) minorities. He has guided (>35) Ph.D. candidates to earn their doctorate. He is an elected member of the Royal Dutch Academy of Arts and Sciences and of Academia Europeae; moreover, a Knight in the Order of the Dutch Lion.

Chapter 7
Experimental Economics: A Test-Bed for the Unconditional Basic Income?

Sascha Füllbrunn, Lei Delsen, and Jana Vyrastekova

Abstract Experimental economics is a method used by economists to explain or predict the behaviour of economic agents under a controlled institutional environment. This method can be used to test policies in order to inform policy-makers about the impact of proposed alternatives, referred to as 'whispering in the ears of princes' (Nobel prize winner Al Roth). In this chapter, we take a detailed look at this method and how it can help to understand the consequences of an Unconditional Basic Income. Additionally, we demonstrate a small scale experiments on risk-taking with and without the influence of the Unconditional Basic Income.

Keywords Experimental economics · Unconditional basic income · Policy testing · Investment behaviour · Stated preferences

7.1 Introduction

It is not unusual for people to be stuck in job positions they are forced to do in order to feed their family, and also to avoid financial sanctions in the common social welfare system. Other jobs appear to be just meaningless, i.e. 'bullshit jobs' (Dur & van Lent, 2019; Graeber, 2018). Such jobs are either psychologically destructive with negative effects on well-being, on health, and/or trap generations in low socio-economic status groups with barely a chance to break free. However, advances in Artificial Intelligence (AI) and robotics will have a drastic effect on the work force. Already today, technology would be able to replace 45% of workers' activities, suggesting a loss of 800 million jobs by 2030 (McKinsey Global Institute, 2017). Unconditional Basic Income (UBI) has been proposed as a solution to increasing inequality and poverty as a consequence of precarious working conditions and of digitalisation (Delsen, 1997; Standing, 2017; van der Veen & Groot, 2000; Van Parijs

---

S. Füllbrunn (✉) · L. Delsen · J. Vyrastekova
Institute for Management Research, Radboud University, Nijmegen, The Netherlands
e-mail: s.fullbrunn@fm.ru.nl; l.delsen@fm.ru.nl; j.vyrastekova@fm.ru.nl

& Vanderborght, 2017; White, 2016; Widerquist, Noguera, Vanderborght, & De Wispelaere, 2013; World Bank, 2019). Reducing poverty and tackling inequality are the main drivers of the UBI pilot in Scotland (see Danson, Chap. 4).

UBI is defined as "a periodic, cash income paid individually to all members of a political community without means test or work requirement" (Basic Income Earth Network, https://basicincome.org/basic-income/). The UBI needs to be financed by a redistribution system, and is therefore linked to a producing and political unit that organises it (see Delsen, Chap. 1). Advocates argue that UBI reduces poverty and income inequality, improves health, that it leads to positive job growth and lower school drop-out rates, or that it empowers important unpaid, voluntary roles such as care-givers. Opponents argue that UBI increases poverty by depriving the poor of needed targeted support, removes incentives to work leading to a labour and skills shortage, and that UBI is simply too expensive. However, those discussions are mostly of philosophical nature as the lack of empirical basis is driving the whole field.

Nonetheless, some empirical evidence is available. Field experiments test individual reactions of mostly poor/unemployed people on additional cash allowances, using variations of a basic income scheme (Chap. 8, Widerquist, 2018: 5). Moreover, their designs are quite similar, and the samples sizes and the amounts are rather small. For example, Finland just ended a two-year experiment and also in the Netherlands several municipalities test UBI-related schemes (2017–2020) (see Muffels & Gielens, Chap. 5). In Germany, HartzPlus (2019–2022) is a trust-based UBI-related experiments with social assistances, similar to the Dutch experiment. However, those pilot studies and the UBI policy proposals in the member states of the European Union do not consider 'unconditional' basic income scenarios, as payments often come with requirements (see Shanahan, Smith & Srinivasan, Chap. 3). They also operate in a fixed timeframe such that behaviour of the subjects is adjusted to a short-term experiment, and not a life-time basic income. Furthermore, none of those studies consider economic systems with redistribution institutions to finance UBI (Noguera & De Wispelaere, 2006). Finally, local politicians often intervene in the experimental design, keep the experimental scope limited, and even end the experiment earlier when the political environment changes. Hence, optimal experimental conditions are barely available, such that results are often diluted and need to be handled with care. The (academic) discussion is thus built upon policy reports, white papers, discussion papers, and books (e.g. ILO, 2017; Standing, 2017; UNDP China, 2017; Van Parijs & Vanderborght, 2017; Widerquist et al., 2013; World Bank, 2019), but not on scientific evidence. Often, researchers are clear advocates or opponents of UBI, which is also communicated in the media.[1] However, we barely find any scientific articles on the effect of UBI in top (economics) journals. Not only empirical, but also theoretical and behaviourally-founded analyses are largely missing in the field of UBI research.

---

[1] Researchers and politicians give their opinions based on partial elements of a society, e.g. Goldin (2018). Five reasons why universal basic income is a bad idea, *Financial Times*, 11 February; Standing (2018) Universal basic income would enhance freedom and cut poverty, *Financial Times*, 14 February 2018.

The challenge to implement new policies motivates the constant search for novel methodological responses. Of course, policy-makers can only implement a new policy based on theoretical considerations or micro-economic or macro-economic simulations. However, in searching to establish what policy would be optimal—why, and under what circumstances—economists face the challenge to identify the policy's causal impacts, its key behavioural parameters, and structural factors that condition or explain the consequences of a new policy. The method of experimental economics allows us to test for such causal impacts.

We thus propose to test UBI using the methods of experimental economics, in order to improve the knowledge base of economists and policy-makers, and to allow for the discussions about boundary conditions for a successful implementation of UBI to be tested empirically. In this approach, experimental subjects take the role of residents in a virtual economy, making real choices (labour supply/investments) with real economic consequences (monetary incentives) in order toto test-bed UBI in a wind-tunnel for institutional design. This approach serves as a middle step between theorising and implementation.

Moreover, experimental methods can be used to build up the test-bed environment in the first place, i.e. to construct a virtual economy that is sufficiently complex to capture the necessary real-world feedback mechanisms between various economic activities, but sufficiently controlled to collect meaningful data from all relevant decision makers. Such experiments allow for details that are often unavailable in the natural context. The behaviour of people (e.g. decision on job-related effort, leisure time, socially relevant activities) depends on the impact of the UBI (policy intervention), their socio-economic environment, i.e. Socio-Economic Determinants (SED) and their preferences and characteristics (P) together with some noise.[2] How the behaviour of people influences the outcome is an empirical issue. For example, if Gross Domestic Product (GDP) is the outcome variable and UBI indeed reduces the incentives to work, we would observe a negative effect on GDP. However, if UBI reduces work-pressure allowing to take more leisure and thereby reducing stress, or stimulates people to have a job they really like, the productivity might go up as people are more productive than before which would have a positive effect on GDP. These two models can be described in UBI stylised equation models (based on Barrett & Carter, 2010):

$$\text{Behaviour} = f(\text{Outcome}, \text{Policy Intervention (UBI)}, \text{Socio-Economic Determinants}, \text{Preferences}, \text{Error Term});$$

$$\text{Outcome} = f(\text{Behaviour}, \text{Policy Intervention (UBI)}, \text{Socio-Economic Determinants}, \text{Preferences}, \text{Error Term}).$$

---

[2] In Chapter 2, Delsen and Schilpzand use survey data to establish the expected changes in labour market behaviour of UBI in the European Union.

What can help to find relevant data for such a model? Panel data analysis is not helpful as preferences are barely available in the field, and even if they are, the functional relationship between the policy intervention and preferences is unclear. Survey results are helpful to learn about the people's preferences and attitudes. However, ordinary people and sometimes even so-called experts barely understand the complexity and consequences of UBI in its full range, and consider a rather narrow frame by looking at a reduced model. Controlled laboratory experiments attempt to circumvent these limitations by controlling the policy instrument, UBI, across the population in an effort to guarantee the statistical independence of UBI from SED and P. Such models allow to map the relationships between the input factors. However, economists often assume subjects to be rational beings who are only interested in their own (monetary) benefits, which is partly falsified (see below). These 'convenient' assumptions of the rational economic man allow for tractable mathematical models that can be solved due to predictable reactions of subjects to e.g. policy interventions. However, subjects are not rational and here 'behavioural economics' comes into play. This field attempts to incorporate people's actual behaviour based on limitations to computing (e.g. bounded rationality), misperception of information (e.g. money illusion), lack of self-control (e.g. hyperbolic discounting), frame dependency (e.g. reference points and loss aversion), social context (e.g. trust, social norms), and other regarding preferences (e.g. fairness, altruism). However, in contrast to well-defined models in economics, behavioural economics often suffers from arbitrary applied models from psychology or sociology to explain so called anomalies (Erev & Greiner, 2015). Further on, the field is meant to explain individual economic behaviour and less so aggregate behaviour, e.g. individual behavioural biases might disappear in aggregation, which is the relevant dimension for policy intervention. We complement the methodology of 'experimental economics', which is an established method to test policies, and the effect of institutions (e.g. Roth, 2015).

In Sect. 7.2, we take a detailed look at the method; what is actually experimental economics, why should we run experiments and what are relevant design elements? In Sect. 7.3, we review the literature on laboratory experiments that consider UBI. In Sect. 7.4, we provide evidence on a small online experiment that we have conducted with 'M-Turkers'. In Sect. 7.5, we conclude.

7.2 Experimental Economics Methodology

7.2.1 What Is an (Economic) Experiment?

Experiments are quite simple. Take as an example a model which makes a prediction on the causal relationship between work effort (Y) and the compensation scheme (X), *e.g.* saying that a piece rate compensation increases work effort in comparison to a fixed payment. The experimenter now randomly allocates experimental subjects to group A (piece rate) and group B (fixed payment), *i.e.* $X \in \{A, B\}$. Due to randomisation, the subjects in both groups have a similar background (vector Z)

which is uncorrelated with X. In the experiment, subjects work, and decide themselves how much effort they will apply. They will be compensated by the treatment they were allocated to. In the analysis, a simple OLS regression model like $Y_i = \alpha + \beta D_X + \gamma' Z_i + \epsilon_{iX}$ with D_X being a dummy for A (or B) can show whether the payment scheme has a significant influence on work effort, i.e. whether β is significantly different from zero, controlling for background variables Z (gender, age, psychological traits, ...). Hence, the variable X is directly controlled or manipulated by the experimenter while other background conditions are kept under control, leading to high internal validity.

To be more precise, the experimenter implements a so-called 'micro-economic system' in the laboratory to analyse three major components: the environment, the institution, and the outcome (e.g. Smith, 1994). The outcome (behaviour of subjects) is modelled as a function of the environment and the institution. The institution is a set of rules governing behaviour by setting incentives, punishments, and their enforcement. The environment is a complex set of factors including the decision environment, the value of parameters, the role of subjects, the rules of interactions between subjects, individual endowments, utility functions and technology.

The micro-economic system implemented in the laboratory is not a hypothetical construct for the subjects. The subjects make decisions according to the rules of the system and will be paid according to their performance. Nobel Laureate Vernon Smith formulated the 'induced value theory' which is the precept of experimental economics (Smith, 1976). It stipulates that the experimental environment needs to be designed in such a way that subjects' earnings are salient and thus increase with their performance or good outcomes, and decrease with bad outcomes. Such monetary incentives satisfy the monotonicity requirement, and if subjects are paid amounts carefully calibrated to the replacement value of time of the subjects, then salience of the incentives is guaranteed as well. Economists therefore use monetary incentives in their laboratory environments and involve real subjects making real economic decisions with real economic consequences (Plott, 1982).

7.2.2 Why Run Economic Experiments?

Nobel Laureate Al Roth argues that economists who run experiments have three (overlapping) reasons to do so (Roth, 1986). They run experiments to test and modify theories ('speaking to theorists'), to collect data on interesting phenomena and important institutions ('searching for facts'), and to test policies ('whispering into the ears of princes'). In this chapter we will focus on the last reason. For policy-makers to be willing to implement a new redistribution system like UBI, they want to know about the effects of such a system on the economy or the society. Experimental economics offers a complementary (and relatively cheap) way to test-bed various systems by controlling all underlying parameters. Such results will advance the knowledge base of policy-makers to allow for evidence-based decision-making, before implementing such a system. These 'policy-oriented' experiments have something in common with the experiments that test theory. Both test hypotheses which arose from formal economic theories, or from the arguments of lawyers, lobbyists, and experts.

Since the 1980s, experimental economists have tested institutional design, for example the allocation of airport slots (Grether, Isaac, & Plott, 1989), the pricing of space stations (Plott & Porter, 1996), for the regulation of inland water transportation (Hong & Plott, 1982), of the gas industry (Grether & Plott, 1984) and of gas transportation networks (Plott, 1988), for the construction of the new Arizona Stock Exchange (Smith & Williams, 1992), for the regulation of the market for new physicians and surgeons (Roth & Peranson, 1999), for the allocation of telecom licences (Guala, 2001; Plott, 1997), and the allocation of scarce school positions (Calsamiglia, Haeringer, & Klijn, 2010). These examples show that there can be an important cycle of development of ideas, theories and discussions of implementation constraints between theory and practice. The case of allocating school positions to students represents a good case study (matching markets). The 'Boston' mechanism is now a very popular student-placement mechanism, even though it is still under critical observation (e.g. Abdulkadiroğlu, Che, & Yasuda, 2011). What started as an analysis of the existing allocation mechanism by game theoretic tools, developed into a rich stream of (experimental) research, involving new theoretical results as well as (field) experiments evaluating and comparing the existing and theoretically proposed solutions (e.g. Dur, Hammond, & Morrill, 2018). Testing a new redistribution system for society, like the UBI, can be a further case study to develop a rich stream of socially relevant research. However, experiments on policy design for revising economic systems are rare.

7.2.3 Relevant Design Elements

The method of experimental economics has several design elements. In the following, we will briefly introduce some of those. These design elements illustrate how this method works, but also delineate the boundary conditions that need to be satisfied so that data collected in an experiment can be considered a valid contribution to a policy discussion, such as a discussion of UBI and its possible impact on the economy.

Monetary Incentives In experimental economics, financial incentives are used to motivate subjects, in such a way that the payment of the subjects is a function of the choices made in the experiment. In contrast, in almost all experiments in psychology, subjects earn a flat fee for participation (which may involve credit in a class) or are not paid for participating. For the decision maker, such hypothetical decisions without any consequences sometimes lead to biased results, as subjects often do not read the instructions thoroughly, make rather socially desirable decisions, or take more risks as they fear no consequences. Often the treatment effect can be found with and without incentives. For a discussion see e.g. Camerer and Hogarth (1999) or Hertwig and Ortmann (2001). Sometimes, however, incentives are relevant to get subjects in the laboratory (Abeler & Nosenzo, 2015). Importantly, the use of monetary incentives linked to decisions in economic experiments decreases noise in the data, and allows for replication of the experimental design. As such, they are an important contribution to the internal validity of an experiment—the ability to link variations in the experimental design to the variations in the observed outcome variables (subjects' behaviour).

No Deception Rule Deception includes providing false information in the instructions, e.g. subjects play against a computer even though the instruction says they play against a human being, or withholding relevant information with severe impact on their decisions among others. Experimental psychology allows such procedures. A debriefing is necessary to inform subjects about the experimental design, and in particular on why deception was necessary. However, if such subjects come back to other experiments, it is unclear whether they can trust the instructions, and thus are less inclined to behave in line with the instructions. Experimental economists believe that researchers should not employ deception in experiments. This rule exists to protect future researchers to conduct experiments with participants who perceive their instructions to be an accurate representation of the game being played. As always, there are grey zones on what might be allowed and what not. See e.g. Hertwig and Ortmann (2008) for a discussion on deception and also Cason and Wu (2018) for a recent contribution in the field. In line with monetary incentives, the no deception rule in economic experiments increases control over the subjects' expectations in the laboratory, and thus contributes to the internal validity of an experimental design.

Laboratory and Field Experiments Field and laboratory experiments add to our ability to understand the 'real' world. The methods should be seen as complements and not as substitutes. Different forms of experimental designs can be considered (e.g. Harrison & List, 2004). In a conventional laboratory experiment, we invite student subjects to a computer laboratory, applying an abstract framing with an imposed set of rules. In an artefactual field experiment, we replace students with a 'relevant' subject pool, but keep the abstract framing, e.g. inviting managers for a managerial decision experiment. In a framed field experiment, we add context to the abstract framing. For example, to understand trading behaviour in experimental asset markets, we bring a mobile laboratory to a trading company and run controlled experiments with the traders (lab-in-the-field experiment). In a natural field experiment, however, the subjects naturally undertake some tasks which can be manipulated by a researcher; those subjects do not know that they participate in an experiment. For example, research assistants purchased *dürüm döner* under different conditions to test whether the weight of the *dürüm döner* increases when tipping the vendor or making compliments beforehand (Kirchler & Palan, 2018). Using laboratory and/or field experiments have different pros and cons. For example Part IV in the *Handbook of experimental methodology* (Fréchette & Schotter, 2015) discusses those differences. In Sect. 7.2.4 below we have a closer look at field experiments on UBI.

External vs. Internal Validity Problems of internal validity have to do with drawing inferences from experimental data to the causal mechanisms of a given decision-making environment. Do we understand what is happening in a particular experimental situation? Are we drawing correct inferences within the experiment? Related to UBI, does UBI change behaviour in the system and if so, why and how? Such a situation can be tested several times with different parameters. Problems of external validity instead have to do with drawing inferences from experimental data to the outside world. Can we use experimental knowledge to understand what goes on in the 'real world'? Are we drawing correct inferences from the experiment? Related to UBI, would UBI have similar effects in the real world as in the laboratory? Experiments as used in experimental economics have high internal validity. They allow for causal inferences due to high control on the parameters of the experimental environment, and for replication, due to reduction of the impact of nuisance variables and due to random assignment of subjects. However, more control and abstraction to consider the relevant variables in an environment comes with a reduction in external validity due to less 'realism'. We discuss this in more detail in the next Sect. 7.2.4.

Further elements contain the abstraction of context, transparency of the experimental design (protocol, instructions, etc.), and proper analysis using conventional techniques, but also techniques applied to special features of an experiment, e.g. experimetrics (Moffatt, 2016). For the interested reader, we refer to Holt (2019) or Weimann and Brosig-Koch (2019) for further information on running laboratory experiments.

7.2.4 A Comparison of Field Experiments and Laboratory Experiments on UBI

Noguera and De Wispelaere (2006) consider the differences between laboratory experiments and large-sale field experiments. One example of the latter is the recent UBI implementation in Finland (see e.g. https://www.policyforum.net/finlands-universal-basic-income/), but also experiments with Negative Income Tax (NIT) have been considered in the field, mainly in the United States (US) and Canada (see e.g. Groot, 2006; Widerquist, 2018). Such experiments have high costs, they cannot be replicated and thus results might be confounded by omitted variables, researchers have limited control over the relevant variables of interest, side-effects for non-voluntary subjects might be severe, political manipulation might take place from opponents or advocators, and the effect that an experiment might end, which cannot be taken into account when acting in such an environment. Noguera and De Wispelaere (2006) thus "plea for the use of laboratory experiments in basic income research". Such policy-relevant experimental research should contain a valid experimental design, production of scientific evidence, translation of evidence into policy recommendations, and assessment of recommendations by third parties. Large-scale field experiments cannot guarantee that the first three stages are free from political influence. Laboratory experiments, in contrast, have a closed environment which enables high control on the variables of relevance and scientific integrity without external influence. In comparison to large-scale field experiments, laboratory experiments have lower costs, can separate and control the variables of interest to make causal inferences, control for preferences, personal beliefs, value orientations and choices of subjects, generate several independent observations, not only one-shot observations, and allow to change the experimental design after gaining insights from earlier sessions. Noguera and De Wispelaere (2006) conclude that, as in field experiments, the outcomes of laboratory experiments approximate the real world and help only to safeguard against inappropriate conclusions. Finally, the question is whether conclusions drawn from field experiments conducted in Finland or the US can be translated to other countries. By contrast, laboratory experiments can be replicated in any country with any population, and could be considered a necessary precursor for a design of an empirically founded large-scale policy experiment (for more information on field experiments, see e.g. Teele, 2014).

In conclusion, laboratory experiments have higher internal validity, while field experients have higher external validity (see Sect. 7.2.3 above). The method of laboratory experiments has high internal validity allowing for causal inferences, provides high control on the parameters of the experimental environment, allows to detect variables of interest which cannot be observed in the field, reduces (unknown) confound effects, allows for replication, reduces the impact of nuisance variables due to random assignment of subjects, and reduces the impact of third-party interest on the design (as e.g. in politicians or interest parties on field experiment). More control and abstraction to consider the relevant variables in an environment comes with a reduction in external validity due to less 'realism'. However, the issue of realism is not a distinctive feature of laboratory vs. field data, but the real issue is determining the best way to isolate the causal effect of interest (Falk & Heckman, 2009). Nonetheless, Hebst and Mas (2015) show that experiments have more external validity than previously recognised. The students' behaviour in the laboratory is often not different from more relevant real world pendants (Charness & Kuhn, 2011).

We think that the advantages of laboratory experiments to test the effects of UBI outweigh some caveats (which can be controlled for). This method can investigate and illuminate any unintended consequences, and can suggest parameters that policy-makers might consider in their final implementation (Croson & Gächter, 2010). After allowing for careful laboratory experiments on elements of UBI, we expect some further experiments in this field, increasing the external validity of the findings from the laboratory. That step is a consequence of arguments that findings from the laboratory do not necessarily readily translate into the field context, and extensive laboratory research thus precedes the field research.

7.3 UBI: Experimental Evidence?

Experiments on the impact of UBI are meant to compare conditions with and without UBI—control and treatment, respectively. There are two possibilities to conduct such comparisons; either the control and treatment group differ in whether UBI is implemented at the start, or UBI is introduced over time in the treatment, but not in the control. In both cases, the researcher can compare the variable of interest between the control and treatment groups. In the latter case, the researcher can also consider the change in the variable of interest. Research questions using experiments can address questions about the change in income generation, i.e. does UBI increase or decrease effort to generate income, but also whether a tax system is able to fund UBI, i.e. what tax system can finance the UBI? Finally, it boils down to the main question: does UBI increase welfare? In the following, we review the scarce literature on laboratory experiments. In the UBI literature, contributions are categorised in 'judgement formation' and 'choice', defined by Camerer and Loewenstein (2004). The latter considers the question about the effect of UBI e.g. on welfare, which is fully operational. The former considers the effect of discourse on the arguments or decisions for or against UBI implementation.

7.3.1 Choice: Effort Provision Under UBI

Haigner, Höchtl, Jenewein, Schneider, and Wakolbinger (2012) consider labour-supply effects comparing a 'CONTROL' treatment, a 'TAX' treatment, and a 'UBI' treatment using a 'real-effort' experiment. In each of the eight periods, subjects calculated the sum of five 2-digit integers on the screen for five minutes. The number of correct answers times a piece rate of € 0.30 yields the period income of a subject. Being matched in a group of three, each subject individually chose among three options before doing the calculations. In option '*ind*', the subject kept his own income, in option '*group*', the subject shared the income equally among the three group members, and in option '*leisure*', the subject was free to browse the web, check e-mails, use social networking, etc., i.e. the experimental screen was relegated to the background and no income was generated. In TAX, a 50% tax rate is applied to any income which is redistributed equally to the group members. In UBI, subjects are in a similar scenario as in TAX. However, they receive an unconditional payment of €15 upfront and the tax revenue is held back to 'finance' that unconditional basic income. In CONTROL, neither the tax rate nor the unconditional payment was applied. The results show that overall about 85% chose option *ind* in CONTROL, and about 80% in TAX and UBI. The remaining subjects chose option *group*; a negligible percentage of the subjects chose option *leisure* in TAX and UBI. The number of correct answers was slightly higher in CONTROL—about 1.5 more questions were solved in comparison to UBI. However, the difference across treatments is not significant at the 5% level ($p = 0.07$ comparing UBI to CONTROL). Finally, they looked at the income distribution and found net income variances to be significantly lower in UBI than in the other treatments (Gini coefficient 0.193 in CONTROL and 0.118 in UBI). The results suggest that UBI lowers income inequality at some loss of output (about 12%) and that only a small budget deficit is needed to finance the upfront payment (average tax revenue 14.43 in UBI). However, from the results we cannot see whether the poorest subjects in a group have lower income in CONTROL than in UBI. In contrast, the unpublished study by Kawagoe (2009), which is integrated in Chap. 8 with a similar design, shows that the UBI treatment reduces the observed number of solved mathematical questions, i.e. an indication that UBI reduces incentives for labour supply. However, comparing UBI to a NIT treatment in which the target income equals the UBI, yields no difference in effort. Even though these papers provide a nice start to consider this matter, both studies show some caveats which need to be addressed in future experiments. Future experiments should have sufficient power and take dynamic (learning) behaviour into account. They should also look at different real-effort tasks as the calculation task itself seems to provide some hedonic benefit rather than effort. These experiments are in line with the methodology of experimental economics in which different conditions might have an influence on properly incentivised experiments.

7.3.2 Judgment: Voter Support and the Impact of UBI return

Kederer, Klein, Kovarich, and Kumm (2017) provide an interesting design to consider opinions about income distribution schemes, including UBI. However, what they consider is more of an experimental design idea than an experiment, due to only one observation, no treatment comparison, and no monetary incentives. Nonetheless, we would like to briefly discuss the experimental design. Via a chat discussion, nine subjects first have to unanimously agree on one of three income redistribution schemes under the veil of ignorance (Rawls, 1971), i.e. not knowing what the income generation process will be. The *potential* gross income yields amounts from 0 to 4000. The distribution schemes generate net incomes either from 1000 to 2600 (high UBI), from 450 to 3250 (subsistence UBI), or from 450 to 3800 (simply redistribution of income tax). After agreeing on one of the schemes, subjects solve math problems in a trial and see their potential gross income including ranking of all subjects afterwards. This task should provide information about the relative position of the subjects. Now, a majority vote is sufficient to change the redistribution scheme. Finally, the subjects conduct the same task but such that the gross incomes are final. Again, they vote for the distribution scheme. The general research question is whether subjects change their voting behaviour in a self-serving manner after observing their own income relative to the others. The group agreed on the high UBI scheme, with the highest redistribution effect. The majority vote after the first trial yields the high UBI scheme as well, even though 1/3 opted for the subsistence UBI. After the second trial, only 1/9 opted for the subsistence UBI, and none of the participants opted for the simple redistribution via an income tax. However, without monetary incentives and this small number of observations, the result has no explanatory power. Even so, the experimental design has potential to request redistribution preferences based on real monetary incentives. Note that the experimental design cannot make causal inferences, as a treatment comparison is not implemented. One possibility to amend this would be to manipulate the schemes available. For example, the treatments can have different combinations of schemes from a set with no redistribution, taxed income equally distributed, NIT, and different levels of UBI including redistribution. Is UBI always the best choice among those systems under consideration? Kederer et al. (2017) made several suggestions to improve their design. This experiment, however, aims to extract the preferences of the participants for redistribution systems. It does not consider whether one system yields higher welfare than another system.[3]

In a recent experiment, Legein, Vandeleene, Heyvaert, Perrez, and Reuchamps (2017) consider the effects of framing on the arguments for or against UBI. They first provided a short description and then asked their subjects to argue about the UBI. The description was manipulated by using different frameworks. Two of those refer to the UBI as "We could see it as an income supplied by the State so that citizens can freely live their life without having to be concerned about material constraints" and as "We could see it as an income that citizens receive from the State by the very fact that they are members of it." With about 100 observations in each treatment, they take the arguments and categorise them. The arguments in the first frame highlight the positive consequences of the UBI; the increase in the quality of life and the fulfilment of the basic needs in life. The arguments in the second frame tend to indicate the negative political considerations that would support the fact that a UBI is needed. Those participants highlight the economic crisis or the fact that there are neglected people in our society, and these participants also tend to focus their argumentation more on the current failure of the welfare state. This experimental study by Legein et al. (2017) shows impressively that the discourse used in the discussion plays an important role on how people form their opinion.

The experiment from Kederer et al. (2017), when properly implemented, can help to understand judgement formation under incentivised conditions, given they implement a valid treatment variable. The Legein et al. (2017) experiment is rather in line with priming experiments in psychology.

Our review on experimental research regarding UBI is quite sobering. Given the history of experiments on income distribution (e.g. Clark & D'Ambrosio, 2015), distributional preferences (e.g. Engelmann & Strobel, 2004), or income tax regimes (e.g. Fochmann, Weimann, Blaufus, Hundsdoerfer, & Kiesewetter, 2013), we wonder why the implementation of UBI has barely been taken into account in the literature, even after Noguera and De Wispelaere (2006) plead for the use of laboratory experiments. For example, experiments that simulate labour market environments ('experimental labour economics') have a long tradition in experimental economics (Charness & Kuhn, 2011; Falk & Gächter, 2010). Such studies consider for example the effect of payment schemes, income tax schemes, or of competition on work behaviour among others. 'Work' in the laboratory is proxied by so called real-effort games (real effort) (Charness & Kuhn, 2011) or by decisions on costly disutility on labour (stated effort) (Charness, Gneezy, & Henderson, 2018). Other studies consider labour market effects in macro-economic settings (Duffy, 2014). Even though some consider redistribution elements (e.g. Riedl & van

---

[3]Actually, given the schemes provided, the total net income in Kederer et al. (2017) is lower in the UBI schemes than in the simple tax scheme.

Winden, 2001), none of them consider UBI. Hence, the techniques and design elements are available to run proper experiments on UBI.

Following Noguera and De Wispelaere (2006), we would like to provide some food for thought on experimental designs that could be considered in the future. Such designs capture different aspects in the discussion on UBI and make use of the advantages of laboratory experiments (see above). We also only refer to experiments in the choice frame as they provide information on the effect of UBI, rather than the opinion of subjects about UBI, the judgement frame.

Task and Skill Heterogeneity In a society, people have different skills. On the one hand such skills can be reflected by the subjects' ability to solve particular tasks. For example, the gross income Y_{it} can be a function of the outcome from a real-effort task, i.e. $Y_{it} = a + b \times E_{it}^c$ assuming $a \geq 0$, $b > 0$, and $c > 0$. The higher the subject's ability, the higher the gross income. On the other hand, such skills can be manipulated in the experiment. Suppose some subjects are randomly assigned to have inferior skills (I) while other subjects are assigned to have superior skills (S). In such a case, we can set $a_I < a_S$, $b_I < b_S$, and/or $c_I < c_S$ such that given the same effort level, the inferior subjects always earn less than the superior subjects. What happens if UBI is implemented in such a society with clear income inequality?

Uncertainty Among others, Varian (1980) argues that a redistributive welfare state positively impacts economic efficiency by providing insurance against adversities related to human capital or market failure. Sinn (1995, 1996) additionally argues that a redistributive welfare state even raises income levels and boosts economic growth via reducing the reluctance of individuals to make economically beneficial, but individually risky, investment choices. They argue that individual investment levels in a society increase under certain circumstances when gains of successful investors are taxed and redistributed to cover the losses of unsuccessful investors. Again, UBI can be compared to several other treatments. Suppose investments earn $Y_{it} = (E_{it} - I_{it}) + r_t \times I_{it}$ with E_{it} being the endowment at the beginning of the period, I_{it} being the investment, and r_t being the return which is randomly distributed with some mean μ_t and some standard deviation σ_t. Even inflation can be implemented by reducing the period endowment. In a control treatment, subjects make individual investment decisions and the society's income is just the total income of all individuals. In a potential tax treatment, subjects make individual investment decisions and gains are taxed while losses are partly covered (excess taxes can be equally distributed), i.e. $Y_{ti} = E_{it} - I_{it} + (1 - \tau) \times r_t \times I_{it}$. A UBI treatment would earn a sure payment U which is added to the income and financed by tax $Y_{it} = E_{it} - I_{it} + (1 - \tau)_{r_t > 0} \times r_t \times I_{it} + U$. Now, we can compare whether the additional safety net of the UBI income increases investment incentives which, given positively expected returns, increases the society's income in total.

Magnitude of UBI The experiments so far consider an arbitrary UBI level. To understand what UBI level allows for an optimal trade-off between incentives and safety net, experiments need to consider different UBI levels. Individual decision-making experiments (controls) with investments or real effort can be used to set the different UBI levels. For example, UBI levels can equal the control's incomes at the low, middle, and high quartiles (q). Then it can be tested whether the distribution of effort levels is indeed shifted to the right at or below threshold q. Of course, a theoretical background needs to define the optimal UBI level and also what the target variable for optimality is (e.g. growth, GDP, ...).

Transition Experiments often make a clear treatment comparison, for example by either implementing or not implementing UBI. However, in a dynamic setting, UBI can also be implemented in some periods only. For instance, subjects start with a real-effort task that generates income for five periods. In the UBI treatment the sixth period introduces UBI, i.e. subjects generate income and UBI for the next five periods, while in the control, subjects still earn income from the real-effort task. Does the implementation of the additional income shift effort in UBI in comparison to the control and in comparison to periods 1–5? We can also imagine to drop UBI in later periods, say 10–15? Do effort levels fall back to the levels before the UBI?

Heritage People in a society have different endowments in their lives, i.e. some people are well equipped while others need social benefits right from the start. Such a heterogeneity can also be taken up in a UBI experiments. Does UBI reduce such inequalities? Are both groups better off with UBI?

Consumption People in a society have different needs, i.e. different levels of consumption. Such heterogeneities can be taken up in a UBI experiment. Further on, people have different aspiration levels when it comes to consumption. Some people need less than others while others need to put in more effort to reach their aspiration level.

Sustainability Within a society, the introduction of UBI might lead to shifts in labour supply, shifts in production of human capital, and ultimately, affect the GDP of a country. Is UBI sustainable? What kind of shifts can be expected? This question relates to the accumulation of the effects in consumption, risky investments, etc. into a macro-economic consequence of UBI.

Migration The discussion in the media on the UBI natural experiment in Finland has raised the question whether foreign people immigrate to exploit a UBI system (see also Widerquist, 2018). To test such an environment, we could consider two closed experimental societies, e.g. one 'control' society without redistribution and one 'UBI' society with redistribution in line with UBI. At some point in time, we open the border and subjects can migrate to the other society. Do we observe people migrating to UBI as they perform below average in the control society but want to achieve at least UBI? Do we observe people migrating to the control society as they perform above average but do not want to pay tax? If so, does UBI break down due to polarisation of societies to a good performing and a worse performing society?

Task Heterogeneity The experiments discussed above use one simple real-effort task which might even earn hedonic utility (for some subjects it might be fun to sum up numbers). However, some people like their job and would not change their working behaviour with UBI, while others do not like their job and would either reduce working hours or improve their working skills to switch to a different job. Hence, different tasks can be implemented in the laboratory to reflect heterogeneity in jobs.[4] Does UBI affect boring tasks more than interesting or difficult tasks? Does UBI make people switch tasks, and if so, can it happen that some tasks cannot be fulfilled anymore?

7.4 Example: The Effect of UBI on Risk-taking

7.4.1 Introduction

Risky investments may be socially efficient—take as an example investments into education, or investments into innovation, or new entrepreneurial ideas. However, these investments might be prohibitively costly from an individual perspective if they affect the minimal aspiration or survival level of the individual's income. People might forego such investments if they could be left with too few resources, unable to function in the society, e.g. unable to pay for accommodation or health insurance. Alternatively, this could happen when people would invest time and effort into education or new ideas instead of being active in the labour market, therefore delaying the income stream in exchange for a future uncertain improvement of own labour market position. According to Rutger Bregman (2018), UBI should be considered as an amount of "venture capital for the people". UBI could thus allow for risky investments, by guaranteeing the subsistence income.

Supporting some individual risk-taking could be welfare improving and UBI could serve as an insurance mechanism, allowing individuals to satisfy their basic needs while pursuing these socially desirable risky alternatives. Note that UBI could also stimulate excessive risk-taking and hurt self-selection incentives, so that sorting by talent or skills into the risk-taking might be weakened. We will not consider this aspect at this moment, and rather focus on the following question: do people take more risks when receiving a UBI? In the following, we discuss an incentivised economic experiment designed to address this question.

First, we will briefly discuss the source of our experimental data. As mentioned before, economic experiments can be implemented in a variety of environments, ranging from a laboratory to the actual field context. We collect our dataset using the online platform Amazon Mechanical Turk (M-Turk) (Paolacci & Chandler, 2014). This platform allows researchers to assign online tasks to a pool of subjects who have self-selected themselves to accept such online tasks, referred to as M-Turkers. It is important for our purposes that these are people who are interested in earning money for their time and attention on the online platform. They come from a general population of internet-connected individuals across the world. We endow these M-Turkers with a certain amount of money and provided the option to invest any

---

[4]For recent articles on real-effort tasks see Gächter, Huang, and Sefton (2016), Dutcher, Salmon, and Saral (2015), or Erkal, Gangadharan, and Koh (2018).

part of it into assets, two of them being risky and one being riskless. Eventually, the M-Turkers' real monetary earnings for this task equals their returns from all assets depending on the assets' outcome, determined by a random draw from the computer (more below). The M-Turkers are therefore incentivised to take decisions that represent their preferences by investing in the risky assets we offer to them.

Who are these M-Turkers? They are not students, as in standard laboratory experiments, but people throughout the population. In our case we focused on US citizens and on M-Turkers that have good reputation in terms of finishing the tasks that they accept. We also obtained basic demographic information about our participants: gender, age, education level, employment status, lining in urban/rural area and number of children. Compared to a typical laboratory experiment, these are individuals that represent the general population better than students, in terms of age, income, education and employment. These aspects balance out that we as experimentalists, when doing online experiments, have limited control over the subject's attention to the experiment. Also, short tasks can be implemented easier than in the laboratory, because of lower fixed costs. Subjects do not need to travel to the laboratory, but can participate from home.

We expose the subjects of our experiment to two experimental tasks—one including UBI and one without UBI. By comparing decisions across the tasks, we give an answer to the question whether UBI affects risk-taking in our experiment. There is a caveat, though. We obtain our answer for one particular conceptualisation of risk-taking. In order to increase the internal validity of our approach, we therefore conceptualise risk-taking in a way that has been implemented frequently in economic experiments before (e.g. Gneezy & Potters, 1997). In order to extend our research in the future, other conceptualisations could be used, to study whether our observations remain robust under other risk tasks.

Our experiment is an example of the experimental approach when one particular element of the policy impact is selected and focused on. We abstract from complexities of the UBI, and this allows us to address one aspect that could be affected in the presence of UBI—namely how they expose themselves to risk. This approach—studying individual aspects of a policy impact in isolation—will only deliver observations relevant outside of the laboratory to the extent that there are no behavioural and environmental variables interacting with risk-taking, e.g. via other variables associated with UBI. However, even if such interactions take place, investigating the impact of UBI in an experiment is not inferior to other data-driven approaches to this question (see also above). Falk and Heckman (2009) make this argument persuasively, stressing that if interactions are likely, they will also be present in any other data collected, not only in the experimental data.

7.4.2 Experimental Design

Let us now describe the design of our experiment, addressing the impact of UBI on risk-taking of individuals. Each participant starts the experiment with an endowment of $E = 100$ tokens. The final number of tokens held by a participant is converted into real money at the end of the experiment, according to a known exchange rate (1 token = $0.06). This resulted in an expected pay-off of $7.30 for a task with an average duration of 7.7 min, similar to acceptable earnings on this platform (Paolacci & Chandler, 2014) . Each subject makes two risky investment decisions in the experiment, referred to as the baseline task (investment without UBI, B) and the UBI task (investment with UBI, U) in random order. The subjects only know the description of the task they start. In other words, they do not know the characteristics of the second task when exposed to the first task. They know, however, that the experiment is finished after the two tasks. We do not provide any feedback about the outcome of any task before the end of the experiment. For this reason, we treat the two tasks as independent of each other, without taking psychological effects from observing the outcome of playing the first task into account. Nevertheless, the participants learned about the baseline task when making the decisions in the UBI task or vice versa. To control for this order ('order effect'), we conduct two conditions of the experiment, varying the order of the tasks: one implements the order of tasks 'baseline task—UBI task—questionnaire' and the other 'UBI task—baseline task—questionnaire'. Our design therefore allows us to study the spill-overs from one to the other task. We refer to the first task in each condition as Task 1 and to the second task as Task 2.

In the baseline task, the subjects' earnings equal the sum of the outcomes from the three assets A, B and C. In the UBI task, each subject is informed that he/she receives an additional fixed amount of 30 tokens on top of the outcome from the assets. For the analysis, we compare the investment levels between treatments to see whether UBI changes the propensity to take risk. As for half of the subjects the baseline task is played first, and for the other half of the subjects the UBI task is played first, we can compare the investments between subjects using the first task only. We can also compare the investment levels within subjects by comparing the first to the second task, controlling for the order. Due to this random assignment, we assume that comparison across subjects is not affected by individual characteristics of each sub-sample. If in doubt, we can control for these characteristics in further analysis.

In order to observe the risky decisions of subjects, we adopt a frequently used risky investment task partly in line with Gneezy and Potters (1997). Subjects allocate an endowment of 100 tokens into two risky assets (A and B) and one riskless asset (C). The asset A pays eight times its investment with probability 1/6; asset B pays 3.5 times its investment with probability 1/3; and asset C pays 0.9 its investment with probability 1 (see also Fig. 7.1). In contrast to the literature, we implement the riskless asset with a negative interest to reflect inflation; subjects need to invest in order to have more money than in the endowment. The expected return of one unit invested in asset A, B and C is $r_A = 8/6 - 1 = 0.33$, $r_B = 3.5/3 - 1 = 0.17$ and $r_C = 0.9 - 1 = -0.1$, respectively. We can apply a simple mean-variance utility function $U(R_p, \sigma_p) = E(R_p) - \frac{1}{2}\gamma\sigma_p$ with $E(R_p) = w_A r_A + w_B r_B + w_C r_C$ (w_i equals the weights of the assets), γ being the risk aversion parameter, and $\sigma_p = \sqrt{w_A^2 \sigma_A^2 + w_B^2 \sigma_B^2}$ being the portfolio's standard deviation given the fact that A and B are not correlated. For a risk neutral person, we have $\gamma = 0$ and thus the subject

	Scheme 'A' pays:	
8 times the number of tokens you allocate to scheme 'A'	if the blue dice shows 1 (chance 1 in 6, 17% probability)	
zero (you lose the tokens you allocate to scheme 'A')	if the blue dice shows 2, 3, 4, 5, or 6 (chance 5 in 6, 83% probability)	

	Scheme 'B' pays:	
3.5 times the number of tokens you allocate to scheme 'B'	if the red dice shows 1 or 2 (chance 2 in 6, 33% probability)	
zero (you lose the tokens you allocate to scheme 'B')	if the red dice shows 3, 4, 5 or 6 (chance 4 in 6, 67% probability)	

Scheme 'C' pays:
0.9 times the number of tokens you allocate to scheme 'C'

Fig. 7.1 Outcomes of investments with probabilities (Screenshot)

picks the portfolio with the highest return, i.e. $X_A = E$. With increasing γ, the trade-off between return and standard deviation comes into play such that subjects aim for more diversification, even choosing for asset C if A is sufficiently high. However, due to the none-riskiness of the UBI payment, the decision maker makes no difference between the two treatments. Alternatively, we can apply SP/A theory (e.g. Shefrin, 2008) which is a combination of incorporating the security-potential relationship of the risky asset (SP) but also the aspiration level (A). For the latter holds that if subjects have a particular aspiration level, which can be a particular amount of money at the end of the experiment, then they would take less risk in baseline task than in UBI task. This is due to the fact that in the UBI task they already receive a particular amount while they have to earn it additionally in the baseline task to achieve the same aspiration level.

In the experiment, we presented the three assets and their properties to the subjects in figures, representing the individual assets as dice outcomes (see Fig. 7.1). To increase understanding, we also provided the feasible outcomes of the investments in a graphical way (see Fig. 7.2).

7.4.3 Data Analysis

In total, 402 subjects participated in our experiments. They were all US citizens with an equal share of men and women, they have an average age of 36.8 (standard deviation 12.28), 66% have a university degree, while about 30% finished at most high school, and with about 80% being employed. The experiment lasted on average 7.7 min and 81% of the subjects finished within five minutes, with a mode duration of five minutes. Each subject in the experiment made a decision in the baseline task and in the UBI task in random order, and filled in a short post-experimental

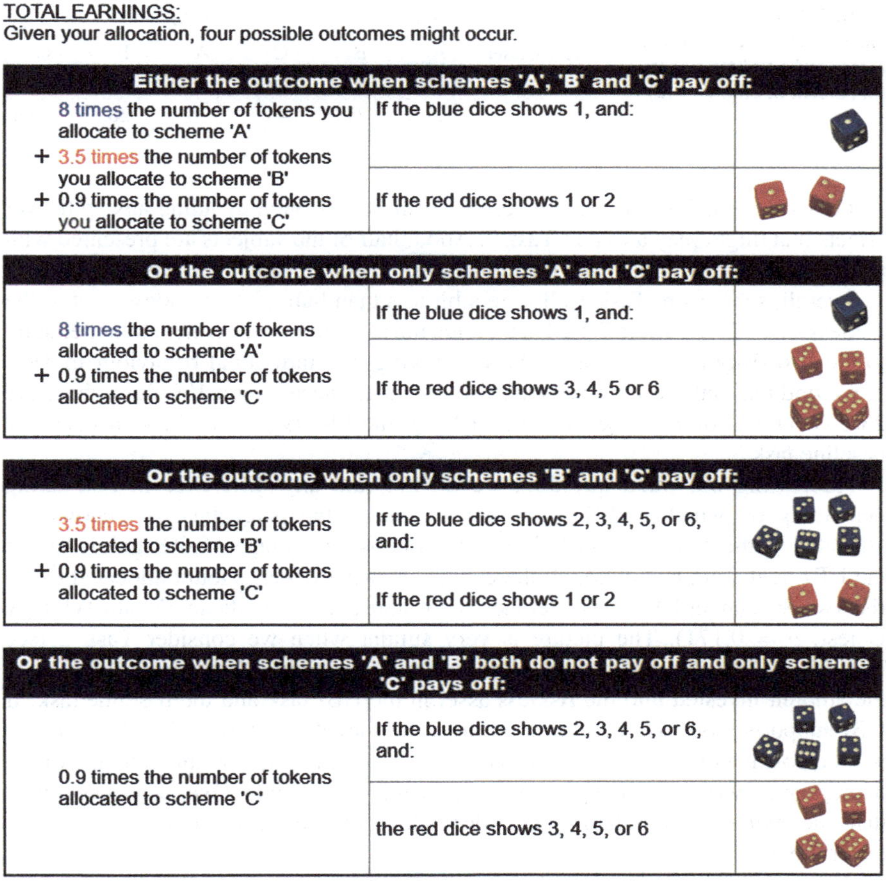

TOTAL EARNINGS:
Given your allocation, four possible outcomes might occur.

Either the outcome when schemes 'A', 'B' and 'C' pay off:		
8 times the number of tokens you allocate to scheme 'A' + 3.5 times the number of tokens you allocate to scheme 'B' + 0.9 times the number of tokens you allocate to scheme 'C'	If the blue dice shows 1, and:	
	If the red dice shows 1 or 2	

Or the outcome when only schemes 'A' and 'C' pay off:		
8 times the number of tokens allocated to scheme 'A' + 0.9 times the number of tokens allocated to scheme 'C'	If the blue dice shows 1, and:	
	If the red dice shows 3, 4, 5 or 6	

Or the outcome when only schemes 'B' and 'C' pay off:		
3.5 times the number of tokens allocated to scheme 'B' + 0.9 times the number of tokens allocated to scheme 'C'	If the blue dice shows 2, 3, 4, 5, or 6, and:	
	If the red dice shows 1 or 2	

Or the outcome when schemes 'A' and 'B' both do not pay off and only scheme 'C' pays off:		
0.9 times the number of tokens allocated to scheme 'C'	If the blue dice shows 2, 3, 4, 5, or 6, and:	
	the red dice shows 3, 4, 5, or 6	

Fig. 7.2 Feasible outcomes of investments (Screenshot)

questionnaire on attitudes to UBI. Due to the fact that we implement our experiment online, some experimental control is lost in this environment; for example, the subjects could be paying very little attention to the experiment description, and only click on content at random, to finish the tests and earn any amount of money. Such subjects create noise in the data, and can be present in any study, whether in the laboratory or in an online experiment. When using the platform Amazon Mechanical Turk, we therefore admitted only high-quality workers of the platform (Peer, Vosgerau, & Acquisti, 2014). We observe that only 4.5% of all subjects finished the experiment under three minutes, supporting that subjects paid sufficient attention to experiment. Additionally, subjects understood the instructions: 79% of the subjects at least somewhat agree with the question "allocation task was easy to understand" (answered on a seven-point Likert scale).

Table 7.1 Endowment allocation to assets A, B and C across tasks and treatments (in percent of endowment)

Task\Asset	Baseline			UBI		
	A	B	C	A	B	C
1	26.0	27.4	46.6	28.2	28.4	43.4
2	27.6	28.7	43.7	26.3	28.3	45.4

Let us now analyse the risky investments in Task 1 only, avoiding any spill-over effects that might play a role in Task 2. About half of the subjects are presented with the baseline task as Task 1, and the remaining subjects decide in the UBI task as Task 1. Overall, subjects in Task 1 allocate a bit less than half of their endowment to the riskless asset C (see Table 7.1). They divide the remaining endowment rather equally to the two risky assets A and B. When looking into individual behaviour in Task 1, we find that only few subjects take no risk at all, accepting a 10% loss: these are 23/203 (11.3%) of the subjects in the UBI task and 14/199 (7%) of the subjects in the baseline task.

Addressing our main question, we do not find any difference in risk-taking depending on whether UBI is present or absent: the percentage of endowment allocated to the riskless asset C in the baseline is on average 46.6% and 43.4% in the UBI treatment, and although there is a somewhat lower amount allocated to the riskless asset under UBI, the difference is not statistically significant (Mann-Whitney U test, $p = 0.171$). The picture is very similar when we consider Task 2 (see Table 7.1). We also run a regression analysis, explaining the difference between the amount invested into the riskless asset in the UBI task and the baseline task. If UBI supports more risk-taking on an individual level, we expect that this variable will be positive on average, but this is not the case. It is also not linked to any of the demographic variables, like gender or age within our sample. Overall, we conclude that the extent of risk-taking is independent of the presence of UBI in our experiment.

Are the subjects taking their decisions in this experiment at random, or with a lot of noise? We find some evidence that there is a structure behind subjects' allocations. Among those who take at least some risk, the share of the investment into the most risky scheme A is significantly positively correlated with the total amount invested in the risky lotteries A and B in total (Spearman correlation coefficient is -0.804 in the baseline and -0.786 in UBI Task 1, and both significant at $p = 0.01$). That means that subjects taking risks choose to do so by allocating more of their risky investment into the most risky asset. We therefore have confidence that subjects do not ignore the experiment design and its incentives, and thus do not allocate their incentives at random.

Finally, we can address whether individual subjects behave differently when exposed to the baseline and UBI tasks. We observe that about half of all subjects are unaffected by the change in the presence of the UBI. The remaining half of the subjects do change their investments into the risky assets, but not unidirectionally. Overall, 207 subjects do not change the amount of risk systematically; 92 subjects decrease risk-taking in the presence of UBI (by about 18 points), and 101 subjects increase risk-taking in the presence of UBI (on average by 19 points).

In conclusion, in our first study on risk-taking and the impact of UBI, we do not find evidence on more risk-taking when UBI is present or added to the incentives of the subjects in the experiment. We can only speculate about the reasons. Even though the task is perceived as being understandable, the complexity might still have been too high for the subject pool in the online experiment. Another possibility is that the way we introduced UBI in our experiment is not sufficiently salient for the subjects, or, that the level of UBI income we used was too low to affect the willingness to take more risk. However, we also observe decisions that suggest that subjects do not take decisions at random. The incentives in the experiment were rather low, but comparable with other online experiments on the M-Turk platform. Further on, subjects might not integrate UBI in their decision; in line with prospect theory (Kahneman & Tversky, 1979) subjects either segregate or integrate information which shifts the reference points (or the aspiration level in line with SP/A theory). If they segregate, and thus do not take UBI into account, the decisions would be the same in both treatments, which is what we observe.

To summarise, we expected that risk-taking would be higher under UBI than without UBI. We collected incentivised decisions of subjects in an online experiment to test this hypothesis. UBI does not result in a higher frequency of risk-taking in our sample. Future research is needed to study the robustness of this observation to other methods of introducing risk in the experiment.

This was a simple demonstration on integrating UBI in a laboratory experiment which definitely incurred some caveats. Of course, we only focussed on risk-taking behaviour with small stakes. However, we hope that this demonstration of the experimental method will motivate further researchers to adopt experimental methods, and address other channels that are hypothesised to generate an impact of UBI on the economy.

7.4.4 Attitudes Towards UBI

Using experiments also allows us to elicit the opinions of the participants which might be correlated with the behaviour in the experiment. In our case, we already see that there is no treatment effect and thus it does not make sense to look at the correlations. However, we would like to briefly provide the results of the basic income questionnaire from the European Dalia Research 2017 survey (see https:// daliaresearch.com/home/). The same definition of UBI was used. *"A Universal Basic Income (UBI) is an income unconditionally paid by the government to every individual regardless of whether they work and irrespective of any other sources of income. It replaces other social security payments and is high enough to cover all basic needs (food, housing etc.)."* This implies that every citizen above eighteen years receives the amount of the UBI once a month. This is the case whether the person works or not, and whether the person has a low or high salary. This also

Table 7.2 Rank of arguments for and arguments against UBI

Rank	Arguments for UBI	Mean rank	Arguments against UBI	Mean rank
1st	It reduces anxiety about financial basic needs	1.92	It might encourage people to stop working	2.65
2nd	It creates more equality of opportunity	2.57	It is impossible to finance	2.70
3rd	It encourages financial independence and self-responsibility everyone	3.71	It increases the dependence on the state	3.47
4th	It increases solidarity, because it is funded by everyone	3.93	It is against the principle of linking merit and reward	3.70
5th	It increases appreciation for household work and volunteering	4.35	Only the people who need it most should get something from the state	4.16
6th	It reduces bureaucracy and administrative expenses	4.50	Foreigners might come to my country and take advantage of the benefits	4.32

allows us to link the attitudes of our US citizen subjects to the European sample (see Delsen & Schilpzand, Chap. 2).

We find that UBI is a relatively known phenomenon among the subjects of our study; 22% of the subjects respond that they never heard about UBI (compared to 10% of the voters and 36% of the non-voters in the European survey). Furthermore, we asked each subject to rank six arguments in favour and six arguments against the introduction of UBI (see Table 7.2). The two highest ranked arguments for the introduction of UBI are the reduction of anxiety about financial needs and more equality of opportunity. These are also the two positive aspects of the UBI that the respondents generally agree upon in ranking them, when we look at the average respondent ranks. Also in the EU these two are the most frequently mentioned arguments in favour of UBI. In the US and the EU the reduction of bureaucracy and administrative expenses was the least important. The two highest-ranked arguments against the introduction of UBI in the US are that the labour supply might decrease, and related to it, the financing of the system questioned. In the EU, the answer "It might encourage people to stop working" is also the most frequently mentioned argument against UBI, however this is, followed by "foreigners might come to my country". In the US the latter is the lowest ranked argument against UBI.

In Table 7.3 the motivations for valuing UBI are presented. The assumed rationality and self-interest in mainstream economic models does not hold. Self-interest (37%) is the least important motivation behind the appreciation of UBI. 40% even disagrees, the highest percentage, while intergenerational concern (55%) (bequest value) is the most important motivation, only 28% disagrees, the lowest percentage. Altruism is the second most important motivation for the valuation of UBI; 44% of the respondents think UBI is also important when it is only useful for other people, 29% disagrees. Less than 30% of the subjects disagree that UBI is important, due to the characteristics relevant for others (other people, future

Table 7.3 When is UBI important?

I think that the basic income is important	Agree (%)	Neutral (%)	Disagree (%)
... mainly when it is useful for me	37	23	40
... also when it is only for other people	44	27	29
... also because (the needs) of future generations	55	16	28
... independently of whether it is useful for anybody	44	23	33

generations). UBI also has existence value, as well as non-use value. UBI generates preferences because it exists, independent of any use. An equally large minority (44%) of the subjects value UBI for its own sake, i.e. independent of usefulness. One third disagrees. Existence value does not fit welfare economics, its economic value cannot be captured for there is no (marginal) change. Existence value in welfare economics, i.e. linking economic value to preferences and preferences to utility leads to circularity (see Bartkowski, 2017; Sen, 1977). Existence value of UBI also implies that rational trade-offs are not accepted by the individual. As a result, the willingness to pay cannot be estimated.

One of the negative aspects of UBI is the possible withdrawal of labour supply from the market. We asked the subjects what they would do after the introduction of UBI. The question asked was: "What could be the most likely effect of basic income on your work choices? Order all your options starting with the one you prefer the most and ending one prefer the least. To order your options drag and drop them to the right place. I would...". Based on the reported responses, subjects expect to enjoy the freedom and opportunities (e.g. spending time with a family/quit job; investing into new skills/freelancing) but they do not foresee an imminent threat to sustainability by stopping to work at all. Instead, they report to spend more time with family, or develop additional skills, without stopping to work. Indeed, the positive aspects of UBI that are usually put on the opposite side of the scales in the discussion (see Table 7.4). Comparison of the ranking of the answers in Tables 7.2 and 7.4 shows clear differences between the indicated effect of UBI on their own work choices (ranked lowest but one) and the expected effect of UBI on work choices of other people (ranked highest). People consider themselves morally superior to their fellow human beings, i.e. better than the average person, which is a phenomenon known as 'self-enhancement': other people are lazier than me (Tapin & McKay, 2017; Standing, 2017: 165–167). This self-enhancement is also found in the EU UBI survey. Ranked number 1 is "Spend more time with their family". This may be related to the fact that people are not fully satisfied with their current work-life balance. UBI may be welfare enhancing. UBI also stimulates investing in human capital and self-employment and allows to look for another job. These positive labour market effects may be efficiency enhancing. It may be concluded that, like in the EU, on balance, the expected change in labour market behaviour does not seem to be that negative in the short term, and may even be positive in the longer term.

In the 2017 EU survey the proportion of people including non-voters voting in favour or probably in favour if there would be a referendum on introducing UBI was 68% and 74% among voters (see Delsen & Schilpzand, Chap. 2). UBI could be

Table 7.4 Impact of UBI on own work choices

	Mean rank
Spend more time with my family	2.81
Get additional skills	3.47
Work less	3.70
Work as a freelance	4.15
Look for a different job	4.26
Do more volunteering work	4.34
Stop working	5.27

Note: Ranking personal consequences if UBI is introduced

Table 7.5 UBI referendum voting behaviour of employed and unemployed

	Unemployed (N = 79)	Employed (N = 324)
Against UBI	28%	33%
For UBI	66%	63%
No vote	6%	4%

Note: Voting support for UBI

interpreted as an unconditional transfer from the working (productive) part of the society to the not-working (unproductive) part of the society. Therefore, one might expect preference of UBI to depend on people's own status—revealing self-serving bias: potential receivers are more likely to vote for UBI than potential suppliers. We find limited empirical support for such bias in our US sample (see Table 7.5). For simplicity, we categorised our subjects as 'unemployed' when they reported to be unemployed, retired, stay-at-home partner or student. When reporting full-time, part-time or self-employment, we categorised them as 'employed'. About one third (33%) of the employed subjects would vote against and 28% of those without a job. The proportion of non-voters is higher among the unemployed. About two thirds of the voting employed and 70% of the voting unemployed—a majority similar to the one in the EU—would vote for UBI if there would be a referendum on introducing UBI. In a 2017 Gallup survey of more than 3000 US adults the following question was posed: "Do you support or not support a universal basic income program as a way to help Americans who lose their jobs because of advances in artificial intelligence?". 48% was in support and 52% was not in support of such a UBI programme (Northeastern University, 2018). These differing results may be related to the representativeness of the samples, differences in definitions and framing of the surveys.

7.5 Conclusions

In this chapter, we discussed the usage of laboratory experiments, or more general the methodology of experimental economics for studying the implementation of UBI. Laboratory experiments have become one of the main tools used by behavioural economists, and these experiments have the advantage of providing a controlled environment that is not possible to create using other empirical methodologies. Due to the lack of empirical effects of UBI, this methodology will be fundamental to our understanding of this topic. We believe that the method will help to carve out relevant aspects of such a policy in order to help policy-makers to make evidence-based decisions.

This method is a complement and not a substitute of other research methods and thus we would like to close this chapter with the conclusion of Falk and Heckman (2009: 537), whose paper is a methodological discussion published in *Science* entitled 'Lab experiments are a major source of knowledge in the social science': *"Causal knowledge requires controlled variation. In recent years, social scientists have hotly debated which form of controlled variation is most informative. This discussion is fruitful and will continue. In this context, it is important to acknowledge that empirical methods and data sources are complements, not substitutes. Field data, survey data, and experiments, both lab and field, as well as standard econometric methods, can all improve the state of knowledge in the social sciences. There is no hierarchy among these methods, and the issue of generalizability of results is universal to all of them."*

References

Abdulkadiroğlu, A., Che, Y.-K., & Yasuda, Y. (2011). Resolving conflicting preferences in school choice: The "Boston mechanism" reconsidered. *American Economic Review, 101*(1), 399–410. https://doi.org/10.1257/aer.101.1.1

Abeler, J., & Nosenzo, D. (2015). Self-selection into laboratory experiments: Pro-social motives versus monetary incentives. *Experimental Economics, 18*(2), 195–214. https://doi.org/10.1007/s10683-014-9397-9

Barrett, C. B., & Carter, M. R. (2010). The power and pitfalls of experiments in development economics: Some non-random reflections. *Applied Economic Perspectives and Policy, 32*(4), 515–548. https://doi.org/10.1093/aepp/ppq023

Bartkowski, B. (2017). *Existence value, biodiversity, and the utilitarian dilemma* (UFZ Discussion Papers, 2/2017). Leipzig: Helmholtz-Zentrum für Umweltforschung – UFZ. Accessed June 8, 2019, from https://nbn-resolving.org/urn:nbn:de:0168-ssoar-51155-0

Bregman, R. (2018). *Utopia for realists: And how we can get there*. London: Bloomsbury.

Calsamiglia, C., Haeringer, G., & Klijn, F. (2010). Constrained school choice: An experimental study. *American Economic Review, 100*(4), 1860–1874. https://doi.org/10.1257/aer.100.4.1860

Camerer, C. F., & Hogarth, R. M. (1999). The effects of financial incentives in experiments: A review and capital-labor-production framework. *Journal of Risk and Uncertainty, 19*(1–3), 7–42. https://doi.org/10.1023/A:100785060

Camerer, C. F., & Loewenstein, G. (2004). Behavioral economics: Past, present, and future. In C. F. Camerer, G. Loewenstein, & M. Rabin (Eds.), *Advances in behavioral economics* (pp. 3–51). Princeton University Press: Princeton, NJ.

Cason, T. N., & Wu, S. Y. (2018). Subject pools and deception in agricultural and resource economics experiments. *Environmental and Resource Economics, 73*, 1–16. https://doi.org/10.1007/s10640-018-0289-x

Charness, G., & Kuhn, P. (2011). Lab labor: What can labor economists learn from the lab? *Handbook of Labor Economics, 4*, 229–330. https://doi.org/10.1016/S0169-7218(11)00409-6

Charness, G., Gneezy, U., & Henderson, A. (2018). Experimental methods: Measuring effort in economics experiments. *Journal of Economic Behavior and Organization, 149*, 74–87. https://doi.org/10.1016/j.jebo.2018.02.024

Clark, A. E., & D'Ambrosio, C. (2015). Attitudes to income inequality: Experimental and survey evidence. In A. Atkinson & F. Bourguignon (Eds.), *Handbook of income distribution* (Vol. 2, pp. 1147–1208). Amsterdam: North Holland.

Croson, R., & Gächter, S. (2010). The science of experimental economics. *Journal of Economic Behavior & Organization, 73*(1), 122–131. https://doi.org/10.1016/j.jebo.2009.09.008

Delsen, L. (1997, February). A new concept of full employment. *Economic and Industrial Democracy, 18*(1), 119–135. https://doi.org/10.1177/0143831X97181007

Duffy, J. (2014). Macroeconomics: a survey of laboratory research. *Handbook of Experimental Economics, 2*, 1–97. https://doi.org/10.2514/1.36125

Dur, R., & van Lent, M. (2019). Socially useless jobs. *Industrial Relations: A Journal of Economy and Society, 58*(1), 3–16. https://doi.org/10.1111/irel.12227

Dur, U., Hammond, R. G., & Morrill, T. (2018). The secure Boston mechanism: Theory and experiments. *Experimental Economics*, 1–36. https://doi.org/10.1007/s10683-018-9594-z

Dutcher, G., Salmon, T., & Saral, K. (2015, December 10). Is 'real' effort more real? https://doi.org/10.2139/ssrn.2701793

Engelmann, D., & Strobel, M. (2004). Inequality aversion, efficiency, and maximin preferences in simple distribution experiments. *American Economic Review, 94*(4), 857–869. Accessed June 8, 2019, from https://www.jstor.org/stable/3592796

Erev, I., & Greiner, B. (2015). The 1-800 critique, counter-examples, and the future of behavioral economics. In G. R. Fréchette & A. Schotter (Eds.), *Handbook of experimental economic methodology* (pp. 151–165). Oxford: Oxford University Press.

Erkal, N., Gangadharan, L., & Koh, B. H. (2018). Monetary and non-monetary incentives in real-effort tournaments. *European Economic Review, 101*, 528–545. https://doi.org/10.1016/j.euroecorev.2017.10.021

Falk, A., & Gächter, S. (2010). Experimental labour economics. In S. N. Durlauf & L. E. Blume (Eds.), *Behavioural and experimental economics. The New Palgrave Economics Collection*. London: Palgrave Macmillan. https://doi.org/10.1057/9780230280786_14

Falk, A., & Heckman, J. J. (2009). Lab experiments are a major source of knowledge in the social sciences. *Science, 326* (5952), 535–538. Accessed June 8, 2019, from http://science.sciencemag.org/content/326/5952/535

Fochmann, M., Weimann, J., Blaufus, K., Hundsdoerfer, J., & Kiesewetter, D. (2013). Net wage illusion in a real-effort experiment. *The Scandinavian Journal of Economics, 115*(2), 476–484. https://doi.org/10.1111/sjoe.12007

Fréchette, G. R., & Schotter, A. (Eds.). (2015). *Handbook of experimental economic methodology*. New York: Oxford University Press. https://doi.org/10.1177/009207002236914

Gächter, S., Huang, L., & Sefton, M. (2016). Combining 'real effort' with induced effort costs: The ball-catching task. *Experimental Economics, 19*(4), 687–712. https://doi.org/10.1007/s1068

Gneezy, U., & Potters, J. (1997). An experiment on risk taking and evaluation periods. *The Quarterly Journal of Economics, 112*(2), 631–645. https://doi.org/10.1162/003355397555217

Graeber, D. (2018). *Bullshit jobs: A theory*. New York: Simon and Schuster.

Grether, D. M., & Plott, C. R. (1984). The effects of market practices in oligopolistic markets: An experimental examination of the ethyl case. *Economic Inquiry, 22*(4), 479–507. https://doi.org/10.1111/j.1465-7295.1984.tb00700.x

Grether, D. M., Isaac, R. M., & Plott, C. R. (1989). *The allocation of scarce resources: Experimental economics and the problem of allocating airport slots*. Boulder, CO: Westview Press.

Groot, L. F. M. (2006). Reasons for a basic income experiment. *Basic Income Studies, 1*(2), 1–7. https://doi.org/10.2202/1932-0183.1037

Guala, F. (2001). Building economic machines: The FCC auctions. *Studies in History and Philosophy of Science, 32*(3), 453–477. https://doi.org/10.1016/S0039-3681(01)00008-5

Haigner, S., Höchtl, W., Jenewein, S., Schneider, F. G., & Wakolbinger, F. (2012). Keep on working: Unconditional basic income in the lab. *Basic Income Studies, 7*(1), 1–14. https://doi.org/10.1515/1932-0183.1230

Harrison, G. W., & List, J. A. (2004). Field experiments. *Journal of Economic Literature, 42* (4), 1009–1055. Accessed June 8, 2019, from https://www.jstor.org/stable/3594915

Hebst, D., & Mas, A. (2015). Peer effects on worker output in the laboratory generalize to the field. *Science, 350*(6260), 545–549. https://doi.org/10.1126/science.aac9555

Hertwig, R., & Ortmann, A. (2001). Experimental practices in economics: A methodological challenge for psychologists?. *Behavioral and Brain Sciences, 24* (3), 383–451. Accessed June 8, 2019, from http://library.mpib-berlin.mpg.de/ft/rh/RH_Experimental_2001.pdf

Hertwig, R., & Ortmann, A. (2008). Deception in experiments: Revisiting the arguments in its defense. *Ethics & Behavior, 18*(1), 59–92. https://doi.org/10.1080/10508420701712990

Holt, C. A. (2019). *Markets, games, and strategic behavior: An introduction to experimental economics*. Princeton, NJ: Princeton University Press.

Hong, J. T., & Plott, C. R. (1982). Rate filing policies for inland water transportation: An experimental approach. *The Bell Journal of Economics, 13*(1), 1–19. https://doi.org/10.2307/3003426

ILO. (2017). *World social protection report 2017–19: Universal social protection to achieve the sustainable development goals*. Geneva: International Labour Office.

Kahneman, D., & Tversky, A. (1979). Prospect theory: An analysis of decision under risk. *Econometrica, 47* (2), 263–291. Accessed June 8, 2019, from https://www.jstor.org/stable/1914185

Kawagoe, T. (2009, August 3–5). *An experimental study of basic income guarantee*. Tokyo: Far East and South Asia Meeting of the Econometric Society.

Kederer, J.-F, Klein, A., Kovarich, D., & Kumm, L. (2017). *Social justice in the context of redistribution* (The Constitutional Economics Network Working Papers No. 01-2017). Department of Economic Policy and Constitutional Economic Theory, Freiburg: University of Freiburg.

Kirchler, M., & Palan, S. (2018). Immaterial and monetary gifts in economic transactions: Evidence from the field. *Experimental Economics, 21*(1), 205–230. https://doi.org/10.1007/s1068

Legein, T., Vandeleene, A., Heyvaert, P., Perrez, J., & Reuchamps, M. (2017, December 21). *The basic income debate in Belgium – An experimental study on the framing impact of metaphors on the opinion formation process*. Conference. Brussels, Belgium: The State of the Federation. Accessed June 8, 2019, from http://hdl.handle.net/2078.1/193660

McKinsey Global Institute. (2017, December). *Jobs lost, jobs gained: Workforce transitions in a time of automation*.

Moffatt, P. G. (2016). *Experimetrics: Econometrics for experimental economics*. London: Palgrave.

Noguera, J. A., & De Wispelaere, J. (2006). A plea for the use of laboratory experiments in basic income research. *Basic Income Studies, 1*(2), 1–8. https://doi.org/10.2202/1932-0183.1044

Northeastern University. (2018). *Optimism and anxiety: Views on the impact of artificial intelligence and higher education's response*. Boston. Accessed June 8, 2019, from https://www.northeastern.edu/gallup/pdf/OptimismAnxietyNortheasternGallup.pdf

Paolacci, G., & Chandler, J. (2014). Inside the turk. *Current Directions in Psychological Science, 23*(3), 184–188. https://doi.org/10.1177/0963721414531598

Peer, E., Vosgerau, J., & Acquisti, A. (2014). Reputation as a sufficient condition for data quality on Amazon Mechanical Turk. *Behavior Research Methods, 46*(4), 1023–1031. https://doi.org/10.3758/s13428-013-0434-y

Plott, C. R. (1982). Industrial organization theory and experimental economics. *Journal of Economic Literature, 20* (4), 1485–1527. Accessed June 8, 2019, from https://www.jstor.org/stable/2724830

Plott, C. R. (1988). *Research on pricing in a gas transportation network* (FERC Office of Economic Policy Technical Report 88-2 (July)). Washington: Federal Energy Regulatory Commission. Accessed June 8, 2019, from http://resolver.caltech.edu/CaltechAUTHORS:20140324-105726069

Plott, C. R. (1997). Laboratory experimental testbeds: Application to the PCS auction. *Journal of Economics and Management Strategy, 6*(3), 605–638. https://doi.org/10.1111/j.1430-9134.1997.00605.x

Plott, C. R., & Porter, D. (1996). Market architectures and institutional testbedding: An experiment with space station pricing policies. *Journal of Economic Behavior & Organization, 73*, 122–133. https://doi.org/10.1016/j.jebo.2009.09.008

Rawls, J. (1971). *A theory of justice*. Cambridge, MA: Harvard University Press.

Riedl, A., & Van Winden, F. (2001). Does the wage tax system cause budget deficits? A macroeconomic experiment. *Public Choice, 109*(3/4), 371–394. Retrieved from https://link.springer.com/content/pdf/10.1023/A:1013029206012.pdf

Roth, A. E. (1986). Laboratory experimentation in economics. *Economics & Philosophy, 2*(2), 245–273. https://doi.org/10.1017/S1478061500002656

Roth, A. E. (2015). Is experimental economics living up to its promise? In G. R. Fréchette & A. Schotter (Eds.), *Handbook of experimental economic methodology* (pp. 13–40). Oxford: Oxford University Press.

Roth, A. E., & Peranson, E. (1999). The redesign of the matching market for American physicians: Some engineering aspects of economic design. *American Economic Review, 89*(4), 748–780. https://doi.org/10.1257/aer.89.4.748

Sen, A. K. (1977). Rational fools: A critique of the behavioral foundations of economic theory. *Philosophy and Public Affairs, 6* (4), 317–344. Accessed June 8, 2019, from http://www.jstor.org/stable/2264946

Shefrin, H. (2008). 26 – SP/A Theory: Introduction. In H. Shefrin (Ed.), *A behavioral approach to asset pricing* (2nd ed., pp. 429–436). Berlington: Academic Press.

Sinn, H. W. (1995). A theory of the welfare state. *Scandinavian Journal of Economics, 97*(4), 495–526. https://doi.org/10.2307/3440540

Sinn, H. W. (1996). Social insurance, incentives and risk taking. *International Tax and Public Finance, 3*(3), 259–280. https://doi.org/10.1007/BF00418944

Smith, V. L. (1976). Experimental economics: Induced value theory. *American Economic Review, 66* (2), 274–279. Accessed June 8, 2019, from https://www.jstor.org/stable/1817233

Smith, V. L. (1994). Economics in the laboratory. *Journal of Economic Perspectives, 8*(1), 113–131. https://doi.org/10.1257/jep.8.1.113

Smith, V. L., & Williams, A. W. (1992). Experimental market economics. *Scientific American, 267* (6), 116–121. Accessed June 8, 2019, from http://www.jstor.org/stable/24939337

Standing, G. (2017). *Basic income and how we can make it happen*. London: Pelican Books.

Tapin, B. M., & McKay, R. T. (2017). The illusion of moral superiority. *Social Psychological and Personality Science, 8*(6), 623–631. https://doi.org/10.1177/1948550616673878

Teele, D. L. (Ed.). (2014). *Field experiments and their critics: Essays on the uses and abuses of experimentation in the social sciences*. New Haven, CL: Yale University Press.

UNDP China. (2017, July). *Universal basic income (UBI): A policy option for China beyond 2020?* (Working Paper).

van der Veen, R., & Groot, L. (2000). *Basic income on the agenda: Policy objectives and political chances*. Amsterdam: Amsterdam University Press.

Van Parijs, P., & Vanderborght, Y. (2017). *Basic income: A radical proposal for a free society and a sane economy*. Cambridge, MA: Harvard University Press.

Varian, H. R. (1980). Redistributive taxation as social insurance. *Journal of Public Economics, 14* (1), 49–68. https://doi.org/10.1016/0047-2727(80)90004-3

Weimann, J., & Brosig-Koch, J. (2019). *Methods in experimental economics – An introduction, Springer Texts in Business and Economics*. Berlin: Springer International Publishing.

White, A. (2016, January 22). How basic income can solve one of the digital economy's biggest problems. *The Conversation*. Accessed June 8, 2019, from https://theconversation.com/how-basic-income-can-solve-one-of-the-digital-economys-biggest-problems-53081

Widerquist, K. (2018). *The devil's in the caveats: A critical analysis of basic income experiments for researchers, policymakers, and citizens*. Berkeley: Bepress. Accessed June 10, 2019, from https://works.bepress.com/widerquist/86/

Widerquist, K., Noguera, J. A., Vanderborght, Y., & De Wispelaere, J. (Eds.). (2013). *Basic income: An anthology of contemporary research*. Chichester: Wiley.

World Bank. (2019). *World development report 2019: The changing nature of work*. Washington: International Bank for Reconstruction and Development/World Bank.

Sascha Füllbrunn (1976) is an Associate Professor at the Chair of Finance of Nijmegen School of Management. He studied Economics and Management at the University of Hannover, completing his Diploma in Economics and Management in 2004. He obtained his Dr. rer. pol. from the University of Magdeburg with honors in 2009. After successfully applying for an AFR research grant from the National research fund in Luxembourg (FNR), he was a research fellow at the Luxembourg School of Finance until 2012. Before his appointment in Nijmegen, he got a scholarship at the Strategic Interaction Group at the Max Planck Institute of Economics in Jena, Germany, but then moved to Nijmegen. Sascha is interested in asset market design and financial decision making using experimental methods (experimental economics/experimental finance). Nowadays his research crosses the barriers between disciplines by looking for examples at 'decision making for others' projects, but also by being involved in the cross-discipline Healthy Brain Study project at Radboud University. Among others, he published in the *American Economic Review, Experimental Economics, Economic Inquiry* and *Journal of Economic Behaviour & Organization*, but also in non-economic journals like the *International Journal of Obesity*.

Lei Delsen (1952) studied economics at the University of Groningen (the Netherlands) and received his Ph.D. in economics from the University of Maastricht (the Netherlands). He was a research fellow at the European Centre for Work and Society in Maastricht (1984–1987), and Assistant Professor at the Department of Applied Economics of the University of Nijmegen, the Netherlands (1987–2002). From 2003–2018 he was Associate Professor of Socio-Economic Policy, Department of Economics, Nijmegen School of Management, Radboud University, Nijmegen. He retired June 2018. He is a research fellow of NETSPAR (Network for Studies on Pensions, Aging and Retirement). His research deals with a number of topical European labour market problems and issues, including new forms of work, retirement from work, work-life balance, choices within pension schemes, responsible investment and the relationship between globalisation and the national welfare states. He is the author of *Atypical employment: An international perspective. Causes, consequences and policy* (Groningen: Wolters-Noordhoff, 1995) and *Exit polder model? Socioeconomic changes in the Netherlands* (Westport: Praeger, 2002). Articles include: A new concept of full employment, *Economic and Industrial Democracy* (1997); Choices within collective labour agreements à la carte in the Netherlands, *British Journal of Industrial Relations* (2006) (with J. Benders & J. Smits); Corporatism and economic performance: does it still work?, *Acta Politica* (2008) (with J. Woldendorp); Does the life course savings scheme have the potential to improve work-life balance?, *British Journal of Industrial Relations* (2009) (with J. Smits); Value matters or values matter? An analysis of heterogeneity in preferences for sustainable investments, *Journal of Sustainable Finance & Investment* (2019) (with A. Lehr).

Jana Vyrastekova (1971) received her Master in Biophysics (1993) from Comenius University, Slovakia, finished programs in Economics at Academia Istropolitana (Slovakia), and the Institute for Advanced Studies (Austria), and obtained her Ph.D. in Economics (2002) at Tilburg University, the Netherlands. She is an experimental economist working interdisciplinary in the field and in the laboratory, to tackle societally relevant questions. Her research addresses the development of prosociality, fairness norms, cooperation in social dilemmas, and the impact of socio-economic context on behaviour. She is also Comenius Teaching Fellow (2018–2019) and contributes with her research to the understanding how online learning environments support learning, accounting for human behaviour and bounded rationality.

Chapter 8
Experimental and Game Theoretical Analyses of the Unconditional Basic Income

Toshiji Kawagoe

Abstract In this chapter we show the results of economic analyses of the Unconditional Basic Income (UBI). Moral hazard and adverse selection problems are addressed, which may arise under the UBI scheme. As for the moral hazard problem, the Negative Income Tax (NIT) and the UBI are compared in a laboratory experiment. In a setting where the NIT and the UBI are identical, we find that UBI increases labour supply significantly more than NIT. We also find that more individualistic and competitive people increase their labour supply even when the UBI is introduced. The conjecture that the UBI makes people lazier is rejected. As for the adverse selection problem, we apply a simple evolutionary game model in order to check whether the introduction of the UBI promotes freedom and self-maintenance of the people who have a weaker position in the household, such as women, children, people of advanced age, and people with disability. We show that there is an equilibrium where women are willing to marry in order to get a higher income for the household, even if such decisions keep them in their weaker positions.

Keywords Basic income · Negative income tax · Moral hazard · Adverse selection · Evolutionary game

8.1 Introduction

The Unconditional Basic Income (UBI) is an income maintenance program which guarantees a constant income for each individual, regardless of age, gender, or any geographic characteristics.[1] Each individual is only required to pay income tax over

---

[1]If a constant income is guaranteed conditional on participation in social activity as a citizen, it is called Participation Income (Atkinson, 1995a: 301–303, 1996; Delsen, 1995: 270–274, 1997; Bowles & Gintis, 1998).

T. Kawagoe
Department of Complex and Intelligent Systems, Future University Hakodate, Hakodate, Hokkaido, Japan
e-mail: kawagoe@fun.ac.jp

additional income, earned besides the UBI.[2] Ozawa (2002) estimates that a UBI of ¥ 80,000 (approx. € 610) can be provided to each individual, given the Japanese financial conditions which assume that a 50% flat income tax is imposed on income other than the UBI.

Advocates of the UBI basically agree about four benefits stemming from the introduction of the UBI (see Fitzpatrick, 1999; Werner, 2006; Delsen, Chap. 1). The UBI reduces income inequality and poverty; the UBI reduces labour supply in the labour market and encourages work-sharing because the UBI may cause a shift from labour to leisure in individual choices; each individual can reduce working hours or withdraw from the labour market and have enough leisure time for self-development when they receive the UBI; as an income is guaranteed not for households, but for individuals in the UBI scheme, the right and dignity of the people who are in weaker positions in the household, such as women, children, persons of advanced age, and people with a disability, can be respected. As a result, the UBI may also promote gender equality in the labour market by enhancing women's negotiating power.

So far, the UBI is discussed in the fields of public finance, social security, and Political Science.[3] However, in these discussions about the UBI it seems that an economic analysis has not been made at a satisfactory level, which has been done in other fields of research [compared, for example, with studies on affirmative action policy (see Calsamiglia, Franke, & Rey-Biel, 2013)]. In the literature, the main discussed economic issue is moral hazard. That is, if the UBI is guaranteed for everyone without any condition or reservation, incentives for labour supply decline significantly, i.e. the UBI makes people lazier (see Noguera & De Wispelaere, 2006). Other effects of the UBI scheme are little or not at all addressed.

In this chapter, the results of two experiments are reported, conducted to examine how the introduction of the UBI scheme would affect labour supply. Though the experiments were conducted in a controlled laboratory setting, tasks assigned to experimental subjects were not fictitious. They required real labour effort. In this sense, these are laboratory experiments with the flavour of field experiment as, e.g. in Cadsby, Song, and Tapon (2007).

In the first experiment, we compared the UBI scheme with an identical Negative Income Tax (NIT) scheme. So, the two schemes have identical labour supply incentives. In economic theory, however, the following argument is frequently stated: an agent with low income has little incentive to raise his/her labour supply in a NIT scheme, because the subsidy he/she receives decreases gradually when income increases. No such effect is expected in the UBI, as it is a fixed amount of money and no distortion is caused for labour supply. So, the UBI scheme is superior to the NIT. In fact, our experimental results confirm it. Whereas no significant

---

[2]Usually a flat tax is proposed (see e.g. Atkinson, 1995b). A progressive tax is proposed by Murphy and Nagel (2002).

[3]On the NIT/UBI and work effort, see e.g. Burtless (1986). On the effects of basic income on labour supply, see e.g. Yi (2017). On the impact of basic income on the propensity to work, see e.g. Gamel, Balsan, and Vero (2006).

change in labour supply was observed when the NIT was introduced, labour supply increased significantly when the UBI was introduced.

In the second experiment, we try to identify which personal traits determine labour supply when the UBI is implemented in the laboratory. In this experiment, we also adopt the experimental task requiring real labour effort as in the first one. In addition to this labour effort task, subjects are asked to answer several questionnaires concerning general reasoning/cognitive ability, risk-aversion, altruism and conscientiousness. Again we find that the introduction of the UBI does not reduce labour supply. On the contrary: labour supply increases in this experiment. Especially people who have more individualistic and competitive motivations strongly increase their labour supply, even when the UBI scheme is introduced. So, these two experiments falsify the statement that the UBI makes people lazier (see also Delsen & Schilpzand, Chap. 2).

Another problem to be mentioned, though it has hardly been addressed in the literature, is an adverse selection problem. That is, there could be an incentive for the household to have more children to increase the household income, for UBI is provided based on the number of people living in a family. In this case, women may be willing to get married to increase total income for the household, even though it could be oppressive for them, for it puts them under their husbands' control. There is evidence that the 1982 Alaska Permanent Fund Dividend Fund, unlike other UBI and UBI-related field experiments characterised by a long duration and a large scale, has a positive effect on the birth rate (see Goldsmith, 2010). If so, contrary to the opinion of the advocates of the UBI (e.g. Fitzpatrick, 1999; Werner, 2006), the introduction of the UBI scheme increases the number of women bearing more offspring, and prevents them from advancing into workplaces, and limits their freedom. For analysing this type of adverse selection, we develop a game theoretic model and analyse it by evolutionary game theory. Our conjecture is confirmed as there exists an equilibrium where women are willing to get married, even if such a decision weakens their positions.

The rest of this chapter is organised as follows. The next Sect. 8.2 introduces the models of the UBI and the NIT schemes. The experimental design and results of the first experiment are also reported. In Sect. 8.3, the second experimental study is explained. In Sect. 8.4, the adverse selection problem and its evolutionary game analysis are presented. In the final Sect. 8.5 we conclude.

8.2 Study 1: Moral Hazard in the UBI and the NIT Schemes

In this section, the UBI and the NIT schemes are compared with respect to moral hazard. As this is a highly empirical question, experimental examination either in the laboratory or in the field is called for, just as a series of social experiments were conducted for testing the NIT scheme,[4] before testing it in the real world. In fact, a special issue on this topic was published in *Basic Income Studies*, Volume 1, No. 2, of the debate "Toward a Basic Income Experiment?" by guest editor Loek Groot (2006).[5] Among the articles in this issue, Peeters and Marx (2006) and Noguera and De Wispelaere (2006) deserve to be mentioned.[6] Peeters and Marx (2006) propose and argue that surveying the winners of the Belgian lottery "Win for Life" can be used as a means for testing the UBI scheme in a social experiment. Every lottery winner receives—life-long—€ 1000 per month. They insist that it can be regarded as the UBI scheme and one will have a good and interesting sample by monitoring the winner's behaviour to explore the change in labour supply when UBI is introduced. Noguera and De Wispelaere (2006) propose that a controlled laboratory experiment should be conducted for measuring the effect of the UBI on labour supply directly. However, they did not conduct any experiment, and did not propose a concrete experimental design for testing the UBI scheme.

Recently, the Stanford Basic Income Lab was established for providing an academic home for the research and the study of the development and impact of UBI. It also published a toolkit to conduct a Randomised Controlled Trial (RCT) for a UBI pilot at the city level (Stanford Basic Income Lab, 2018). This encourages city officials and policymakers to experiment with the UBI.

In Japan, the Children Treat Law came into force in 2010, when the Democratic Party of Japan administered Japanese government. According to this law, a flat rate of ¥ 13,000 (approx. € 100) per month per child up to the age 15 was unconditionally granted to households. This was the first, nation-wide experiment of the UBI in Japan. Unfortunately, because of the 2011 earthquake and tsunami disaster, the law was repealed in 2012. However, interest in the UBI still persists in Japan (see Vanderborght & Yamamori, 2014).

Several individual attempts to test the effectiveness of the UBI have been done since then. For example, Takafumi Horie, a Japanese entrepreneur and advocate of UBI, founded an Internet university HIU (Horie Internet University[7]), where he started a basic income project in 2017. In his HIU Basic Income, five recipients chosen from the HIU members are granted ¥ 100,000 (about € 770) per month. One of the recipients is a musician with only a left hand. He went on a piano playing tour with the aid of the HIU Basic Income. Kairyu Kimura, age 29, runs a real estate business in Japan, and started a similar type of the UBI in 2018. His project is called Basic Income House. Five recipients can rent a house with five rooms for free for two years (average rent in Japan is about ¥ 70,000 (around € 540) per month). A car

---

[4]For social experiments of the NIT scheme, see Robins (1985) and Widerquist (2005).

[5]It is the first peer-reviewed journal devoted to basic income and related issues of poverty relief and universal welfare.

[6]Other papers in this issue are Widerquist (2006) and Virjo (2006).

[7]See http://salon.horiemon.com/

and Wi-Fi are also freely provided. They are also granted ¥ 15,000 (about € 115) in cash per month. The chosen residents are young artists, musicians, and the like.[8]

Although both the HIU Basic Income and the Basic Income House are more of a 'sugar daddy' treatment for protecting and promoting artistic activity, interests for knowing how and with what condition the UBI works are real. However, their 'experiments' are not experiments in a scientific sense, because there is no control treatment in their projects.

For measuring the effect of the UBI scheme on labour supply directly, we conducted a laboratory experiment of the UBI in a fashion of field experiments, inspired by Cadsby et al. (2007).[9] Next we will show our models of the UBI and the NIT schemes to be tested in the laboratory.

First, for the NIT scheme, post-tax income Z is determined by earned income Y, a target income G, and marginal tax rate T as follows:

$$Z = \begin{cases} Y + T(G - Y) & \text{if} \quad Y \leq G \\ Y - T(Y - G) & \text{if} \quad Y > G \end{cases}$$

For the UBI scheme, post-tax income, z, is determined by a guaranteed income, g, and marginal tax rate, t, as follows:

$$z = g + (1 - t)Y.$$

If we set $T = t$ and $TG = g$, then $Z = z$, which would mean that the UBI and the NIT schemes are identical.[10] Figure 8.1 shows the relationship between earned income, Y, and post-tax income, Z, when $T = 0.5$ and $G = 50$ ($g = 25$).

Our research questions are as follows. Facing the identical type of the UBI or the NIT scheme, what response does a worker show? As opponents of the UBI wonder, when an income g is guaranteed, does the worker reduce his/her labour supply? In addition, is there any difference of impact on labour supply between the UBI and the NIT schemes?

For all these questions concerning moral hazard, the following laboratory experiment has been conducted on March 10, 2009. Participants were recruited from the undergraduate students of Future University Hakodate. They all voluntarily participated in the experiment by responding to the electronically distributed announcement. They had no previous experience with this experimental task. A total of 60 students participated in the experiment.[11] As explained later in detail, their

---

[8]Both the HIU Basic Income and Basic Income House are on-going projects; we cannot yet report their consequences.
[9]For controlled field experiments of labour supply, see Gneezy and List (2006).
[10]Basic features of these models are the same as those used by Ozawa (2002) and Tondani (2009).
[11]Pool bias due to the fact that only students participate is limited or non-existing. The results of laboratory experiments can be generalised to the field (Charness & Kuhn, 2011; Hebst & Mas, 2015; see also Füllbrunn, Delsen & Vyrastekova, Chap. 7).

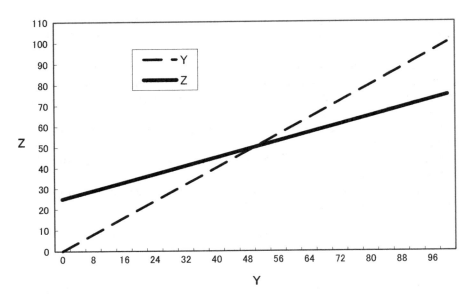

Fig. 8.1 The relationship between earned income (Y) and post-tax income (Z)

earnings were paid in cash during the experiment, following the standard procedures in experimental economics (see Friedman & Sunder, 1994).

When subjects entered the room, their seats were randomly assigned. The seats were separated with enough distance. No communication and eye-contact between subjects were allowed during the experiment. The instructions for the task were distributed and an experimenter read the instructions out loud as well. The experiment was conducted via computer terminals. Each subject was asked to work out a series of multiplication exercises of two digits and one digit natural numbers (for example, 24 × 6 = ?). The task was set as work which would demand enough concentration. 25 questions were selected at random in each round, and the participants had to answer each question within four seconds. In the pilot experiment, the average points score was 60 out of 100. These points were regarded as Y. Z was calculated according to the UBI or the NIT scheme, after which the subject was paid ¥ 4 (€ 0.03) for each point. The duration of the experiment was 90 min, including payment procedures. Actual decision time was one hour. The average of the rewards was ¥ 3000 (approximately € 23 at that time).

In this experiment, the A-B-A design was employed for separating subject's experience or learning effect and the effect caused by the introduction of each scheme. Under condition A, no scheme was introduced. Under condition B either the UBI or the NIT scheme was introduced. We also adopted between-subjects design in the experiment. There were two groups in the experiment. Each group consisted of 30 subjects. The UBI scheme was introduced in one group, and the NIT scheme was introduced in the other group. Under condition A of the experiment, the subject's payoff was determined by $Z = (1 - t)Y$.

Our hypothesis to be tested in this experiment is as follows. An agent with low income, that is, less than G, has little incentive to raise their labour supply in both schemes, because the subsidy they receive decreases gradually when their income increases.

Table 8.1 shows average earned income, Y, under conditions A and B. The numbers between parentheses are standard deviations. The data shows that average labour supply is monotonically increasing in both cases.

According to the standard economic analysis, the introduction of the NIT or the UBI scheme reduces the incentive for people to work through income and substitution effects. That is why it is surprising to see that average labour supply is increasing. However, this behaviour is understandable for the following reasons. Firstly, the labour supply was generally increased by the experience/learning effect, as subjects more easily solved the calculation problems by their experience during the experiment. Subjects were also motivated to reduce their labour supply because of the introduction of the scheme. Both effects might be confounding, especially in early rounds. Then, under condition A2 after B, after taking away the scheme, an increase in average labour supply was observed.

To measure the reduction of the labour supply incentive, we compare the distributions of labour supply in the condition B and A2. Figure 8.2 shows average

Table 8.1 Average earned income under conditions A (no scheme) and B (UBI or NIT scheme)

	Condition A1 (Baseline) Round 1–5	Condition B (with scheme) Round 6–10	Condition A2 (Baseline) Round 11–15
NIT	67.467 (18.370)	72.133 (18.753)	74.000 (18.755)
UBI	67.304 (19.503)	72.504 (16.676)	75.970 (15.729)

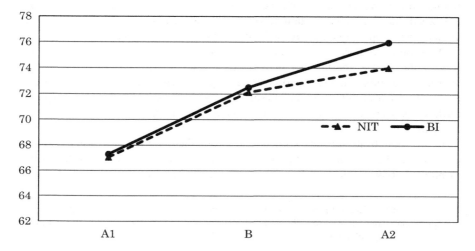

Fig. 8.2 The average of earned income in the UBI and the NIT schemes

Y in both schemes. Under the NIT scheme, there is no significant difference between conditions B and A2. However, for the UBI scheme the difference of average Y between conditions B and A2 is significant (t-test, $p < 0.05$). This means that the introduction of the UBI scheme did not reduce labour supply, but increased labour supply. A relevant and interesting next question to be answered in the following Sect. 8.3 is: which factor(s) affected their labour supply decision under the UBI scheme? To examine possible psychological factors or personality traits affecting their labour supply, we conducted another laboratory experiment.

8.3 Study 2: UBI and Personal Traits

In order to follow up on the previous findings, another laboratory experiment was designed and conducted on July 20, 2018. In this case, we focused on the UBI only and tried to determine which personality trait had the most significant effect on labour supply choices.

8.3.1 Experimental Procedures

A. Real Labour Effort Task
Unlike the previous experiment, subjects were asked to solve a series of simplified Sudoku puzzles as a real labour effort task. The task was the same as used by Calsamiglia et al. (2013), who tested the effectiveness of affirmative action policy on labour effort. In the original version of the Sudoku puzzle, the objective is to fill natural numbers 1–9 in the 9×9 matrix. In the simplified version we used in the experiment, subjects were asked to fill natural numbers 1–4 in the 4×4 matrix. Similar to the original Sudoku puzzle, each row, each column and each of the four 2×2 sub-matrices must contain all of the natural numbers 1–4, and each natural number must appear in each row and each column only once (see Fig. 8.3).

As subjects require an adequate level of mental effort and concentration for solving the puzzle, the number of correctly solved puzzles can be a measure of their labour efforts.[12] In the experiment, participants were presented a total of twenty puzzles in one trial and were asked to solve as many as possible within three minutes. Such trials were repeated four times because of given time constraint for the experiment.

In the first trial, subjects earned 150 times the number of correctly solved problems as their experimental points. In the second trial, in addition to the points mentioned above, subjects were given 500 points. This represented the UBI in the

---

[12] Even if effort cost function is nonlinear, the relationship between labour effort and labour supply is proportional. Thus, it is reasonably assumed that subject's effort level can be reflected in the number of correctly solved puzzles.

Fig. 8.3 Example of a 4 × 4 Sudoku puzzle (**a**) a 4 × 4 problem (**b**) the problem correctly solved

(a)

			2
4		3	
	4		
1			

(b)

3	1	4	2
4	2	3	1
2	4	1	3
1	3	2	4

experiment. The third and fourth trial were exactly the same as the first and the second trial respectively. In summary, the rewards for each subject were calculated as follows:

Trial 1: 150 times the number of correctly solved problems;
Trial 2: 150 times the number of correctly solved problems + 500;
Trial 3: 150 times the number of correctly solved problems;
Trial 4: 150 times the number of correctly solved problems + 500.

Subjects were informed about each payment scheme before entering the trials through instructions. After participants had completed all four trials, one of them was randomly chosen and they were paid according to the points they earned in the selected trial. One point was converted into ¥ 1 in cash.

B. Personality Tests

Along with the real labour effort task, we examined subjects' personality traits using popular psychological tests. For measuring general personality traits, we used a simplified version of the Big Five (Gosling, Rentfrow, & Swann, 2003). The five traits measured in this test are openness, conscientiousness, extraversion, agreeableness, and neuroticism (OCEAN). As for subjects' general cognitive ability, we used the Raven's Progressive Matrices (Raven, 1936). For measuring risk-aversion, the Multiple Price List (MPL) proposed by Holt and Laury (2002) was used. Finally, as for social preference, the extended version of Social Value Orientation (Chen, Chiu, Smith, & Yamada, 2013) was used.

Big Five

In the Big Five personality test, subjects are asked to answer several verbally expressed questions on a seven-point Likert scale as follows:

1. Disagree strongly;
2. Disagree moderately;
3. Disagree a little;
4. Neither agree nor disagree;
5. Agree a little;
6. Agree moderately;
7. Agree strongly.

In the simplified version of the Big Five that we used, subjects are asked to submit their assessment for the following ten questions by using above seven-point Likert scale.

I see myself as:

1. Extraverted, enthusiastic;
2. Critical, quarrelsome;
3. Dependable, self-disciplined;
4. Anxious, easily upset;
5. Open to new experiences, complex;
6. Reserved, quiet;
7. Sympathetic, warm;
8. Disorganised, careless;
9. Calm, emotionally stable;
10. Conventional, uncreative.

The answers given by the participants are used to decompose the subject's personality into the five categories: Openness to experience, Conscientiousness, Extraversion, Agreeableness, and Neuroticism. In the simplified version, for each category, there are two corresponding questions. Then, in our experiment, we only used the result concerning Conscientiousness, because other categories (Openness to experience, Extraversion and Neuroticism) are irrelevant in this research and Agreeableness is also measured by another test, Social Value Orientation (SVO), explained below. Questions concerning Conscientiousness are answers 3 and 8. The measure for Conscientiousness is obtained from the Likert scale values for questions 3 and 8, L3 and L8, as follows:

$$\text{Conscientiousness} = [L3 + (8 - L8)]/2$$

If a subject's measure for Conscientiousness is high, the subject has a tendency to be organised and dependable, show self-discipline, act dutifully, aim for achievement, and prefer planned rather than spontaneous behaviour. So, we may reasonably assume that people with low levels of conscientiousness reduce their effort level when the UBI is introduced, while highly conscientious individuals maintain their effort levels.

Multiple Price List

The Multiple Price List (MPL) introduced by Holt and Laury (2002) is the standard method for eliciting a subject's risk-attitude in individual choice problems. With the MPL method, subjects are asked to choose one out of two lotteries with different rewards. Several lotteries in a particular order are presented to the participants. In each lottery the rewards are fixed, but the probability of obtaining a higher prize in each lottery is gradually increased. For example, the rewards in Choice A are either € 2.00 or € 1.60 and the prizes in Choice B are either € 3.85 or € 0.10. The probability of obtaining the higher prize in each lottery is increased from 10 to 100% by steps of 10% (see Table 8.2). After all the choices are completed, one of the lotteries is

Table 8.2 Lottery choices in the Multiple Price List (MPL) method

Price	Choice A		Choice B	
	€ 2.00 (%)	€ 1.60 (%)	€ 3.85	€ 0.10
Lottery 1	10	90	10	90
Lottery 2	20	80	20	80
Lottery 3	30	70	30	70
Lottery 4	40	60	40	60
Lottery 5	50	50	50	50
Lottery 6	60	40	60	40
Lottery 7	70	30	70	30
Lottery 8	80	20	80	20
Lottery 9	90	10	90	10
Lottery 10	100	0	100	0

randomly selected with uniform distribution. Then, either a high or a low prize for the chosen lottery was selected with a corresponding probability distribution and participants were paid according to their choices. With the MPL, a risk-neutral subject who initially chose Choice A will switch his choice to Choice B at Lottery 4. A risk-averse subject will switch later. Hence, this switching point gives a measure for a subject's risk-attitude. As risk-averse individuals tend to be pessimistic about their abilities, it is expected that they generally put in more effort than other individuals. However, as the UBI guarantees them a certain number of points in the task, as risk of getting lower points is reduced, we can assume that they will reduce their effort level when UBI is introduced.

Raven's Test

Raven's Progressive Matrices (Raven's test) is a non-verbal test used in measuring abstract reasoning and cognitive ability, developed by Raven (1936). It is a very popular test in psychological research and recently experimental economists also started using it (for example, Benito-Ostolaza, Hernandez, & Sanchis-Llopis, 2016; Burks, Carpenter, Goette, & Rustichini, 2009; Carpenter, Graham, & Wolf, 2013). A series of questions with visual geometrics are presented to the subjects. The task in each question is to find an appropriate piece of visual pattern and to fill in a missing place in the whole picture. Subjects are asked to choose one out of eight options. There are several levels of difficulty in this test. We used a selection of Advance Progressive Matrices. In our case, a total of sixteen problems were presented, and participants were asked to solve them within ten minutes.

We are interested in the relationship between subjects' reasoning/cognitive ability and the outcome of the Sudoku task. A subject whose reasoning/cognitive ability is higher will earn more points in the Sudoku task. However, when the UBI is introduced, how will they respond to it? Do they save their mental efforts in solving the Sudoku when the UBI is available, and is such a reduction of mental effort correlated to their reasoning/cognitive abilities? That is the question we are mainly concerned with.

Table 8.3 A typical choice task in the Social Value Orientation (SVO) test

	A	B	C	D
Your share	480	540	480	480
Partner's share	80	280	480	540

Social Value Orientation
Social preferences are of fundamental importance in understanding interdependent decision making behaviour among people. For measuring a subject's social preference, we used the extended version of the Social Value Orientation (Chen et al., 2013). The Social Value Orientation (SVO) was developed by Van Lange, Otten, De Bruin, and Joireman (1997) and is widely used in social psychology since then. The test consists of a series of distribution tasks in which subjects are asked to allocate monetary resources between themselves and another person. Participants are presented several options of how to share the resources, and their individual choices are final and binding. That is, the problem subjects face is a simple Dictator Game (DG). The only difference between SVO and DG is that choices in the SVO are hypothetical; their choices are independent of their earnings in the experiment (but choice-related rewards were paid in our experiment). Each distribution option corresponds to 'Individualistic' (option maximises the outcome for the self), 'Prosocial' (option maximises the sum of the outcomes for the self and the other), 'Competitive' (option maximises the difference between the outcomes for the self and for the other), or 'Altruistic' (option maximises the outcome for the other). Table 8.3 shows an example of the task. Each subject is asked to choose one of the four options A–D. A is the Competitive, B is the Individualistic, C is the Prosocial, and D is the Altruistic option.

In conducting the SVO, several measurement methods have been proposed. We employed the Triple-Dominance Measure (Messick & McClintock, 1968). In this method, each subject is presented nine problems. Each problem contains three (four in our extended version) options on how to share the resources, as in Table 8.3. If, after completing the task, the subject chooses a particular type of option at least six times, then he/she is categorised as such.[13] Chen et al. (2013) extended the original version by adding the Altruistic option. As a result, their extended version of SVO becomes essentially the same as the test proposed by Charness and Rabin (2002), a widely accepted test for measuring a subject's social preference in experimental economics. After all the choices are completed, one of the nine problems is randomly selected with uniform distribution. Then, participants are paid according to their choices in this selected problem. Our research question is: do different social preferences motivate differently in the Sudoku task? Our tentative hypothesis is that Individualistic and Competitive subjects will keep their effort levels, and Prosocial and Altruistic participants will not.

---

[13] In practice, if we set the criterion for identification of a subject's type as five of nine problems, it is sometimes the case that subjects are classified in multiple types. For reducing such possibility, we increased the criterion into six of nine problems.

C. Experimental Procedures

Similar to our first laboratory experiment, participants were recruited from the undergraduate students of Future University Hakodate. They all voluntarily participated in the experiment by responding to the electronically distributed announcement. They had no previous experience with this experimental task. A total of 28 students participated in the experiment and they were paid their earnings in cash during the experiment, following the standard procedures in experimental economics (see Friedman & Sunder, 1994). When subjects entered the room, their seats were randomly assigned. The seats were separated with enough distance. Communication and eye-contact between subjects were not allowed during the experiment. The instructions for each task were distributed at the time that the corresponding task was about to be assigned. The experimenter also read the instructions out loud. The order of the tasks was as follows:

1. Big Five;
2. Sudoku task;
3. the MPL;
4. Raven's test;
5. the SVO.

In each of the instructions, subjects were informed that they were paid according to their choices and their outcomes in the Sudoku task, the realised prizes in the MPL task, and the realised earnings in the SVO task. At the end of each task, the experimenter announced the realisation of the random variable contained in each task, and participants were paid according to their choices. The experiment was conducted manually with pen and papers. The duration of the experiment was 90 min, including payment procedures. Actual decision time was one hour. The average of the rewards was ¥ 1723 (approx. € 13 at that time).

8.3.2 Experimental Results

In Table 8.4, the average number of correctly solved problems and the standard deviations (SD) in each trial are shown. Apparently, there are increasing trends in both averages and standard deviations. So, the introduction of the UBI did not reduce labour supply. This finding is consistent with the result of Experiment 1 in Sect. 8.2.

Next, we will assess which personal traits affect labour effort. For this purpose, we estimate the following linear regression model:

Table 8.4 Average number and standard deviation (SD) of correctly solved problems in each of the four trials

Trial	Average	SD
1	6.071	2.638
2 (with the UBI)	7.393	3.023
3	7.857	3.064
4 with the UBI)	8.214	3.143

$$r_i^t = \beta_0 + \beta_1 \cdot Raven + \beta_2 \cdot Risk + \beta_3 \cdot Altruism + \beta_4 \cdot Consc + \beta_5 \cdot Round$$

where r_i^t is subject i's number of correctly solved problems at Trial t. *Raven* is the proportion of correctly solved problems in the Raven's test. A total of 16 problems were presented in our experiment,

Raven = the number of correctly solved problems/16.

Risk is a dummy variable that takes on the value of 1 when the subject i is identified as risk-averse in the MPL and is equal to 0 otherwise. *Altruism* is a dummy variable that takes value 1 when the subject i is identified as Altruistic or Prosocial in the SVO and otherwise is 0.[14] *Consc* is the value for Conscientiousness in the Big Five test. *Round* is the number of Trials. The raw data for each variable is provided in Table 8.5.

The average score in the Raven's test is 11.7 (73.0%). The median score is twelve and the mode is thirteen. In our sample of undergraduate students, the score is around average, or a little bit higher (see Benito-Ostolaza et al., 2016; Burks et al., 2009; Carpenter et al., 2013). The minimum score is seven, and the maximum score is fifteen.

According to the MPL test, out of 28 subjects, thirteen are risk-averse (46.4%), eight are risk-neutral (28.6%), four are risk-loving (14.3%) and three are not identified because they switched their choices more than twice.

According to the SVO test, out of 28 subjects, ten are Prosocial (35.7%), seven are Altruistic (25.0%), nine are Individualistic (32.1%), no Competitive and two are not identified because their scores for each category were less than six.[15]

Valuation for Conscientiousness was taken from the Big Five test, and the average score is 2.95. As the seven-point Likert scale was used, this average is close to the "3. Disagree a little" assessment. The median and mode were 2.5. The minimum score was one and the maximum score was six.

The estimated values of the coefficients, the standard errors (SE), the t-values and the p-values are shown in Table 8.6. *Raven* has a positive effect on labour effort. Thus, subjects who have more reasoning/cognitive ability solved more problems. However, this effect is not significant. The positive coefficient for *Risk* implies that more risk-averse subjects solved more problems, which is consistent with our hypothesis. However, again this effect is not significant. The coefficient for *Altruism* is negative and strongly significant. This means that Altruistic and Prosocial subjects solved fewer problems. As the rest of population is either Individualistic or Competitive, this implies that Individualistic and Competitive subjects solved more problems. This is an intuitively acceptable result. Conscientiousness also has a negative coefficient, but it is very close to zero and not significant. Finally, *Round* is positive and significant. Thus, we conclude that a subject's effort level has an increasing trend. This confirms the results in Table 8.4.

---

[14]Here we identify subjects as Altruistic when they are either Altruistic or Prosocial in the SVO measure, because their behaviours are similar.

[15]Survey data for the Unites States show that altruism is a more important motivation for the appreciation of UBI than self-interest (see Füllbrunn, Delsen & Vyrastekova, Chap. 7).

Table 8.5 Raw data of experiment 2

Subject	Trial 1	Trial 2	Trial 3	Trial 4	Raven	Risk	Altruism	Conscientious
1	8	8	8	11	0.875	1	1	5.0
2	5	5	5	6	0.813	0	1	6.0
3	5	7	6	7	0.563	0	1	3.0
4	6	7	8	7	0.625	0	1	2.5
5	9	12	13	12	0.750	0	0	4.0
6	6	10	11	11	0.750	0	0	1.0
7	4	5	5	6	0.813	1	1	1.5
8	4	7	8	9	0.750	1	1	3.0
9	5	4	5	6	0.750	1	1	2.0
10	4	8	8	9	0.813	0	0	4.5
11	8	7	7	7	0.688	0	0	3.0
12	7	7	8	8	0.750	0	0	2.0
13	7	7	7	7	0.563	0	1	2.5
14	16	18	19	21	0.813	1	0	3.5
15	7	7	8	7	0.813	0	1	2.0
16	7	8	8	8	0.750	1	0	1.5
17	5	6	5	7	0.438	0	0	1.5
18	4	3	8	8	0.813	1	1	2.5
19	6	9	8	8	0.938	1	1	1.0
20	4	5	9	7	0.688	1	0	4.0
21	6	10	9	10	0.500	0	1	2.5
22	2	5	3	5	0.563	1	1	4.5
23	5	6	6	7	0.875	1	0	2.0
24	7	9	8	12	0.938	0	0	1.0
25	6	7	7	6	0.500	0	1	4.0
26	6	6	6	8	0.813	1	1	4.5
27	2	3	6	5	0.813	0	1	5.5
28	9	12	12	12	0.688	1	1	2.5

Table 8.6 Estimation results of regression of personality traits on labour effort

Variable	Coefficient	SE	t-Value	p-Value
Constant	5.320	1.812	2.937	0.004**
Raven	1.910	2.220	0.861	0.391
Risk	0.475	0.586	0.810	0.420
Altruism	−2.110	0.581	−3.633	0.000**
Cons	−0.003	0.199	−0.171	0.865
Round	0.764	0.238	3.212	0.002**

**means 1% significance

In summary, we do not observe any reduction in labour effort when the UBI is introduced. Subjects who have individualistic and competitive motivations rather increased their labour efforts as they obtained experience in solving Sudoku tasks during the experiment and gained more rewards. So, as in the first experiment, we can conclude that the UBI does not reduce labour effort, but rather increases it when subjects have individualistic and competitive motivations. However, as the number of the observations in our experiment is relatively small, to increase the external validity of the results an additional experiment with a larger sample size is required.

8.4 Adverse Selection Under the UBI Scheme

Finally, we examine the adverse selection problem under the UBI scheme by using evolutionary game theory (Smith, 1982; Weibull, 1995). A fundamental concept in evolutionary game theory is the ESS (Evolutionary Stable Strategy). This is a refinement of the Nash equilibrium concept, which is a central piece of modern game theory. The ESS is an asymptotically stable state of population dynamics. It is suitable to analyse a long-run consequence in a given game situation. Therefore, as our concern here is analysing the long-run consequence of the introduction of the UBI in a society, we utilise the ESS. Marriage and childbearing choices within a couple are the focal point in our study.

First, suppose that there are two types of agents in a society. The M type is an agent who is willing to get married and is content with obtaining only the income guaranteed in the UBI scheme. The B type is an agent who is willing to participate in the labour market in order to gain more income than what the UBI scheme guarantees. It is assumed that to enter the labour market, each agent should take training to be qualified as skilled worker. Let additional income gained by skilled labour be T, the probability of getting a skilled labour job p ($0 \leq p \leq 1$), and training costs c. We also assume that a flat tax has been extracted from T. There are infinitely many agents in the society and they are matched at random and decide whether or not they get married in the marriage market. They are all selfish individuals and do not care about the future state of their children, nor demand care for themselves in their old ages.[16]

If both matched agents are type M, we assume that they mutually agree to get married, and deliver q children on average. For each child, they suffer cost d for needed care and education. Of the average amount of income guaranteed by the UBI scheme, qg, these parents use a proportion a ($0 \leq a \leq 1$) for needed care and education for the child respectively. Thus, each M type agent receives $g + (ag - d)q$. If both matched agents are type B, they do not marry, but take training for skilled labour, and enter the labour market. Then they receive $g + pT - c$. If a type M and a type B are matched, they do not agree to get married. As the type M agent cannot enter the labour market and deliver no children, he/she receives only the income guaranteed by the UBI, g. The type B agent receives $g + pT - c$.

---

[16]These individualistic assumptions seem to be strong. However, our intention here is to show a possibility that the opposite result may arises: we will show that even under these assumptions, it is possible that women get married and bear children.

Table 8.7 Payoff matrix of the UBI game with M type agents (willing to get married) and B type agents (willing to participate in labour market)

1	2 M	B
M	$g + (ag - d)q$, $g + (ag - d)q$	g, $g + pT - c$
B	$g + pT - c$, g	$g + pT - c$, $g + pT - c$

Table 8.7 shows the payoff matrix of this game. In analysing this game, we use the ESS. First, if $(ag - d)q > pT - c$, then type M strategy is an ESS. If $pT > c$, then type B strategy is an ESS. If neither of these conditions hold, that is, if $pT < c$ and $(ag - d)q < pT - c$, then there exists a mixed strategy ESS. In the mixed strategy ESS, the proportion of type M strategy is as follows:

$$\frac{c - pT}{(ag - d)q}$$

If the expected value of additional income T is greater than training cost c, that is, $pT > c$, the proportion of type M increases. In other words, if women have little prospect of net gain from additional income T, the number of agents who are willing to get married and deliver children likely increases. Further, if g and d are constant, as average delivery rate q increases, then population grows, so the probability of getting a skilled labour job likely decreases. This makes this condition for the existence of mixed strategy ESS more likely. So, type M increases in the population at least in the short run. However, when type M increases, type B relatively decreases, so then productivity in the society as a whole may decrease. Additionally, population has grown, which means it will be less likely that UBI can still be provided, for the budget balance of the government cannot be maintained. So sooner or later, a government intervention will be made to reduce the birth rate. This may reduce the proportion of M type in the population.

On the other hand, when costs for care and education for the child, d, is greater than income gained from the child, ag, the proportion of type M decreases. The more frequently women participate in the labour market, the more g increases. Then type M decreases in the short run, type B increases and productivity in the society as a whole increases. However, this increases g, and then the society comes to the point where ag exceeds d, again type M increases.

Thus, the introduction of the UBI scheme does not necessarily promote freedom and participation in the labour market of oppressed people such as women, children, people of advanced age, and people with a disability, but there is an equilibrium where women are willing to get married in order to get higher income for the household, even if such decision keeps them in their weaker position.

8.5 Conclusion

In this chapter, we examined the UBI as an income maintenance program by controlled laboratory experiments and evolutionary game theory. First, we investigated the moral hazard problem by comparing the UBI scheme with an identical NIT scheme in the laboratory. In our first experiment, we found that the UBI increases labour supply incentives significantly more than the NIT. In our second experiment, using several psychological questionnaires, we examined which personality traits affect labour incentives when the UBI is introduced. We found that individualistic and competitive motivations had a significant positive effect on labour supply. So, both experiments show that the UBI does not reduce the work incentive, but increases it. However, the external validity is limited due to the small number of participants.

Moreover, we developed and analysed an adverse selection problem with a simple evolutionary game theoretic model. The analysis showed that contrary to the opinion of the advocates of the UBI scheme, who expected that women will enjoy more freedom and self-determination, and in line with the Alaska Permanent Fund Dividend Fund experience, there exists an equilibrium in which women are willing to get married in order to increase total income of the household, even though they are then in an oppressive situation under their husbands' control. As for the adverse selection problem, we made an *ad hoc* assumption about timing of entering marriage and labour markets. It is necessary to refine this model by using matching theory in the future research.

References

Atkinson, A. B. (1995a). *Incomes and the welfare state. Essays on Britain and Europe*. Cambridge: Cambridge University Press.

Atkinson, A. B. (1995b). *Public economics in action. The basic income/flat tax proposal*. Oxford: Clarendon.

Atkinson, A. B. (1996). The case for a participation income. *The Political Quarterly, 67*(1), 67–70. https://doi.org/10.1111/j.1467-923X.1996.tb01568.x

Benito-Ostolaza, J., Hernandez, P., & Sanchis-Llopis, J. (2016). Do individuals with higher cognitive ability play more strategically? *Journal of Behavioral and Experimental Economics, 64*, 5–11. https://doi.org/10.1016/j.socec.2016.01.005

Bowles, S., & Gintis, H. (1998). *Recasting egalitarianism*. London: Verso.

Burks, S., Carpenter, J., Goette, L., & Rustichini, A. (2009). Cognitive skills affect economic preferences, strategic behavior, and job attachment. *Proceedings of the National Academy of Sciences, 106*(19), 7745–7750. https://doi.org/10.1073/pnas.0812360106

Burtless, G. (1986). The work response to a guaranteed income: A survey of experimental evidence. In A. H. Munnell (Ed.), *Lessons from the income maintenance experiments* (pp. 22–52). Boston: Federal Reserve Bank of Boston.

Cadsby, C. B., Song, F., & Tapon, F. (2007). Sorting and incentive effects of pay-for-performance: An experimental investigation. *Academy of Management Journal, 50*(2), 387–405. https://doi.org/10.5465/amj.2007.24634448

Calsamiglia, C., Franke, J., & Rey-Biel, P. (2013). The incentive effects of affirmative action in a real-effort tournament. *Journal of Public Economics, 98,* 15–31. https://doi.org/10.1016/j.jpubeco.2012.11.003

Carpenter, J., Graham, M., & Wolf, J. (2013). Cognitive ability and strategic sophistication. *Games and Economic Behavior, 80,* 115–130. https://doi.org/10.1016/j.geb.2013.02.012

Charness, G., & Kuhn, P. (2011). Lab labor: What can labor economists learn from the lab? *Handbook of labor economics, 4,* 229–330. https://doi.org/10.1016/S0169-7218(11)00409-6

Charness, G., & Rabin, M. (2002). Understanding social preferences with simple tests. *Quarterly Journal of Economics, 117*(3), 817–869. https://doi.org/10.1162/003355302760193904

Chen, C.-C., Chiu, I.-M., Smith, J., & Yamada, T. (2013). Too smart or be selfish? Measures of cognitive ability, social preferences, and consistency. *Journal of Economic Behavior & Organization, 90*(Issue C), 112–122. https://doi.org/10.1016/j.jebo.2013.03.032

Delsen, L. (1995) *Atypical employment: An international perspective. Causes, consequences and policy.* Groningen: Wolters-Noordhoff (PhD dissertation).

Delsen, L. (1997). A new concept of full employment. *Economic and Industrial Democracy, 18*(1), 119–135. https://doi.org/10.1177/0143831X97181007

Fitzpatrick, T. (1999). *Freedom and security. An introduction to the basic income debate.* London: Palgrave.

Friedman, D., & Sunder, S. (1994). *Experimental methods: A primer for economists.* New York: Cambridge University Press.

Gamel, C., Balsan, D., & Vero, J. (2006). The impact of basic income on the propensity to work: Theoretical issues and micro-econometric results. *The Journal of Socio-Economics, 35*(3), 476–497. https://doi.org/10.1016/j.socec.2005.11.025

Gneezy, U., & List, J. A. (2006). Putting behavioral economics to work: Testing for gift exchange in labor markets using field experiments. *Econometrica, 74*(5), 1365–1384. https://doi.org/10.1111/j.1468-0262.2006.00707.x

Goldsmith, S. (2010) The Alaska permanent fund dividend: A case study in implementation of a basic income guarantee. In *Paper presented at the 13th Basic Income Earth Network Congress,* Sao Paulo, Brazil. Retrieved June 18, 2019, from https://scholarworks.alaska.edu/handle/11122/4170

Gosling, S. D., Rentfrow, P. J., & Swann, W. B. (2003). A very brief measure of the Big-Five personality domains. *Journal of Research in Personality, 37*(6), 504–528. https://doi.org/10.1016/S0092-6566(03)00046-1

Groot, L. (2006). Reasons for launching a basic income experiment. *Basic Income Studies, 1*(2), Article 8. https://doi.org/10.2202/1932-0183.1037

Hebst, D., & Mas, A. (2015). Peer effects on worker output in the laboratory generalize to the field. *Science, 350*(6260), 545–549. https://doi.org/10.1126/science.aac9555

Holt, C. A., & Laury, S. K. (2002). Risk aversion and incentive effects. *American Economic Review, 92*(5), 1644–1655. https://doi.org/10.1257/000282802762024700

Messick, D. M., & McClintock, C. G. (1968). Motivational bases of choice in experimental games. *Journal of Experimental Social Psychology, 4*(1), 1–25. https://doi.org/10.1016/0022-1031(68)90046-2

Murphy, L., & Nagel, T. (2002). *The myth of ownership, taxes and justice.* Oxford: Oxford University Press.

Noguera, J. A., & De Wispelaere, J. (2006). A plea for the use of laboratory experiments in basic income research. *Basic Income Studies, 1*(2), Article 11. https://doi.org/10.2202/1932-0183.1044

Ozawa, S. (2002). *Welfare society and social security reform: A new ground of basic income concept.* Kyoto: Takasuga Publishing. (in Japanese).

Peeters, H., & Marx, A. (2006). Lottery games as a tool for empirical basic income research. *Basic Income Studies, 1*(2), Article 10. https://doi.org/10.2202/1932-0183.1040

Raven, J. C. (1936) *Mental tests used in genetic studies: The performances of related individuals on tests mainly educative and mainly reproductive.* MSc thesis, University of London.

Robins, P. K. (1985) A comparison of the labor supply findings from the four negative income tax experiments, *Journal of Human Resources*, 20 (4): 567-582. Retrieved May 15, 2019, from. http://www.jstor.org/stable/pdfplus/145685

Smith, J. M. (1982). *Evolution and the theory of games*. Cambridge: Cambridge University Press.

Stanford Basic Income Lab. (2018) *Basic income in cities. A guide to city experiments and pilot project*. Retrieved June 8, 2019, from https://basicincome.stanford.edu/sites/g/files/sbiybj7921/f/basic_income_in_cities_toolkit_shareable_11-2-18.pdf

Tondani, D. (2009). Universal basic income and negative income tax: Two different ways of thinking redistribution. *The Journal of Socio-Economics, 38*(2), 246–255. https://doi.org/10.1016/j.socec.2008.10.006

Van Lange, P. A. M., Otten, W., De Bruin, E. M. N., & Joireman, J. A. (1997). Development of prosocial, individualistic, and competitive orientations: Theory and preliminary evidence. *Journal of Personality and Social Psychology, 73*(4), 733–746. https://doi.org/10.1037/0022-3514.73.4.733

Vanderborght, Y., & Yamamori, T. (Eds.). (2014). *Basic income in Japan: Prospects for a radical idea in a transforming welfare state*. Basingstoke: Palgrave MacMillan.

Virjo, I. (2006). A piece of the puzzle: A comment on the basic income experiment debate. *Basic Income Studies, 1*(2), Article 12. https://doi.org/10.2202/1932-0183.1045

Weibull, J. W. (1995). *Evolutionary game theory*. Cambridge, MA: The MIT Press.

Werner, G. W. (2006). *Ein Grund für die Zukunft: Das Grundeinkommen*. Stuttgart: Verlag Freies Geistesleben & Urachhaus.

Widerquist, K. (2005). A failure to communicate: What (if anything) can we learn from the negative income tax experiments? *Journal of Socio-Economics, 34*(1), 49–81. https://doi.org/10.1016/j.socec.2004.09.050

Widerquist, K. (2006). The bottom line in a basic income experiment. *Basic Income Studies, 1*(2), Article 9. https://doi.org/10.2202/1932-0183.1038

Yi, G. (2017) *The effects of basic income on labour supply*. Paper for the 17th BIEN Congress: Implementing a Basic Income, 25–27 September, Lisbon. Retrieved June 8, 2019, from https://basicincome.org/wp-content/uploads/2015/01/Gunmin_Yi_The_Effects_of_Basic_Income_on_Labour_Supply.pdf

Toshiji Kawagoe (1970) was born in Japan and studied economic theory and game theory at Fukushima University (B.A.) and Osaka City University (M.A.) and then received Ph.D. (in economics) from Osaka City University. He was a research associate at the Faculty of Economics, Saitama University (1995–2000), lecturer (2000–2006) and Associate Professor (2006–2013) at the Department of Complex and Intelligent Systems, Future University Hakodate. From 2013, he is professor at Future University Hakodate. His research is on game theoretic modelling of social and economic phenomena and its experimental evaluation. Particularly, game theoretic models of bounded rationality and social preferences (altruism and reciprocity), experimental analysis of mechanism/market design, and methodology of experimental economics are major interests. His research articles are published in well-established international journals such as *Games and Economic Behavior*, *Experimental Economics*, and *International Journal of Industrial Organization*. He also published many specialised books on economics and game theory in Japan.

Author Index

A
Abdulkadiroğlu, A., 176
Abeler, J., 176
Abma, F.I., 112, 116
Acemoglu, D., 10
Acquisti, A., 189
Amable, B., 5
Ambrosio, C.D., 182
Andersson, J.O., 30, 35, 51
Arcarons, J., 16, 72
Armstrong, S., 90
Arum, R., 148
Aslam, S.H., 11
Atkinson, A.B., 5, 6, 14, 82, 84, 87, 103, 110, 135, 201, 202

B
Backhouse, R.E., 11
Baker, J., 75
Bakker, B., 148
Balsan, D., 7, 44, 202
Banerjee, A., 2
Barthet, E., 69
Bartkowski, B., 193
Baute, S., 30
Beatty, C., 92
Beblavý, M., 68
Becker, G.S., 148
Benito-Ostolaza, J., 211, 214
Berg, A., 9, 12
Betkó, J.G., 20, 143
Betzelt, S., 8
Bheemaiah, K., 68
Bidadanure, J., 75

Bigotta, M., 134
Björklund, A., 18
Blaufus, K., 182
Blumkin, T., 15
Boffey, D., 141, 143
Bohnet, I., 116
Bond, G.R., 134
Bonoli, G., 134
Booth, A.L., 41
Borchardt, K., 112
Borgers, N., 148
Borghans, L., 41
Bothfeld, S., 8
Bottoni, G., 36, 37, 41, 42, 51, 54
Bowles, S., 201
Bradley, J.R., 15
Brady, D., 88
Braude, L., 134
Bregman, R., 2, 6, 140, 143, 185
Brickman, P., 15
Brooks, L., 62
Brosig-Koch, J., 178
Brouwer, S., 112, 116
Browne, J., 4, 9
Bültmann, U., 112, 116
Burdorf, A., 112, 116, 148
Burks, S., 211, 214
Burstein, P., 17, 30
Burtless, G., 18, 45, 202

C
Cadsby, C.B., 202, 205
Calhoun, C., 83
Calonge, S., 16

© Springer Nature Switzerland AG 2019
L. Delsen (ed.), *Empirical Research on an Unconditional Basic Income in Europe*,
Contributions to Economics, https://doi.org/10.1007/978-3-030-30044-9

Calsamiglia, C., 202, 208
Camerer, C.F., 19, 176, 180
Campbell, D.T., 15, 140, 152
Caputo, R.K., 62
Card, D., 134
Carlier, B., 148
Carpenter, J., 211, 214
Cason, T.N., 177
Castles, F.G., 111
Cesarini, D., 17
Chandler, J., 185, 187
Chandola, T., 8
Charness, G., 19, 179, 182, 205, 212
Che, Y.K., 176
Chen, C.-C., 209, 212
Chiu, I.-M., 209, 212
Cholbi, M., 74
Chung, W., 18
Cingano, F., 8
Clark, A.E., 182
Clasen, J., 67
Cole, G., 89
Colombino, U., 6, 14
Colombo, C., 30, 41, 42, 45, 50, 51, 57, 62
Cook, T.D., 140, 152
Costanza, R., 12
Croson, R., 179

D
Dagevos, J., 148
Daniels, A.S., 134
Danson, M., 20, 82–104
Deater-Deckard, K., 147
De Bruin, E.M.N., 212
Deci, E.L., 112, 116
de Grauwe, P., 10, 12
Delespaul, S., 30
Delphin-Rittmon, M.E., 134
Delsen, L., 2, 5, 7, 8, 10, 19, 20, 29, 41, 110, 112, 113, 142, 143, 171, 201
DeMaris, A., 56
de Mooij, R., 45
DeRocchi, T., 30, 41, 42, 45, 50, 51, 57, 62
Dessens, J., 164
de Wispelaere, J., 2, 7, 18, 19, 30, 41, 62–66, 68, 72, 74, 75, 103, 140, 171, 172, 178, 179, 182, 183, 202, 204
Dickie, P., 87
Diener, E., 120
Dirven, H.J., 113
Dodge, K.L., 147

Dohmen, T., 41, 51
Dougherty, R.H., 134
Downes, A., 2
Drake, R.E., 134
Drejer, T., 87
Dubois, R., 13
Duque, M., 88
Dur, R., 14, 171
Dur, U., 176
Dutcher, G., 185

E
Eamets, R., 68
Easterlin, R.A., 15
Elgarte, J.M., 75
Elliott, L., 84, 87
Elster, J., 9
Engelmann, D., 182
Erev, I., 174
Erkal, N., 185
Esping-Andersen, G., 68
Evers, M., 45

F
Falk, A., 41, 51, 179, 186, 195
Fehr, E., 10, 112, 116, 146, 164, 166
Fernández-Macías, E., 76
Ferrera, M., 68
Filer, R.K., 5
Finn, M., 68
Fischbacher, U., 10
Fisher, I., 8
Fitoussi, J.P., 13
Fitzgerald, R., 36, 41, 42, 51, 54, 62, 63, 73
Fitzpatrick, T., 202, 203
FitzRoy, F., 5
Fochmann, M., 182
Forget, E., 18, 43, 74, 76
Fossati, F., 134
Fothergill, S., 92
Frank, R.H., 15
Franke, J., 202, 208
Fraser, G., 83
Freundt, A., 87
Frey, B.S., 116
Frey, C.B., 6
Friedman, D., 206, 213
Friedman, M., 11, 30
Füllbrunn, S., 20

G

Gächter, S., 164, 166, 179, 185
Galloway, L., 86
Gamel, C., 7, 44, 202
Gangadharan, L., 185
Ganun, Y., 15
Garbarino, E., 165
Gärter, S., 10
Gazier, B., 112
George, P., 134
Gerber, A.S., 17
Gertler, P.J., 43
Gertler, S., 18
Gesthuizen, M., 20
Gheaus, A., 74, 75, 77
Gielens, E., 20
Gilroy, B.M., 43, 44
Gingerich, D.W., 5
Gintis, H., 201
Gneezy, U., 182, 186, 187, 205
Goette, L., 211, 214
Goldberg, R.W., 134
Goldsmith, S., 4, 8, 16–18, 203
Golsteyn, B.H.H., 41
Goodin, R.E., 113
Gosling, S.D., 209
Gottlieb, J.D., 10
Gough, I., 12
Graeber, D., 14, 171
Graetz, M.J., 15
Graham, M., 211, 214
Granovetter, M.S., 44
Greenberg, D.H., 140, 163
Green, D.P., 17
Green, S., 140, 144
Greiner, B., 174
Grether, D.M., 176
Groot, L., 2, 44, 110, 111, 114, 118, 141, 171, 178, 204
Gugushvili, D., 30

H

Ha, H., 18
Haigner, S., 19, 180
Hall, P.A., 5
Halmetoja, A., 62, 64, 140
Hamermesh, D.S., 5
Hamilton, K., 89
Hamilton, T.B., 141
Hammond, R.G., 176
Hanna, R., 2
Hansen, H., 87

Hanushek, E.A., 18
Harrison, G.W., 177
Harvey, H., 146, 164
Harvey, P., 6
Hastings, T., 8
Haushofer, J., 2, 146, 166
Haydecker, R., 83
Haywood, L., 7, 14, 41
Headey, B., 113
Hebst, D., 19, 179, 205
Heckman, J.J., 18, 41, 45, 140, 145, 152, 163, 179, 186, 195
Heimann, A., 43, 44
Heller, N., 61
Hemerijck, A., 68, 110–113
Henderson, A., 182
Henke, K.D., 112
Herd, P., 146, 164
Hernandez, P., 211, 214
Hertwig, R., 176, 177
Hetherington, P., 83
Heyes, J., 8
Heyne, L., 45
Higgins, J.P.T., 140, 144
Höchtl, W., 19, 180
Hofstede, G., 35
Hofstede, G.J., 35
Hogarth, R.M., 176
Hohendanner, C., 8
Hohmann, N., 140, 145
Holt, C.A., 178, 209, 210
Hombert, J., 10
Hood, A., 86, 92
Houston, D., 87, 88
Hoynes, H.W., 4, 6–8, 13, 18
Huang, L., 185
Huck, S., 116
Huffman, D., 41, 51
Humal, K., 68
Hundsdoerfer, J., 182

I

Imbens, G.W., 17
Immervoll, H., 4, 9
Inglehart, R., 140, 148, 160
Isaac, R.M., 176
Islam, N., 14

J

Jansen, W., 164
Jauhiainen, S., 17, 18, 30

Jegen, R., 116
Jenewein, S., 19, 180
Jin, J., 5
Joireman, J.A., 212
Jones, D., 17, 18

K
Kahneman, D., 145, 191
Kangas, O., 17, 18, 30, 35, 51, 61, 64, 74, 76
Kappeler, A., 11, 86
Kapteyn, A., 41, 51
Kawagoe, T., 19, 20, 181
Kederer, J.-F., 181, 182
Kelly, M., 12
Keohane, R.O., 162
Khoo, M., 140, 145
Kiesewetter, D., 182
Killingsworth, M.R., 18, 45
Kim, B., 18
King, G., 162
Kirchler, M., 177
Klandermans, B., 140
Klein, A., 181, 182
Klosse, S., 5
Kluve, J., 134, 140
Knight, K.W., 7
Koh, B.H., 185
Kovarich, D., 181, 182
Krehm, W., 6
Krug, G., 8
Kuhl, J., 116
Kuhn, P., 19, 179, 182, 205
Kumm, L., 181, 182
Kurer, T., 30, 41, 42, 45, 50, 51, 57, 62
Kuznets, S., 12

L
Laenen, T., 30
Lalive, R., 134
Langer, W., 56
Lansley, S., 2, 76, 82, 103
Laury, S.K., 209, 210
Layard, R., 15
Lee, S., 34, 35, 56, 63, 69, 73, 93, 112
Leininger, A., 45
Leitner, R., 112
Leschke, J., 68, 73, 77
Lewis, J., 70
Linder, W., 45
Lindqvist, E., 17
Lindsay, C., 87, 88

List, J.A., 177, 205
Liu, G., 89
Lloyd, G., 94, 103
Lockwood, B.B., 15
Loewenstein, G., 19, 180
Lötters, F., 148
Lubbers, M., 164
Lucas, R.E., 120
Luciano, A., 134

M
Mani, A., 116
Mankiw, N.G., 13–15
Marinescu, I., 17, 18
Marshall, T., 134
Martinelli, L., 74, 76, 103
Martinez, S.W., 18, 43
Marx, A., 16, 204
Marx, K., 12
Mas, A., 19, 179, 205
Maselli, I., 68
Matud, M.P., 147
Maydell, v.B., 112
McAlpine, R., 83, 87, 88
McCandless, B., 165
McClintock, C.G., 212
McGregor, J.M., 13
McHardy, F., 87
McKay, A., 87, 93
McKay, R.T., 50, 193
McKendrick, J., 87
McKnight, A., 88
Meade, J., 89
Meadowcroft, J., 12
Medema, S.G., 11
Meijers, H., 41
Mèlich, L.T., 72
Merrett, D., 165
Messick, D.M., 212
Meuleman, B., 30
Miller, A., 82, 89, 90, 93, 100
Minkov, M., 35
Mirrlees, J., 13
Mitchell, W., 5
Moffatt, P.G., 178
Moffitt, R.A., 45, 55
Mooney, G., 83, 87
Morel, N., 110, 112
Morrill, T., 176
Mostafavi-Dehzooei, M.H., 2, 4, 74, 76
Moynihan, D., 146, 164
Muffels, R.J., 20, 110–114, 118, 123, 134, 141

Author Index

Mullainathan, S., 116, 146, 166
Murphy, L., 202
Muysken, J., 5

N
Nagel, T., 202
Nathanson, C.G., 15
Naumann, I.K., 111
Niehaus, P., 2
Nikiforos, M., 16
Noguera, J.A., 2, 16, 18, 19, 30, 41, 62, 64–66, 68, 74, 75, 103, 171, 172, 178, 179, 182, 183, 202, 204
Nolen, P., 41
Nooteboom, B., 43
Nosenzo, D., 176
Notowidigdo, M.J., 17

O
Oesch, D., 134
O'Hara, B., 83
Okun, A.M., 9
Olds, G., 10
Olken, B.A., 2
O'Reilly, J., 73, 77
Ortlieb, R., 73, 77
Ortmann, A., 176, 177
Osborne, M.A., 6
Östling, R., 17
Ostry, J.D., 9, 12
O'Sullivan, P., 83
Otten, W., 212
Ozawa, S., 202, 205

P
Palan, S., 177
Palier, B., 110, 112
Pallier, B., 76, 77
Palme, J., 110, 112
Pañella, D.R., 72
Paolacci, G., 185, 187
Patten, B.C., 12
Pech, W.J., 16, 44
Peer, E., 189
Peeters, H., 16, 204
Pencavel, J., 18, 45
Perkiö, J., 64, 74
Peters, K., 11
Pfeifer, M., 34

Piachaud, D., 2
Piasna, A., 8
Pickett, K., 9
Pierson, C., 111
Piketty, T., 15–16
Pionnier, P.A., 11, 86
Plott, C.R., 175, 176
Polan, M., 10
Porter, D., 176
Potters, J., 186, 187
Pouw, N., 13
Ptacek, J.T., 147
Pulkka, V.V., 62, 64, 140
Pullinger, M., 7

Q
Quante, M., 112
Quiggin, J., 11

R
Rabin, M., 212
Ranshuijsen, A., 143
Rauhala, P.L., 112
Raven, J.C., 209, 211
Raventós, D., 16
Rawls, J., 181
Raworth, K., 13
Reed, H., 76, 82, 103
Rees, A.E., 5
Regnér, H., 18
Renema, J.A., 164
Rentfrow, P.J., 209
Rey-Biel, P., 202, 208
Rice, D., 110
Richards, J., 86
Robbins, L., 10
Robeyns, I., 7, 41, 74, 75
Robins, P.K., 18, 45, 204
Rodrik, D., 10
Roosma, F., 30
Rosa, E.A., 7
Rossetti, F., 30
Roth, A.E., 174, 175
Rothschild, K.W., 6
Rothstein, J., 4, 6–8, 13, 18
Rowlingson, K., 9
Rubin, D.B., 17
Rubio-Codina, M., 18, 43
Rucci, M., 88
Russell, B., 103

Russell, H., 68
Rustichini, A., 211, 214
Ryan, R.M., 112, 116

S
Sacerdote, B.I., 17
Saez, E., 15
Salehi-Isfahani, D., 2, 4, 74, 76
Salmon, T., 185
Sanchis-Llopis, J., 211, 214
Sandbu, M., 74
Sang, J.K., 86
Saral, K., 185
Scarr, S., 147
Scharpf, F.W., 76
Schaufeli, W.B., 112, 116
Scheepers, P., 20, 148
Schiller, B.R., 9
Schilpzand, R., 19, 29
Schmid, G., 5, 15, 112
Schmidt, K.M., 112, 116
Schneider, F.G., 19, 180
Schoar, A., 10
Schömann, K., 5, 15
Schopf, M., 43, 44
Schor, J.B., 7
Schulz, P., 75
Schupp, J., 41, 51
Schuring, M., 148
Schwellnus, C., 11, 86
Scott, G., 87
Seeleib-Kaiser, M., 73, 77
Sefton, M., 185
Sen, A.K., 110, 112, 116, 145, 193
Shadish, W.R., 140, 152
Shafir, E., 116, 146, 166
Shanahan, G., 20, 57, 61–77
Shapiro, J., 2
Shavit, Y., 148
Shefrin, H., 188
Shimer, R., 10
Shroder, M., 140, 163
Siegel, N.A., 67
Simanainen, M., 17, 18, 30
Sinfield, A., 88
Sinn, H.W., 9, 183
Slonim, R., 165
Smith, H.L., 120
Smith, J., 209, 212
Smith, J.A., 18, 140, 145, 152, 163
Smith, J.M., 216
Smith, M., 20, 57, 61–77

Smith, R.E., 147
Smith, V.L., 175
Soentken, M., 110
Sommer, M., 16
Song, F., 202, 205
Soskice, D., 5
Spence, M., 148
Spicker, P., 83, 87, 88, 91, 92
Spierings, N., 20
Sraer, D., 10
Srinivasan, P., 20, 61–77
Stafford, F., 19
Standing, G., 2, 5, 7, 41, 44, 50, 61, 75, 76, 82, 86, 87, 89, 93, 103, 141, 171, 172, 193
Stanley, J.C., 140
Stantcheva, S., 15
Steffens, N.K., 11
Steinbaum, M., 16
Stiglitz, J., 13
Stirton, L., 7, 72
Stirzaker, R., 86
Stovicek, K., 68
Straubinger, S.G., 87
Strobel, M., 182
Sturgeon, N., 94
Suchman, E.A., 165
Suh, E.M., 120
Sullivan, W., 83, 87, 88
Sunde, U., 41, 51
Sunder, S., 206, 213
Sunstein, C.R., 116, 145
Suri, T., 2
Sushmita Shoma Ghose, E.D., 134
Swann, W.B., 209
Swift, S., 36, 41, 42, 51, 54

T
Tapin, B.M., 50, 193
Tapon, F., 202, 205
Teele, D.L., 179
Teppa, F., 35, 41, 51
Thaler, R.H., 116, 145
Thesmar, D., 10
Tinbergen, J., 5
Tinnemans, W., 143
Titmuss, R.M., 10
Torry, M., 2, 6, 7, 41, 44, 63–65, 72, 76, 82, 86, 89, 103
Townsend, R.R., 10
Tsangarides, C.G., 9, 12
Turrini, A., 68
Tversky, A., 145, 191

Author Index

U
Ultee, W., 164

V
Vacas-Soriano, C., 76
Valero, J., 62
van Bavel, B., 2, 9, 11, 12
Vanderborght, Y., 2, 3, 30, 35, 36, 41, 44, 89, 103, 171, 172
van der Klink, J.J., 112, 116, 123, 134
van der Veen, R., 2, 171
van der Wilt, G.J., 112, 116
van Doorn, M., 148
van Gestel, N., 8
van Geuns, R., 146, 166
van Hooren, F., 110
van Lange, P.A.M., 212
van Lent, M., 14, 171
van Oorschot, W., 30
van Parijs, P., 2, 3, 30, 35, 36, 44, 67, 89, 103, 135, 171, 172
van Vugt, J., 8
van Vuuren, D., 45
Varian, H.R., 9, 183
Veenhoven, R., 120
Verba, S., 162
Verlaat, T., 110, 111, 114, 118, 141
Vero, J., 7, 44, 202
Verschraegen, G., 112
Villa, P., 70, 73, 77
Virjo, I., 19, 204
Vis, C., 35
Vlandas, T., 35–37, 42
Vliegenthart, A., 143
Vosgerau, J., 189
Vyrastekova, J., 20

W
Wagner, G.G., 41, 51
Wakolbinger, F., 19, 180
Walter, T., 41
Wang, C., 165
Ward, B., 13
Waters, T., 86, 92
Watts, M., 5
Weber, A., 134
Weibull, J.W., 216
Weimann, J., 178, 182
Weinzierl, M., 13, 14
Werner, G.W., 202, 203
Westerveld, E., 140, 143, 162
Weyl, E.G., 15
White, A., 87, 171
Widerquist, K., 2, 18, 19, 35, 41, 45, 64, 99, 103, 171, 172, 178, 184, 204
Widmer, T., 30, 41, 42, 45, 50, 51, 57, 62
Wilkinson, R.G., 9
Williamson, L., 69
Wolf, J., 211, 214
Wright, E.O., 103
Wu, S.Y., 177

X
Xu, T., 10

Y
Yagan, D., 13, 14
Yamada, T., 209, 212
Yamamori, T., 204
Yasuda, Y., 176
Yi, G., 202
Ylikännö, M., 17, 18, 30
Young, C., 82

Z
Zelleke, A., 75
Zezza, G., 16
Zhang, N., 8
Zhao, J., 116
Zijlstra, F.R., 112, 116
Zukowski, M., 112

Subject Index

A
Activation, 9, 20, 62, 64, 74, 83, 110, 113, 141
Active labour market policies, 110, 112, 113, 134, 208
Administration costs, 5, 6, 72
Administrative costs, 164
Alaska Permanent Fund Dividend, 4, 8, 17, 18, 203, 218
Allowance, 70, 99, 100, 102, 103, 117, 131, 141–143, 145–154, 161–164, 167, 172
Amazon Mechanical Turk, 185, 189
  See also M-Turk
Artificial Intelligence (AI), 36, 77, 89, 171, 194
Attitudes, 17, 30, 34, 36, 37, 41, 56, 63, 83, 99, 100, 120, 174, 189, 191, 210, 211
  See also preferences; public support
Awareness, 39, 45, 46, 48, 52, 54, 57, 93, 95, 167
  See also familiarity

B
Basic income, 2–7, 11, 18, 20, 29–31, 33, 34, 37, 50, 51, 54, 61–77, 82–104, 110, 113, 117–118, 134–136, 139–141
  experiments, 94, 110, 118, 140, 162, 172, 204
  public support of, 112
    (*see also Unconditional Basic Income*)
  See also Citizen's basic income
Basic Income Earth Network (BIEN), 2, 3, 62, 67, 69–71, 89, 90, 92, 93, 98, 103, 172
Basic Income Scotland, 83
Basic Income Studies, 67, 103, 204

Behavioural economics, 19, 112, 116, 117, 122, 135, 145, 174
Benefit, 3–9, 14–16, 31, 34, 36, 37, 40–42, 44, 47, 50, 51, 53, 55–57, 63, 68, 72, 74, 75, 82–104, 110–112, 114, 116–119, 130–132, 142, 148, 174, 181, 184, 202
  withdrawal of, 83
Bias(es), 17, 19, 20, 51, 99, 100, 119, 140, 141, 144–145, 147, 151, 152, 166, 167, 174, 194, 205
  test, 141, 155, 158, 161, 162, 165, 166
  See also selection effects
Big trade-off, 9
  See also trade-off
Birth rate, 18, 19, 86, 203, 217
Birth weight, 18
Bullshit jobs, 171
  See also professions; socially useless jobs

C
Capabilities, 10, 110, 111, 113, 115–117, 120, 122, 126, 127, 135, 143, 144
Capability approach, 112, 116, 135
Capacitating, 110–114
Capitalism, 2, 8, 11–13
Care work, 14, 75, 149, 172, 216, 217
Citizen's basic income, 82–104
  See also Basic income; Unconditional Basic Income
Citizen's Basic Income Network Scotland (CBINS), 82, 83, 89–92, 94, 98, 99, 103
Class struggle, 12
Climate change, 12

Consumption tax, 4, 13, 15, 16
Council of Europe, 62
Counting rule, 5
Credit Suisse Research Institute (CSRI), 8

D
Dalia Research, 17, 29–33, 35–37, 40, 43, 45, 48, 54, 55, 62, 63, 73, 191
Democracy, 17, 86
Democratic society, 37, 41, 42, 65, 87, 91
Demogrant, 3
Disability, 87–89, 98, 120, 134, 202, 217
 benefit, 110, 119
Disabled, 7, 82, 88, 132
Disincentive effect, 44, 45, 56
Distrust, 115, 143, 146, 163

E
Economic growth, 9, 11, 12, 15, 49, 183
 See also Gross Domestic Product (GDP)
Education, 13, 18, 31–33, 38, 42, 45, 46, 51, 52, 82, 99, 117, 135, 147, 148, 153, 154, 158, 163, 166, 185, 186, 216, 217
 level, 31, 42, 51, 111, 122, 130–132, 163, 186 (*see also training*)
 See also human capital
End Child Poverty, 92
Entrepreneurship, 10, 43, 49, 86, 90, 98, 99
 See also free-lancer; self-employed; self-employment
Environmental Kuznets curve, 12
Eurofound, 6
Europe, 2, 6, 9, 12, 29–31, 34–37, 41, 42, 46, 49, 52, 57, 61–77, 84, 88, 90, 91, 111
 Central, 68
 Continental, 57, 63, 68–70, 73
 Eastern, 42, 68–71, 73, 74
 Liberal, 68
 Southern, 68–71, 73
European Social Survey (ESS), 30, 34, 35, 37, 41, 42, 51, 62, 63, 73, 75, 93, 112
 See also poll; survey
European Union (EU), 2, 29–33, 35–37, 42, 44, 46, 49, 51, 52, 57, 61–64, 66–71, 73, 75, 76, 84, 85, 95, 103, 172, 173
Eurostat, 31, 33, 35, 42, 88
Experiment(s), 2–4, 10, 15, 17–20, 34, 39, 49, 57, 61, 62, 64, 70, 72, 82–84, 90, 93, 96–99, 103, 110, 111, 172–176, 179, 182, 183
 external validity of, 166, 178
 field, 19, 20, 35, 45, 49, 61, 90, 172, 177, 178, 202, 205
 internal validity of, 178
 laboratory (lab), 19, 165, 174, 177, 178, 182, 194, 202, 204, 205, 208, 218
  (*see also pilot(s); social experiment*)
Experimental
 design, 140, 141, 152, 172, 177–179, 181, 183, 186, 203, 204
 economics, 20, 173, 174, 176, 206, 212, 213
External effects, 17–19
External limits, 12
 See also externalities
Externalities, 12, 15
 See also external effects

F
Fairness, 7, 15, 31, 56, 90, 174
Familiarity, 36, 45, 147
 See also awareness
Feasibility, 62–77, 93–96
Feasibility study, 3, 16, 17, 19, 20, 30, 82, 83, 93–96, 98, 99, 103, 113
 See also pilot
Field experiment, 2, 3, 17–19, 35, 45, 49, 90, 172, 177, 178, 202, 205
 See also experiment; natural experiment; participants
Fife Council Research, 93
Financial feasibility, 16, 65, 95
Flat rate benefit, 4, 14
Flat tax, 13, 14, 102, 103
Flexicurity, 112
Framing, 35, 37, 63, 177, 182, 194
Free-lancer, 43
 See also entrepreneurship; self-employed; self-employment
Full employment, 5, 12, 57, 98
Full-time, 32, 33, 38, 41, 42, 45, 46, 48, 51, 52
 (paid) work, 87, 113, 117–119, 144, 146
 job, 143

G
Gender, 31–33, 38, 41, 45, 51, 63, 70, 75, 98, 111, 130, 131, 141, 145, 147, 153, 154, 158, 166, 175, 186
 division, 7, 147
 effect, 74
 equality, 202
 inequality, 70, 76
Generation, 8, 83, 89, 104, 171

inter, 90, 192
intra, 8
Gross Domestic Product (GDP), 6, 11, 12, 15, 88, 91, 173
See also economic growth

H

HartzPlus, 17, 69, 70, 172
Hawthorne effect, 18
Health problems, 8, 9, 123, 135, 171
Helicopter money, 30, 41
Homo economicus, 43, 55, 145
Human capital, 7, 8, 10, 18, 43, 49, 55, 89, 100, 113, 117, 146, 148, 183, 184, 193
    investments in, 8, 10, 193 (see also training)
    See also education
Human flourishing, 7, 10

I

Immigration, 8, 51, 56, 184
    See also migration
Income inequality, 8, 11, 12, 15, 88, 172, 180, 183, 202
Income tax, 3, 13–16, 97, 100, 181, 182, 201
    See also optimal taxation
Induced value theory, 175
ING, 17, 30, 36, 37, 41
Institutional choice, 5, 6, 13
Intergenerational concern, 90
International Monetary Fund (IMF), 9, 11, 16
Intrinsic motivation, 44, 113, 116, 135
Investment behaviour, 183, 185
Ipsos MORI, 30

J

Job insecurity, 6, 8, 35
    See also flexible jobs; low-paid jobs; precarious jobs

L

Laboratory experiment, 4, 10, 15, 19, 20, 75, 165, 174, 177, 178, 180, 182, 194, 202, 204, 205, 208, 218
    See also experiment; participants
Labour effort, 202, 203, 208, 213–215
Labour market activation, 62, 141
Labour supply, 7, 15–18, 20, 43–45, 49, 56, 193, 202, 203, 205, 207, 213, 218

Latent Class Analysis (LCA), 111, 122, 125, 126
Lazy, 9, 43, 55
Leisure, 6, 43, 44, 55, 173, 180, 202
Lottery, 16, 17, 95, 190, 204, 210
Low-paid jobs, 8
    See also flexible jobs; job insecurity; precarious jobs

M

Macro-simulation, 173
Marginal withdrawal rate, 88
    See also earning withdrawal; reduced benefits
McKinsey Global Institute, 6
Means-tested benefits, 4, 6, 7, 16, 44, 62, 102
Micro-simulation, 4, 5, 16, 173
Migration, 184
    See also immigration
Minimum income guarantee, 34, 118, 142
Mixed method approach, 141, 163
Moral hazard, 6, 7, 20, 202–208
Motivation(s), 11, 13, 44, 82, 111–113, 115–117, 122, 135, 158, 162, 163, 166, 167, 192, 203, 214–216, 218
M-Turk, 174, 185, 186, 191
    See also Amazon-Mechanical-Turk

N

National Audit Office (NAO), 82, 91
National dividend, 3
Natural experiment, see participants; field experiment
Negative Income Tax (NIT), 2, 3, 45, 117, 136, 178, 202–205, 207, 218
    Experiments, 202–208, 218
Neoclassical economics, 10
Neoliberal, 65, 91, 110, 112
New Economics Foundation (NEF), 14
Nordic countries, 57, 68–71, 73, 84
Northeastern University, 17, 30, 36, 41, 42
Nudging, 116, 134

O

Opportunity costs, 6
Optimal taxation, 3, 14, 15
    See also progressive consumption tax; progressive income tax
Organisation for Economic Cooperation and Development (OECD), 2, 4, 6–9, 87

P

Paradigm shift, 3, 83, 90, 110, 111, 143
Participants, 66, 110, 111, 114, 115, 118–120, 122–126, 129, 132–133, 135, 141, 143–147, 151–155, 158, 162–164, 166, 205, 206, 209–213, 218
 in laboratory experiment, 205, 206, 208, 210, 211, 213 (*see also students*)
Participation Act, 110, 112–114, 117
Participation income, 6, 7, 20, 110, 111, 118, 134, 201
Part-time
 job, 5, 44, 72, 143, 145, 146, 148–150, 153, 164
 work, 7, 18, 41, 55, 87, 144, 146, 147
Pigouvian subsidy, 15
Pigouvian tax, 15
Pilot(s), 20, 35, 62, 64, 66–70, 76, 82, 83, 90, 93–100, 103, 104, 140, 204, 206
 See also experiment
Political feasibility, 16, 17, 19, 20, 30, 34, 37, 49, 63–66, 68, 75, 76, 95
Political will, 5, 20
Poll, 36
 Gallup, 36, 41, 194 (*see also survey*)
Poverty, 3, 4, 6, 7, 9, 12, 14, 16, 31, 41, 42, 49, 82–84, 86–95, 100–104, 116, 126, 135, 142, 146, 166, 171, 172, 202, 204
 line, 4, 7, 8, 142
 reduction, 6, 13, 20, 44, 49, 56, 83, 88, 92, 140, 143, 172
 trap, 7
Precarious jobs, 7, 41, 88, 91, 99
 See also flexible jobs; job insecurity; low paid jobs
Preferences, 17, 19, 29–31, 33–37, 43, 44, 49, 56, 57, 74, 93, 173, 174, 179, 182, 186, 193, 209, 212
 See also attitudes; public opinions; public support
Professions, 14, 15
Prosperity state, 10
Public opinions, 17, 29, 30, 66
 See also attitudes; preferences

R

Randomised Controlled Trial (RCT), 99, 110, 114–120, 134, 140, 144, 145, 163, 165, 166, 204
Rational-choice, 150, 164, 166, 167
 mechanism, 164, 166
 theory, 145, 147, 150, 163

Reciprocity, 3, 10, 31, 50, 56, 113, 116, 117, 119, 146, 164, 166
Referendum, 33, 54, 57, 62, 194
 Swiss, 41, 42, 45, 51, 57
Reform Scotland, 93
Regression analysis, 36, 51, 175, 190, 213
 logistic, 149, 154, 155
 logit, 111, 122, 130
Risk, 6, 8–10, 12, 18, 20, 31, 35, 41–43, 49, 55, 56, 64, 65, 74–77, 91, 113, 142, 146, 176, 183–194, 214
 averse, 41, 43, 51, 146, 187, 203, 209, 214
Robot tax, 36
Robots, 6, 90, 100
Royal Society for the encouragement of Arts, Manufactures and Commerce (RSA), 30

S

Scottish Government, 84, 86, 92, 94, 96, 97
Scottish Parliament, 94
Scottish Parliament Social Security Committee, 93
Selection effects, 140–142, 144, 145, 163, 165, 166
 bias, 119, 140, 141, 144–145, 151, 152, 158, 161, 162, 165–167 (*see also bias (es)*)
Self-employed, 42, 43, 55, 86, 87, 143
Self-employment, 55, 88, 91, 144, 193
 See also entrepreneurship; free-lancer
Self-enhancement, 50, 51, 57, 193
Self-interest, 116, 192, 214
Simulations, 4, 16
 macro, 173
 micro, 173
Social assistance, 4, 6, 17, 20, 94, 110, 114, 117, 119, 120, 122, 127, 129–136, 141–144, 146–150, 152–155, 161–163, 166, 167, 172
 benefit, 111, 112, 130, 142
Social cohesion, 13, 83
Social dividend, 3, 14, 89
Social experiment, 17, 140–142, 144–145, 151, 162, 163, 165–167, 203, 204
 See also field experiment; natural experiment
Social ills, 83
Social investment, 9, 110–114, 117, 134, 135
Socially useless jobs, 14
 See also bullshit jobs; professions
Solidarity, 10, 15, 20, 31, 34, 39, 47, 49, 53, 83, 89, 104, 143

Subject Index

Splendid Research, 30
Stanford Basic Income Lab, 204
Stigmatisation, 6, 7, 88
Stress, 13, 103, 116, 140, 143, 146, 147, 162, 165–167
    reduction, 147, 162, 173
Students, 10, 19, 205, 213, 214
Survey, 4, 16, 17, 19, 29–31, 33–38, 42, 49–51, 57, 62, 63, 66, 73, 99, 110–112, 119, 120, 122, 151, 152, 155, 174, 191–194
    data, 30, 31, 34, 35, 41, 51, 63, 66, 74, 75, 122–126, 135 (*see also poll*)
Sustainable Development Goals, 13

T

Trade-off(s), 7, 9, 10, 13, 183, 188, 193
    See also big trade-off
Training, 42, 55, 75, 82, 87, 99, 134, 144, 216, 217
    See also education; human capital
Trap, 74
    poverty, 7
    unemployment, 44
Trust, 13, 17, 20, 90, 94, 111–113, 115–117, 120, 127, 135, 136, 143, 146, 147, 164, 172, 174

U

Unconditional Basic Income (UBI), 2, 29–31, 33–37, 41–46, 49–52, 54–57, 62–77, 82–84, 87–91, 93–104, 112, 113, 118, 119, 171, 202–218
    arguments against, 180, 182, 192, 202
    arguments for, 180, 182, 192, 202
    (*see also basic income; citizen's basic income*)
    definition of, 172, 191, 201
    full, 64, 68, 76, 202
    policy, 65, 66, 68, 70, 75, 76
    short-term effects, 202, 207, 213, 215, 217, 218 (*see also Unconditional Basic Income*)
Unconditional Job Guarantee (UJG), 5
    definition of, 5
Unemployment trap, 44
United States (US), 2, 4, 6, 10, 18, 35, 36, 41, 42, 44, 45, 49, 51, 69, 110, 118, 178
Universal Credit, 82, 91

Unpaid work, 45, 74, 88, 111
    See also voluntary work; volunteering

V

Validity, 17, 19
    external, 166, 178, 179, 216, 218
    internal, 175, 177–179, 186
Value, 3, 5, 11, 14, 15, 18, 33, 35, 36, 44, 55–57, 86, 88, 90, 91, 100
    bequest, 192
    existence, 193
    non-use, 193
Valuing UBI, 192, 193
Voluntary work, 50, 99
    See also unpaid work; volunteering
Volunteering, 34, 39, 40, 43, 44, 46, 47, 49, 52, 53, 55, 144
    See also unpaid work; voluntary work

W

Wages, 6, 8, 11, 42, 86–88, 91, 100
Wealth inequality, 6, 92
Welfare, 2–5, 7–10, 12, 15–17, 19, 30, 31, 34, 51, 55–57, 62, 63, 65, 66, 68, 69, 72, 74, 76, 83, 84, 86, 88, 110, 111, 113, 114, 116, 118, 120, 122, 125, 126, 130, 132, 135, 141, 142, 164, 180, 193, 204
    benefits, 86, 117, 119, 142, 185
    economics, 193
    system, 171
Welfare and labour market regimes, 66, 68
Welfare regime, 62, 65, 68, 69, 72, 76, 113, 143
Welfare state, 2, 3, 9, 10, 12, 17, 19, 34, 51, 56, 62, 63, 66, 69, 72, 88, 90, 91, 97, 104, 111, 112, 116, 117, 134, 135, 142, 143, 182, 183
    design, 112
Well-being, 5, 7, 8, 12, 13, 18, 49, 88, 89, 91, 99, 111, 113, 116–120, 126–127, 129, 133, 135, 146, 171
Withdrawal rate, 86, 99, 117, 118
Work, 3–10, 13–15, 18, 20, 31, 33, 34, 37, 39–41, 43–47, 49, 50, 52, 53, 55–57, 63, 64, 67, 68, 70, 72, 74–76, 82–84, 86–88, 90–97, 99, 103, 104
    paid, 113, 118–120, 129–132, 134, 135
Workfare, 7, 8, 110, 112, 113, 115, 134, 135, 143
World Economic Forum, 84